Men and masculinities in modern Britain

Manchester University Press

Men and masculinities in modern Britain

A history for the present

Edited by

Matt Houlbrook, Katie Jones,
and Ben Mechen

MANCHESTER UNIVERSITY PRESS

Copyright © Manchester University Press 2023

While copyright in the volume as a whole is vested in Manchester University Press, copyright in individual chapters belongs to their respective authors, and no chapter may be reproduced wholly or in part without the express permission in writing of both author and publisher.

Published by Manchester University Press
Oxford Road, Manchester M13 9PL

www.manchesteruniversitypress.co.uk

British Library Cataloguing-in-Publication Data
A catalogue record for this book is available from the British Library

ISBN 978 1 5261 74697 hardback

First published 2023

The publisher has no responsibility for the persistence or accuracy of URLs for any external or third-party internet websites referred to in this book, and does not guarantee that any content on such websites is, or will remain, accurate or appropriate.

Typeset
by Cheshire Typesetting Ltd, Cuddington, Cheshire

Contents

List of contributors — *page* vii

Introduction: Histories for the present — 1
Matt Houlbrook, Katie Jones, and Ben Mechen

Part I: Institutions

1 Male breadwinners of 'doubtful sex': Trans men and the welfare state, 1954–1970 — 49
   Adrian Kane-Galbraith

2 Reading colonial masculinity through a marriage in Burma — 67
   Jonathan Saha

3 'Crutches as weapons': Reading Blackness and the disabled soldier body in the First World War — 88
   Hilary Buxton

Reflection: Male historians explain things to me: Masculinity, expertise, and the academy — 111
Charlotte Lydia Riley

Part II: Histories

4 'Formal qualifications for full masculine status'? Challenging the fragmentation of the male life cycle through the First World War pension archives — 121
   Jessica Meyer

5 Reimagining working-class masculinities in the twentieth century — 136
   Helen Smith

6 Perceptions of crisis in the history of masculinity: Power and change in modern Britain — 158
Ben Griffin

Reflection: Masculinities and history for the present — 178
John Tosh

Part III: Everyday lives

7 Gender, locality, and culture: Revisiting masculinities in the Liverpool docklands, 1900–1939 — 189
Pat Ayers

8 Struggling 'heroes': Everyday masculine encounters in the public library, 1890s–1920s — 208
Michelle Johansen

9 Fathers, sons, and 'normal', 'ordinary' family life, 1945–1974 — 228
Richard Hall

Reflection: Doing gender history and the history of masculinity — 249
Michael Roper

Part IV: Bodies

10 Dirty magazines, clean consciences: Men and pornography in the 1970s — 253
Ben Mechen

11 'It's more what me and my partner feel comfortable with': Gay masculinities, safer sex, and Project SIGMA, 1987–1996 — 269
Katie Jones

Reflection: Writing the history of male sexuality in the wake of Operation Yewtree and #MeToo — 288
Hannah Charnock

Conclusion: Histories, historians, and the politics of masculinity — 299
Lucy Delap and John Tosh, in conversation

Index — 314

Contributors

Pat Ayers is an independent scholar.

Hilary Buxton is Assistant Professor of History at Kenyon College, Ohio.

Hannah Charnock is a lecturer in British history at the University of Bristol.

Lucy Delap is Professor of Modern British and Gender History at the University of Cambridge.

Ben Griffin is a lecturer in modern British history at the University of Cambridge.

Richard Hall is an independent scholar.

Matt Houlbrook is Professor of Cultural History at the University of Birmingham.

Michelle Johansen is an independent scholar.

Katie Jones is an independent scholar.

Adrian Kane-Galbraith is a doctoral candidate at the University of Washington, DC.

Ben Mechen is a lecturer in modern British history at University College London.

Jessica Meyer is Professor of British Social and Cultural History at the University of Leeds.

Charlotte Lydia Riley is a lecturer in twentieth-century British history at the University of Southampton.

Michael Roper is Professor of Sociology at the University of Essex.

Jonathan Saha is Associate Professor of South Asian History at the University of Durham.

Helen Smith is a senior lecturer in history at the University of Lincoln.

John Tosh is Emeritus Professor of History at the University of Roehampton.

Introduction: Histories for the present

Matt Houlbrook, Katie Jones, and Ben Mechen

Making men, making masculinities

James Kitten and Bracewell Smith were self-made men. In the mid-1920s, their paths crossed most days: they lived on opposite sides of Great White Lion Street, in London's Seven Dials, where they ran successful businesses – a restaurant and hotel, respectively. The stories of Kitten and Smith's paths to Seven Dials were entwined. From humble beginnings, Kitten travelled the world in search of opportunity. Captured at the start of the Great War, he spent years in a German internment camp, before arriving in London with his passport and a bullet wound that would lead to his early death. Through low-paid catering jobs at the Savoy Hotel and Lyons' Cadby Hall factory, Kitten, and his new wife, Emily, saved up enough money to open their own eating house. There they found happiness, status within their community, and modest prosperity. Smith's journey to Seven Dials was remarkably similar: born in Keighley, he worked as a pupil teacher and attended the University of Leeds. After wartime service in the Royal Engineers, Smith began his career as an entrepreneur and property developer by purchasing the Shaftesbury Hotel.[1]

Smith and Kitten's lives diverged dramatically in the late 1920s, however. Smith would become spectacularly wealthy, building a prestigious property portfolio that included the opulent Park Lane Hotel. He would be a prominent Conservative politician and, after the Second World War, Lord Mayor of London, Baronet, and Chair of Arsenal Football Club. Obituaries celebrated the achievements of a remarkable man, who succeeded through graft, intuition, and character.[2] Kitten's life played out differently. He was also a self-made man, whose respectability was rooted in hard work, economic independence, and commitment to playing by the rules. As Smith's empire expanded, however, Kitten's restaurant was harassed by police and condemned by magistrates, his character was impugned by a muckraking newspaper, and his business subjected to a vicious letter-writing campaign by neighbours – orchestrated by the well-connected developer with whose life his own was entwined. Kitten fought to protect his reputation and livelihood, most dramatically by suing the newspaper for libel. Yet his world was unmade: the Kittens went bankrupt, lost their café, and spent the rest of their lives in poorly paid catering jobs.[3]

For a short time, it would have been easy for newspapers and historians to tell the same story about Kitten and Smith's lives as self-made men. That that story became impossible, though, is instructive. What made them different? Kitten was born in Sierra Leone, and he was a Black man married to a white woman in a racist society.

The short-lived convergence of two lives on a Seven Dials backstreet provides an outline for the arguments this book makes about masculinities in modern Britain. Smith and Kitten's diverging fates show how masculinity was a relational category.[4] Individual lives and notions of manliness took shape at the intersection between identities of gender and differences of class, race and ethnicity, nation, and sexuality.[5] That process meant that masculinities were made and constrained through huge inequalities of power. Kitten claimed the status of wartime sacrifice, the respectability of a self-made property owner, and the equality before the institutions of law and state that was his due as a British subject. His marriage to Emily might have emblematised how idealised visions of the family formed the bedrock of post-war reconstruction and ideas of Britishness.[6]

That Kitten's claims were dismissed, then, demonstrates both the pervasive effects of the 1920s 'colour bar' and the formal and informal ways in which state institutions and popular newspapers policed the boundaries of men's lives and normative ideas of masculinity. Identified as a threat to public morality, Kitten's café was persecuted as police and courts sought to suppress his business. Despite Kitten's faith in British justice, his libel case was laughed out of court by a racist judge. In court and press he was depicted not as a hard-working man and husband, but a dangerous criminal and sexual predator. Kitten was characterised as an alien in the place he made home.[7]

The coming apart of Smith and Kitten's lives underscores three further themes elaborated in this book. The first is the productive relationship between masculinities and broader axes of social difference. The second is the power of institutions of state and culture to make (and unmake) ideas of manliness and men's lives. Although this process was open-ended and contested, we see the intensity with which the boundaries of normative manhood were produced and policed. The third theme is the historical specificity of such processes. Viewed synchronically, we can see radically different ways in which men made sense of the world and their place in it. Viewed diachronically, we can see how masculinities could change equally radically over time. Kitten and Smith's lives as men reflected both the historical conjuncture they inhabited and the interlocking spaces of home and work, neighbourhood and city, and nation and empire through which they moved.

The starting point for this book is simple: *like masculinities, men are made*. Taking this as our prompt, we argue that the formation of masculine ideals, experiences, and subjectivities should be understood as an ongoing and unfinished historical process. As such, it provides a locus for radical historical work that grounds liberatory futures of gender in new understandings of the gendered past. Treating masculinity as a process, rather than a category of analysis, foregrounds the critical work of construction through which men's lives took shape. As Kitten and Smith's encounter suggests, that process coalesced where different strands of historical analysis met – social, cultural, political, economic, institutional, material, and environmental. It took place on different geographical and chronological scales of analysis, including the domestic, local, regional, national, and transnational and both macro-level historical transformations, the individual life cycle, and the event or conjuncture. Men were made through institutions and bureaucracies, social and economic relations, and the interaction between culture and self-fashioning. Men were made in the warp and weft of life, through history, in a process marked by conflict and negotiation and shaped by massive inequalities of power and hierarchical social differences. Masculinities, like men, were always of a particular time, and a particular place.

Contexts and conjunctures

This book provides a critical overview of ongoing debates in the history of masculinities and the historical formation of men's lives and ideas of masculinity in Britain between the 1890s and the present day. It sets out a new agenda for the field, making an ambitious argument for the importance of writing histories of masculinity which are present-centred and politically engaged, and which foreground the intersecting processes through which men and masculinities are made across time and space. The book has two points of departure. The first is the intensification of 'crisis talk' around men's lives in contemporary Britain. Prompted by issues ranging from educational attainment to mental health and the shape and size of the male body, the language of crisis presents both individual men and ideas of masculinity as increasingly brittle and embattled. From this perspective, men and masculinities are perceived as threatened by progressive social change, particularly third-wave feminism and the growing purchase of new male identities. The anger that characterises men's rights activists, 'incels', and the social media 'manosphere', however, is underpinned by deep-rooted inequalities of gender in social, economic, cultural, and political life, and the reinvigoration of patriarchal power and male violence against women. In thinking historically about these tensions, *Men and Masculinities* offers a critical genealogy for contemporary gender politics. In so doing, it establishes new ways of understanding how men's lives and ideas of masculinity have (and have not) changed over the past 130 years.

The book's second point of departure is ethical and methodological. The opening discussion of James Kitten and Bracewell Smith underscores how each chapter is animated by our insistence on the capacity of individual life stories to reorientate our understanding of the time- and place-specific ways in which male subjectivities and ideas of masculinity took shape. In teasing out how individuals made sense of the world and their place in it as men – the articulation points between men and masculinities – the book takes its cue from the experiences of the ordinary and extraordinary, framing its arguments through (and with) careful consideration of the contradictions and complexities of individual lives. This introduction models that endeavour, introducing the stories of other men including the barman and dance organiser 'Lady' Austin Salmon, the South Yorkshire coal miner and rabbit fancier Will Topham, and the anxious Welsh house painter John Domney. Exploring their lives in vivid colour and precise detail establishes that approach from the very start.

If masculinities and men's experiences are shaped by a process which is ongoing and of its time, so, too, are the histories of masculinity that have developed over the past three decades. For historians of nineteenth- and twentieth-century Britain, at least, the publication in 1991 of Michael Roper and John Tosh's collection of essays *Manful Assertions: Masculinities in Britain since 1800* marked the moment when the history of masculinity took shape as a recognisable field. *Manful Assertions* should not be understood in isolation. Tracked by similar interventions across different national and chronological historiographies in Britain, North America, and beyond, the volume exemplified a wider historical conjuncture that made the emergence of a new field possible. This was a significant point when disparate intellectual, social, and cultural trajectories, especially the project of women's liberation, intersected to isolate men's lives and masculinities as subject to historical enquiry, interdisciplinary theoretical reflection, and political activism.[8] As John Tosh and Lucy Delap explore in the conversation that concludes this volume, *Manful Assertions* interwove an emerging body of work within women's and gay history, gender theory, and the sociology of masculinity.[9] Like other formative interventions in the field, it did so, crucially, at a moment in the mid-1980s when dominant ideas of masculinity were identified as a problem for men and women alike. For at least some contributors, the men's anti-sexist movement's structures and ideas, particularly Sheila Rowbotham's assertion that 'the creation of a new woman of necessity demands the creation of a new man', were part of the genealogy of *Manful Assertions*.[10]

The starting point for *Manful Assertions* was simple, and one we revisit in this volume: masculinities have a history, and the forms and experiences of manliness and men's lives are always time- and place-specific. It was on this basis that Roper, Tosh, and their contributors explored changing ideals of manliness, the intersection between identities of gender and those of class, race and ethnicity, religion, and sexuality, and how masculinities were multiple, relational, and contested. They did so in ways that remained alive to the power relations within which the gender order emerged, especially in the Victorian and Edwardian periods, through *both* the patriarchal social, cultural, political, and economic relations from which all men derived status *and* the distance and antagonism between men themselves. What *Manful Assertions* did, then, was foreground those diachronic and synchronic axes of difference and conflict within which men's lives took shape, and ideas of masculinity took hold, in modern Britain.[11]

Manful Assertions has been – and remains – a vital part of the intellectual formation of the contributors to this volume. Revisiting the historical conjuncture when *Manful Assertions* was published, we argue, is a productive way of exploring what the field has become. This comparative approach gives us a way of historicising the history of masculinity, placing the development of an academic field since the mid-1980s within its broader context. In so doing, *Men and Masculinities* seeks both to show how pervasive notions of masculinity shape the practice of history as a discipline and profession and to think historically about the persistence of patriarchy and male power in contemporary Britain. *Manful Assertions* is thus both a model for our work and a starting point for a sustained interrogation of the shifting politics and practice of writing histories of masculinity. Rather than offering a comprehensive survey of work published over the past thirty years, our aim is to map key historiographical trajectories and suggest future directions.[12] In returning to the foundational moment exemplified by *Manful Assertions*, then, and interrogating the social, economic, cultural, and political conditions within which its subject matter and mode of enquiry became possible, we want to show how histories of masculinity are themselves time- and place-specific. Thinking about the similarities and differences between *Manful Assertions* and our own conjuncture affords new possibilities for writing histories of men and masculinities which are present-centred and politically engaged.[13]

Why should those histories be present-centred? There is an ethical or political imperative here, because the radical potential of *Manful Assertions* and the men's anti-sexist movement has dissipated, and the damaging effects of dominant forms of masculinity and male power continue to be lived in contemporary Britain. These effects are visible in patterns of male behaviour that have driven feminist campaigns around #MeToo, routine sexual violence and Everyday Sexism, and the persistence of gendered inequalities in labour markets, incomes, and political participation.[14] In contemporary Britain, misogyny and patriarchal power often appear reinvigorated. Violence against women remains pervasive, while commentators fret over supposed crises of men's bodies, minds, and lives, and the growing incidence of suicide and mental ill-health among young men. The deforming effects of masculinities are embodied in the disjuncture between rising rates of obesity and images of hyper-masculine physicality predicated on steroid abuse and the gym. Reminiscent of rising suicide rates among unemployed men in the 1930s, contemporary concerns around young men's mental health point to the difficulty of reconciling older ideals of masculinity with new economic, political, and institutional realities.[15] Thinking critically about how masculinities are made historically, we argue, might afford possibilities for unmaking those masculine forms which still deform and constrain the lives of men and women alike. Thinking historically also offers a riposte to the idea, central to misogynist 'men's rights' activism, that there is some essential truth to manhood and to male power.[16] In addressing such challenges, and in positioning the history of masculinity as an alternative to the distortions of the 'manosphere', we might rediscover the activist engagement that characterised *Manful Assertions*. The chapters in this volume thus build into an extended argument for the importance of histories which reflect on their intellectual and political formation and think critically about pressing issues around men's lives today.

This approach should also prompt us to think critically about the historicity and politics of our own work. Despite the activist commitments of those involved with *Manful Assertions*, the politics of the field that has emerged since the 1980s is ambiguous. This is particularly striking when compared to women's and gender history. From the 1970s, the first generation of historians of women's lives, like those social historians concerned with class, race and ethnicity, or sexuality, engaged in a deliberate project of historical recovery that was explicitly progressive and reformist. Reclaiming previously 'hidden' histories was a way to rethink established historical narratives and establish a genealogy for activist politics. Building on this scholarship, feminist historians explored how power was shaped by (and contributed to) deep-rooted differences of gender and maintaining patriarchal social, cultural, economic, political, and interpersonal structures.[17] Similar approaches characterised the work of scholars on what became lesbian and gay history, and Black history, in the 1970s and 1980s.

Historical recovery, historical and political critique, and liberationist politics were entwined.[18]

Manful Assertions was indebted to this work, as Tosh and Delap note below. Despite their affinities, though, the position of histories of masculinity within such progressive projects has been uneasy. The intimate relationship between women's history and the women's movement, histories of race and the civil rights and anti-colonial movements, and LGBTQ histories and gay liberation does not exist in the same way for historians of masculinity. While men might have been historically marginalised by dint of their position within hierarchies of class, race and ethnicity, sexuality, age, and place, they have not been marginalised only *as men*. While men might have remained unmarked as *gendered actors* in the historiography, this is not the same as being effaced from the historical record. Politicised modes of historical recovery that characterised social history have very different implications when our subjects are male. Peripheral figures associated with populist politics or men's rights activism might lay rhetorical claim to the status of marginalisation and make similar claims for their historical case studies, usually situated within a reactionary teleology of loss. That argument is untenable, however.[19]

This means that the ethical imperatives of histories of masculinity have often been unclear. Paradoxically, while *Manful Assertions* has shaped the work of historians of modern Britain, we have somehow forgotten the political commitments of those involved in the project. In revisiting this foundational conjuncture, our aim is also to reimagine the contemporary possibilities of histories of masculinity. It is striking that many of our contributors take up this challenge by approaching men's lives from the vantage point of feminist history, histories of sexuality, or queer and trans histories, which provide a sharp analytic and political edge. The critique of Adrian Kane-Galbraith or Hilary Buxton, as developed in their chapters below, for example, has far-reaching possibilities for unlocking the historical formation of gender relations and imagining new ways of being men.[20] As Lee Edelman argues of queer studies, as a radical project, the history of masculinity should be concerned not with defining identities but disturbing them.[21]

Men and Masculinities shows how thinking critically about the historical formation of masculinities provides new ways of understanding histories of modern Britain. While our focus is on men's lives and ideas of masculinity, treating these as historically specific case studies also allows us to suggest new ways of thinking about the formation of British modernities – to intervene in debates around the transformation of society, culture, economics, and politics during a period of massive upheaval.[22] Our argument that men, like masculinity, are made allows us to move from histories of masculinity out to bigger debates in the field and, in so doing, understand how masculinities might have been made differently. Histories of masculinity engage with questions including the effects of global flashpoints of war and pandemic, the resonance of Britain's changing global and imperial status, the transformation of hierarchies of class, gender, race and ethnicity, age, and sexuality, and the reconfigured boundaries between public and private life. These histories, moreover, underscore the shifting balance of power between state institutions, cultural entrepreneurs, and markets of labour and property in making men and masculinities. As Hannah Charnock rightly notes, the significance of these histories resonates beyond the realm of gender relations. 'Understanding how patriarchy is embedded within *all* social institutions', Charnock argues, 'offers not just an opportunity to address contemporary cultures of masculinity and gender relations, but to think about other major contemporary issues including climate change, technology, privacy, and the role of the state.'[23] If gender, as Joan Scott rightly insists, is both a 'constitutive element of social relationships' and a 'primary way of signifying relationships of power', then modern British history is always a history of masculinity too.[24]

Same and different

In the thirty years since *Manful Assertions* was published, the history of masculinities in modern Britain has become a burgeoning, exciting field. Despite this intellectual dynamism, however, in some ways the field has become bogged down. One issue is how the field has primarily developed through the thematic case study. Perhaps more than in other fields, this is the characteristic form of monographs and edited collections alike. The result is a proliferation of work organised around particular themes, including, for example, masculinity and war, masculinity and religion, masculinity and leisure, masculinity and empire, or masculinity and politics. Alternatively, masculinity has figured as a peripheral issue in studies more concerned with other things.[25] While these discrete interventions might be excellent, what we are still missing is a systematic overview of the history of masculinities in modern Britain.[26]

One aim of this book, then, is to consider how the whole of our field might be more than the sum of its parts. While this challenge is a perennial one for an edited collection, we have worked to address the problems of fragmentation through the ongoing and collaborative process through which *Men and Masculinities* was brought into being. Exemplified by this introduction and the concluding conversation that frame our substantive chapters, the book draws on an iterative process of workshopping ideas, sharing work-in-progress and written reflections, and continuing in-person and virtual conversations between contributors. It originated in a panel on 'Manhood in Crisis: Masculinities in Late Twentieth-Century Britain', at the Modern British Studies conference 'British Studies in a Broken World', held at the University of Birmingham in 2017. That panel sought to historicise masculinity's crises and, in conversation with the conference themes, explore how gender politics emblematised far-reaching contemporary crises in British public life and identity.[27] We revisited these themes in summer 2018, situating them in a broader chronological and thematic context through a one-day workshop that discussed pre-circulated papers. Most of the contributors to this volume participated in that session, but the workshop and the reflection and critical discussion that followed between 2018 and 2022 brought together a much larger group of historians, all of whom made telling contributions to this book's scope, shape, and arguments. In a very real sense, *Men and Masculinities* is the outcome of a generative and genuinely collaborative intellectual exchange.[28]

A second issue with the historiography is a striking tendency to circle around a familiar set of theoretical, methodological, and historiographical debates. These include the relationship between discourses of masculinity and the experiences of ordinary men, the value of social and cultural approaches to the historical formation of manliness, and notions of the 'crisis of masculinity'.[29] Most prominent is the recurrence of intensely structural debates about the intersection between dominant, subordinate, and hegemonic masculinities. Such debates reflect the intellectual indebtedness of foundational histories of masculinity – including, but not only, *Manful Assertions* – to theoretical models derived from sociology, particularly the powerful interventions of Raewyn Connell.[30] Addressing this relationship has been productive, because it has forced historians to think carefully about the intersection between men's lives and social differences, the relationality of past masculinities, and the gender order as a site where power operates. This work, moreover, frames many of the chapters that follow, particularly Jessica Meyer's critical engagement with Tosh's analysis of the relationship between social and cultural approaches and Ben Griffin's nuanced reworking of Connell's models of hegemonic and dominant masculinity to explore questions of power and change over time.[31]

Yet it remains our sense that the development of historical scholarship has become constrained within and by these conceptual models. The repetition of these frameworks has little echo in adjacent fields like women's history, histories of sexuality, or queer histories, so its overdetermining effects on histories of masculinity are striking and problematic. In shifting attention from structure to process – following the sociologist Andrew Abbott to think about structures *as* and *in* process – we do not discount matters of men's power or the organisation of patriarchy.[32] Instead, this move seeks to better understand the resilience of male power across modern British history. Masculinity has perhaps escaped successful challenge as a mechanism for distributing power by always being on the move. Foregrounding process, then, underscores this fugitive quality, while holding open the possibility of more substantive change. Thinking of masculinity as processual and plastic balances the pessimism demanded by the analysis of historical experience and the optimism necessary for any radical historical project.

This book thus reflects our shared commitment to finding new vantage points on what are now old debates. In so doing, it sets out an approach which is both present-centred and emphasises the processes through which men and masculinities were made. We argue that this provides a more dynamic mode of analysis that disrupts the structural approaches that have come to overdetermine the field. Therefore, we draw on recent work in queer theory and histories, particularly that which interrogates the relationship between sexual subjectivities and time.[33] What we have called 'a history for the present' reworks a productive tension in queer history: the insistence on the distance of the queer past versus the recognition that that past might be made integral to imagining new forms of community and selfhood in the present. Moving beyond the political registers of queer history, however, we argue that histories of masculinity most often reveal patterns of power and violence – of men over women, of men over men – and of men's suffocation by gendered expectations. Perhaps the field's most important task, then, is to make an evidence-based case for the undoing of masculinity, and levelling the edifice of men's power, altogether.

Elaborating this approach thus presses against the conventional vocabularies, categories, and theoretical frameworks within which a vibrant field emerged and has become bound. In different ways, our contributors explore the historically specific conjunctures through which British masculinities took shape over the past 130 years. Pushing past the methodological impasse that characterises the existing historiography, they explore how men's lives and masculinities were made and remade in and by the state and its institutions, social and cultural relations, and patterns of everyday life. Histories (and historians) of masculinities are also present-centred, however. Despite their affinities – and despite our indebtedness to that volume – the distance between *Manful Assertions* and this book demonstrates how much the vocabularies of historical scholarship have changed over the past thirty years. Two things stand out. The first is the central prominence of questions of sexuality, transgender, and race in this book. Rather than marginalised subfields, Kane-Galbraith's work on transmasculinities and Jonathan Saha and Hilary Buxton's work on race and empire gives this book much of its analytic impetus. Our insistence that men and

Introduction   11

masculinities are made is prompted by Kane-Galbraith's path-breaking analysis of trans men's engagement with the bureaucratic logics of National Insurance and Saha and Buxton's compelling reading of the racialisation of male embodiment. Their work also defines the geographical terrain our contributors cover, particularly in attending to the competing valence of the British nation, world, and empire.[34]

The second difference between this book and *Manful Assertions* is a more pronounced preoccupation with questions of selfhood and emotion. We might read this as an historiographical expression of what scholars have sometimes presented as the individualisation of post-war society and culture – of the historicity of our scholarly work.[35] It also reflects growing interest in these issues within history and adjacent disciplines. Like historiographies of modern Britain more broadly, work on masculinities has been transformed by the emergence of new theoretical frameworks and categories of analysis derived from cultural history. The language of subjectivity and emotion is now pervasive. For sure, those questions were present in *Manful Assertions*, and have been teased out by Michael Roper in the past two decades. Yet they are articulated with a self-consciousness that is very different in Richard Hall's contribution to this book, for example.[36]

It is tempting to see these shifts as evidence of the generative nature of the field. We might be more cautious, though. What do we achieve by using these ideas (and not others) to understand the historical formation of masculinities? How do we avoid the traps of 'the evidence of experience', including the notion that our access to lost 'voices' is somehow unmediated?[37] Addressing these questions means thinking critically about what we gain (or lose) by shifting the scale of analysis onto the family, adopting the oral history interview as a mode of analysis, or treating social survey responses as a window onto the past. It also means considering whether foregrounding selfhood, for example, makes us rethink patterns of continuity and change in the history of masculinities, rather than simply adding new terrain to the landscape across which historians move. Here, as always, the challenge is to define a whole greater than its constitutive parts.

The affinities between *Manful Assertions* and this volume are instructive, however. Read side by side, they demonstrate the enduring privileges of masculinity over the twentieth century. As historians have shown, certain forms of masculinity have carried institutional entitlements in the emerging welfare state and different opportunities in markets of labour and capital. Despite its changing scope and size, the state has continued to arbitrate and make men and masculinities. Examples include the institutionalisation of the male breadwinner ideal into welfare provision and taxation regimes, generational experiences of compulsory military mobilisation, and the regulation of transgressive masculinities through criminal law, prison, or removal to an asylum.[38] The state was never a monolithic actor, however, and the governance of men's lives was marked by conflict and change. Because that process was shaped by differences of power and status, it was also subject to sustained political critique. Power relations between men informed the construction of masculine styles, generational reproduction, and boundaries between normative and non-normative identities. These struggles often took place where masculinity intersected with differences of class, race, sexuality, age, and place. James Kitten's life showed how institutional entitlements could be claimed. Punitive legal systems faced demands for reform, most strikingly through campaigns around the extension of the franchise before 1918 and the partial decriminalisation of homosexuality in 1967. At moments of rupture, the process of making masculinity could itself be remade.[39]

Masculinity was ordinary, however, and treating it as process means recognising the quotidian ways in which men's lives were made and remade. It was within the everyday that historical subjects became men, where social differences were negotiated, and where tensions between cultural ideals and material realities became most resonant.[40] Consider the letters, photographs, and diary that document Will Topham's adult life between the 1910s and 1960s. Working underground at Brodsworth Main Colliery, in South Yorkshire, Topham's diary suggests the importance of work to his identity as a man, particularly the value placed on physical strength, bravery, and class solidarities that characterised the emotional communities of work and trade union politics. Equally important was his involvement in all-male worlds of leisure and association. Their importance changed, but at different moments Topham's sense of self was invested in cycling, his allotment, and exhibiting rabbits. Topham's marriage to Kitt left fewer archival traces, but his familial relationships were also integral to his identity. His relationship with Enid, his daughter, transcended that of distant breadwinner to encompass rich emotional bonds formed through their shared endeavours of rabbits or cycling.[41]

Topham's archive also reflects moments when habitual processes of self-making were disrupted. Workplace solidarity broke down when his pick was stolen, and he sought redress through the Yorkshire Mineworker's Association. Accidents, illness – a diagnosis of rheumatoid arthritis – and old age eroded the strength and independence necessary to work below ground, ride a bicycle, or maintain his allotment. Lockouts, strikes, short-time, and unemployment in the 1920s and 1930s undermined his role as breadwinner and participation in associational life. Enid's growing independence – grammar school, college, and a teaching career – upended axes of gendered and generational power within the family.[42]

Topham's archive provides a powerful sense of the demands of being a man. Masculinity was never named in his diary or letters, nor did he reflect on related terms like 'manliness'. We should still understand the act of writing and the experiences documented as part of making himself visible *as a man* – both to other men or women and, perhaps, himself. The concerns that braced Topham's writing emerged through unstated yet compelling ideas of what it meant to be a man in public or private. Everyday writing was also an effortful exercise in documenting, identifying, or negotiating those tensions. Implicit in the ordinariness of Topham's diary – the rhythms of planting and harvesting, for example – is the ongoing process of making oneself as a man.[43] This example underscores how masculinity was always in the making. What Kane-Galbraith calls 'microprocesses of recognition' were freighted with 'anxiety', reflecting 'an ongoing situational uneasiness about the boundaries of manhood'. At work or within associational life, men like Topham 'had to make themselves visible *as men* to an audience of other men, with the attendant concern that some gesture, bodily trait or sartorial choice might make them non-legible within this structurally privileged category'. In this sense, fulfilling the expectations of masculine archetypes had far-reaching emotional, political, and economic costs.[44]

Time and space

In December 1932, police officers raided a ballroom on Holland Park Avenue, London, initiating the most notorious of several 'pansy cases' in the early 1930s. For weeks, crowds of working-class men – mainly waiters and hotel workers living nearby – had gathered in the ballroom. Many were flamboyantly camp in dress and demeanour, most notably through their use of cosmetics; several wore drag. In so doing, they evoked the complex ways in which male identities were defined through self-presentation and burgeoning consumer cultures. The ballroom was hired, and the dances run, by a small group of friends. They included Austin Salmon, more commonly known as Lady Austin, a twenty-four-year-old barman.[45] During the raid Lady Austin showed remarkable sang-froid. 'There is nothing wrong in that', he told the arresting officer. 'You may think so, but it is what we call real love man for man. You call us Nancies and bum boys but … before long our cult will be allowed in this country.' Continued into the courtroom, this was a striking assertion of the legitimacy of same-sex desire and transgressive masculinities.[46]

The ballroom raid underscores how the modern state sought to maintain normative ideas of gender. Like the harassment of James Kitten's café, persecution of the 'Camp Boys' shows how institutions of state, law, and culture policed the boundaries of what was permissible. Their transgressions warranted punitive intervention. Twenty-seven men were convicted and sentenced to between three and twenty months' imprisonment, usually for nothing more than wearing make-up or dancing with another man. At the trial's conclusion, the judge praised police for purging this dangerous 'nest of sodomitical haunts'. It was, he concluded, 'essential that a sharp lesson should be administered' against all '[who] have degraded their manhood'.[47]

The case also reveals the historically specific nature of binaries of gender and sexuality that shape contemporary Britain and which, we often assume, shaped social relations and subjectivities in the past. Lady Austin refused distinctions between 'gay' and 'straight', 'queer' and 'normal', and 'masculine' and 'feminine', exchanging names and presenting himself in ways that disrupted the stability of gender. Like many of his friends, Austin's camp name went alongside masculine pronouns; the 'Camp Dance Club' were 'Queenies' and 'my camp boys'. Unexpected forms of naming underscore a radical dissonance between contemporary and historical categories of gender.[48] Kane-Galbraith makes a similar argument, showing how the language of 'persons of doubtful sex' signifies something different to contemporary notions of trans men.[49] While men's lives might seem familiar across time, we should be wary of reinscribing late modern categories of gender and sexual orientation onto the self-perception of historical subjects or establishing stable genealogies for trans and non-binary identities. Here we see the intersections between masculinity, sexuality, and class, and the importance of processes of embodiment, self-presentation, and consumption to masculine subjectivities – most strikingly through men's engagement with mass market fashion and the beauty industry.[50] These are familiar themes in contemporary cultures of masculinity. Lady Austin's strangeness, though, reminds us of the distance of the recent past and how masculinities might change radically over time.

How should historians begin to characterise how masculinities and men's lives have changed over the past 130 years? Thinking about its relationship with time has often been dominated by ideas of masculinity in crisis. Viewed from this perspective, the history of masculinity is defined by recurring moments of instability within the gender order. Such crises are exemplified by phenomena as disparate as the experience of shell shock during the Great War, the challenge of second-wave feminism and gay liberation, and the cyclical effects of de-industrialisation and mass unemployment.[51] Even this summary suggests how notions of crisis are now a hoary cliché, repeated so often that the gender order appears always and everywhere threatened.[52] In history, crisis is an analytic category emptied of critical purchase. Troublingly, however, in contemporary gender politics the idea persists not as a category but a trope, central to the grammar of men's rights activism. Here 'masculinity in crisis' has become a pretext for 'fighting back' against 'misandry'. There is both a political and intellectual case for moving past the language of 'crisis' in our work, at least as anything other than an object of conceptual history.[53]

The persistence of 'crisis talk' ironically underscores the usefulness of thinking about masculinity as an ongoing process rather than a fixed state. This idea informs Griffin's discussion of the 'operations' mediating between historical change and moments when masculinity was deemed imperilled.[54] Called into being by moral entrepreneurs – politicians, journalists, men's rights activists – such moments demonstrated *both* how social, economic, cultural, and political change could disrupt the processes through which masculinities were made *and* more direct challenges to male hegemony. Presenting masculinity as in crisis had (and has) high stakes. Crisis talk can be a lucrative commodity for the media. Crisis talk does political work, often predicated upon defining men's social position as embattled and needing reassertion. If crises make men and masculinities – and draw attention to moments when those processes come under pressure – the effects of crisis talk are often deeply conservative, mobilising resistance to progressive social change.[55]

As this suggests, we are sceptical that crisis can provide a constructive framework for thinking about the relationship between masculinities and time. Instead, we suggest three alternatives. First: if men and masculinities were made through history, the nature of that process and the primary sites around which gendered subjectivities and experiences took shape have shifted radically but unevenly over the past century. Elaborating this approach, we might see how key chronologies in the history of masculinity have been defined by the changing shape and scope of the state, the growing reach of new forms of mass culture and media, often transnational or global in form, and the reconfiguration of boundaries between legitimate and illegitimate forms of masculinity through changes to criminal and civil law. As Helen Smith and Pat Ayres argue below, this approach might also foreground the importance of changing markets in housing and labour and the nature of men's work.

As we have suggested, starting with such processes also affords new ways of thinking about British society, culture, politics, and economics. Rather than a discrete subject of analysis, histories of masculinity allow us to interrogate the field and period more broadly conceived. From this perspective, the supposed turning points of the First and Second World Wars are important less as events per se than in accelerating changes to the nature of the state or providing symbolic focus for ideas of national character, heroic masculinity, and leadership after 1945.[56] As commentators have argued, when refracted through notions of masculinity these ideas have deformed post-war society, culture, and politics, most recently through discussions around decline and national prestige associated with Brexit and a resurgent populism. In this context, continuities in men's lives and ideas of masculinity appear more important than the changes on which historians have usually focused.

The second alternative approach to the relationship between masculinities and time focuses on the *expressions* of these processes. From this perspective, the proliferation or transformation of ideas of manliness reflected specific changes to the processes through which men and masculinities were made. The renewed influence of new forms of consumerism, often originating in the United States, over the twentieth century sustained new identities associated with style, performance, and personality.[57] The 'brief window of tolerance' towards trans men identified by Kane-Galbraith simultaneously challenges historiographical assumptions about the 1950s, exemplifies how masculinities were historically specific, and reveals the formative influence of new forms of state bureaucracy, identification, and data management. Finally, the growing salience of ideas of 'ordinariness' to men's identities after the Second World War might be understood as the social and cultural expression of new forms of social democracy. If, as Richard Hall demonstrates, normality and ordinariness were the 'dynamic terrain' on which intergenerational relations were negotiated in mid-century Britain, they were themselves historically specific.[58]

The third alternative approach to the relationship between masculinities and time takes up a challenge John Tosh sets out below. Tosh argues that we need to 'explain the historical process by which masculinity came to prevail' as a way of understanding men's lives and the gender order. One striking change has been the growing purchase of a new conceptual vocabulary for understanding male lives and subjectivities: the prominence of the language of *masculinity* itself has a history, in other words. For much of the nineteenth and twentieth centuries, 'masculine' was understood as something one was, so that ideas of masculine character or domains were mobilised with considerable force around the campaigns for the vote before the Great War. In this schema, masculinity's reference point was external. As historians have begun to show, however, over the past century masculinity has been reconfigured as an inherent trait of personality or interiorised sense of selfhood.[59]

It was on this basis that Michael Roper situated the period 1914–1950 'between manliness and masculinity'.[60] Roper is right to identify a profound shift in ideas of masculinity, but the process was more uneven and, we would argue, took place much later. Indeed, the isolation of masculinity as subject for historical or sociological reflection in the 1980s was itself part of the process through which it was brought into being as a component of selfhood. In that decade, as Lucy Delap and Katie Jones observe, a combination of social, economic, cultural, and political shifts prompted commentators to identify a crisis in men's lives and hegemonic notions of manhood.[61] This crisis talk underpinned the growing currency of 'masculinity' in everyday life and public debate. It is a crude measure, but a Google n-gram search for 'masculinity' or 'crisis of masculinity' suggests the use of these terms exploded after the mid-1980s. Ironically, the work of historians of masculinity has been integral to making the very changes we have sought to understand. Thinking historically about masculinities has been part of transforming historical ideas of masculinity.

Masculinity's growing reach within public life, popular culture, the psy-sciences, and politics thus reflects the shifting apparatus for thinking about men's lives over the past century. Rather than an external set of expectations, ideas about being a man have been reframed as a component of personhood. Masculinity, in Tosh's resonant phrasing, 'is not just a code of conduct but expresses the "authentic" self'. Naming gender like this dramatically raises what is at stake in processes of change or activism that challenge the structural foundation of male power. It makes 'crisis talk' both more individualised and more threatening. This means 'we could better interpret men's condition today if we understood how masculinity acquired its conceptual hegemony'.[62]

As the encounter between Kitten and Smith suggests, the geographical terrain upon which men's lives and ideas of masculinity took shape was also expansive. The spatialised processes through which masculinities were made cut across boundaries between the local and the national, and the imperial, transnational, and global. As many of our contributors show, it is impossible to understand what was at stake in debates around race and manliness without considering the constant movement of men and ideas across the British world and empire. That process could be (and often was) transnational in scope: the productive relationship between masculine identities and new forms of consumer culture, for example, reflected both the cultural influence of the United States and how the transformative power of consumer capitalism cut across national borders. While the empirical case studies on which *Men and Masculinities* focuses deal with modern Britain and its empire, moreover, the book's arguments about the practice and politics of histories of masculinity are informed by historiographical and theoretical debates that are similarly transnational. The critical conversation between histories of gender and histories of the emotions or queer theory, for example, echoes a growing body of work in North America, Australia, and New Zealand. Finally, *Men and Masculinities*' transnational resonance is evident through our contemporary political reference points. The reinvigoration of patriarchal power, misogyny, and male violence, the growth of a virulent men's rights movement, and fears around masculinity's so-called crises are striking and troubling features of transnational public life. Histories and historiographies of masculinity cannot be fully understood within the constraints of national histories.

Men and masculinities

John Domney was an anxious man. Throughout 1936, the young house painter wrestled with his lack of concentration, confidence, and success. Domney attributed his 'trouble' to a sense of inferiority and fear of 'being outclassed'. Such failings were, he wrote, compounded by his 'reserved nature' and nagging doubts that came through 'comparison of others with myself'. The effects were profound, since Domney's worries 'made me jealous & envious and inclined to … give up the seemingly hopeless struggle'. The process that led Domney to confide his fears in writing also underscored his earnest commitment to making himself anew. As well as completing courses in shorthand and book-keeping, he undertook the correspondence course in self-improvement known as Pelmanism. Domney's anxieties were documented through grey exercise books and completed worksheets that traversed the postal network between his home in Rhos-on-Sea, where he lived with his parents, and the Pelman Institute's offices in Bloomsbury.[63]

Domney's dedication to self-improvement might have been unusual, but he was by no means the only person to pursue Pelmanism after the Great War. The tireless scrutiny evidenced through his worksheets underscores the work of self-fashioning undertaken by one ordinary man in the mid-1930s. As this example suggests, the process of making men and masculinities was also one in which men themselves engaged. Reflecting on the limits of discursive approaches to the history of masculinities, Jessica Meyer calls for an analytic 'practice that acknowledges the agency of men as problematic historical actors in their own right and across time, rather than as representations of the generically male subject at a given moment in time'. In taking seriously the experiences of men like Domney – or Kitten, Topham, or Salmon, for that matter – we might begin to see the pay-off of such an historical practice. What happens when, following Meyer, we work towards 'seeing [our subjects] as men rather than as facets of masculinity', while – in Joan Scott's words – still 'attend[ing] to the historical processes that, through discourse, position subjects and produce their experiences'?[64]

First, we see how the process of making masculinity was quotidian. Domney voiced his struggle to negotiate the distance between ideals of manliness and the realities of everyday life. 'What do you desire more than anything in the world?' Domney was asked. His response ventriloquised the Pelman Institute's advertising: 'self-respect, efficiency, respect of others, single-mindedness of purpose'.[65] Pelmanism held out the tantalising prospect of individual transformation, fuelling dreamlike fantasies of social mobility and personal fulfilment.[66] Domney's aspirations also imply the unease that impelled him towards self-improvement. His worksheets offer a moving description of a life felt to be falling short and an earnest attempt to address those feelings. While the painful feelings were Domney's own, they reflected more pervasive tensions between ideals of manliness, lived experiences, and material constraints of class, age, and place. Those feelings took shape at the intersection between the self and the social. 'Anxious masculinities', Griffin argues, 'have been the product not simply of the profusion of cultural models of masculinity, but an inability to establish some preferred models or characteristics as more legitimate than others.'[67] For an unmarried house painter living in a seaside town, particular ideals like the man of business, gentleman, or romantic hero might have proven elusive, just as unemployment challenged the breadwinner ideal in the 1930s. Pat Ayers rightly observes the remarkable complicity of the audience for performances of masculinity – the lengths to which women, for example, could go to sustain the illusion of manliness within families.[68] Still, when manifested as anxiety or depression the concerns of men like Domney reflected tensions between cultural scripts and social and economic conditions. Here we see the frustrations that ensued when masculine ideals reproduced through new forms of commercial mass culture reached into material worlds where they were impossible.

Anxious masculinities and men's anxieties thus reflected frictions between culture and society and the irresolvable distance between hope and reality. Following Domney we can see how those expectations cut across boundaries between work, education, social life, consumption, relationships, and housing. Expectations were embedded in local communities and economies, but they were also braced by cultural forms – commercial self-improvement, for example – that were global in scope. Exploited by entrepreneurial boosters like the Pelman Institute, such conflicts found more poignant expression in a marked shift in the incidence of male suicide in the 1930s. In this sense they anticipated what is often presented as a novel contemporary crisis of men's mental health and allow us to think historically about what is at stake there.[69]

Meyer's approach starts by acknowledging men's agency 'as problematic historical actors'. Equally important, however, is tracking their lives 'across time'. We need, she argues, a fuller understanding of how the process of making men and masculinities could be reconfigured along discrete temporal axes. The ideas of self-improvement that characterised Pelmanism had longer genealogies but coalesced in the mid-1930s as aspirational and historically specific ideals of masculinity. The process of making men and masculinities shifted across chronological or historical time. Domney's anxieties, however, reflected a particularly freighted moment in his life. There is no comparable archive covering his middle or old age but we can still discern the life cycle's formative influence on men's lives and subjectivities. The process of making men and masculinities was reconfigured across biographical time. Domney's laments were those of a young man making his way – unmarried, living with his parents, bereft of confidence and direction. The public record suggests later life brought modest success, security, and fulfilment: marriage and children in the late 1930s, wartime service in a Home Defence unit, a career in amateur dramatics in the 1950s and 1960s. Across this time, we might conclude, Domney's aspirations and anxieties shifted as his understanding of what it meant to be a man changed.[70]

Starting with individual lives underscores how the relationship between masculinity and time was configured on different scales and moved through competing rhythms and tempos. Conventions of historical periodisation intersected with the generation, life cycle, and autobiography as axes around which men's lives were transformed.[71] Of course, the challenge is developing an analysis in which all these parts are in motion. Richard Hall's chapter suggests how this might work. Hall's ethnography of the emotional dynamics between fathers and sons interrogates Laura King's influential argument that a 'new, if fragile, family-oriented masculinity' emerged in mid-century Britain.[72] Through oral histories, Hall explores what this ideal meant for individual men, their engagement with new forms of domestic labour and emotional attachment, and the relationship between domesticated ideals of masculinity and self-fashioning. Ideas of ordinariness had more purchase for fathers, he argues, while sons were more invested in individualism. A fundamental historical shift played out in individual and familial lives. Emphasising these generational dynamics allows Hall to tease out processes of change that were both historical and biographical.[73] In making this argument we do not want to rehearse that perennial cry for a rapprochement between social and cultural historical approaches to masculinity. Nor are we interested in returning to older debates about the relationship between discourse and experience. Taking individual lives as a starting point, however, allows us to think differently about the processes through which men and masculinities are made and to break apart some of the historiographical and theoretical constraints within which historians of masculinity have worked.

Structure

The chapters in this book are organised into four thematic clusters or parts, each focusing on one site at which men and masculinities were made: institutions, histories, the everyday, and bodies. Part I explores how normative masculinities were maintained through the work of modern state institutions and forms of bureaucratic knowledge. Developing this approach takes Adrian Kane-Galbraith, Jonathan Saha, and Hilary Buxton in different geographical and thematic directions. Kane-Galbraith's state is welfarist and national, manifested through the documentation of identity and entitlements of National Insurance. For Saha and Buxton, the state is colonial and militarised. Here legal processes and the allocation of military pensions and disability benefits governed boundaries between racialised and imperial masculinities and shaped men's lives in metropolitan Britain, Burma, and the West Indies.

Focusing on the 1950s and 1960s, Kane-Galbraith shows how the bureaucratic apparatus of citizenship could be a productive space for trans men. The law could be punitive – criminalising those who made a false statement on a marriage licence – but new forms of state welfare gave men startling opportunities for remaking their lives and identities. Masculinity might be claimed at home and work. It could also be secured through material cultures of identification. Processes of 'state registration and recognition' prioritised 'social performance rather than male embodiment' in issuing National Insurance cards. If this was a pragmatic recognition of trans men's economic contribution, the breadwinner state ironically afforded new opportunities for self-making. The result was a short-lived window in which trans men could effectively self-identify. The 'social self' was also a card and paper self. Identity documents conferred powerful 'recognition of lived identity'. Those opportunities remained contingent. A National Insurance card and birth certificate might jar; concerns over sexual impropriety could derail opportunities for self-definition. And this was ultimately a story of loss rather than gain: computer systems could only process sex as binary, so automated processes of identification removed the ambiguities that afforded trans men opportunities a decade earlier. The state 'did not "see" ... with a steady gaze'.[74]

While the number of 'sex change' cases civil servants encountered was small, they did 'disproportionate cultural work' in defining official policy and revealing its underlying assumptions about maleness. Jonathan Saha focuses on a similar limit case – the ill-fated marriage of novelist Mabel Cosgrave and Arakanese barrister Chan-Toon – in analysing the intersections between masculinity, race, and empire. Saha's chapter follows the transformation of ideas of masculinity as they moved between metropole and colony. Teasing out the 'range of social relations [which] produce masculinity' he shows how masculinities were racialised and racial differences gendered, most strikingly through the distinction between Chan-Toon and the 'generalised figure of the Burman'. While colonial law was ostensibly objective, its work was inflected by inequalities of race and gender. Chan-Toon's difficulties in claiming the status of the independent rational man mirrored the colour bar that denied Kitten the formal equality before the law that was his right as a British citizen. 'In the case of colonial masculinity', Saha concludes, it was 'through the vagaries of when and where the racial exclusivity of Britishness was made manifest ... that we can see the work done by whiteness'.[75]

Like all our contributors, Saha denaturalises men and masculinity by 'tracing the process of embodiment, rather than assuming a sexed male body to be the subject of histories of masculinity'. Hilary Buxton develops this approach, focusing on the experience of Black disabled soldiers from the British West Indies Regiment. Buxton shows how ideas of military service were refracted through pervasive associations between whiteness and Britishness after the Great War. The soldier hero was an exclusive category, and Black men were often unable to mobilise the idea that their disabilities were markers of heroic sacrifice and national service. Buxton's version of embodiment shows how medical treatment and rehabilitation sought to remake injured men's bodies around the ideal of the breadwinner, just as disability pensions sought to restore a proper manly independence. Despite their claims to imperial citizenship, West Indian servicemen's difficulties in securing these entitlements had far-reaching material stakes. Economic and physical independence were frustrated through unequal access to necessary prostheses and wheelchairs. These exclusions were shaped through both the colonial state and the interactions between men and racialised masculinities. Buxton's analysis of tensions within a Liverpool auxiliary hospital, for example, shows how 'Black embodiment' was refracted through interactions with white servicemen, patients, and hospital staff. Buxton concludes: 'racially bound representations of disabled servicemen ... both enabled and hindered soldiers from making concrete claims for care and assistance'.[76]

In Part II, Jessica Meyer, Helen Smith, and Ben Griffin explore the relationship between time, space, and masculinities. Meyer's groundbreaking work on the Ministry of Pensions files of disabled Great War veterans challenges the idea that the war was a turning point in histories of masculinity. Confronting the tendency to define ex-servicemen entirely through their short-lived military experience Meyer argues for a biographical approach that follows individual men over the life cycle, rather than isolating one fragment of a life. In so doing, she argues, we can more fully appreciate how the interplay between historical and biographical change shaped men's lives. Often stretching over decades, pension files provided fragmented life stories through which to explore 'quotidian' experiences of disability, work, and family and the negotiations between individuals,

Introduction 23

families, the state, and employers. Here was an ongoing and often painful process of making men and masculinities.[77]

Grounded in the best traditions of social history, Helen Smith's chapter on Sheffield's steelworkers shows how differences of class and region shaped men's lives and masculinities, foregrounding the importance of work and labour markets. The dangers of the steelworks generated ideals of manliness that prized physical strength, care, and cooperation between mates. Social and emotional bonds around the workplace played out through union organisation, associational culture, and leisure. Workplace solidarities were, Smith argues, overlaid rather than displaced by the growing importance of consumption in men's lives after the 1950s. Viewed from South Yorkshire, the turning points of war and crisis that dominate histories of masculinity look less important than protracted changes in work's organisation and availability. Until the collapse of heavy industries from the 1970s, men's lives remained remarkably stable. Deindustrialisation and unemployment shocked everyday notions of masculinity predicated on work. By the 1990s, an 'insecure identity had no place for the cultures of care and self-betterment valued by steelworkers'. Those angry, violent masculinities visible in recent decades betray deep anxieties and a profound sense of loss.[78]

Smith's regional case study reinvigorates tired ideas about masculinity's crises. Ben Griffin develops this approach through a nuanced analysis of those ideas' conceptual foundations. Despite all the 'crisis talk', Griffin observes, male power and gender inequalities have proven remarkably resilient. Crisis talk, he argues, reflected the 'unsettling of a broader set of power relations … the gender order rather than one of its parts'. Such talk could be underpinned by the disruption of those *processes* through which men and masculinities are made – shifts in those 'institutional practices, rewards, and sanctions' through which masculinities were produced, for example – or by challenges to *some* men's social or political position. Griffin sees these struggles between different models of manliness as routine rather than symptoms of crisis. From this perspective, the 'communication communities' within which competing ideas of masculinity acquired purchase – the workplace, association, or region – appear equally important. Over the past century, the growing need to move between these communities has made it harder for men to negotiate competing demands on their sense of selfhood. There were material constraints on the masculinities individuals could plausibly claim, which could be accentuated through unemployment. In this context, Griffin concludes, crisis could never be more than localised.[79]

What emerges from these chapters is a compelling sense of masculinity's ordinariness. How men made sense of their lives *as men* – how ideas of manliness were reproduced, negotiated, and challenged – was shaped by interactions within families, homes, workplaces, organisations, neighbourhoods, and streets, and by men's engagement with different forms of mass media and culture. Pat Ayers, Michelle Johansen, and Richard Hall elaborate this insight in Part III. Each explores the mundane spaces where experiences and ideas of masculinity materialised. Reflecting recent scholarship on the purchase of these ideas in mid-century Britain, Johansen and Hall include 'everyday' and 'ordinary' in their titles. More than descriptive categories, these terms contain a far-reaching argument about how (and where) masculinities were made.

Pat Ayers revisits her early work on Liverpool's docklands.[80] Along the Mersey, distinctive cultures of work, leisure, and domesticity shaped diverging ideas of masculinity, despite enduring male dominance and the 'infinite adaptability of patriarchy. Towards the south of the city, everyday lives were shaped by differences of race, growth of new housing estates, and existence of employment opportunities outside the docks. There were fewer sectarian tensions, a stronger union, and class solidarities had greater power. Companies like Bryant & May, whose match factory employed women, were particularly important in disrupting the segregated labour markets that characterised Liverpool's North End. One result was a less acute gendered division of domestic labour and childcare. For Ayers's interviewees, conditions of work and housing played out in their reflections on the centrality of children and family to their identities as men.[81]

Michelle Johansen also foregrounds the 'everyday masculine encounters' that shaped identities of gender and class. Johansen focuses on the socially mobile municipal librarian, reinvigorating older work on Britain's growing lower middle class through a prosopography of 130 senior librarians in London around 1900. Johansen's rich ethnography reconstructs these men's professional and private life-histories. In the late nineteenth century, the transformation of municipal governance, new forms of rational recreation, and expansion of state education created more rate-supported libraries and opportunities for employment and masculine self-making. Asked to establish the institutional world of the new public library, this first generation of librarians negotiated both the transition between manual and mental work within their families and pejorative views of their occupation. Often dismissed as humdrum or inadequate, Johansen's librarians forged new versions of manliness that stressed self-control, resilience, and endurance. They reworked the language of 'heroism' and 'struggle' associated with military or imperial service to characterise how provincial working-class autodidacts made their way in an unfamiliar world. This process played out in how librarians wrote about their lives, workplace interactions, and professional organisations. Crucially, the 'heroic' librarian reflected that period when the modern library was coming into being, rather than the consolidation after the 1930s when the librarian's image was feminised.[82]

Like a growing number of historians, Richard Hall addresses questions of subjectivity and emotion.[83] Exploring how individual men understood the world and their place in it, Hall uses interviews with fathers and sons to consider the intergenerational articulation of selfhood and masculinity within families. Fathers and sons made sense of their lives as men at the same time as they navigated an intimate relationship and fast-changing world. That masculinity was a relational category was a foundational assumption of gender history. What Hall does differently is show how relationality was also inter-subjective. This move sustains a radical transformation of histories of masculinity and selfhood. Narrating one's life to an interviewer becomes a proxy for the process self-making men undertook throughout their lives. For younger generations, Hall argues, that process was increasingly directed at securing a distinctive individuality rather than the ordinariness emphasised by fathers. Sons' testimony 'was more inclined towards narratives of self-fulfilment, reflecting the greater educational, economic, work, and socio-cultural opportunities ... available to them'. When masculinity was reworked as interiority, being ordinary was more of a problem.[84]

These chapters foreground how men and masculinities were made. They also underscore how the male body was a site of self-definition and object onto which ideas of masculinity were inscribed. Kane-Galbraith and Buxton, for example, show how male bodies were remade through gender reassignment surgery and pioneering treatments including prosthetic limbs. Their emphasis on embodiment signals the constant work of self-making emblematised by the popularity of physical efficiency before the Great War or contemporary archetypes like the muscle-bound gym bunny. Men's status and the integrity of ideals of masculinity were displaced onto debates about the vitality and wholeness of their physique. Concerns around disability and shell shock after the Great War and thickening waistlines and risk of heart disease today underscore how men's bodies have been proxies for masculinity itself.[85]

Ben Mechen and Katie Jones bring these issues under scrutiny in Part IV, tightening focus on the relationship between sexuality and masculinity. Mechen starts with the extraordinary letters written by self-defined 'ordinary' men to the Committee on Obscenity and Film Censorship – the Williams Committee – in 1977–1978. This material allows him to move from exploring pornographic texts, markets, and regulation to more challenging questions around the relationship between the consumption of porn and men's lives and identities – what Mechen terms the 'relationship between pornographic discourse and gendered and sexual subjectivity'. Both defensive and assertive, men's letters challenged pejorative notions that pornography was damaging, exploitative, or manifested patriarchal sexual violence against women. Instead, they drew on emerging ideas of well-being and sexual fulfilment to articulate a 'liberal sexual subject'. For Mechen, this figure embodied 'a new idea of normative masculinity' in which the sexual self was 'individualist, free of so-called hang-ups, and something to be ... realised as part of a "sex life" and a "sexual career"'. Embedded in this position, however, was a 'new narrative of male victimhood', mobilised against an increasingly assertive feminist politics, which anticipated the more strident ideas associated with the worst excesses of contemporary men's rights activism.

Like Mechen, Katie Jones focuses on personal testimonies. In her case, these are questionnaires and sexual diaries completed by men who participated in Project SIGMA (Socio-sexual Investigations of Gay Men and AIDS) between 1987 and 1996. Rich qualitative social research data allows Jones to explore men's decisions around safer sex during the HIV/AIDS pandemic. Challenging pejorative notions of the hyper-sexual gay men – not least by revealing the assumptions embedded in SIGMA's research methods – respondents articulated a more conflicted relationship between sex and masculinity. Emotion and intimacy, as well as perceived risks of transmission, were integral to the decisions men made about their sexual encounters with long-term and casual partners. Far from irrational or pathological, dispensing with condom use in an ongoing relationship could reflect understandings of anal sex as a physical symbol of emotional closeness and commitment, or followed mutual negative HIV tests. Such decisions often rested on explicit or implicit negotiations with partners about the importance of safe sex *outside* a relationship. It is on this basis that Jones develops a powerful argument for the importance of affect and intimacy in gay sexual cultures and, by extension, queer masculinities that emerged in the 1980s and 1990s.

Conclusion

In arguing that men and masculinities are made in and through history, this book makes a pointed intervention in ferocious debates in contemporary gender politics. The resurgence of gender essentialism and reassertion of patriarchy as a 'natural' or transhistorical (albeit perennially threatened) state, most notably in the polemics of Jordan Peterson and men's rights activists, requires a history of masculinity that centres questions of process, power, and contingency. Patriarchy has endured in modern Britain. As our contributors show, however, that has required the constant work of politics, culture, and social interaction: men and masculinities took form, and gendered inequalities were upheld, through the unpredictable dynamics of encounters between different groups. *Men and Masculinities* thus charts how some claims to manliness have, despite their historical specificity and apparent fragility, remained the currency of power within a remarkably stable gender order.

At the same time, the book's argument that men are *made* underscores the importance of contingency in shaping gender relations. It offers the possibility of change: might men and masculinities be made differently, or even unmade completely, so that men's social dominance begins to dissolve? This was a central question for the first generation of historians of masculinity, whose work emerged from the men's anti-sexist movement of the 1980s. From this perspective, women's liberation, and the liberation of men from themselves – that is, from patriarchy and heteronormativity – was integral to a formative moment in the emergence of our field. *Manful Assertions'* emphasis on the historicity of masculinities has remained influential over the past thirty years. So, too, has the self-reflexive energy of this early work, rooted in feminist and pro-feminist practices of consciousness-raising, prompted us to ask: how might a collective inquiry into the history of masculinity also encompass an inquiry into the masculinity of history? How do masculinities function to structure history as a discipline and field of professional, social, and pedagogical relations?

The reflections threaded through the book offer some answers, while also clarifying unresolved tensions between the claims made for history as a radically deconstructive practice, and its uncomfortable durability as a site where gender and power continue to operate in unreconstructed, conservative forms. In different ways, Charlotte Lydia Riley, Hannah Charnock, Michael Roper, and John Tosh turn the historian's critical gaze on our discipline's institutions and working practices. Their chapters are bracing because they exemplify how histories written for the present might make the case for profound change within forms of work, research, teaching, and administration often taken for granted.

Charlotte Lydia Riley explores the patriarchal cultures of expertise, evaluation, and promotion that deform everything we do as historians. Gendered patterns of harassment and bullying represent one extreme of more pervasive forms including interpersonal interactions within the conference, seminar room or lecture theatre, and department meeting, conventions of citation and acknowledgement, and decisions about research funding, appointments, and promotion. Scholarly or pedagogic styles are intensely gendered, Riley shows, in ways that reward some of us – usually white men – and disadvantage others.[86] The cliched protest 'not all men' obfuscates the distinctions between individual responsibility and structural privileges from which all men derive benefit. Expertise, authority, professionalism – those identities to which historians lay claim and on which our working lives rely – are embedded in deep-rooted cultures of masculinity.[87]

Hannah Charnock shifts attention to practices of reading, research, and writing. Her starting point is simple: 'How do we write feminist histories of masculinity when we're not addressing institutions or culture, but studying the lives of individual men, many of whom are still alive?' Charnock's experiences as a younger female scholar using oral history to explore sexual experiences make this question particularly salient. Interviewing presents considerable difficulties in navigating tensions of gender and generation. Charnock's work is underpinned by a progressive politics of gender and sexuality. Recurring stories of sexual harassment and violence recounted by her interviewees, however, challenge that politics and the interpersonal interactions on which the interview relies. Reflecting on these awkward encounters, Charnock argues that the ethics and politics of historical recovery can be incompatible with men's lives in the past. Allowing older men to speak for themselves reifies rather than challenges structures of male privilege. Politics and politeness collide: should an interviewer confront their subject with a potentially damaging version of their own past? It is vital that we understand the historical and contemporary pervasiveness of men's sexual violence. Still, the task of interrogating and confronting the forms of manliness that structure those behaviours becomes more difficult when interviewing an older man.[88]

Critical practices associated with histories of masculinity can thus serve to understand and, perhaps, transform our intellectual and professional practices. While Riley and Charnock start from the historical conjuncture at which we work, Michael Roper and John Tosh return to the prehistory of *Manful Assertions*, seeking what Tosh calls 'useful purpose' in the 'continuing relevance of the cultural politics of that time'.[89] Roper reflects on his making as a historian of masculinity through an idiosyncratic journey that was, nonetheless, shaped by wider intellectual currents. Roper's decision to work on male working cultures was indebted to gender history's interest in questions of power and relationality. His journey was also underpinned by the experiences of a particular moment in the history of British universities. As a PhD student at the University of Essex, joining Leonore Davidoff's pioneering gender history MA was transformative. As the only man in that group Roper's very presence was controversial, prompting heated discussions that underscored the everyday politics of pedagogy. Writ small here were growing tensions between women's history and gender history, particularly around how gendered histories of men might compromise the field's radical and feminist potential. Men's presence in such courses might be less contentious today, though the gendered patterns of enrollment remain familiar. Roper's remembered 'discomfort', however, underscores the stakes – political and emotional, and individual and collective – in exploring histories of gender, power, and patriarchy in the seminar room.

As Lucy Delay and Ben Mechen discuss below, the continued relevance of these themes makes teaching a 'form of political engagement'. It also ensures gender history has striking – and sometimes disconcerting – utility for thinking critically about both selfhood and society.

John Tosh, finally, reflects on *Manful Assertions*' origins in an informal study group patterned on the London Feminist History Group. Deliberately occupying the margins of professional and disciplinary structures, these loosely organised 'kitchen seminars' sustained an informal and generative conversation. Tosh does not make this point directly, but the change of name from the Men's History Group to HOMME (History of Men, Masculinity, etc.) might suggest some discomfort with the political implications of the former, particularly the implied claim to the same recovery work that drove women's and feminist histories. *Manful Assertions* was inseparable from attempts *by men* to make a case for transforming men's lives and hegemonic notions of masculinity. Tosh recognises the limits of that project in the 1980s. In so doing, however, he makes a renewed call for historians to engage explicitly and systematically with the 'concerns of the present'.[90]

These threads are drawn together by the imaginative essay with which *Men and Masculinities* concludes. This expansive and open conversation between Tosh, Lucy Delap, and the book's editors brings together a pioneering historian of masculinity, whose work grew out of their involvement in men's groups in the 1980s, and a leading feminist historian (and historian of feminism) who has worked on that moment. What unfurls is a striking and provocative reflection on what histories of masculinity have been and where they might go next. Tosh and Delap do not always agree, but their shared vision emphasises the importance of rediscovering the progressive orientation points that defined the emergence of the field. From this vantage point, the distance between the optimism of *Manful Assertions* and where we are today underscores the vital importance of politically engaged histories that seize on the proliferation of 'crisis talk' around masculinity to understand its genealogies and imagine alternative ways of living as men.

This is what we have tried to do. Although their approaches, arguments, and case studies are very different, the contributors to this book all move between the historical and the contemporary. In so doing, they explore the ongoing and conflictual processes through which men and masculinities were made in modern Britain. Each chapter shows how questions around male power and masculinities are more pressing than their treatment as intellectual and historical problems might suggest. The same masculinities that took shape during the past century shaped – and continue to shape – how historians work as gendered subjects in archives and libraries, how we teach and are evaluated for teaching, how we engage in public life, and how we interact with one another in a profession that remains hierarchical and patriarchal. Making men and masculinities, in other words, is a process in which our working conditions, markets of labour and knowledge, and professional identities are implicated. We hope that our histories of masculinity might have a role in transforming working practices and lives in the present.

Notes

1 See Matt Houlbrook, *Songs of Seven Dials: Intimate Stories of 1920s and 1930s London* (manuscript in progress).
2 'Sir Bracewell Smith', *The Times*, 13 January 1966, 12; 'Former Stadium Chairman', *Harrow Observer*, 20 January 1966, 2; 'Sir Bracewell Smith Leaves £1,197,000: Exchequer Takes £948,939', *Daily Telegraph*, 2 April 1966, 11.
3 This summary draws upon TNA, J 54 1951: James Kitten versus Odhams Press and E.R. Thompson (February 1927); TNA, HO 144 22301: Section 432194/20, SDI Frankton to Superintendent (19 February 1927); LMA, PS BOW A04 059 (25 June 1924); LMA, PS BOW A04 060 (2 July and 9 July 1924). 'The "Black Man's Cafe" Libel Action', *The Times*, 9 February 1927; 'Negro Cafe Owner's Libel Suit', *Guardian*, 10 February 1927, 5. On Kitten's bankruptcy, see *London Gazette*, 28 February 1928, 1471; 8 March 1929, 1733; 20 April 1928, 2883.
4 Joan W. Scott, 'Gender: A Useful Category of Historical Analysis', *American Historical Review*, 91:5 (1986), 1053–1075.
5 Kimberlé Crenshaw, 'Mapping the Margins: Intersectionality, Identity Politics, and Violence against Women of Color', *Stanford Law Review*, 43:6 (1991), 1241–1299.
6 Minkah Makalani, *In the Cause of Freedom: Radical Black Internationalism from Harlem to London, 1917–1939* (Durham: University of North Carolina Press, 2011); Lara Putnam, *Radical Moves: Caribbean Migrants and the Politics of Race in the Jazz Age* (Durham: University of North Carolina Press, 2013); Susan Pennybacker, *From Scottsboro to Munich: Race and Political Culture in 1930s Britain* (Princeton: Princeton University Press, 2009); Laura Tabili, *We Ask for British Justice: Workers and Racial Difference in Late Imperial Britain* (Ithaca: Cornell University Press, 1994); Laura Tabili, *Global Migrants, Local Culture: Natives and Newcomers in Provincial England, 1841–1939* (Houndmills: Palgrave Macmillan, 2011); Kenetta Hammond Perry, *London Is the Place for Me: Black Britons, Citizenship, and the Politics of Race* (Oxford: Oxford University Press, 2015); Susan Okokon, *Black Londoners, 1880–1980* (Stroud: Sutton Publishing, 1998).
7 Perry, *London Is the Place for Me*; Marc Matera, *Black London: The Imperial Metropolis and Decolonization in the Twentieth Century* (Oakland: University of California Press, 2015); Carina Ray, *Crossing the Color Line: Race, Sex, and the Contested Politics of Colonialism in Ghana* (Athens: Ohio University Press, 2015); Gemma Romain, *Race, Sexuality, and Identity in*

Britain and Jamaica: The Biography of Patrick Nelson, 1916–1963 (London: Bloomsbury Academic, 2017).

8 Michael Roper and John Tosh (eds), *Manful Assertions: Masculinities in Britain since 1800* (London: Routledge, 1991). The volume, of largely Victorian and Edwardian focus, included chapters on Thomas Carlyle (Norma Clarke), Edward White Benson (John Tosh), and T. E. Lawrence (Graham Dawson), boys' adventure papers (Kelly Boyd), the Salvation Army (Pamela Walker), the homosocial matrix of the public schools, army, and universities (Peter Lewis), the life of the 'company man' (Michael Roper), and the masculinisation of the labour aristocracy (Keith McClelland). Other notable early work in the history of British masculinity included J. A. Mangan and James Walvin (eds), *Manliness and Morality: Middle-Class Masculinity in Britain and America, 1800–1940* (Manchester: Manchester University Press, 1987); Michael Roper, *Masculinity and the British Organization Man since 1945* (Oxford: Oxford University Press, 1994); Sonya O. Rose, *Limited Livelihoods: Gender and Class in Nineteenth-Century England* (London: Routledge, 1992); Anna Clark, *The Struggle for the Breeches: Gender and the Making of the British Working Class* (Berkeley: University of California Press, 1995); Leonore Davidoff and Catherine Hall, *Family Fortunes: Men and Women of the English Middle Class, 1780–1850* (London: Routledge, 1987); Graham Dawson, *Soldier Heroes: British Adventure, Empire and the Imagining of Masculinities* (London: Routledge, 1994); Lesley A. Hall, *Hidden Anxieties: Male Sexuality, 1900–1950* (Cambridge: Polity Press, 1991); A. James Hammerton, *Cruelty and Companionship: Conflict in Nineteenth-Century Married Life* (Routledge: London, 1992); Susan Kingsley Kent, *Making Peace: The Reconstruction of Gender in Interwar Britain* (Princeton: Princeton University Press, 1993); Jon Lawrence, 'Class and Gender in the Making of Urban Toryism, 1880–1914', *English Historical Review*, 108:428 (1993), 629–652; Frank Mort, *Cultures of Consumption: Masculinities and Social Space in Late Twentieth-Century Britain* (London: Routledge, 1996). In the late 1980s and early 1990s, parallel discussions about Black and diaspora masculinities (and their histories) were going on in Black British cultural studies, though with very little traffic between these and those initiated by Rope and Tosh in the (overwhelmingly white) terrain of UK academic history. See especially Kobena Mercer, *Welcome to the Jungle: New Positions in Black Cultural Studies* (London: Routledge, 1994); Paul Gilroy, *The Black Atlantic: Modernity and Double Consciousness* (London: Verso, 1993); and the films of Isaac Julien and the photographs of Ajamu X.

9 See Roper and Tosh's introduction to *Manful Assertions*, which roots the collection in the gay history pioneered by John Boswell, Alan Bray, and Jeffrey Weeks, the women's history of Sheila Rowbotham and the new gender history of Catherine Hall and Joan Scott, and the sociologies of men and women of Victor Seidler, Mary McIntosh, Nancy Chodorow, and Cynthia Cockburn.

10 Sheila Rowbotham, 'Women's Liberation and the New Politics', in Michelene Wandor (ed.), *The Body Politic: Writings from the Women's Liberation in Britain, 1969–1972* (London: Stage 1, 1972), 3–30. On the men's anti-sexist

movement, see the Conclusion; and Victor Seidler (ed.), *The Achilles Heel Reader: Men, Sexual Politics and Socialism* (London: Routledge, 1991); Victor Seidler, *Recreating Sexual Politics: Men, Feminism and Politics* (London: Routledge, 1991); Lynne Segal, *Slow Motion: Changing Masculinities, Changing Men* (London: Virago, 1990); Lucy Delap, 'Feminism, Masculinities and Emotional Politics in Late Twentieth Century Britain', *Cultural & Social History*, 15:4 (2018), 571–593; Lucy Delap, 'Rethinking Rapes: Men's Sex Lives and Feminist Critiques', *Contemporary British History*, 36:2 (2022), 253–276; Nicholas Owen, 'Men and the 1970s British Women's Liberation Movement', *Historical Journal*, 56:3 (2013), 801–826. Consciousness-raising through group discussion and writing was a foundational practice of the men's movement, building upon techniques developed by feminist women in the 1970s. See Margaretta Jolly, *Sisterhood and After: An Oral History of the UK Women's Liberation Movement, 1968–Present* (Oxford: Oxford University Press, 2019); Lucy Delap, 'Feminist Bookshops, Reading Cultures and the Women's Liberation Movement in Great Britain, c. 1974–2000', *History Workshop Journal*, 81 (2016), 171–196; Sue Bruley, 'Consciousness-Raising in Clapham: Women's Liberation as "Lived Experience" in South London in the 1970s', *Women's History Review*, 22:5 (2013), 717–738; Natalie Thomlinson, *Race, Ethnicity and the Women's Movement in England, 1968–1993* (Basingstoke: Palgrave Macmillan, 2016); D.-M. Withers, 'The Politics of the Workshop: Craft, Autonomy and Women's Liberation', *Feminist Theory*, 21:2 (2020), 217–234.

11 Roper and Tosh, *Manful Assertions*. The work of Catherine Hall and Leonore Davidoff perhaps did most to secure the relevance of gender to the study of modern British history: Davidoff and Hall, *Family Fortunes*; Catherine Hall, *White, Male and Middle Class: Explorations in Feminism and History* (Cambridge: Polity Press, 1992); Catherine Hall, *Civilising Subjects: Metropole and Colony in the English Imagination 1830–1867* (Chicago: University of Chicago Press, 2002); Catherine Hall, Keith McClelland, and Jane Rendall, *Defining the Victorian Nation: Class, Race, Gender and the British Reform Act of 1867* (Cambridge: Cambridge University Press, 2000).

12 For more detailed surveys of masculinities in Britain, from the Middle Ages to the twentieth century, see Karen Harvey and Alexandra Shepard, 'What Have Historians Done with Masculinity? Reflections on Five Centuries of British History, circa 1500 to 1950', *Journal of British Studies*, 44:2 (2005), 274–280; Karen Harvey, 'The History of Masculinity, circa 1650–1800', *Journal of British Studies*, 44:2 (2005), 296–311; Alexandra Shepard, 'From Anxious Patriarchs to Refined Gentlemen? Manhood in Britain, circa 1500 to 1700', *Journal of British Studies*, 44:2 (2005), 281–295; Michelle Cohen, '"Manners" Make the Man: Politeness, Chivalry, and the Construction of Masculinity, 1750–1830', *Journal of British Studies*, 44:2 (2005), 312–329; John Tosh, 'Masculinities in an Industrializing Society: Britain, 1800–1914', *Journal of British Studies*, 44:2 (2005), 330–342; Martin Francis, 'The Domestication of the Male? Recent Research on Nineteenth- and Twentieth-Century British Masculinity', *Historical Journal*, 45:3 (2002), 637–652.

13 Formative for us has been the programme for a 'critical history' and 'history of the present' developed in turn by Michel Foucault, Joan Scott, and Laura Doan, as well as the historiographical praxes of the history workshop movement and feminist, queer, and anti-colonial histories. Michel Foucault, 'Nietzsche, Genealogy, History', in Donald F. Bouchard (ed.), *Language, Counter-Memory, Practice: Selected Essays and Interviews* (Ithaca: Cornell University Press, 1977), 139–164; Michel Foucault, *Discipline and Punish: The Birth of the Prison* (London: Allen Lane, 1977); Joan W. Scott, 'History-Writing as Critique', in Keith Jenkins, Sue Morgan, and Alun Munslow (eds), *Manifestos for History* (London: Routledge, 2007), 19–38; Laura Doan, *Disturbing Practices: History, Sexuality, and Women's Experience of Modern War* (Chicago: University of Chicago Press, 2013); Raphael Samuel (ed.), *People's History and Socialist Theory* (London: Routledge, 1981).

14 For recent popular interventions on these issues, see e.g. Jacqueline Rose, *On Violence and On Violence against Women* (London: Faber & Faber, 2021); Kate Mann, *Entitled: How Male Privilege Hurts Women* (London: Allen Lane, 2020); Caroline Criado Perez, *Invisible Women: Exposing Data Bias in a World Designed for Men* (London: Chatto & Windus, 2019).

15 Some recent examinations include Jamie Hakim, *Work That Body: Male Bodies in Digital Culture* (London: Rowman & Littlefield, 2020); J. J. Bola, *Mask Off: Masculinity Redefined* (London: Pluto Press, 2019); Obioma Ugoala, *The Problem with My Normal Penis: Myths of Race, Sex and Masculinity* (New York: Simon & Schuster, 2022); Grayson Perry, *The Descent of Man* (London: Allen Lane, 2016).

16 Arguably a contention of the 1980s 'mythopoetic' men's movement now resurgent through the enormously popular work of Jungian psychologist Jordan Peterson. Robert Bly, *Iron John: A Book about Men* (Shaftesbury: Element, 1990); Jordan B. Peterson, *12 Rules for Life: An Antidote to Chaos* (London: Allen Lane, 2018).

17 On patriarchy and history, see Sally Alexander and Barbara Taylor, 'In Defence of 'Patriarchy', in Samuel (ed.), *People's History and Socialist Theory*.

18 Sheila Rowbotham, *Hidden from History: 300 Years of Women's Oppression and the Fight against It* (London: Pluto Press, 1977); Jeffrey Weeks, *Coming Out: Homosexual Politics in Britain from the Nineteenth Century to the Present* (London: Quartet Books, 1977); Beverley Bryan, Stella Dadzie, and Suzanne Scafe, *Heart of the Race: Black Women's Lives in Britain* (London: Verso, 1995); Walter Rodney, *The Groundings with My Brothers* (London: Bogle L'Ouverture Publications, 1969).

19 Bly, *Iron John*; Peterson, *12 Rules for Life*. For a recent commentary pivoting around the odd idea of men's cultural devaluation, see Nina Power, *What Do Men Want? Masculinity and Its Discontents* (London: Penguin, 1991). The right-wing men's movement's temporalised framings of the 'loss' and potential 'return' of an authentic masculinity, which usually play on the idea of men as victims of feminism, carry a striking echo of those Hemmings has seen in the

women's movement itself: Clare Hemmings, *Why Stories Matter: The Political Grammar of Feminist Theory* (Durham, NC: Duke University Press, 2011).
20 See Chapters 1 and 3.
21 Lee Edelman, *No Future: Queer Theory and the Death Drive* (Durham, NC: Duke University Press, 2004).
22 For British modernities and broad interpretive accounts of modern British history, see Becky Conekin, Frank Mort, and Chris Waters (eds), *Moments of Modernity: Reconstructing Britain, 1945–1964* (London: Rivers Oram Press, 1999); Simon Gunn and James Vernon (eds), *The Peculiarities of Liberal Modernity in Imperial Britain* (Berkeley: University of California Press, 2011); James Vernon, *Distant Strangers: How Britain Became Modern* (Berkeley: University of California Press, 2010); David Edgerton, *The Rise and Fall of the British Nation: A Twentieth-Century History* (London: Allen Lane, 2018); Jon Lawrence, *Me Me Me? The Search for Community in Post-War England* (Oxford: Oxford University Press, 2019); Deborah Cohen, *Family Secrets: Living with Shame from the Victorians to the Present Day* (London: Viking, 2013).
23 See Reflection by Charnock.
24 Scott, 'Gender', 1067–1069. See also Denise Riley, *'Am I That Name?' Feminism and the Category of 'Women' in History* (Basingstoke: Macmillan, 1988).
25 On **war**, see Michael Brown, Anna Maria Barry, and Joanne Begiato (eds), *Martial Masculinities: Experiencing and Imagining the Military in the Long Nineteenth Century* (Manchester: Manchester University Press, 2019); Julia Banister, *Masculinity, Militarism and Eighteenth-Century Culture, 1689–1815* (Cambridge: Cambridge University Press, 2018); Joanna Bourke, *Dismembering the Male: Men's Bodies, Britain and the Great War* (London: Reaktion Books, 1996); Alison Chand, *Masculinities on Clydeside: Men in Reserved Occupations during the Second World War* (Edinburgh: Edinburgh University Press, 2016); Stefan Dudink, Karen Hagemann, and John Tosh (eds), *Masculinities in Politics and War* (Manchester: Manchester University Press, 2004); Martin Francis, *The Flyer: British Culture and the Royal Air Force, 1939–1945* (Oxford: Oxford University Press, 2008); Holly Furneaux, *Military Men of Feeling: Emotion, Touch and Masculinity in the Crimean War* (Oxford: Oxford University Press, 2016); Grace Huxford, *The Korean War in Britain: Citizenship, Selfhood and Forgetting* (Manchester: Manchester University Press, 2018); Tracey Loughran, 'A Crisis of Masculinity? Re-writing the History of Shell-Shock and Gender in First World War Britain', *History Compass*, 11:9 (2013), 727–738; Max Jones, '"National Hero and Very Queer Fish": Empire, Sexuality and the British Remembrance of General Gordon, 1918–72', *Twentieth Century British History*, 26:2 (2014), 175–202; Anna Maguire, *Contact Zones of the First World War: Cultural Encounters across the British Empire* (Cambridge: Cambridge University Press, 2021); Linda Maynard, *Brothers in the Great War: Siblings, Masculinity and Emotions* (Manchester: University of Manchester Press, 2021); Jessica Meyer, *Men of War: Masculinity and the First World War in Britain* (Basingstoke: Palgrave Macmillan, 2009); Jessica Meyer, *An Equal Burden: The Men of the Royal Army Medical Corps in the First World War*

(Oxford: Oxford University Press, 2019); Helen Parr, *Our Boys: The Story of a Paratrooper* (London: Allen Lane, 2018); Juliette Pattinson, Arthur McIvor, and Linsey Robb, *Men in Reserve: British Civilian Masculinities in the Second World War* (Manchester: Manchester University Press, 2016); Linsey Robb and Juliette Pattinson (eds), *Men, Masculinities and Male Culture in the Second World War* (Basingstoke: Palgrave Macmillan, 2017); Michael Roper, *The Secret Battle: Emotional Survival in the Great War* (Manchester: Manchester University Press, 2010); Sonya O. Rose, *Which People's War? National Identity and Citizenship in Wartime Britain, 1939–1945* (Oxford: Oxford University Press, 2003); Richard Smith, *Jamaican Volunteers in the First World War: Race, Masculinity and the Development of National Consciousness* (Manchester: Manchester University Press, 2004); Alison Twells, 'Sex, Gender, and Romantic Intimacy in Servicemen's Letters during the Second World War', *Historical Journal*, 63:3 (2020), 732–753; Laura Ugolini, *Civvies: Middle-Class Men on the English Home Front, 1914–18* (Manchester: Manchester University Press, 2013); Emma Vickers, *Queen and Country: Same-Sex Desire in the British Armed Forces, 1939–45* (Manchester: Manchester University Press, 2013). On **politics**, see Ben Griffin, *The Politics of Gender in Victorian Britain: Masculinity, Political Culture and the Struggle for Women's Rights* (Cambridge: Cambridge University Press, 2012); T. G. Ashplant, *Fractured Loyalties: Masculinity, Class and Politics in Britain, 1900–30* (London: Rivers Oram Press, 2007); Aidan J. Beatty, *Masculinity and Power in Irish Nationalism, 1884–1938* (Basingstoke: Palgrave Macmillan, 2016); Christopher Fletcher, Sean Brady, Rachel E. Moss, and Lucy Riall (eds), *The Palgrave Handbook of Masculinity and Political Culture in Europe* (Basingstoke: Palgrave Macmillan, 2018); Angela V. John and Claire Eustance (eds), *The Men's Share? Masculinities, Male Support and Women's Suffrage in Britain, 1890–1920* (London: Routledge, 1997); Matthew McCormack, *The Independent Man: Citizenship and Gender Politics in Victorian England* (Manchester: Manchester University Press, 2005). On **religion**, see Lucy Delap and Sue Morgan (eds), *Men, Masculinities and Religious Change in Twentieth-Century Britain* (Basingstoke: Palgrave Macmillan, 2013); Alana Harris, 'A Magna Carta for Marriage: Love, Catholic Masculinities and the Humanae Vitae Contraception Crisis in 1968 Britain', *Cultural & Social History*, 17:3 (2020), 407–429; Jane McGaughey, *Ulster's Men: Protestant Unionist Masculinities and Militarization in the North of Ireland, 1912–1923* (Montreal: McGill-Queen's University Press, 2012). On **law and policing**, see David G. Barrie and Susan Broomhall (eds), *A History of Police and Masculinities, 1700–2010* (London: Routledge, 2012); Katie Barclay, *Men on Trial: Performing Emotion, Embodiment and Identity in Ireland, 1800–45* (Manchester: Manchester University Press, 2018); Eloise Moss, *Night Raiders: Burglary and the Making of Modern Urban Life in London, 1860–1968* (Oxford: Oxford University Press, 2019); Martin J. Wiener, *Men of Blood: Violence, Manliness and Criminal Justice in Victorian England* (Cambridge: Cambridge University Press, 2004); Abigail Wills, 'Delinquency, Masculinity and Citizenship in England 1950–1970', *Past & Present*, 187 (2005), 157–185.

On **leisure and popular culture**, see Brad Beaven, *Leisure, Citizenship and Working-Class Men in Britain, 1850–1945* (Manchester: Manchester University Press, 2005); Kelly Boyd, *Manliness and the Boys' Story Paper, 1855–1940* (Basingstoke: Palgrave, 2002); Sarah Goldsmith, *Masculinity and Danger on the Eighteenth-Century Grand Tour* (London: University of London Press, 2020); Christine Grandy, *Heroes and Happy Endings: Class, Gender and Nation in Popular Film and Fiction in Interwar Britain* (Manchester: Manchester University Press, 2014); Patrick McDevitt, *'May the Best Man Win': Sport, Masculinity and Nationalism in Great Britain and the Empire, 1880–1935* (Basingstoke: Palgrave Macmillan, 2004); Amy Milne-Smith, *London Clubland: A Cultural History of Gender and Class in Late Victorian Britain* (Basingstoke: Palgrave Macmillan, 2011); Melanie Tebbutt, *Being Boys: Youth, Leisure and Identity in the Inter-war Years* (Manchester: Manchester University Press, 2012). On **education and intellectual life**, see Paul Deslandes, *Oxbridge Men: British Masculinity and the Undergraduate Experience, 1850–1920* (Bloomington: Indiana University Press, 2005); Heather Ellis, *Masculinity and Science in Britain, 1831–1918* (Basingstoke: Palgrave Macmillan, 2017); Emily Rutherford, 'Arthur Sidgwick's *Greek Prose Composition*: Gender, Affect, and Sociability in the Late Victorian University', *Journal of British Studies*, 56:1 (2017), 91–116. On **work**, see Linsey Robb, *Men at Work: The Working Man in British Culture, 1939–1945* (Basingstoke: Palgrave Macmillan, 2015); Heidi Egginton and Zoë Thomas (eds), *Precarious Professionals: Gender, Identities and Social Change in Modern Britain* (London: University of London Press, 2021); Karen Downing, Johnathan Thayer, and Joanne Begiato (eds), *Negotiating Masculinities and Modernity in the Maritime World, 1815–1940: A Sailor's Progress?* (Cham: Palgrave Macmillan, 2021); John Field, *Working Men's Bodies: Work Camps in Britain, 1880–1940* (Manchester: Manchester University Press, 2013); Katie Hindmarch-Watson, *Serving a Wired World: London's Telecommunications Workers and the Makers of an Information Capital* (Berkeley: University of California Press, 2020); Michael Roper, *Masculinity and the British Organization Man since 1945* (Oxford: Oxford University Press, 1994); Helen Smith, *Masculinity and Same-Sex Desire in Industrial England, 1895–1957* (Basingstoke: Palgrave Macmillan, 2015). On **domesticity and family**, see John Tosh, *A Man's Place: Masculinity and the Middle-Class Home in Victorian England* (New Haven: Yale University Press, 1999); Lucy Delap, Ben Griffin, and Abigail Wills (eds), *The Politics of Domestic Authority in Britain since 1800* (Basingstoke: Palgrave Macmillan, 2009); Laura King, *Family Men: Fatherhood and Masculinity in Britain, 1914–1960* (Oxford: Oxford University Press, 2015); Julie-Marie Strange, *Fatherhood and the British Working Class, 1865–1914* (Cambridge: Cambridge University Press, 2015); Laura Ugolini, *Fathers and Sons in the English Middle Class, c. 1870–1920* (London: Routledge, 2021); Hammerton, *Cruelty and Companionship*. For surveys of masculinity in **individual nations**, see Rebecca Anne Barr, Sean Brady, and Jane McGaughey (eds), *Ireland and Masculinities in History* (Cham: Palgrave Macmillan, 2019); Lynn Abrams and Elizabeth Ewan (eds), *Nine

Centuries of Man: Manhood and Masculinity in Scottish History (Edinburgh: Edinburgh University Press, 2017).

26 John Arnold and Sean Brady's 2011 collection made an important and thematically wide-ranging contribution to the historiography of masculinity, while reaching far beyond the confines of any discrete chronological or geographical location: John H. Arnold and Sean Brady (eds), *What Is Masculinity? Historical Dynamics from Antiquity to the Contemporary World* (Basingstoke: Palgrave Macmillan, 2011). Along with *Manful Assertions*, a closer analogue for the approach taken here might instead be Tim Hitchcock and Michelle Cohen (eds), *English Masculinities, 1660–1800* (London: Longman, 1999). Some recent monographs on earlier periods have also tried to offer broader interpretative frameworks: Alexandra Shepard, *Meanings of Manhood in Early Modern England* (Oxford: Oxford University Press, 2003); Joanne Begiato, *Manliness in Britain, 1760–1900: Bodies, Emotion and Material Culture* (Manchester: Manchester University Press, 2020); Karen Harvey, *The Little Republic: Masculinity and Domestic Authority in Eighteenth-Century Britain* (Oxford: Oxford University Press, 2012); Henry French and Mark Rothery, *Man's Estate: Landed Gentry Masculinities, 1660–1900* (Oxford: Oxford University Press, 2012).

27 See https://mbsbham.wordpress.com/programme-british-studies-in-broken-world/ (accessed 6 April 2023).

28 Other participants in the original conference panel and workshop – and contributors to the discussions that shaped this volume – included Mark Anderson, Laura Beers, Jacob Bloomfield, Paul Deslandes, Ewan Gibbs, Sophie Greenway, Liam Liburd, Amy Milne-Smith Emily Rutherford, Jack Saunders, and Rory Scothorne.

29 John Tosh, 'The History of Masculinity: An Outdated Concept?', in Arnold and Brady (eds), *What Is Masculinity?*, 17–34; Michael Roper, 'Slipping Out of View: Subjectivity and Emotion in Gender History', *History Workshop Journal*, 59 (2005), 57–72. In debates on the relative merits of cultural and social approaches, or attention to discourse versus experience, the field has therefore played out its own version of those going on in historical method more widely. See, *inter alia*, Peter Mandler, 'The Problem with Cultural History', *Cultural and Social History*, 1:1 (2004), 94–117; Christine Grandy, 'Cultural History's Absent Audience', *Cultural and Social History*, 16:5 (2019), 643–663; Geoff Eley, *A Crooked Line: From Cultural History to the History of Society* (Ann Arbor: University of Michigan Press, 2005).

30 R. W. Connell, *Masculinities*, 2nd edn (Cambridge: Polity Press; Sydney: Allen & Unwin; Berkeley: University of California Press, 2005); R. W. Connell, *Gender and Power: Society, the Person, and Sexual Politics* (Cambridge: Polity Press, 1987). Connell's theory of hegemony emerged from a broader turn to Gramscian models in the social sciences and New Left politics in the 1970s and 1980s, as traced in Dennis Dworkin, *Cultural Marxism in Post-War Britain: History, the New Left, and the Origins of Cultural Studies* (Durham, NC: Duke University Press, 1997). For a more recent spin on this approach, see

Christopher Chitty, *Sexual Hegemony: Statecraft, Sodomy, and Capital in the Rise of the World System* (Durham, NC: Duke University Press, 2020).
31 See Chapter 6; and Ben Griffin, 'Hegemonic Masculinity as a Historical Problem', *Gender & History*, 30:2 (2018), 377–400.
32 Andrew Abbott, *Processual Sociology* (Chicago: University of Chicago Press, 2016).
33 Jack Halberstam, *In a Queer Time and Place: Transgender Bodies, Subcultural Lives* (New York: New York University Press, 2005); Elizabeth Freeman, *Time Binds: Queer Temporalities, Queer Histories* (Durham, NC: Duke University Press, 2010); Carla Freccero, *Queer/Early/Modern* (Durham, NC: Duke University Press, 2006); José Esteban Muñoz, *Cruising Utopia: The Then and There of Queer Futurity* (New York: New York University Press, 2009); Kadji Amin, *Disturbing Attachments: Genet, Modern Pederasty, and Queer History* (Durham, NC: Duke University Press, 2017); Carolyn Dinshaw, *Getting Medieval: Sexualities and Communities, Pre- and Postmodern* (Durham, NC: Duke University Press, 1999); David M. Halperin, *How To Do the History of Homosexuality* (Chicago: University of Chicago Press, 2002); Heather Love, *Feeling Backward: Loss and the Politics of Queer History* (Cambridge: Harvard University Press, 2009); Leah DeVun and Zeb Tortorici, 'Trans, Time, and History', *TSQ: Transgender Studies Quarterly*, 5:4 (2018), 518–539. For a critical overview of some this work, see Valerie Traub, 'The New Unhistoricism in Queer Studies', *PMLA: Publications of the Modern Language Association*, 128:1 (2013), 21–39. For what Brian Lewis has identified as 'the new British queer history', see Brian Lewis (ed.), *British Queer History: New Approaches and Perspectives* (Manchester: Manchester University Press, 2013); Matt Houlbrook, *Queer London: Perils and Pleasures in the Sexual Metropolis, 1918–1957* (Chicago: University of Chicago Press, 2005); Matt Cook, *London and the Culture of Homosexuality, 1885–1914* (Cambridge: Cambridge University Press, 2003); Matt Cook, *Queer Domesticities: Homosexuality and Home Life in Twentieth-Century London* (Basingstoke: Palgrave Macmillan, 2014); Sean Brady, *Masculinity and Male Homosexuality in Britain, 1861–1913* (Basingstoke: Palgrave Macmillan, 2005); Laura Doan, *Disturbing Practices: History, Sexuality, and Women's Experience of Modern War* (Chicago: University of Chicago Press, 2013); Lucy Robinson, *Gay Men and the Left in Post-War Britain: How the Personal Got Political* (Manchester: Manchester University Press, 2011); Seth Koven, *Slumming: Sexual and Social Politics in Victorian London* (Princeton: Princeton University Press, 2006); Richard Hornsey, *The Spiv and the Architect: Unruly Life in Postwar London* (Minneapolis: University of Minnesota Press, 2010); H. G. Cocks, *Nameless Offences: Homosexual Desire in the 19th Century* (London: I.B. Tauris, 2003); Helen Smith, *Masculinity and Same-Sex Desire in Industrial England, 1895–1957* (Basingstoke: Palgrave Macmillan, 2015). Regina Kunzel offers an excellent overview of queer history's methods and insights in 'The Power of Queer History', *American Historical Review*, 123:5 (2018), 1560–1582.
34 See Chapters 1–3. On masculinity, race, and empire, see Heather Ellis and Jessica Meyer (eds), *Masculinity and the Other: Historical Perspectives* (Newcastle

upon Tyne: Cambridge Scholars Publishing, 2009); Onni Gust, *Unhomely Empire: Whiteness and Belonging, from the Scottish Enlightenment to Liberal Imperialism* (London: Bloomsbury, 2020); Leslie Allin, *Penetrating Critiques: Emasculated Empire and Victorian Identity in Africa* (Toronto: University of Toronto Press, 2020); Ronald Hyam, *Empire and Sexuality: The British Experience* (Manchester: Manchester University Press, 1990); Catherine Hall, *Civilising Subjects: Metropole and Colony in the English Imagination 1830–1867* (Chicago: University of Chicago Press, 2002); Kate Imy, *Faithful Fighers: Identity and Power in the British Indian Army* (Stanford: Stanford University Press, 2019); Liam Liburd, 'Beyond the Pale: Whiteness, Masculinity and Empire in the British Union of Fascists, 1932–1940', *Fascism*, 7:2 (2018), 275–296; Anna Maguire, *Contact Zones of the First World War: Cultural Encounters across the British Empire* (Cambridge: Cambridge University Press, 2021); J. A. Mangan, *'Manufactured' Masculinity: Making Imperial Manliness, Morality and Militarism* (London: Routledge, 2012); Marc Matera, *Black London: The Imperial Metropolis and Decolonization in the Twentieth Century* (Berkeley: University of California Press, 2015); Anne McClintock, *Imperial Leather: Race, Gender and Sexuality in the Colonial Contest* (London: Routledge, 1995); John C. Mitcham, *Race and Imperial Defence in the British World, 1870–1914* (Cambridge: Cambridge University Press, 2019); George N. Njung, 'Amputated Men, Colonial Bureaucracy, and Masculinity in Post-World War I Colonial Nigeria', *Journal of Social History*, 53:3 (2020), 620–643; Paul Ocobock, *An Uncertain Age: The Politics of Manhood in Kenya* (Athens: Ohio University Press, 2017); Jonathan Saha, 'Whiteness, Masculinity and the Ambivalent Embodiment of "British Justice" in Colonial Burma', *Cultural and Social History*, 14:4 (2017), 527–542; Bill Schwarz, *The White Man's World* (Oxford: Oxford University Press, 2011); Mrinalini Sinha, *Colonial Masculinity: The 'Manly Englishman' and the 'Effeminate Bengali' in the Late Nineteenth Century* (Manchester: Manchester University Press, 1995); Richard Smith, *Jamaican Volunteers in the First World War: Race, Masculinity and the Development of National Consciousness* (Manchester: Manchester University Press, 2004); Heather Streets, *Martial Races: The Military, Race and Masculinity in British Imperial Culture, 1857–1914* (Manchester: Manchester University Press, 2004); T. J. Tallie, *Queering Colonial Natal: Indigeneity and the Violence of Belonging in Southern Africa* (Minneapolis: University of Minnesota Press, 2019); Thomas Webb, Chris Pearson, Penny Summerfield, and Mark Riley, 'More-Than-Human Emotional Communities: British Soldiers and Mules in Second World War Burma', *Cultural & Social History*, 17:2 (2020), 245–262; Rahul Rao, *Out of Time: The Queer Politics of Postcoloniality* (Oxford: Oxford University Press, 2020); Carina E. Ray, *Crossing the Color Line: Race, Sex, and the Contested Politics of Colonialism in Ghana* (Athens: Ohio University Press, 2015); Saheed Aderinto, *When Sex Threatened the State: Illicit Sexuality, Nationalism, and Politics in Colonial Nigeria, 1900–1958* (Champaign: University of Illinois Press, 2015); Anjali Arondekar, *For the Record: On Sexuality and the Colonial Archive in India* (Durham, NC: Duke University Press, 2009); Joseph Allen

Boone, *The Homoerotics of Orientalism* (New York: Columbia University Press, 2014); Trevor Burnard, *Mastery, Tyranny, and Desire: Thomas Thistlewood and His Slaves in the Anglo-Jamaican World* (Chapel Hill: University of North Carolina Press, 2004); Hilary Buxton, 'Imperial Amnesia: Race, Trauma and Indian Troops in the First World War', *Past & Present*, 241 (2018), 221–258; Graham Dawson, *Soldier Heroes: British Adventure, Empire and the Imagining of Masculinities* (London: Routledge, 1994); Humberto Garcia, *England Re-Oriented: How Central and South Asian Travelers Imagined the West, 1750–1857* (Cambridge: Cambridge University Press, 2020); Durba Ghosh, *Sex and the Family in Colonial India: The Making of Empire* (Cambridge: Cambridge University Press, 2006).

35 Emily Robinson, Camilla Schofield, Florence Sutcliffe-Braithwaite, and Natalie Thomlinson, 'Telling Stories about Post-War Britain: Popular Individualism and the "Crisis" of the 1970s', *Twentieth Century British History*, 28:2 (2017), 268–304; James Vernon, *Modern Britain: 1750 to the Present*, Cambridge History of Britain (Cambridge: Cambridge University Press, 2017), esp. ch. 13; Lawrence, *Me Me Me?*.

36 See Chapter 9. For recent work on selfhood, emotion, and affect in modern British history, see Claire Langhamer, *The English in Love: The Intimate Story of an Emotional Revolution* (Oxford: Oxford University Press, 2013); Richard Hall, 'The Emotional Lives and Legacies of Fathers and Sons in Britain, 1945–1974' (DPhil diss., University of Cambridge, 2019); Simon Szreter and Kate Fisher, *Sex before the Sexual Revolution: Intimate Life in England, 1918–1963* (Cambridge: Cambridge University Press, 2010); Huxford, *The Korean War in Britain*; Cohen, *Family Secrets*; Hannah Charnock, 'Teenage Girls, Female Friendship and the Making of the Sexual Revolution in England, 1950–1980', *Historical Journal*, 63:4 (2020), 1032–1053; Furneaux, *Military Men of Feeling*; Emma Griffin, *Bread Winner: An Intimate History of the Victorian Economy* (New Haven: Yale University Press, 2020); Ewan Gibbs, *Coal Country: The Meaning and Memory of Deindustrialization in Postwar London* (London: University of London Press, 2021); Charlotte Greenhalgh, *Aging in Twentieth-Century Britain* (Berkeley: University of California Press, 2018); Celia Hughes, *Young Lives on the Left: Sixties Activism and the Liberation of the Self* (Manchester: Manchester University Press, 2015); Meyer, *Men of War*; Roper, *The Secret Battle*. For methodological reflections, see Penny Summerfield, *Histories of the Self: Personal Narratives and Historical Practice* (London: Routledge, 2018); Tracey Loughran and Dawn Mannay (eds), *Emotion and the Researcher: Sites, Subjectivities and Relationships* (Bingley: Emerald Publishing, 2018).

37 Joan W. Scott, 'The Evidence of Experience', *Critical Inquiry*, 17:4 (1991), 773–797. Michael Roper gives a typically nuanced consideration of this question in 'Slipping Out of View: Subjectivity and Emotion in Gender History', *History Workshop Journal*, 59 (2005), 57–72.

38 Some touchpoints: Susan Pedersen, *Family, Dependence and the Origins of the Welfare State: Britain and France, 1914–1945* (Cambridge: Cambridge University Press, 1993); Ben Jackson, 'Free Markets and Feminism: The Neo-

Liberal Defence of the Male Breadwinner Model in Britain, c. 1980–1997', *Women's History Review*, 28:2 (2019), 297–316; Rose, *Which People's War?*; Richard Vinen, *National Service: Conscription in Britain, 1945–1963* (London: Penguin, 2014); Cocks, *Nameless Offences*; Amy Milne-Smith, *Out of His Mind: Masculinity and Mental Illness in Victorian Britain* (Manchester: Manchester University Press, 2022).

39 Nadia Ellis charts some of the complexities of the struggle for inclusion in 'Black Migrants, White Queers and the Archive of Inclusion in Postwar London', *Interventions*, 17:6 (2015), 893–915. See also Stephen Brooke, 'Gender and Working-Class Identity in Britain during the 1950s', *Journal of Social History*, 34:4 (2001), 773–795; Rob Waters, *Thinking Black: Britain, 1964–1985* (Berkeley: University of California Press, 2018); Jeffrey Weeks, *The World We Have Won: The Remaking of Erotic and Intimate Life* (London: Routledge, 2007).

40 Claire Langhamer, '"Who the Hell Are Ordinary People?" Ordinariness as a Category of Historical Analysis', *Transcations of the Royal Historical Society*, 28 (2018), 175–195. See also Florence Sutcliffe-Braithwaite, *Class, Politics, and the Decline of Deference in England, 1968–2000* (Oxford: Oxford University Press, 2018); Hilary Young, 'Being a Man: Everyday Masculinities', in Lynn Abrams and Callum Brown (eds), *A History of Everyday Life in Twentieth-Century Scotland* (Edinburgh: Edinburgh University Press, 2010), 131–152; Ben Mechen, '"Instamatic Living Rooms of Sin": Pornography, Participation and the Erotics of Ordinariness in the 1970s', *Contemporary British History*, 36:2 (2022), 174–206; Helen Smith, 'Working-Class Ideas and Experiences of Sexuality in Twentieth-Century Britain: Regionalism as a Category of Analysis', *Twentieth Century British History*, 29:1 (2018), 58–78; Laura Carter, *Histories of Everyday Life: The Making of Popular Social History in Britain* (Oxford: Oxford University Press, 2021).

41 The Topham family's diaries, letters, photographs, and ephemera are part of Matt Houlbrook's family archive. See Diary of Will Topham (1945); Enid Topham, Charles Letts's School-Girl's Diary (1942). On cultures of masculinity in mining communities, see e.g. Neil Penlington, 'Masculinity and Domesticity in 1930s South Wales: Did Unemployment Change the Domestic Division of Labour?', *Twentieth Century British History*, 21:3 (2010), 281–299; Stephanie Ward, 'Miners' Bodies and Masculine Identity in Britain, c.1900–1950', *Cultural and Social History*, 18:3 (2021), 443–462; Ben Curtis and Steven Thompson, '"This Is the Country of Premature Old Men": Ageing and Aged Miners in the South Wales Coalfield, c.1880–1947', *Cultural and Social History*, 12:4 (2015), 587–606.

42 Diary of Will Topham (1945); Will Topham to Enid and Roy Sprake (2 July 1967). For recent work on ageing, disability, and bodies, see Greenhalgh, *Aging in Twentieth-Century Britain*; Tracey Loughran, *Shell-Shock and Medical Culture in First World War Britain* (Cambridge: Cambridge University Press, 2017); Deborah Cohen, *The War Come Home: Disabled Veterans in Britain and Germany, 1914–1939* (Berkeley: University of California Press, 2001).

For unemployment and masculinity, see Marjorie Levine-Clark, *Unemployment, Welfare, and Masculine Citizenship: 'So Much Honest Poverty' in Britain, 1870–1930* (Basingstoke: Palgrave Macmillan, 2015); Gibbs, *Coal Country*. For fathers and daughters and domestic lives, see Strange, *Fatherhood and the British Working Class*; Carolyn Steedman, *Landscape for a Good Woman: A Story of Two Lives* (London: Virago, 1986); King, *Family Men*.

43 For an introduction to these ideas, see Michael Roper, 'Splitting in Unsent Letters: Writing as a Social Practice and a Psychological Activity', *Social History*, 26:3 (2001), 318–339; Jennifer Sinor, *The Extraordinary Work of Ordinary Writing: Annie Ray's Diary* (Iowa: University of Iowa Press, 2002); Summerfield, *Histories of the Self*, esp. ch. 3; Matt Houlbrook, *The Prince of Tricksters: The Incredible True Story of Netley Lucas, Gentleman Crook* (Chicago: University of Chicago Press, 2016); Carolyn Steedman, *An Everyday Life of the English Working Class: Work, Self and Sociability in the Early Nineteenth Century* (Cambridge: Cambridge University Press, 2013); Carolyn Dever, *Chains of Love and Beauty: The Diary of Michael Field* (Princeton: Princeton University Press, 2022).

44 See Adrian Kane-Galbraith, unpublished workshop reflection, 14 June 2018.

45 Matt Houlbrook, 'Lady Austin's Camp Boys: Constituting the Queer Subject in 1930s London', *Gender and History*, 14:1 (2002), 31–61. The trial papers are in TNA, CRIM 1 639, S., Austin and (33) Others: Disorderly House/Conspiracy to Corrupt Morals (1933/1938).

46 TNA, CRIM 1 639, S., Austin and (33) Others: Disorderly House/Conspiracy to Corrupt Morals: Statement of SDDI Francis (7 February 1933).

47 'West End Nest of Vice Smoked Out', *News of the World*, 5 March 1933, 18. On the sentencing, see TNA, CRIM 4 1576 (7 February 1933); LMA, ACC 2385 183: Calendars of Prisoners, Central Criminal Court (7 February 1933).

48 See Laura Doan, *Disturbing Practices: History, Sexuality, and Women's Experience of Modern War* (Chicago: University of Chicago Press, 2013).

49 See Chapter 1. On trans histories in Britain and beyond, see Jen Manion, *Female Husbands: A Trans History* (Cambridge: Cambridge University Press, 2021); Christine Burns, *Trans Britain: Our Journey from the Shadows* (London: Unbound, 2019); James Vernon, '"For Some Queer Reason": The Trials and Tribulations of Colonel Barker's Masquerade in Interwar Britain', *Signs*, 26:1 (2000), 37–62; Alison Oram, *Her Husband Was a Woman! Women's Gender Crossing in Modern British Popular Culture* (London: Routledge, 2007); Emily Skidmore, *True Sex: The Lives of Trans Men at the Turn of the Twentieth Century* (New York: New York University Press, 2017). See also Jacob Bloomfield, '*Splinters*: Cross-Dressing Ex-Servicemen on the Interwar Stage', *Twentieth Century British History*, 30:1 (2019), 1–28. On trans theory and 'female masculinities', see Jack Halberstam, *Female Masculinity* (Durham, NC: Duke University Press, 1998); Jack Halberstam, *In a Queer Time and Place: Transgender Bodies, Subcultural Lives* (New York: New York University Press, 2005); Sofia Aboim, Pedro Vasconcelos, and Sara Merlini, 'Trans Masculinities: Embodiments, Performances and Materiality of Gender in Times of Change',

Changing Societies: Legacies and Challenges (2018), 333–355; Susan Stryker and Dylan McCarthy Blackson (eds), *The Transgender Studies Reader Remix* (London: Routledge, 2022). On the political stakes, see Shon Faye, *The Trangender Issue: An Argument for Justice* (London: Allen Lane, 2021).

50 Justin Bengry, 'Courting the Pink Pound: *Men Only* and the Queer Consumer, 1935–39', *History Workshop Journal*, 68:1 (2009), 122–148; Christopher Breward, *The Hidden Consumer: Masculinities, Fashion, and City Life* (Manchester: Manchester University Press, 1999); Shaun Cole, *Don We Now Our Gay Apparel: Gay Men's Dress in the Twentieth Century* (London: Berg, 2000); Laura Ugolini, *Men and Menswear: Sartorial Consumption in Britain, 1880–1939* (London: Routledge, 2007); Paul Deslandes, *The Culture of Male Beauty in Britain: From the First Photographs to David Beckham* (Chicago: University of Chicago Press, 2021); Mort, *Cultures of Consumption*; Sean Nixon, *Hard Looks: Masculinities, Spectatorship and Contemporary Consumption* (London: UCL Press, 1996); Ina Zweiniger-Bargielowska, *Managing the Body: Beauty, Health and Fitness in Britain 1880–1939* (Oxford: Oxford University Press, 2011); Rosalind McKever, Claire Wilcox, and Marta Franceschini (eds), *Fashioning Masculinities: The Art of Menswear* (London: V&A, 2022); Jessica Clark, *The Business of Beauty: Gender and the Body in Modern London* (London: Bloomsbury, 2020).

51 As Roper and Tosh argued in the introduction to *Manful Assertions* (18), many late twentieth-century scholars and cultural commentators used the trope 'masculinity in crisis' to try to make sense of the difficulties men faced in the 1970s–1990s, or articulations of anti-feminist 'backlash'. See Roger Horrocks, *Masculinity in Crisis: Myths, Fantasies and Realities* (London: St. Martin's Press, 1994); Anthony Clare, *On Men: Masculinity in Crisis* (London: Arrow, 2001); Joseph Pleck, *The Myth of Masculinity* (Boston: MIT Press, 1981); Andrew Tolson, *The Limits of Masculinity: Male Identity and Women's Liberation* (London: Harper Collins, 1977); Segal, *Slow Motion*, xii; Ros Coward, *Sacred Cows: Is Feminism Relevant to the New Millennium?* (London: Harper Collins, 1999), 51; John Beynon, *Masculinities and Culture* (London: Open University Press, 2001); bell hooks, *We Real Cool: Black Men and Masculinity* (London: Routledge, 2004); Susan Faludi, *Backlash: The Undeclared War against Women* (London: Chatto & Windus, 1992). As historians have recognised, the language of crisis seemed to have special power in the 1970s and 1980s. See Robinson *et al.*, 'Telling Stories', 269; Stephen Brooke, 'Living in "New Times": Historicizing 1980s Britain', *History Compass*, 12:1 (2014), 21. On men after feminism and incursions by women onto traditionally masculine terrain, see Katherine Jones, '"Men Too": Masculinities and Contraceptive Politics in Late Twentieth Century Britain', *Contemporary British History*, 34:1 (2020), 44–70; Ben Mechen, '"Closer Together": Durex Condoms and Contraceptive Consumerism in 1970s Britain', in Jennifer Evans and Ciara Meehan (eds), *Perceptions of Pregnancy from the Seventeenth to the Twentieth Century* (Basingstoke: Palgrave Macmillan, 2017); Helen McCarthy, 'Women, Marriage and Paid Work in Post-War Britain', *Women's History Review*, 26:1 (2017), 46–61; Elaine Showalter, *Sexual Anarchy: Gender and Culture at the Fin de Siècle* (London: Virago, 1992).

52 As Sharon Willis has put it, 'masculinity in crisis is really white heterosexual masculinity desperately seeking to reconstruct itself within a web of social differences, where its opposing terms include not only femininity, but black masculinity and male homosexuality'. Sharon Willis, *High Contrast: Race and Gender in Contemporary Hollywood Film* (Durham, NC: Duke University Press, 1997), 31.

53 For the renewed salience of the 'masculinity in crisis' trope, see Freddie Hayward, '"Men Are Trapped in a Gender Prison": Ivan Jablonka on the Crisis of Men and Masculinity', *New Statesman*, 16 February 2022; Ross Raisin, 'Men or Mice: Is Masculinity in Crisis?', *Guardian*, 6 October 2017; 'Doctor Who: Is She Driving Men to Crime?', *The Week*, 3 December 2021; Pankaj Mishra, 'The Crisis in Modern Masculinity', *Guardian*, 17 March 2018. Jordan Peterson, meanwhile, speaks of modern masculinities in relation to his broader thesis of pervasive social 'chaos' – a situation to which his '12 rules' offer an 'antidote'. For feminist analysis of such crisis talk, as well as the right-wing men's movement in general, see Susanne Kaiser, *Political Masculinity: How Incels, Fundamentalists and Authoritarians Mobilize for Patriarchy*, trans. Valentine Pakis (Cambridge: Polity Press, 2022); Amia Srinivasan, 'Does Anyone Have the Right to Sex?', *London Review of Books*, 40:6 (2018). The feminist theorist Jacqueline Rose has recently argued that violence against women most often happens as a symptom of 'masculinity in a panic': Jacqueline Rose, *On Violence and On Violence against Women* (London: Faber & Faber, 2021).

54 See Chapter 6.

55 As shown, for example, by Kent, *Making Peace*; and Alison Light, *Forever England: Femininity, Literature and Conservatism between the Wars* (London: Routledge, 1991).

56 Rose, *Which People's War?*; Roper, *The Secret Battle*; Martin Francis, 'A Flight from Commitment? Domesticity, Adventure and the Masculine Imaginary in Britain after the Second World War', *Gender & History*, 19:1 (2007), 163–185; Jessica Hammett, *Creating the People's War: Civil Defence Communities in Second World War Britain* (Manchester: Manchester University Press, 2022).

57 Adrian Horn, *Juke Box Britain: Americanisation and Youth Culture, 1945–60* (Manchester: Manchester University Press, 2009); Allison Abra, *Dancing in the English Style: Consumption, Americanisation and National Identity in Britain, 1918–50* (Manchester: Manchester University Press, 2017); Mort, *Cultures of Consumption*.

58 See n. 39; and Michal Shapira, *The War Inside: Psychoanalysis, Total War, and the Making of the Democratic Self in Postwar Britain* (Cambridge: Cambridge University Press, 2013).

59 On the growing purchase of ideas of personality and selfhood in modern Britain, see Nikolas Rose, *Governing the Soul: The Shaping of the Private Self* (London: Free Association, 1990); Carolyn Steedman, *Strange Dislocations: Childhood and the Idea of Human Interiority, 1780–1930* (Cambridge: Harvard University Press, 1995); Anna Clark, *Alternative Histories of the Self: A Cultural History of Sexuality and Secrets, 1762–1917* (London: Bloomsbury, 2017); Mathew Thomson, *Psychological Subjects: Identity, Culture, and Health*

in Twentieth-Century Britain (Oxford: Oxford University Press, 2006); Mark Jackson and Martin D. Moore (eds), *Balancing the Self: Medicine, Politics and the Regulation of Health in the Twentieth Century* (Manchester: Manchester University Press, 2020). See also the sociological and philosophical commentaries of Anthony Giddens, *Modernity and Self-Identity: Self and Society in the Late Modern Age* (Cambridge: Polity Press, 1991); Charles Taylor, *Sources of the Self: The Making of the Modern Identity* (Cambridge: Harvard University Press, 1990); and Michel Foucault in his extensive writings and lectures on 'the care of the self' and governmentality. The mythopoetic programmes for manliness of Bly and Peterson fit into exactly this paradigm through their return to Carl Jung's theories of gender and personality.

60 Michael Roper, 'Between Manliness and Masculinity: The "War Generation" and the Psychology of Fear in Britain, 1914–1950', *Journal of British Studies*, 44:2 (2005), 343–362.
61 See the Conclusion; and Jones, '"Me Too"'.
62 See Reflection by Tosh.
63 Conwy Archive Service, GB 2008 CX638: John Domney, Pelman Institute Worksheets and Correspondence, Worksheet 2 (5 May 1936). On Pelmanism, see Thomson, *Psychological Subjects*, ch. 1.
64 See Chapter 4; and Scott, 'The Evidence of Experience', 779.
65 Conwy Archive Service, GB 2008 CX638 (9 April 1936).
66 Houlbrook, *Prince of Tricksters*; Houlbrook, 'Charming Faces and the Problem of Identification', in Rex Ferguson, Melissa Littlefield, and James Purdon (eds), *The Art of Identification: Forensics, Surveillance, Identity* (Pennsylvania: Pennsylvania State University Press, 2021).
67 See Chapter 6.
68 See Chapter 7.
69 Olive Anderson, *Suicide in Victorian and Edwardian England* (Oxford: Clarendon Press, 1987); Lyndsay Galpin, *Male Suicide and Masculinity in 19th-Century Britain: Stories of Self-Destruction* (London: Bloomsbury, 2022); Mark Jackson, *The Age of Stress: Science and the Search for Stability* (Oxford: Oxford University Press, 2013); Jill Kirby, *Feeling the Strain: A Cultural History of Stress in Twentieth-Century Britain* (Manchester: Manchester University Press, 2019); Hall, *Hidden Anxieties*; Christopher Millard, *A History of Self-Harm in Britain: A Genealogy of Cutting and Overdosing* (Basingstoke: Palgrave Macmillan, 2015); Kyla Thomas and David Gunnell, 'Suicide in England and Wales, 1861–2007: A Time-Trends Analysis', *International Journal of Epidemiology*, 39:6 (2010), 1464–1475; Ali Haggett, *A History of Male Psychological Disorders in Britain, 1945–1980* (Basingstoke: Palgrave Macmillan, 2015).
70 See 1939 Register, 623 (2), www.ancestry.co.uk/discoveryui-content/view/46225630:61596 (accessed 7 April 2023); 'Righteous Hate', *North Wales Weekly News*, 2 July 1942, 8; 'Wartime Pal Traced', *North Wales Weekly News*, 13 March 1958, 8 'Rhos Players in Comedy', *North Wales Weekly News*, 24 April 1958, 7; 'Obituary', *North Wales Weekly News*, 18 January 1962, 12.

71 See e.g. Michael Anderson, 'The Emergence of the Modern Life Cycle in Britain', *Social History*, 10:1 (1985), 69–87.
72 King, *Family Men*.
73 See Chapter 9.
74 See Chapter 1.
75 See Chapter 2.
76 See Chapter 3.
77 See Chapter 4.
78 See Chapter 5.
79 See Chapter 6; and Griffin, 'Hegemonic Masculinity'.
80 See Pat Ayers, *The Liverpool Docklands: Life and Work in Athol Street* (Liverpool: Countryvise, 1988); Pat Ayers, 'Work, Culture and Gender: The Making of Masculinities in Postwar Liverpool', *Labour History Review*, 69:2 (2004).
81 See Chapter 7.
82 See Chapter 8.
83 For this literature, see Langhamer, *The English in Love*; and Rose, *Governing the Soul*. For the use of this term, see Cohen, *Family Secrets*, 238. For a similar argument, see Hera Cook, 'From Controlling Emotions to Expressing Feelings in Mid-Twentieth Century England', *Journal of Social History*, 47:3 (2014), 627–646; Francis, 'Tears, Tantrums and Bared Teeth: The Emotional Economy of Three Conservative Prime Ministers, 1951–1963', *Journal of British Studies*, 41:3 (2002), 354–387.
84 See Chapter 9.
85 See Chapters 1 and 3. See also Meyer, *Men of War*, 97–127; Fiona Reid, *Broken Men: Shell Shock, Treatment and Recovery in Britain, 1914–1930* (London: Continuum, 2010); Loughran, *Shell-Shock and Medical Culture*.
86 See also Sara Ahmed, *Living a Feminist Life* (Durham, NC: Duke University Press, 2015); and Sara Ahmed, *Complaint!* (Durham, NC: Duke University Press, 2021).
87 Stefan Collini, *Public Moralists: Political Thought and Intellectual Life in Britain, 1850–1930* (Oxford: Oxford University Press, 1991).
88 See Reflection by Charnock. On the oral history interview and histories of gender and sexuality, see also Clare Summerskill, Amy Tooth Murphy, and Emma Vickers (eds), *New Directions in Queer Oral History: Archives of Disruption* (London: Routledge, 2022); and Summerfield, *Histories of the Self*.
89 See Reflection by Tosh.
90 *Ibid.*

Part I

Institutions

1

Male breadwinners of 'doubtful sex': Trans men and the welfare state, 1954–1970

Adrian Kane-Galbraith

Until the end of 1954, officers at the Ministry of Pensions and National Insurance had no reason to take note of Vincent Jones.[1] The twenty-six-year-old held a steady job at a telephone exchange, paid his weekly insurance contributions at a standard male rate, and rented a small Catford flat with his wife, Joan Lee. However, in mid-December, Jones's performance of quiet, respectable masculine citizenship came to an abrupt, and very public, end.[2] On the afternoon of the thirteenth, at the Greenwich Magistrates Court, Jones and Lee pleaded guilty to the charge of making a false statement on their marriage licence. What the couple had neglected to inform the new vicar of their local church – a fact known to the previous vicar, who alerted the police when he learned of their union – was that Jones was registered as a girl on his birth certificate. 'I am a man,' Jones explained to a *Daily Express* reporter, 'but if you mean physically I still have female organs … I have been to doctors to get my sex changed and I am sick of waiting.'[3] Although Jones carried National Insurance documents affirming his male name and identity, the magistrate ruled that Jones's 'female organs' meant that he could not consummate a legal marriage in the role of a husband: the ceremony was merely a ploy to cover 'unnatural passion … with a false air of respectability'.[4] Jones, for his part, admitted the truth of the former charge, while strenuously contesting the latter. If he could work as a man, contribute to the nation's coffers as a man, but not form a legitimate family as a man, it was the law, not him, that had made false promises. 'I am guilty,' he declared, 'but something should be done for people like us.'

Perhaps more striking than Jones's public demand for justice, however, was the active, albeit unpublicised, response it provoked in the upper echelons of the General Register Office (GRO) and the Ministry of Pensions and National Insurance (MPNI). While Jones was hardly the first English 'female husband' to catch the attention of the Commonwealth press, the exposure of Jones's dual *legal* identities was a novel feature, casting a cloud of suspicion over the new contributory welfare system and its claims to efficiency, fairness, and transparency.[5] Faced with this direct challenge to its expertise, the MPNI's legal and medical officers scrambled to define what, exactly, the block-capital designation 'MAN' on the National Insurance card was supposed to represent. Had the MPNI, in failing to cross-reference Jones's identity claims with the evidence of his birth certificate, facilitated fraud – as well as a technically legal, but morally reprehensible, 'unnatural passion' between female-assigned people? Or did the sex marker on a National Insurance card reflect a set of citizenship rights and responsibilities fundamentally different from those signified by the sex marker on a birth certificate? How, in other words, were the benefits and responsibilities of a 'male breadwinner' to be allocated when maleness proved a less than self-evident quality?

These questions would divide British National Insurance officers for more than a decade following Jones's trial, reflecting the ongoing moral, and practical, anxieties generated by the gap between 'man' as a class of citizen and the messy heterogeneity of individual men. In numerical terms, 'sex changes' were rare: according to one internal census, the Chief Medical Officer of the MPNI approved just 130 changes of sex registration from female to male between 1954 and 1969, all insured persons from England or Wales.[6] Yet the vast MPNI correspondence on the question of 'sex change', bursting from half a dozen fat pink folders at the National Archives, suggests that trans people were crucial to the bureaucratic project of determining the uses of sex at mid-century. Trans men were, effectively, limit cases. Their self-identification as men with 'female organs' forced MPNI administrators to name the assumptions about male bodies and behaviour implicit in their sex classification system, and to determine how best to accommodate exceptions without undermining the binary sex-differentiated rights and responsibilities that underpinned the contributory welfare state. Curiously enough, for much of the 1950s and 1960s, MPNI officers frequently decided to grant trans men the documentation they desired. Given the centrality of productive work to the 'strong male breadwinner state' of mid-century Britain, transmasculine workers could potentially be more 'useful' citizens as members of their chosen, rather than their assigned, sex.[7]

Sex in Britain: 'Historical fact' or social fiction?

The story of how this window of relative tolerance opened in the mid-1950s – and, crucially, how it slammed shut at the turn of the 1970s – is a useful counterpoint to the growing historiography of 'sex change' as a medical and cultural phenomenon in the anglophone world. In recent years, interwar historians Clare Tebbutt and David Andrew Griffiths have pointed out that the concept of 'sex change' current in the medical and popular press of the 1930s–40s did not make a clear distinction between sex – usually referring to an individual's hormonal, gonadal, and genital anatomy – and gender, the feelings, behaviours, and bodily habitus culturally associated with that anatomy.[8] Most Britons would have first encountered the term 'sex change' in connection with female-assigned intersex people like the English Olympic javelin-thrower Mark Weston, who received extensive coverage in both the daily and the Sunday press during the mid-1930s.[9] However, as is evident Jones's 1954 testimony, 'sex change' could also refer to people without intersex diagnoses who felt themselves to be fundamentally different from other members of their birth-assigned sex.[10] In fact, well beyond the interwar years, the popular press made few distinctions between transitions initiated by doctors' determination to 'correct' a sexual anomaly and transitions initiated by gender-variant people themselves. Physicians like C. N. Armstrong, a leading endocrinologist at the Royal Victoria Hospital, Newcastle upon Tyne, continued to interpret not just gender dysphoria but even homosexuality as part of an intersex 'spectrum' until the turn of the 1960s.[11]

However, while these scholars have laid the groundwork for a discursive history of female-to-male transition in Britain – and established that rise of the psychiatric diagnosis of 'transsexualism' in the United States, as recounted by Susan Stryker and Joanne Meyerowitz, was not a universal phenomenon – there has been little reflection on how these intellectual trends played out in the crucial arena of state registration and recognition.[12] Indeed, there has been little discussion of transmasculine people at all, barring the odd biography, in the years *after* the Second World War. As is evident from the reminiscences of contributors to Christine Burns's 2018 collection *Trans Britain*, the tabloid exposure of trans women, like that of Roberta Cowell in March 1954 or April Ashley in 1961, tends to dominate public memory of the mid-twentieth century.[13] This chapter contends, however, that trans men's negotiations with the Ministry of Pensions and National Insurance are critical to consider precisely *because* they were less visible. The ambiguous term 'sex change' drew a veil over the particulars of trans men's bodies, not because those who used it were deceptive or ignorant, but as a deliberate means of centring masculine social performance rather than male embodiment in the determination of male insurance identity. Much like 1950s proponents of homosexual law reform, trans men applying for new insurance cards tried to frame their own congenital 'variation' as a potential social good.[14] As long as a trans applicant could demonstrate that he had the potential to productively contribute to society as a man, he could appeal to the pragmatic interest of the MPNI in order to gain recognition of his lived identity – provided, of course, nothing about his class, career choice, appearance, race, or sexuality threatened to expose the fragile foundations of binary sex.

This, then, was the context in which MPNI solicitor J. Vaughan, just a week following Jones's trial, proposed a meeting with his counterparts at the GRO on the subject of 'change of sex'. As he wrote to his superior, undersecretary D. H. Abbott, on 28 December, both insurance officers and registrars had arrived at the conclusion that the MPNI's 'position regarding the issue of contribution cards was more flexible', than that of the GRO.[15] In contrast to the relatively new National Insurance system, the GRO was bound my centuries of precedent. It had been issuing standardised documents recording an individual's sexual identity at birth, marriage, and death since 1837, with intersex people registered as men or women according to Lord Coke's seventeenth-century ruling that 'an Hermaphrodite may purchase according to that sexe which prevail'.[16] Although the GRO's representative at the meeting with Vaughan professed himself 'sympathetic' to the plight of people on the borderlands of sex, he held firm to the position that the birth certificate – and hence, the marriage certificate – represented only the 'true' or 'prevailing' sex of an infant at the point of birth. There was no such thing as sex change, only misidentified sex, and anyone wishing to re-register had to provide statutory declarations from people present at the birth – one attending physician and one family member – who were willing to testify to the 'error'.

However, as Vaughan wrote to Abbott several weeks later, the National Insurance card was not constrained by the birth certificate's commitment to 'historical' records of legitimacy and patrimony. It was, moreover, far more likely to expose a trans man to public embarrassment if his appearance failed to match the sex marker on the heading of the card. As the 1946 National Insurance Act and its successors centralised an array of public and privately funded benefits under the aegis of the Ministry of National Insurance (renamed the Ministry of National Insurance and Pensions in 1953), the sex-marked National Insurance card had emerged as a key identity document in its own right.[17] It had to be presented to employers each week for a contribution stamp, and was required proof of identity at local insurance offices, employment exchanges, and anywhere else Britons had to demonstrate entitlement to non-means-tested benefits of British citizenship.[18] In Vaughan's words, the National Insurance card was a 'passport to employment', and trans men might 'be prevented from becoming useful citizens by our refusal to issue the "wrong" type of card'.[19] After all, if a trans applicant's sartorial choices, libido, and career ambitions were as much a natural component of sex as his private anatomy – and the latter was far easier to conceal than the former – a policy that preserved the *appearance* of consistent binary sex was less likely to draw the MPNI into awkward public arguments over the reality and morality of 'sex change'.

Several months later, Vaughan's suggestions were given institutional weight by the memorandum Abbott crafted out of their chain of conversations: 'Persons of Doubtful Sex', issued on 18 April 1955. In it, Abbott borrowed extensively from the letter Vaughan had written to him in the days after Jones's trial, even re-using the phrase 'passport to employment'.[20] He concurred that defining sex as an historical record fixed at birth, as did the GRO, would reduce people like Jones to an unemployable class thrown on the straitened mercies of the National Assistance Boards – a prospect as unwelcome to the state as it was to trans men.[21] However, Abbott's pragmatism was tempered by a concern to avoid any public disclosure of the fact that two branches of state bureaucracy assessed sex by different standards. The Deputy Chief Medical Officer of the MPNI, F. M. Collins, had written to Abbott in April to insist that he be personally brought in to certify that 'the case is genuine and under medical supervision' – though he declined to clarify what constituted a 'genuine' case of 'sex change'.[22] Accordingly, all requests for sex re-designation were to be forwarded immediately by local authorities to Division C1B in London, where Collins, alongside the applicant's own doctor, would assess 'whether it would be proper, and to the advantage of the person concerned, that they should be treated as one sex or the other'.[23]

The key element of 'propriety' in this diagnostic process, as Collins's later decisions make clear, was the applicant's demonstration of his ability to function socially in his desired sex. 'Persons of Doubtful Sex' was in no sense a document driven by progressive convictions – Abbot, Vaughan, and Collins almost never used the name and pronouns preferred by the people they were discussing, making clear that they regarded the new card not as fact but as a means of papering over the gap between an applicant's assigned sex and his social presentation.[24] Yet by making sex assignment a question of 'proper' treatment rather than concrete anatomy, Abbott nevertheless gave his officers the flexibility to make subjective assessments of gender based on gender performance. And for a time, this compromise seemed to serve its purpose. Trans men sought an identity card that gave concrete affirmation to their narratives of sexed selfhood. National Insurance officers wanted the newly consolidated welfare system to remain politically viable, financially solvent, and easy to administer. Both groups, thus, had their own reasons for adapting a structure founded on the legal 'fiction' of binary sex to the messy reality of personhood.[25]

However, 'Persons of Doubtful Sex' also rested upon a number of assumptions particular to its mid-1950s context – assumptions which, over the course of the following decade, would make its hazily defined policy increasingly untenable. First and foremost, Abbott's memorandum spoke to the fact that the contributory welfare system was intended to engage with men directly, and women only indirectly.[26] Mere months after the release of William Beveridge's 1942 report *Social Insurance and Allied Services*, feminist commentators began to publish critiques of the way the state's 'cradle to grave' welfare provision economically devalued reproductive labour. Until 1975, male Class 1 card-holders paid higher weekly contributions from their earnings but also received higher unemployment, sickness, and pension rates on the assumption that they were the household's primary earners.[27] Married women, meanwhile, were initially excluded from the insurance system, leaving them dependent upon their husbands and on limited family allowances, while people of either sex classification who were routinely unemployed had no recourse but the perennially cash-strapped National Assistance Boards. Thus, within this 'strong male breadwinner state' – to borrow Jane Lewis's influential term – sex assignment had profound material consequences.[28] Even as the realities of working motherhood, the MPNI's dwindling financial resources, and the increasingly vocal feminist movement chipped away at social insurance's foundational fictions, the facade of male mediation between state and nuclear household remained intact through the mid-1960s.

This systemic inequity had, ironically enough, a positive impact on people who wanted to change their insurance designation from female to male. Admittedly concern about having to pay higher disability and unemployment benefits encouraged officers to screen out transmasculine applicants who appeared less than independent: in 1966, for instance, one trans man with an estranged husband was denied sickness benefit at a male rate until it was determined 'what contribution, if any [the husband] has been making towards her [*sic*] maintenance'.[29] But since working trans men with male cards paid higher weekly contributions 'under the erroneous belief that they are properly payable', as Vaughan put it, the MPNI actually stood to gain financially from recognising trans men's identities.[30] Trans men were also likely to defer retirement until sixty-five, remaining a contributing member of the workforce for five years longer than they were obliged to by statute. Moreover, the fact that trans men made up a majority of the first applicants for National Insurance re-designation during the 1950s and early 1960s – outnumbering trans women forty to twenty-nine as late as 1963 – encouraged MPNI officers to think of sex change as a net gain.[31] To put it in the starkest utilitarian terms – as did one MPNI officer in a 1959 letter to the Treasury – 'rather more women choose to pay as men than vice versa, so that [*sic*] the application of our policy should not result in a net loss to the National Insurance Fund'.[32]

Finally, on the cultural front, many insurance officers seem to have given credence to the widespread belief that 'true' trans men pursued changes to their embodiment for professional, rather than emotional or sexual, reasons. Unlike trans women, whose sexual and family life were routinely scrutinised by officers processing their applications, trans men were able to emphasise the productive rather than the reproductive aspect of masculinity in their self-accounting. At a time of historically low unemployment, such a career move could seem not just logical, but laudable, as long as it was directed towards appropriate channels: work in engineering, medicine, or skilled manual occupations dominated the professions trans men reported, rather than, say, sales, creative, or clerical work.[33]

The highly gendered career motive for female-to-male transition was widely disseminated through exclusives in the Sunday press during the early 1950s and 1960s. In December 1951, for instance, Terry Brown, a patient of prominent interwar sexologist Norman Haire, recalled for the *News of the World* that 'all the time I wanted to be doing a man's job. At 17 I thought work as an office girl was a mild form of hell.' The reporter went on to describe Brown's 'square, capable hands' which, Brown averred, 'were not made for pen-pushing'.[34] Another exclusive interview in the *Sunday Pictorial*, from 1953, reported that a transitioning man had given up his former career as a housewife and artist's model for a job working 'side by side' with his former husband at an aircraft manufacturing plant.[35] At least at first, this pervasive emphasis on masculine work habits seems to have contributed to a more positive attitude towards trans men among specialists: A. J. Evans, one of the only surgeons performing phalloplasty on the NHS during the 1950s, recalled that he was 'sympathetic' towards his transmasculine patients, describing them as 'very solid, pipe-smoking individuals' with 'a very strong career interest'.[36] In a sense, then, trans men's desire to be recognised as male could be, and often was, rationalised as a career-driven person's attempt to escape the dependency imposed by a female insurance status.

Within the National Insurance system, the very structural assumptions that penalised any deviations from the nuclear family model of breadwinner husband, housewife, and children also created pathways for some people to quietly, cautiously, abandon the sex-differentiated life path that had been set out for them. This was less a capitulation on the part of either party than it was a working misunderstanding, contingent upon mutual gestures of respect – at least in public – for the norms of 'respectable' masculinity. The MPNI might have appeared, at the population level, to be a top-down exercise of the state's panoptic power over life, but at the level of interactions between individual officers and insured persons, they more closely resembled cautious – and, over time, increasingly fraught – negotiations.[37]

'Unnatural passions' and the limits of tolerance

No sooner had 'Persons of Doubtful Sex' been committed to print, however, than the contradictions between the MPNI's gender-based classification system and the anatomically based system of other state agencies raised difficult questions – in this case, in C. M. O Collins's judgment on Vincent Jones. Jones, wrote Collins in late April 1955, had forfeited his right to carry a male insurance card under the current regulations. He should, said Collins, 'be told the implications of her [sic] plea of guilty which quite undermines her case to make out that she is male'.[38] Legally speaking, the problem was that Jones's plea had implicitly denied his masculinity, but no doubt the imputation of 'unnatural passions' underlying his deception also put him at a disadvantage on grounds of propriety.[39] Even so, Collins refused to foreclose on the possibility that Jones could return with a better story: if he provided evidence that contradicted his guilty plea, Collins suggested, he could be reissued a male card. And Jones himself apparently remained optimistic. He was planning to save his wages, he told the *Daily Herald*, 'so I can go abroad for treatment. Then I shall apply for an alteration of my birth certificate.'[40] His persistence, at any rate, could not be denied.

This negative judgement of Jones's male identity highlights how quickly suspicions of sexual impropriety could undermine the narrative of transmasculine social responsibility, particularly when benefits, rather than just identification cards, were in question. While sexual relationships between trans men and non-transgender women were technically legal, sexuality – and its legitimate social vehicle, marriage – brought the GRO's anatomical standards back into play, complicating the trans insured person's claims. The year 1958 saw the first test of the MPNI's approach towards married couples of the same birth-assigned sex, when Josephine Owen put in an apparently straightforward claim for a widow's pension. Josephine's husband Charles had passed away in his mid-forties the previous year; they had married in 1942 and were raising three children together, one of whom had been registered at birth as Charles's illegitimate child with another woman.[41] All the registration documents were obtained through normal procedures, Charles had paid standard male contribution rates since the inception of the National Insurance system, and there is no evidence that anyone (even, by her own account, Josephine herself) doubted Charles's manhood. However, the coroner examining Charles's remains confidently proclaimed him to be a woman. At a loss for how to process this revelation, the Beswick local insurance officer sent Owen's claim up the chain of command, launching a year-long controversy with effects that would reverberate far beyond the case itself.

In contrast to the more holistic terms in which Abbott had advised insurance officers to assess trans men's ability to become 'useful citizens', the examination process Charles's family had to undergo focused exclusively – and invasively – on sexual function. The primary respondent in the appeals process was not, it appears, Mrs Owen but rather Charles's corpse, which was interrogated with the scalpel to determine whether a mysterious 'operation' in '1939 or 1940' had rendered him capable of penile–vaginal intercourse.[42] According to F. M. Collins, who dissected the coroner's report with a perhaps unseemly tinge of scientific curiosity, it had not. In a summary for his colleagues Collins described Owen's abdominal scars and 'female though small and atrophic' genitalia, suggesting not only that the marriage was never consummated but that Owen might have been 'the *mother* of one of the children though she [*sic*] cannot possibly have been a father of anyone'.[43] He speculated that the unspecified operation 'may have been to remove the breasts to make the figure conform more to the male; this operation is sometimes done but it by no means changes the sex.'[44] The disarticulated parts of Owen's body having been thus compelled to speak, Manchester deputy commissioner Micklethwait decided to dismiss Josephine's appeal. Since Charles 'could never have played the part of a man in sexual intercourse or been the father of a child', the sixteen-year marriage had legally never existed – and Josephine Owen was 'not therefore YZ's widow'.[45]

Micklethwait's decision is all the more noteworthy in that he professed to regard Josephine as the victim of sexual deception, but did not suggest that Charles's National Insurance card implicated the MPNI in that deception. In the text of his judgement, Micklethwait assured his colleagues that he had taken full account of the documents Josephine had submitted to the local tribunal describing her 'married' life with Charles. 'I shall not embarrass her by recording them in this decision,' he wrote, 'beyond saying that she stresses that she never had any reason to believe that XZ was not a man, and I have no reason to doubt that this is true.' Owen's testimony may reflect a timeworn narrative of sexual ignorance articulated by the wives of 'female husbands' in the press, rather than the couple's real intimate practices – but what matters is that Micklethwait gave credence to her story and yet abrogated ministerial responsibility for the family's well-being.[46] For all the high-minded rhetoric about 'male breadwinners' as the pillar of the welfare state, when it came to allocating contributory benefits the MPNI seems to have stripped it down to a matter of anatomical conjunction. By choosing a partner with the 'wrong' anatomy Josephine Owen had lost title to the rights she supposedly enjoyed as the dependent spouse of a male contributor, and she would have had to resort to means-tested National Assistance for supplemental income.

The 1959 judgement against Josephine Owen had a lingering effect on National Insurance policy with regard to trans men with non-trans female spouses. Future claims made by both parties in trans man/non-trans woman marriages – including two claims for maternity benefit and sickness benefit in 1965–1966 and another claim for widow's benefit in 1969 – met similar results, with the Charles Owen decision cited as precedent.[47] Ironically, in one case despite the loss of benefits this judgement broke even in material terms: Norma Raitt, wife of Oliver Vance, was under investigation for fraudulently continuing to collect widow's pension on her previous marriage despite residing permanently with a man, and the ministry's determination that Vance was legally female led to her pension being reinstated.[48] And there is no evidence in the files that MPNI officers reported 'illegally' married couples to the GRO. The net effect of these statutory denials of benefit was, however, corrosive, as much for the National Insurance system as for the couples shut out of the promised land of full British citizenship. Each decision undermined the notion that the English welfare state could continue to sustain two competing definitions of sexual identity, and the more exceptions there were, the less tenable 'Persons of Doubtful Sex' seemed.

'Gender identity' and the loss of recognition

The cumulative effects of these internal contradictions, and the fragility of the assumptions about masculinity that sustained them, grew more acute during the following decade. For the National Insurance bureaucracy and for trans people as a whole, the mid-1960s was an important inflection point – and both institutional and social change influenced the readiness with which trans men were able to transition bureaucratically. The first such change was a gradual 'Americanisation' of clinical approaches to gender and sexuality. As Jennifer Germon has suggested, the concept of 'gender' as a category of person emerged out of American psychology during the 1950s, with John Money's experiments on intersex children and Robert Stoller's analyses of gender non-conforming young adults building evidence for a social-constructionist – albeit deeply socially conservative – understanding of gender and sex.[49] 'Gender identity' proved a useful rubric for trans people in the United States to use to articulate their desires. Harry Benjamin's Gender Identity Clinic at Johns Hopkins University, established in 1966, offered gender-confirmation surgeries to a small cohort of trans women (including one English migrant, Dawn Langley Simmons), further popularising Benjamin's understanding of 'transsexualism' as a (usually female) mind 'trapped' in a (usually male) body.[50]

For trans men in the United Kingdom, by contrast, the popularisation of 'gender identity' seems to have had ambivalent cultural effects. Although it would take the better part of a decade for daily and Sunday papers to begin routinely employing the diagnostic language of gender, the transatlantic collaborations of a number of British psychiatrists, most notably John Randell, began to have a public impact. In 1966, Randell opened the country's first Gender Identity Clinic at Charing Cross Hospital, establishing a streamlined set of diagnostic criteria that allowed him to sort record numbers of gender-dysphoric patients into 'transsexuals', bound for surgery, or 'transvestites', who were compelled to retain their clinical and legal sex at birth.[51] In tandem with this development, 'sex change', which had previously elided non-elective surgeries performed on intersex people and elective gender-confirmation therapies, lost some of its flexibility. The 1966 *Horizon* programme 'Sex-Change?', for instance, included an interview with a trans woman who explained the difference between 'corrective' intersex surgeries and speculative transsexual surgeries, exposing television audiences to a more rigid sex/gender divide.[52]

As the figure of the 'transsexual' gained currency, and as transfeminine celebrities like April Ashley figured more frequently in the Sunday papers, trans women for the first time began to outnumber trans men in the MPNI's archived correspondence. In part this reflected benefits-related problems specific to trans women, notably retirement age; in 1965, the longest-running exchanges of memos on the subject of transition in the files began, prompted by a trans woman's insistence on her right to retire at the standard women's pension age of sixty.[53] It also, in part, reflected the real gender balance of people applying for cards. In 1969, roughly 25 per cent more women had applied for cards than men, while by 1973, when the MPNI next produced internal statistics, the figure was closer to two to one.[54] This had an impact on the account balance of the MPNI – given that trans women represented a net loss in contributions – but also on the rhetoric insurance officers employed when discussing trans people in general. The misogynistic stigma of deviance and dependency that trans women disproportionately suffered had adverse effects on trans men as well.[55]

Changing social attitudes towards transition were further reinforced by institutional changes within the Ministry of Pensions and National Insurance itself. The 1960s were transformative years for the insurance system, beginning in 1961, when the ideal of a flat-rate insurance contribution system was deemed financially untenable and graduated pension units were introduced. This shift to a partially earnings-related pension scheme rendered the administration of individual accounts far more complex, prompting the introduction, the following year, of the EMIDEC computer system – one which could process sex only as a binary. As Mar Hicks has argued, this move effectively rendered trans people 'uncountable' within the insurance system unless their files were separated out for special handling.[56] Moreover, between 1966 and 1970 the ministry itself went through multiple periods of reorganisation, emerging first in 1966 as the Department of Social Security and again, two years later, as the vast Department of Health and Social Security.[57] With each reorganisation the personnel involved in processing trans people's applications changed: Abbott was promoted, Collins retired, and their signatures in the files are replaced by those of Douglas Burns, a computer administrator, C. M. Regan, the private secretary to the new Minister of Pensions and National Insurance, as well as district heads based in Newcastle, where the central computer system was located. With more automated processes used to keep up with the department's scale and shifting administration, conflicts between individuals' records in different governmental departments became a more serious issue. A new insurance card and a small cadre of specialist officers could no longer reliably paper over the gaps between trans male body and transmasculine affect.

The story of female-to-male transition within the Ministry of Pensions and National Insurance is, thus, chronologically bound to the heyday of Britain's 'classic welfare state', coming more or less to a close as the National Insurance card – once the main means of mediating between individual and welfare bureaucracy – gave way to less-transparent digital record-keeping.[58] In 1968, the reconsolidated DHSS under the Wilson government began working to 'rationalise' the provision of contributory welfare, setting a timeline for eliminating many sex-linked differentials and benefit rates and, above all, ending the requirement for all citizens to produce a physical National Insurance card at point of hire.[59] This was, for most Britons, a process welcomed as the sweeping-away of one of the last reminders of wartime austerity, and in terms of gender parity, any relaxation of the male breadwinner ideal's stranglehold over women's earnings was long overdue. Many officers of the DHSS – now including D. C. H. Abbot as undersecretary – seem to have assumed that trans people would take the revisions in the same spirit. Douglas Burns, summarising the new policy in autumn of 1969, saw it as a positive that 'the abolition of the contribution card would diminish the need of the ip [sic] to approach DHSS'. The applicant would no longer fear being exposed to their employer through a misdirected insurance communication, and DHSS record officers could at last be rid of the inconvenience of having to determine on a case-by-case basis when an insured person was to be considered male, and when female.[60]

But for many trans men, the departure of the National Insurance card as a feature of everyday working life seems to have been experienced as a loss. With birth certificates almost impossible to alter, transitioners often had only their contribution cards to testify that the state, or at least part of it, saw them as men. Sir Roger Ormrod's decision in the 1970 divorce case of *Corbett* v. *Corbett*, which established the legal principle that sex was to be defined according to XX or XY karyotype, was a particularly devastating blow: C. M. Regan opined in its aftermath that the decision 'would necessarily lead us to a very serious reconsideration of the whole of this extremely difficult and sensitive field of doubtful sex status, and of the liberal attitude which we feel we can at present take in these cases'.[61] As the MPNI gradually wound down its provision of new National Insurance cards during the years between 1970 and 1975, trans people and their advocates – John Randell included – continued to apply for cards as though the old 'liberal attitude' still obtained. Despite the fraught and uneven relationship between the National Insurance card as a symbol of masculine citizenship and the benefits it allegedly implied, it was valued by trans men as a tool in building their social self – and its absence fuelled the first attempts to frame the recognition of trans identities as a matter of human rights.

For after all, the pragmatic emphasis on the National Insurance card as a 'passport to employment' never superseded trans men's reliance on the card for recognition as a citizen and human being. Morever, that need could never be satisfied while a computer in Newcastle continued to churn out insurance documents that tied them, in inexorable and inhumane binary code, to the identities they sought to shed. As Keith Breckenridge and Simon Szreter point out in their introduction to a 2012 British Academy volume on the subject of 'registration and recognition', states are not the only actors with a stake in identity registration.[62] Indeed, the attachment of trans men to their National Insurance registration speaks to a whole field of historiography – from Edward Higgs's *Identifying the English* to Sarah Igo's *The Known Citizen* – wrestling with the balance of agency and exploitation in individuals' engagements with bureaucracy.[63] The opportunity as well as the challenge facing British trans men in the mid-twentieth century was the fact that 'The State' did not 'see' – to borrow a phrase from James C. Scott – with a steady gaze.[64] The question of 'doubtful sex' illustrates how different branches of the welfare system could pursue divergent strategies for managing structural challenges, including, at times, a strategic blindness to the bodies it was intended to discipline.

This hidden history of transition in the National Insurance system is, admittedly, a fractured lens through which to view the broad field of postwar British masculinities. Trans men were a tiny minority by any measure, and most insurance officers probably passed their entire career without knowingly encountering a trans person. But the disproportionate cultural work performed by the figure of the trans man in MPNI correspondence suggests that it is time to remedy their near-invisibility in the history of masculinities.[65] Recent reflections on the state of the field, after all, have often turned on the perceived conflict between studies of discourse and of – as John Tosh puts it – the 'political, economic, and physical realities of men's lives'.[66] Trans men's experiences with National Insurance, however, reveal that such political and economic realities – the kinds of jobs a person had access to, the benefits they could claim, the relationships they could form – were intimately bound to how physical bodies were discursively framed. Paradoxically, it was the very strength of the institutionalised 'male breadwinner' norm that rendered any breadwinning body liable to be labelled a male body, an outcome which, for many trans men, was richly desired.

But trans men's work to win recognition from the post-war welfare state also illustrated the fragility of identity claims based on external measurements of masculinity or femininity. If the ideal of the 'male breadwinner' offered trans men a way to prove their masculine citizenship without having to prove their ability to perform a specific reproductive role, it also bound them to a system which had little regard for women, disabled people, or non-normative bodies of any kind. And as soon as that restrictive ideal began to slip, so too did the basis for trans men's specific gender-based claims to recognition. Without condemning the survival strategies of a previous generation of queer men, it is important to reflect on the insight at the core of their thwarted struggle: attempts to essentialise either masculinity *or* maleness, to stake out the boundaries of manhood in policy papers, only expose the inadequacy of administrative categories to reflect the complexity of human bodies and selves.

Notes

1 The names of trans people who were covered extensively in the media have been retained as reported; all other names of trans people are pseudonymous.
2 '"Marriage" of Two Women', unknown pub., 14 December 1954, Lesbian and Gay Newsmedia Archive, CHRON-1954; Express Staff Reporter, 'Girl Who "Wed" Another Says: I Am a Man', *Daily Express*, 14 December 1954; 'The Bridegroom Was a Woman', *News Chronicle*, 14 December 1954; 'Newly-wed "Husband" to Change Her Sex', *Straits Times*, 15 December 1954.
3 'Girl Who "Wed" Another'.
4 'The Bridegroom Was a Woman'.
5 Alison Oram, *Her Husband Was a Woman! Women's Gender-Crossing in Modern British Popular Culture* (London: Routledge, 2007), 35.
6 V. Stanley, handwritten memo: 'Transsexual Statistics', 28 August 1971, NA PIN 43/591. This is, moreover, certainly an undercount. Scottish law had very different procedures for administering sex, in which the local sheriff enjoyed greater scope for independent action than did English judges. Because of this

decentralised process – and of the more restrictive data protection statutes that apply in Scotland – it proved impractical to incorporate Scottish stories into the present chapter. Northern Ireland, which had analogous practices to England but only figures in Ministry of Pensions and National Insurance correspondence on 'sex change' in the early 1970s, posed similar logistical challenges. See E. R. Medderly, letter to J. S. Marshall, 17 June 1963, NA PIN 43/590; and E. J. Dowling, letter to J. E. Ashford, 30 September 1971, NA PIN 43/590.

7 Jane Lewis, 'Gender and the Development of Welfare Regimes', *Journal of European Social Policy*, 2:3 (1992), 16.

8 David Andrew Griffiths, 'Diagnosing Sex: Intersex Surgery and "Sex Change" in Britain 1930–1955', *Sexualities*, 21:3 (2018), 481; Clare Tebbutt, 'Popular and Medical Understandings of Sex Change in 1930s Britain' (PhD diss., University of Manchester, 2014), 26; Clare Tebbutt, 'The Spectre of the "Man-Woman Athlete": Mark Weston, Zdenek Koubek, the 1936 Olympics and the Uncertainty of Sex', *Women's History Review*, 24:5 (2015), 721.

9 Tebbutt, 'The Spectre of the "Man-Woman Athlete"', 725.

10 'Girl Who "Wed" Another'.

11 C. N. Armstrong, 'The Clinical Diagnosis of Sex: President's Address', *Proceedings of the Royal Society of Medicine*, 51 (1958), 2.

12 Bernice L. Hausman, *Changing Sex: Transsexualism, Technology, and the Idea of Gender* (Durham, NC: Duke University Press, 1995); Joanne J. Meyerowitz, *How Sex Changed: A History of Transsexuality in the United States* (Cambridge, MA: Harvard University Press, 2002); Susan Stryker, *Transgender History* (Berkeley: Seal Press, 2008).

13 For example, Jane Fae, 'The Press', in Christine Burns (ed.), *Trans Britain: Our Journey from the Shadows* (London: Unbound, 2018), 191.

14 This mode of queer male respectability politics – exemplified by the Homosexual Law Reform Society that emerged in response to the Wolfenden Commission – has long been a central theme of queer British historiography. Ironically, this respectability often involved fervently attacking the notion that gay men were inherently effeminate or gender non-conforming. See, for instance, Simon Avery and Katherine L. Graham (eds), *Sex, Time and Place: Queer Histories of London, c. 1850 to the Present* (London: Bloomsbury, 2016); Harry Cocks, 'Conspiracy to Corrupt Public Morals and the "Unlawful" Status of Homosexuality after 1967', *Social History*, 41:3 (2016), 267–284; Tommy Dickinson, *'Curing Queers': Mental Nurses and Their Patients, 1935–74* (Manchester: Manchester University Press, 2015); Matt Houlbrook, *Queer London: Perils and Pleasures of the Sexual Metropolis, 1918–1957* (Chicago: University of Chicago Press, 2005); Brian Lewis, *Wolfenden's Witnesses: Homosexuality in Postwar Britain* (Basingstoke: Palgrave Macmillan, 2016); Chris Waters, 'The Homosexual as a Social Being in Britain, 1945–1968', in Brian Lewis (ed.), *British Queer History: New Approaches and Perspectives* (Manchester: Manchester University Press, 2013), 188–218; Jeffrey Weeks, *Coming Out: Homosexual Politics in Britain, from the Nineteenth Century to the Present* (London: Quartet Books, 1977); Chris Waters, 'Disorders of the Mind, Disorders of the Body Social: Peter

Wildeblood and the Making of the Modern Homosexual', in Becky Conekin, Frank Mort, and Chris Waters (eds), *Moments of Modernity: Reconstructing Britain 1945–1964* (London: Rivers Oram Press, 1999), 134–151.

15 J. Vaughan, minutes of meeting with Fletcher and Dunnell of the GRO, 23 December 1954, NA PIN 43/590.

16 Anne Fausto-Sterling, *Sexing the Body: Gender Politics and the Construction of Sexuality* (New York: Basic Books, 2000), 36.

17 Bernard Harris, *The Origins of the British Welfare State: Social Welfare in England and Wales, 1800–1945* (Basingstoke: Palgrave Macmillan, 2004), 163.

18 Rodney Lowe, *The Welfare State in Britain since 1945* (Basingstoke: Palgrave Macmillan, 2004), 129.

19 J. Vaughan, letter to D. C. H. Abbot, 28 January 1955, NA PIN 43/590.

20 D. C. H. Abbot, 'Persons of Doubtful Sex', 18 April 1955, NA PIN 43/590.

21 Jameel Hampton, *Disability and the Welfare State: Changes in Perception and Policy, 1948–79* (Bristol: Policy Press, 2016), 55.

22 F. M. Collins, letter to D. C. H. Abbott, 18 April 1955, NA PIN 43/590.

23 Abbot, 'Persons of Doubtful Sex'.

24 F. M. Collins, minute addressed to D. C. M. Abbot, 21 April 1955, NA PIN/592.

25 Judith Butler, *Gender Trouble: Feminism and the Subversion of Identity* (New York: Routledge, 1990), 11.

26 Stephanie Spencer, *Gender, Work, and Education in Britain in the 1950s* (Basingstoke: Palgrave Macmillan, 2005), 40. The evolution of this 'male breadwinner' model is by no means a straightforward one. Feminist authors like Katharine Abbot and Elizabeth Bompass noted, in the wake of the Beveridge report's publication, that the nuclear family ideal of male breadwinner, housewife, and children was not, and had never been, the way most family economies functioned. Scholars writing in the decades since have, moreover, emphasised the nineteenth-century roots of the post-war state's ideals, and pointed out the persistence of these voluntary social welfare agencies and practices in shaping gender roles during the 1950s. See, for instance, Susan Pedersen, *Family, Dependence, and the Origins of the Welfare State: Britain and France, 1914–1945* (Cambridge: Cambridge University Press, 1993); Mary Daly, *The Gender Division of Welfare: The Impact of the British and German Welfare States* (Cambridge: Cambridge University Press, 2000); Derek Fraser, *The Evolution of the British Welfare State: A History of Social Policy since the Industrial Revolution*, 5th edn (Basingstoke: Palgrave Macmillan, 2017); A. N. Hagget, *A History of Male Psychological Illness in Britain, 1945–1970* (Basingstoke: Palgrave Macmillan, 2015); Harris, *The Origins of the British Welfare State*; Seth Koven and S. Michel (eds), *Mothers of a New World: Maternalist Politics and the Origins of the Welfare States* (London: Routledge, 1993); Julia Parker, *Citizenship, Work, and Welfare: Searching for the Good Society* (Basingstoke: Macmillan Press, 1998).

27 Fraser, *Evolution of the British Welfare State*, 672.6.

28 Jane Lewis, 'Gender and the Development of Welfare Regimes', *Journal of European Social Policy*, 2:3 (1992), 164.

29 V. L. Burden, letter to L. Perry, 14 December 1966, The National Archives, Kew, PIN 61/27.
30 Vaughan, letter to D. C. H. Abbot, 28 January 1955.
31 J. Drummond, letter to N. Nelson, 17 April 1963, NA PIN 43/592.
32 H. E. Morgan, draft letter to the Treasury, 17 March 1959, NA PIN 43/590.
33 Michael Roper, 'Yesterday's Model: Product Fetishism and the British Company Man, 1945–1985', in Michael Roper and John Tosh (eds), *Manful Assertions: Masculinities in Britain since 1800* (London: Routledge, 1991), 192.
34 'The Fantastic Story of Terry Brown', *News of the World*, 11 March 1951, LAGNA.
35 Barrie Harding and Sidney Rodin, 'The Astonishing Case of Michael who was Kathleen', *Sunday Pictorial*, 3 December 1953, LAGNA.
36 A. J. Evans, interview with Dave King, 18 May 1982, Dave King Papers, WL PP/KIN/K/1/3.
37 Michel Foucault, *Society Must Be Defended: Lectures at the College de France, 1975–1976*, trans. David Macey (New York: Picador, 1997), 246. For more typically sceptical readings of registration's coercive effects in Britain, see e.g. James C. Scott, *Seeing like a State: How Certain Schemes to Improve the Human Condition Have Failed* (New Haven: Yale University Press, 1998); Nikolas Rose, 'Governing by Numbers: Figuring Out Democracy', *Accounting, Organizations and Society*, 16:7 (1991), 673–692.
38 Collins, n.d., NA PIN 43/592.
39 'The Bridegroom was a Woman'.
40 'The Bridegroom Was a Woman'.
41 J. F. Crampton, '[name redacted], deceased', 27 February 1958 NA PIN 61/27.
42 F. M. Collins, letter to local insurance officer Mr Prendergast, 31 March 1958, NA PIN 61/27.
43 F. M. Collins, letter to Mr Prendergast, 30 April 1958, NA PIN 61/27.
44 Collins, letter to Prendergast, 31 April 1958, NA PIN 61/27.
45 Mickelthwait, 'Decision of the Commissioner in Claim for Widow's Benefit', NA PIN 61/27.
46 Oram, *Her Husband Was a Woman!*, 35.
47 H. Gerrie, letter to H. S. McPherson, 21 September 1966, NA PIN 61/27; H. Gerrie, letter to T. H. Sims, 4 November 1969, NA PIN 61/27.
48 W. Smith, letter to V. L. Burden, 14 September 1966, NA PIN 61/27.
49 Jennifer Germon, *Gender: A Genealogy of an Idea* (Basingstoke: Palgrave Macmillan, 2009), 80.
50 Meyerowitz, *How Sex Changed*, 118.
51 Richard Ekins and Dave King, 'Pioneers of Transgendering: John Randell, 1918–1982', conference paper proof for GENDYS Conference (2002), WL PP/KIN/A/2/46/7; John Randell, 'Cross-dressing and the Desire to Change Sex' (MD thesis, University of Wales, 1960).
52 'Sex-Change?', *Horizon*, 21 November 1966, WL PP/KIN/K/3/1.
53 H. Gerrie, letter to M. J. A. Partridge, 18 December 1964, NA PIN 61/27.
54 D. V. Stanley, 'Transsexual Statistics', 17 October 1973, NA PIN 43/591.

55 W. H. M. Clifford, letter to F. M. Collins, 10 October 1958, NA PIN 43/593.
56 Mar Hicks, 'Hacking the Cis-tem: Transgender Citizens and the Early Digital State', *IEEE Annals of the History of Computing*, 41 (2019), 23.
57 Fraser, *Evolution of the British Welfare State*, 767.6.
58 Anne Digby, *British Welfare Policy: From Workhouse to Workfare* (London: Faber, 1989).
59 Douglas Burns, letter to C. H. Adams, 19 September 1968, NA PIN 43/590.
60 Douglas Burns, 'Change of Sex', 17 September 1969, NA PIN 43/590.
61 C. M. Regan, 'Memorandum of the Secretary of State on the Nullity of Marriage Bill', 25 January 1971, NA PIN 43/590.
62 Keith Breckenridge and Simon Szreter, 'Editors' Introduction', in Keith Breckenridge and Simon Szreter (eds), *Registration and Recognition: Documenting the Person in World History* (Oxford: Oxford University Press, 2012), 12.
63 Ilsen About, James Brown, and Gayle Lonergan, *Identification and Registration Practices in Transnational Perspective: People, Papers and Practices* (Basingstoke: Palgrave Macmillan, 2013); Jane Caplan and John Torpey (eds), *Documenting Individual Identity: The Development of State Practices in the Modern World* (Princeton: Princeton University Press, 2001); Edward Higgs, *Identifying the English: A History of Personal Identification, 1500 to the Present* (London: Continuum, 2011); Sarah E. Igo, *The Known Citizen: A History of Privacy in Modern America* (Cambridge, MA: Harvard University Press, 2018).
64 Scott, *Seeing like a State*.
65 Lucas Gottzén and Wibke Straube, 'Trans Masculinities', *NORMA: International Journal for Masculinity Studies*, 11:4 (2016), 221.
66 John Tosh, 'The History of Masculinity: An Outdated Concept?', in John H. Arnold and Sean Brady (eds), *What Is Masculinity? Historical Dynamics from Antiquity to the Contemporary World* (Basingstoke: Palgrave Macmillan, 2011), 25.

2

Reading colonial masculinity through a marriage in Burma

Jonathan Saha

Revisiting Mrinalini Sinha's *Colonial Masculinity* over two decades after its publication, much of its historiographical critique still applies. The book is ubiquitously cited in the literature reviews of articles and books examining masculinities in Britain and its empire. However, when relating her central argument – that British manliness in colonial Bengal was co-constituted with the figure of the 'effeminate Bengali' – the wider methodological import of her approach has not always been fully engaged with. The generic point, that ideas of masculinity emerged entangled with the racialised divisions of colonial society, is one that is now almost axiomatic to the field;[1] but some of Sinha's essential contextualising caveats have often been left unaddressed. There are two principal points that have been less well heeded. The first is her warning about too easy an alignment between 'imperial' and 'national' frames in the history of masculinity, lest either be effectively submerged beneath the other. The second is her emphasis on analysing the ways that colonial gender ideologies were rooted in material and ideological shifts *within* communities, particularly through their changing class divisions. While histories of masculinity in colonial Asia emphasise heterogeneity and contingency, these more pointed insights have not been consistently attended to.[2]

Historians unpacking white masculinities in British India – often somewhat euphemistically referred to as 'imperial' – have now identified a range of typologies of masculinity,[3] with studies being more sensitive to class hierarchies within white populations.[4] Commonly missing from these studies is a consideration of how these specific ways of being a man in the empire inform, overlap with, or are in tension with masculinities 'at home' in Britain. Nor do they treat imperial representations of Asian masculinities as discursive figures contested and appropriated by colonised populations, something that Sinha details with regards to Bengali Hindu middle classes and the trope of effeminacy. For example, studies of imperial hunters show how this lethal sport entailed a particular performance of virile manliness and racial superiority. Though this, historians of the imperial hunt have carefully uncovered its aristocratic precedents, its links to South Asian practices, and its reliance on South Asian labour.[5] But they have not traced how this manly archetype fed back into discussions of masculinity in Britain or within colonised communities.[6]

Studies tracing the colonial histories of Asian masculinities mirror those of white masculinities. Many have followed Sinha's lead in examining the construction of particular figures of masculinity; some valourised and lauded, such as 'martial races', others marginalised and policed, like *thuggees* and *hijra*s.[7] In addition, some have shifted beyond deconstructions of the gendered gaze of imperial authors and the effects of the colonial state's disciplinary power, to uncovering the practices and writings of colonised actors.[8] Such studies have often examined the place of masculinity in animating different strands of anti-colonial nationalist thought and struggles.[9] It is a sign of the maturity of the historiography on colonial South Asia that these studies can dispense with a dialogue with work on masculinity in imperial Britain and white masculinity in the empire.[10] Nevertheless, this contributes to a growing cleavage between studies of white masculinities and studies of Asian masculinities in colonial contexts.

As a result of these trends, the framing devises of 'imperial' and 'national' are either treated as necessary heuristic divisions or left unexamined. In either case, the tensions between these two social imaginaries are elided. The use of the adjectives 'British' and 'imperial', either together or interchangeably to prefix 'masculinity' in secondary literature, masks myriad contradictions and fractures.[11] In addition, there is an implicit reification of the counterpart masculinity co-constructed across the divide between coloniser and colonised. In other words, research into white masculinities, while noting local agency, tends to leave Asian masculinities unexplored. Likewise, research into Asian masculinities, while contextualised alongside normative imperial discourses, often does not interrogate the heterogeneity of white masculinities. Without attending to these entanglements and complexities, the contention that the masculinities of coloniser and colonised were co-constituted is reduced to a superficial and abstract acknowledgement, one easily made but rarely meaningfully explored.

Not long after her book, Sinha reviewed the growing field for the journal *Gender & History*, exploring what histories of masculinity might contribute to the discipline. One of her critiques in this essay was of the 'easy equation of men and masculinity'. This critique still resonates. Most studies of masculinity implicitly frame themselves as studies of men. To counter this, she urges historians to denaturalise men and masculinity by tracing the processes of embodiment, rather than assuming a sexed male body to be the subject of histories of masculinity. Moreover, she argues that giving masculinity a history means uncovering how a broader range of social relations produce masculinity, beyond the narrower set of practices entailed in manhood. For Sinha these wider social relations were the fraught material and ideological contests within and between British colonisers and Bengali Hindu middle classes. Masculinity provided her with a single analytical frame through which these social relations could be better understood.[12] But this critique also suggests the utility of more micro-historical approaches to masculinity focussed on uncovering bodily performances and performativity.

While new vistas in this field have emerged, the methodological approach that *Colonial Masculinity* outlined still has analytical purchase and interpretive power, especially for those attempting to disentangle precisely what might be *British* about the various masculine figures constituted throughout the empire. However, realising this approach is beset with challenges. There is a difficult subtlety required to treat masculinity as a single analytical frame while not artificially reducing the national to the imperial, or vice versa. Giving a balance of analysis to the material and ideological tensions within a particular colonised community *and* among the colonisers, while also tracing the contests and collaborations across this division, requires handling disparate archival materials. It is an aspiration made harder still by the more recent, and entirely justified, call for more attention to be paid to *inter*-Asian social relations.[13] Scale also poses a problem. Masculinity has been described as a 'world historical category of analysis', with global purchase.[14] Fitting awkwardly within this planetary view are the interconnected geographies covered by overviews of imperial histories, which are on occasion mapped beyond the British Empire.[15] Moreover, within these sweeping frameworks, there is the imperative to maintain the analytical precision to avoid equating the history of masculinity with that of men.

Numerous imperial historians have successfully overcome these challenges by limiting the scope of their research. Sinha did this through an unwavering focus on Bengal 'proper' and three greatly contested, high political conjectures. Others, such as Catherine Hall, have followed suit by identifying particular colonial sites and moments.[16] Biography has proved another effective approach.[17] A tight empirical focus is evidently beneficial for enabling studies of colonial masculinity to retain their analytical power without reducing the complexities at work. But within this necessary narrowing of topic, there is a need to be attentive to wider connections and comparisons that might be abstracted from the empirics of a study. To achieve this, a focus on sites and institutions replicated across imperial spaces enables studies to simultaneously explore what might be specific to certain colonial contexts and what might be generic to colonialism. There are many such framing devises that might be deployed; however, 'family' is one that has already been serving this role.[18]

There is now a significant body of literature exploring the history of family within the empire; although much of the focus has been on either white families or families whose members cut across colonial racial divides. Analysis of masculinity is inevitably present in much of this work. Building in part on the history of sexuality, families have been conceptualised as 'dense transfer points of power' in which the tensions between the uneven construction of discourses of bodily difference, such as race, and the curation of exclusive social imaginaries, such as nation, have played out.[19] In addition to this, a focus on family has enabled historians to trace the emergence of gendered subjectivities while attending to the history of emotions,[20] rooting studies of these otherwise abstract ideological constructs in lived experiences. Of course, family does not have a transhistorical, universal form. Families take many forms across time and place, and in this chapter, I am narrowing the ambit of my research further to look at the institution of marriage.[21] Or, more narrowly still, one marriage: that of controversial novelist Mabel Cosgrave and celebrated Arakanese barrister Chan-Toon, in *fin de siècle* Rangoon and London.

Mabel Cosgrave and Chan-Toon were married in St Mary of the Angels in Bayswater, London, on 27 July 1893. Their nuptials were reported in the press from Scotland to Singapore.[22] It was an unhappy marriage, at least for Mabel Cosgrave Chan-Toon. In 1905, she published a fictionalised, but apparently autobiographical, account of the relationship, *A Marriage in Burmah: A Novel*. Unusual in that it depicts a marriage between a white British woman and a colonised man of colour – a well-policed taboo of the high-imperial era[23] – her account exposes some of the fractures between Britishness and whiteness through an exploration of masculinity. Writing under the name 'Mrs Chan-Toon', in the course of the book she simultaneously deploys a critique of Burmese masculinity and of gender relations within British imperial society in Rangoon to plot her (or rather, her protagonist Mrs Moung Gyaw's) emergence as an independent woman. In the process, through her unfavourable rendering of her husband in the form of the character Moung Gyaw, also an Arakanese barrister, she argues that 'Oriental' men were imperfect mimics of British aristocratic norms of gentlemanly behaviour due to their innate flaws. As a result of these themes, it is a book that reveals how women could deploy critical renderings of colonial masculinity, and reproduce discourses of racial difference, to sustain feminine subjectivities with precarious, hard-won mobility.[24] It also provides a window onto the ambivalent discursive responses to colonised actors' attempts to embody British masculinity.[25]

The book follows Mrs Moung Gyaw's experiences of her doomed marriage to her Arakanese husband, whom she marries not out of love, but due to his promising legal career and the expectation of a large inheritance.

Almost as soon as she arrives in Rangoon, this veneer of good prospects is destroyed as her husband's dishonesty is revealed to her. He is instead exposed as being in a financially precarious position, heavily indebted to a Bengali moneylender and struggling to sustain a profitable legal practice. Marked as an outsider and a curiosity because of her racially transgressive marriage, she is ostracised from the close-knit, white Rangoon society, suffering from constant petty slights from vindictive, upper-class British wives. The either doddering or aloof white men provide no relief. The sociality of British married couples in Rangoon is portrayed as stilted, overly formal, and vapid; a litany of excruciating dinners and tedious race meetings. It is a poor simulacrum of London society. Cringingly seeking acceptance within white official circles, her vain and weak-willed husband rebuffs her advice and hides his further deteriorating circumstances, squandering an inheritance that he has not yet secured. As their relationship rapidly breaks down, she lives with worsening rough and rudimentary domestic arrangements, and is left largely bereft of company. Her husband descends into alcoholism, his practice falls apart, and she is physically assaulted by him. Most of the novel is set in colonial Rangoon, with a brief sojourn to London where he attempts to rebuild his reputation while they rely on her upper-middle-class (although not especially wealthy) family for meagre support, attempting to hide the true extent of their poverty. The book ends with Mrs Moung Gyaw giving birth to a baby girl that she feels no love for and that she abandons to the care of a Karen *ayah* and Christian nuns while she leaves her family to make her own future.[26]

The novel makes claims to authenticity through deliberate and pointed suggestions that the story is autobiographical in content. This is indicated in the para-texts to the book through her choice of 'Mrs M. Chan-Toon' to appear as her name. She had previously published under her maiden name, Mabel Cosgrove, and then under the Burmese pseudonym 'Mimosa';[27] although this was no secret and was known to be her. By the time she wrote *A Marriage in Burmah* in 1905 her husband had been dead for around a year, dying of heart failure in Rangoon's law library.[28] Now publishing under Mrs M. Chan-Toon she foregrounded her unconventional relationship, which was also the subject of her book. The name of the author's counterpart in the novel echoes this, as she is almost exclusively referred to throughout the text as Mrs Moung Gyaw. The Burmese provenance of the name provides her with a claim to expertise, a move further sustained by making the husband hail from Arakan, a region in the west of the colony bordering Bengal. It was also where Chan-Toon himself was known to come from.[29] Detailing Arakanese customs in the book builds her credibility by demonstrating a knowledge not of the generalised figure of the Burman but of a particular ethnic identity. This attempt to build credibility is further reinforced in the para-texts of the book through the brief, two-sentence preface. In this she outlines her purpose in sketching 'the life of an English girl who married a native of Burmah' so as to reveal 'the gulf that divides the Eastern from the Western', while professing to 'merely record things as they actually occurred'.[30]

In the substance of the book itself the sense of autobiographical authenticity is sustained through a number of narrative devices. In one chapter, she purports to be directly quoting snippets from her (Mrs Moung Gyaw's) diaries of the time to illustrate the mental anguish of her isolation, and does so at length. Other than in these extracts, she uses the third-person point of view, while still anchoring the plot in her heroine's introspective thoughts. In contrast, the motives of other characters are presented as inferences on the basis of their behaviour. The effect is to give the impression that the author is not writing about a different person, but about a past self. The emotionality of the text also gives the effect of truthfulness through her use of an almost confessional style. There are silences produced in the book around particularly harrowing moments that add to the sense of realism. Marital rape is hinted at. Two difficult pregnancies and one miscarriage are apparent, although only through passing mentions. The episodes of domestic violence are rendered in sparing but affecting detail. As the book draws to a conclusion, Mrs Moung Gyaw gains resolve through her involuntary but unshakable dislike of her baby. She pours scorn on the notion of women as being innately maternal, describing it as 'the most puerile of delusions, the most illogical of human fallacies'. The candid disclosure of unwelcome feelings and forceful prose in these passages stand out from the rest of the book, perhaps indicating their provenance in a deeply personal place, maybe even that they were born out of painful lived experience.[31]

Nevertheless, Mrs Chan-Toon is knowingly playing with fictive elements in her writing. This comes through in the less-than-subtle names given to Mrs Moung Gyaw's enemies in Rangoon society, such as the gossip Mrs M'Chatter. In a more subtle move, Mrs Moung Gyaw is made English, whereas the author herself was Irish. This distancing of the author from Mrs Moung Gyaw, when elsewhere the two were quite deliberately conflated, infers an attempt to emphasise the protagonist's uncomplicated whiteness that may have otherwise been compromised, although not undone, through her Irish heritage.[32] Throughout her literary career the deliberate blurring of the boundary between truth and falsehood is what Mabel Cosgrove Chan-Toon's writings specialised in. Her 1912 book, *Love Letters of an English Peeress to an Indian Prince*, purported to be a collection of romantic correspondence penned by an aristocratic white woman to a rebel leader in the 1857 uprising, Nana Saheb, a man implicated in the massacre of women and children during the siege of Kanpur; a provocative premise and use of history.³³ She is something of a trickster figure, most famous for likely penning the play *Love of the King: A Burmese Masque*, published in 1922, and successfully passing it off as a manuscript authored by Oscar Wilde to publishers and, subsequently, to much of the literary establishment. She was accused of fabricating not only the play itself, but the accompanying letters from Wilde evidencing a friendship between the two. In these letters Cosgrove Chan-Toon carefully interwove truthful elements of both of their lives to produce a credible account of when and why Wilde had written it. In 1926, the play became the subject of a widely publicised defamation case brought by its publisher, Methuen against one of Wilde's biographers, who accused them of knowingly publishing a forgery; a case that Methuen won.³⁴ Mabel Cosgrove, now going by the name Mabel Wodehouse Pearse following a re-marriage, was unable to testify at the trial because she had been jailed for theft.³⁵

In later life she was, by most accounts, an eccentric figure, often dressed in a long coat and with a parrot perched on her shoulder.³⁶ Three years after the publication of *A Marriage in Burmah*, she was reported as having been charged with blackmail in Mexico.³⁷ It seems that it was here that she acquired the parrot, called Monsieur Coco.³⁸ It is intriguing, therefore, that she incorporated an eccentric Australian woman as a key character called Mrs Rooney into *A Marriage in Burmah*, complete with pet cockatoo. The character's age and aspects of her physical description fit onto Mabel Chan-Toon's at the time she would have drafted the novel. Rooney is good-hearted, but belligerent and vulgar when drunk. Her world-weary attitude stands in contrast to Mrs Moung Gyaw's naïve outlook and she acts as a salutary lesson to the young woman; a warning of the dangers of remaining in Rangoon. Mrs Rooney's presence in the book complicates any straightforward reading of the novel as directly autobiographic. But it does suggest that through her portrayal of the neglectful and tyrannical aspects of her husband's character, traits she indicates are typically 'Eastern', she is exploring different subject positions beyond the pale of acceptable bourgeois femininity in colonial Burma and late Victorian, early Edwardian England. The fiercely independent-minded and earnest Mrs Moung Gyaw, having transgressed racial boundaries in her marriage, ultimately rejects the expectations upon a wife and mother to build her own future. So does Mrs Rooney, the easy-going, jovial outcast of polite white society, but sadly downtrodden and bitter drunk. Both, in their own way, represent a 'flight from domesticity' through different forms of escapism in the empire; travel and drink.³⁹

The setting is crucial to the book. Rangoon is not an incidental backdrop. Contextualising the novel within the gender politics of colonial Burma allows us to see how the racialised binary between coloniser and colonised was animated through portrayals of contrasting masculinities. Central to this co-constitutive relationship between British and Burmese masculinity was the spectre of India. As studies of South Asia have shown, conceptions of masculinity on the subcontinent were highly variegated by caste, class, religion, and region.[40] Nevertheless, in most colonial-era writings on Burma this complexity was homogenised into a monolithic stereotype of the Indian man against which the Burmese man was contrasted. This is suggestive of the fractal nature of colonial masculinities. The closer the historian hones their focus, the more differentiations appear. Within writings on Burmese masculinity, comparisons were drawn separating out Bama, Karen, Shan, Arakanese, and other ethnicities in colony.[41] The distinction between India and Burma made by British writers and state officials was the prominent and public presence of Burmese women, particularly in their economic activities and rights to property.[42] Often these depictions held Burmese women to be the overbearing partner in marriages, accused of beating their hapless men. India was associated with purdah and a subjugated femininity, Burma with raucous female market traders and hen-pecked husbands.[43]

Burmese masculinity was rendered in particular ways in relation to this. In terms of descriptions of their physicality, British writers depicted the typical Burmese man as stout and muscular.[44] In habits, they were said to be lazy, easy-going, and of mild temperament, to a point. Once roused, the Burmese man was supposed to be prone to outbursts of violent anger, followed quickly by remorse and regret. The apparently casual nature of marriages, and freedom of women within them, was said to be a frequent cause of domestic violence. A repeated narrative in colonial police reports held that men would divorce their spouses, regret their decision, and attack their former partner in the resulting jealous rage when she formed a new connection.[45] Mrs Chan-Toon also deployed this trope. As the book unfolds, Moung Gyaw's behaviour becomes increasingly stereotypical. He becomes slothful and laconic, his passivity occasionally broken by moments of violence towards his wife. The implicit figure of British masculinity constituted through these portrayals, at least for the male officials deploying these tropes, was of a secure, virile manliness able to hold women in a respectful, companionate but firmly subservient position. As we have seen above, for Mrs Chan-Toon this figure of Burmese man was doing rather different work.

In the context of the late nineteenth century, this articulation of masculinity was also a response to first-wave British feminism, the figure of the New Woman, and legislative restrictions on male sexuality.[46] Indeed, feminists in Britain and some nationalists in India used this portrayal of Burmese women as evidence to support their causes.[47] In contrast white British male writers in the colony explicitly rendered the position of Burmese women a spectre of the potential culmination of suffragist reform. For these men, Burma as a nation had been stunted by women's independence and predominance which had emasculated the men, sapping their energies and stifling societal dynamism. Others spun the comparison to contemporary British feminists differently, emphasising the ease with which Burmese women were able to elegantly embody their high status without undermining their femininity, contrasting this to the clamouring noise of white women activists in Britain.[48] Here, there was a tension between the local toleration of white male sexual desire for Burmese women within imperial society in Burma, and the growing condemnation of the resulting cross-racial relationships in segments of British society.[49] References to the allure and beauty of Burmese women were commonplace in imperial texts situated in the colony, perhaps most famously appearing in Rudyard Kipling's poem 'Mandalay' through the nostalgic longings of a British Tommy. Mrs Chan-Toon also relies on this trope through her description of Mrs Moung Gyaw's Burmese rival for her husband's affections, a scene that, in spite of its rather minor place in the book as a whole, was reproduced in the frontispiece.[50]

While having a Burmese wife might lead to official approbation and a limiting of opportunities for government employment for white colonists,[51] 'temporary marriages' were reportedly a widespread practice. Mrs Chan-Toon does not address this practice, but her depiction of the inverse relationship would have been read within a wider imperial awareness of the scandals related to it. Christian imperial critics concerned about the toleration of prostitution and white slavery in the empire used Burma as an example of the degrading effects of the practice on white British men, dubbing them 'Western men with Eastern morals'.[52] Within official circles, at the turn of the century Viceroy Curzon set himself against these relationships.[53] However, white colonists who formed connections with Burmese women were largely absolved of responsibility for their 'lapses' by the lack of white society and the resulting loneliness of the colony, the oppressive and stultifying effects of the climate, and the seductive behaviour of Burmese women and girls. The Burmese woman as succubus was a frequent narrative device in imperial novels set in the colony, recurring across texts with diametrically opposing positions on female sexuality.[54] Mrs Chan-Toon does not touch upon this issue, nor does she portray Mrs Moung Gyaw's Burmese rival as a seductress. Instead, she uses the husband's infidelity to demonstrate *his* moral weakness.

The weakness of Burmese men in relation to women fed into the adoption of a paternalistic attitude towards them on the part of white British officials. According to this view, the Burmese were at risk of being taken advantage of by guileful and predatory Chinese and Indian traders and moneylenders. The lackadaisical Burmese population, who it was believed lacked any entrepreneurial spirit, needed protecting from these exploitative outsiders, particularly when it came to vices. Burmese men were portrayed as being particularly weak-willed and thus especially vulnerable to ruin through drink, gambling, and opium. This racial understanding structured government policies in these areas, with restrictions on participating in these activities differentiated by categories of race.[55] Mrs Chan-Toon too reproduced this view. The most vitriolic and overtly racist descriptions in her novel are reserved for her characterisation of Moung Gyaw's Bengali moneylender and his wife. She portrays Moung Gyaw's feeble vanity as making him susceptible to the preening flattery of the ruthless, calculating greed of Mr and Mrs Chundera.[56] Moung Gyaw's inability to curb his growing addiction to brandy, likewise, was a sign of his weak mental fortitude. His indifference to money was another inherent flaw of his character that resonated with these wider imperial tropes.

As much as Chan-Toon was posthumously framed by wider imperial notions of Burmese masculinity through his wife's fictionalised, quasi-autobiographical novel based on their marriage, he was also an active figure in participating in the construction of these gendered perceptions of Burma. He further pushed at the racialised limits of inclusion and recognition as an imperial subject. Somewhat contrary to the portrayal of his career in *A Marriage in Burmah*, by the time that they married in 1893 he had established a formidable reputation for himself as a scholar and public intellectual in London. He arrived in London to study for the bar around 1885, a pivotal time in Burmese history. While all of coastal Burma had been colonised by the British by 1852, with Chan-Toon's home district of Arakan having been under British rule since 1826, the cultural heartland of the Konbaung dynasty remained an independent rump state until 1885 when the last king, Thibaw, was deposed and taken into exile by the Indian Army. Shortly after the deposition, Chan-Toon was present at a meeting of the National Indian Association – an imperial society set up by the social reformer and advocate of female education and women's suffrage Mary Carpenter and British feminist Charlotte Manning in the 1870s – at which the fate of this new colony was discussed.

Dr Cullimore, who had been a resident surgeon in Mandalay, the courtly capital of Thibaw's kingdom, spoke about the country and its peoples, and held forth in favour of the recent British annexation. However, the report of the meeting in the *Standard* dedicated most of its column to Chan-Toon's contributions to the ensuing discussion. He framed his opinion as that of a native, a position well-received in the liberal space of the association: 'he [Chan-Toon] thought his [Dr Cullimore's] experiences must be balanced by Burmese opinion (hear, hear).' He went on to argue that while he had no objection to annexation, he believed that the seeming ease with which Thibaw was deposed was but a superficial impression of calm, as the people had not yet been placed under British rule. He anticipated that colonisation would not be welcome.[57] The protracted and brutal pacification campaign combatting the widespread rebellion that followed in the years to come proved his insight to have been correct.[58] Gender relations were central to his argument. He reproduced the already well-developed narrative that Thibaw was king only in name, with the true ruler being his formidable wife, Queen Supayalat. This too was well-received: 'even the King in Burmah had to do all that his wife told him to do (laughter).'[59] In this space, afforded by imperial feminism yet redolent of the masculine culture of British learned societies, a colonised subject voiced a critique of a white imperial actor's knowledge, in part, by deploying the racialised and gendered notion of the hen-pecked Burmese husband.

Meanwhile in London Chan-Toon excelled in his studies, winning a scholarship in 1886. This achievement was eclipsed by the manner in which he was called to the bar in the summer of 1888. During his studentship at the Middle Temple he entered all eight principal prizes for law students and won every one, receiving a total of £338.[60] He was the first student to achieve this. To mark his unprecedented success he was honoured in a resolution passed by a parliament of the benches of the Middle Temple, drafted by Sir Henry James, and in a letter from Queen Victoria. No student prior to him had been complimented in this way.[61] While in the press he generally received plaudits, in some quarters his success was framed within the discourse of a crisis of white masculinity. The London correspondent of the *Liverpool Mercury* wrote, melodramatically, 'Bow your heads, ye Anglo-Saxon students, not to you go the prizes of the future. Here is a Burmese, Mr Chan-Toon – who has done in the law examinations what was never done yet by any Englishmen … English eyes will henceforth turn to Burmah for its scholars.' Explicitly linking Chan-Toon's achievements to women's recent entry into some higher education institutions, the correspondent went on, 'Our boys, indeed, seem to be far behind the race. At universities they are beaten by their sisters, and in law examinations they are beaten by a Burmese.'[62] This passage made explicit what was implied in other reports, that part of the interest in Chan-Toon's success stemmed from his being a racial other. Although he was a British imperial subject, to the English newspaper-reading public he was framed as not one of 'our boys'.

In the few years that he remained in London following his qualification, he was a frequent public lecturer, particularly to the Balloon Society who met at St James's Hall in London. His talks on Burma reproduced the gendered colonial representations unpacked above. The summary of one of his talks reported in the *Morning Post* is worth quoting at length as it consists of a neat synthesis of the key themes. After recounting the benefits of British rule, he made the following observations:

> The Burmese were a proud and conceited race, and they had no desire to amass wealth. They took life easily, and, when there was no necessity for work, were the laziest of human beings. If, through the tide of fortune, they became rich, they availed themselves of the means at their disposal to build a resting-place for travellers or to erect a padoga [sic]. Having alluded to the freedom and importance of the position occupied by women in Burma and touched upon the influence of Buddhism upon Burmese society, the lecturer spoke of the future of the country, and advocated the more direct control of Burma by Great Britain. The sentiments, religion, and institutions of the Indian races, and the two countries were dissimilar in every respect.[63]

Returning to speak on this topic to the Balloon Society again in 1895, he picked up on these themes with a particular concern about Asian immigrant populations in British Burma. He was reported as arguing that 'since the province had been opened up both Indians and Chinese were flooding into the country' and that the Burmese population 'had failed to compete successfully with foreigners, notably with the industrious Chinamen and the thrifty Indians'. Again, he advocated for Burma to be governed separately from British India.[64] In adopting these positions, Chan-Toon appears as an intermediary figure foreshadowing some of the concerns that would become manifest in Burmese anti-colonial nationalism. While his position was firmly liberal and loyalist,[65] his desire for separation from India and for controls on immigration became central political platforms for nationalists in the interwar years. The Indian man as a sexual threat to Burmese women, and miscegenation as a threat to the Burmese nation, emerged in this period as expressions of masculine anxieties.[66]

In his public life in London Chan-Toon was more than simply a native informant on the state of Burma. He was also invited to speak on 'the progress of man' and international law.[67] In 1889, he published his most successful book, *The Nature and Value of Jurisprudence*. This was not a volume of pure legal scholarship, but a sweeping philosophical and historical work drawing on a range of prominent British thinkers. The book opens with an eloquent chapter on the importance of 'relative' and 'kindred subjects', calling for breaking down of barriers between academic disciplines.[68] Practising what he preaches, the rest of his study drew from published works on early human societies, anthropological studies of 'primitive tribes', English liberal political thought, and, extensively, Herbert Spencer's social Darwinism. Chapter 5, titled the 'Disintegration of the Family', provides a grand narrative of the emergence of monogamous marriage as an attendant feature of human progress. The chapter passes through a study of slavery in Roman law and Mexico, and anthropological studies of polygyny and polyandry in Indo-China and Tibet, before tracing the establishment of property rights of married women, the tendency for marriages to take the form of contracts in modern societies, and the rights of children.[69] Burmese family structures are not mentioned. Chan-Toon was showing his mastery of trends and developments in British scholarship, and applying them to the study of jurisprudence. And did so with some flair. The *Graphic* gave it a rave review, recommending it to general readers for its erudition, scientific approach, and lucidity. However, Chan-Toon's pleasure in the review, if he had read it, may have been marred by the reviewer's misrecognition of his race: 'It is a sign of the times when a Chinese writes a book full of teaching and suggestion on such a thoroughly English subject.'[70] Again, Chan-Toon was not fully recognised as a British subject; his (in this case, inaccurately) ascribed racial difference marked the reception of his work.

Mrs Chan-Toon's portrayal of Moung Gyaw's disastrous career does not wholly line up with that of Chan-Toon, at least not according to the extant evidence available in court records. His return to Arakan in Burma was widely reported and apparently marked by public celebrations, with crowds greeting him in the port town of Akyab.[71] Between 1893 and 1900 he appears representing clients in thirty-one cases in the printed records of the Lower Burma judicial court, which saw the final appeals in the southern half of the colony that had been governed since at least 1852. This meant that he was involved in approximately 10 per cent of cases at this highest level of judgement. This would suggest a healthy practice during these years, which were most of the years that he was married, factoring in a spell back in London during 1895–1896. During these years he won slightly more of these appeal cases than he lost. Strikingly, he won all five of his appeals in criminal cases against the Crown. The printed judgements do not often provide details of where in Burma the appellants and respondents in these cases came from, but where they do it indicates that his client base was mostly drawn from Arakan, suggesting strong ties with his home region.[72] Of course, it is still possible that both this practice was poorly managed and unprofitable, and that, given his meteoric successes as a student, a middling career as a barrister in Rangoon was a hard-felt disappoint.

Mabel Chan-Toon's novel makes clear that racial prejudice was part of the context in which the fictional Arakanese lawyer Moung Gyaw struggled; something also noted in sections of the press.[73] There was an awareness that obstacles stood before Chan-Toon making his way as a barrister in colonial society. In this context, the heroine of *A Marriage in Burmah* is introduced as someone without prejudice and ignorant of the existence of racism. This positioning was an acknowledgement that the figure of the 'pukka sahib' and the exclusive sociality of Anglo-Indians were losing cultural credibility in sections of Edwardian Britain.[74] Nevertheless, Moung Gyaw remains a wholly irredeemable character. More importantly, in spite of the disavowals of racial prejudice on behalf of the author, the faults in him are not individual flaws, nor are they understood as part of a wider patriarchal culture. Instead, they are indicative of his racial difference. In this, transgressive desires had to be policed.[75] The implication that there may have been any romantic appeal to Moung Gyaw at the start of the relationship is rejected early in the book. This was a relationship of convenience. She declares Mrs Moung Gyaw as being unaware of the gallant behaviours of British men – by which she means *white* British men – and through this lack of worldly knowledge, initially being unsure of whether her experience was atypical.

Ultimately, it is the difference between Moung Gyaw's external presentation of himself – as a respectable, English-educated gentleman – and his slovenly, dissipated private persona that reveals his true Oriental nature. Mrs Chan-Toon repeats this point throughout the novel through different spaces. Their first marital home is a metonym for his imperfect embodiment of masculinity. She describes it as 'splendour without, squalor within', adding that this is 'truly Oriental'.[76] The gradual decline in the quality of their lodgings through the marriage charts the erosion of his own civilised facade. Sartorial choices, diet, and his body all mark a similar dynamic. His clothing at home becomes more informal, Burmese, and sparse; a state of undress that revealed his true lack of civilisation.[77] He reverts to a Burmese diet of curries and ceases to adhere to the formalities of dining. Through his intemperate drinking and gluttonous diet, he becomes overweight – a repeated trope used for decadent and overpowering Burmese men in British novels.[78] His now ill-fitting clothes and habit of going about in partial nudity reveal the tattoos that cover his body, yet another sign of his savage nature.[79] In this reading, Moung Gyaw qua Chan-Toon's British masculinity was but a hollow performance.

However, it was a particular form of colonial masculinity that Chan-Toon was inhabiting, or at least aspiring to inhabit. British legal actors in the empire, particularly judges and magistrates, enacted their masculinity through an attempt to appear detached, objective, and even-handed. It was a form of white masculinity that could not name itself, as the implication was that these men were the embodiment of independent judgement. Instead, it was only apparent as white and male through contrasts made with other bodies, the partiality of colonised women in particular. When, through either imperial scandals or anti-colonial critique, these white male bodies were criticised as a sign of inherent biases, there were moments of acute discomfort and denial. A strict adherence to a dispassionate style of judicial writing was one performative element in the sedimentation of this ambivalent mode of masculinity.[80] One reading of Chan-Toon's *Nature and Value of Jurisprudence* is that his positionality in the text attempted to establish the same disembodied authorial locale. In other words, it was an attempt to shed his othered bodily differences and colonised cultural mores to disappear himself into the words and ideas of the British philosophical canon. But it could not happen. Whiteness was a barely apparent but impermeable barrier blocking a colonised subject from fully embodying British masculinity. From this perspective, Chan-Toon's public life might be read not as a superficial, surface performance but as a troubling performative embodiment disallowed.[81]

In 1890, Chan-Toon's brother, Shway Ban, emulated his sibling's successes by winning the University College School's prizes for Latin and geography. This was reported in the press with reminders of Chan-Toon's achievements a year prior. The *Daily News's* closing lines of its short report on the story encapsulate the ambivalence within the construction 'British imperial': 'Here is another example of what the rule of the English in the East means – of what English citizenship means to the "subject races".'[82] In this celebratory passage there is a gap maintained between English citizenship and 'subject races', even though the former is implied as bestowed on the latter. Moreover, this benefit of citizenship is predicated upon the continued rule of the English over the East, the two being fundamentally distinct and discrete. This captures the politics of what Partha Chatterjee has coined 'the rule of colonial difference', arguing that the governmentalising thrust of the colonial state was always limited by the imperative to perpetuate a division between the rulers and the ruled, a division marked by ideas of inherent racial difference.[83] The marriage of Mabel Cosgrove and Chan-Toon reveals the intimate politics of colonial differentiations.

A focus on masculinity reveals these tensions. On the one hand, masculinity was variegated by racial difference. Burmese masculinity was contrasted to British masculinity and Indian masculinity, all unstable and heterogeneous figures but nonetheless tropes that structured colonial 'common-sense'.[84] Both Mabel Chan-Toon and Chan-Toon himself cited and reiterated these contrasts in their public writings and talks. On the other hand, masculinity held the possibility of transcending racial difference for Chan-Toon. British legal masculinity, supposedly independent, objective, and detached, was a field of practice in which he sought to realise his imperial citizenship unmarked by bodily difference. His class status and elite education, supported by the capital accumulated of his merchant father profiting from the dramatic expansion of the rice frontier in British Burma,[85] made this a possibility. But ultimately it proved unattainable. His failed marriage, through Mabel Chan-Toon's retelling, rendered him as Eastern as East can be beneath his veneer of civilisation. He was cast to the other side of the gulf between the East and her West. Lurking in the margins and between the lines of the texts analysed here was whiteness. British masculinity in the empire and at home was mediated by whiteness. As a concept, whiteness shares much with masculinity as an object of study. They have historically been taken as unacknowledged, universal subject positions. Scholars of both have struggled with issues of reification, wishing to avoid further cementing these exclusive subjectivities.[86] However, whiteness and masculinity interact and are entangled – although not rigidly or mechanistically. In the case of colonial masculinity, it may be through the vagaries of when and where the racial exclusivity of Britishness was made manifest in discourse or practice that we can see the work done by whiteness.

Notes

1 Ashwini Tambe, 'Colluding Patriarchies: The Colonial Reform of Sexual Relations in India', *Feminist Studies*, 26.3 (2000), 587–600; Catherine Hall, 'Of Gender and Empire: Reflections on the Nineteenth Century', in Philippa Levine (ed.), *Gender and Empire* (Oxford: Oxford University Press, 2004), 46–76.
2 Mrinalini Sinha, *Colonial Masculinity: The 'Manly Englishman' and the 'Effeminate Bengali' in the Late Nineteenth Century* (Manchester: Manchester University Press, 1995).
3 Tracey Rizzo, *Intimate Empires: Body, Race, and Gender in the Modern World* (New York: Oxford University Press, 2017).
4 Stephen Heathorn, 'How Stiff Were Their Upper Lips? Research on Late-Victorian and Edwardian Masculinity', *History Compass*, 2.1 (2004); Harald Fischer-Tiné and Susanne Gehrmann (eds), *Empires and Boundaries: Race, Class, and Gender in Colonial Settings* (London: Routledge, 2008).
5 John M. Mackenzie, *The Empire of Nature: Hunting, Conservation and British Imperialism*, Studies in Imperialism (Manchester: Manchester University Press, 1988); M. S. S. Pandian, 'Gendered Negotiations: Hunting and Colonialism in the Late 19th Century Nilgiris', *Contributions to Indian Sociology*, 29.1–2 (1995), 239–263; Joseph Sramek, '"Face Him like a Briton": Tiger Hunting, Imperialism, and British Masculinity in Colonial India, 1800–1875', *Victorian Studies*, 48.4 (2006), 659–680.
6 Julie E. Hughes, *Animal Kingdoms: Hunting, the Environment, and Power in Indian Princely States* (New Delhi: Permanent Black, 2013).
7 Heather Streets, *Martial Races: The Military, Race and Masculinity in British Imperial Culture, 1857–1914* (Manchester: Manchester University Press, 2004); Gavin Rand, '"Martial Races" and "Imperial Subjects": Violence and Governance in Colonial India, 1857–1914', *European Review of History: Revue Européenne d'histoire*, 13.1 (2006), 1–20; Daniel J. R. Grey, 'Creating the "Problem Hindu": Sati, Thuggee and Female Infanticide in India, 1800–60', *Gender & History*, 25.3 (2013), 498–510; Jessica Hinchy, 'Obscenity, Moral Contagion and Masculinity: Hijras in Public Space in Colonial North India', *Asian Studies Review*, 38.2 (2014), 274–294.

8 Joseph S. Alter, 'Indian Clubs and Colonialism: Hindu Masculinity and Muscular Christianity', *Comparative Studies in Society and History*, 46.3 (2004), 497–534; Shruti Kapila, 'Masculinity and Madness: Princely Personhood and Colonial Sciences of the Mind in Western India 1871–1940', *Past and Present*, 187.1 (2005), 121–156; Shefali Chandra, 'Mimicry, Masculinity, and the Mystique of Indian English: Western India, 1870–1900', *The Journal of Asian Studies*, 68.1 (2009), 199–225; Douglas E. Haynes, 'Selling Masculinity: Advertisements for Sex Tonics and the Making of Modern Conjugality in Western India, 1900–1945', *South Asia: Journal of South Asian Studies*, 35.4 (2012), 787–831.

9 Subho Basu and Sikata Banerjee, 'The Quest for Manhood: Masculine Hinduism and Nation in Bengal', *Comparative Studies of South Asia, Africa and the Middle East*, 26.3 (2006), 476–490; Chie Ikeya, *Refiguring Women, Colonialism, and Modernity in Burma* (Honolulu: University of Hawaii Press, 2011).

10 Although, the field is still comparatively small. See Chie Ikeya, 'Masculinities in Asia: A Review Essay', *Asian Studies Review*, 38.2 (2014), 243–252.

11 Sramek, '"Face Him like a Briton"'; Marjorie Levine-Clark, 'From "Relief" to "Justice and Protection": The Maintenance of Deserted Wives, British Masculinity and Imperial Citizenship, 1870–1920', *Gender & History*, 22.2 (2010), 302–321; Ashok Malhotra, 'Performing Imperial Masculinity in British Theatre in the Late Eighteenth and Early Nineteenth Century', *Cultural and Social History*, 9.2 (2012), 227–250; J. A. Mangan, *The Games Ethic and Imperialism: Aspects of the Diffusion of an Ideal* (London: Routledge, 2013).

12 Mrinalini Sinha, 'Giving Masculinity a History: Some Contributions from the Historiography of Colonial India', *Gender & History*, 11.3 (1999), 445–460.

13 Christopher E. Goscha, 'Widening the Colonial Encounter: Asian Connections Inside French Indochina during the Interwar Period', *Modern Asian Studies*, 43.5 (2009), 1189–1228; Tamara Loos, 'Transnational Histories of Sexualities in Asia', *American Historical Review*, 114.5 (2009), 1309–1324.

14 Simon Yarrow, 'Masculinity as a World Historical Category of Analysis', in John H. Arnold and Sean Brady (eds), *What Is Masculinity? Historical Dynamics from Antiquity to the Contemporary World* (Basingstoke: Palgrave Macmillan, 2011), 114–138.

15 Antoinette Burton, 'Not Even Remotely Global? Method and Scale in World History', *History Workshop Journal*, 64.1 (2007), 323–328; Simon J. Potter and Jonathan Saha, 'Global History, Imperial History and Connected Histories of Empire', *Journal of Colonialism and Colonial History*, 16.1 (2015).

16 Catherine Hall, *Civilising Subjects: Metropole and Colony in the English Imagination, 1830–1867* (Cambridge: Polity Press, 2002); Tony Ballantyne and Antoinette Burton (eds), *Bodies in Contact: Rethinking Colonial Encounters in World History* (Durham, NC: Duke University Press, 2005); Catherine Hall and Sonya O. Rose (eds), *At Home with the Empire: Metropolitan Culture and the Imperial World* (Cambridge: Cambridge University Press, 2006).

17 Warwick Anderson, 'The Trespass Speaks: White Masculinity and Colonial Breakdown', *American Historical Review*, 102.5 (1997), 1343–1370; Catherine Hall, *Macaulay and Son: Architects of Imperial Britain* (New Haven: Yale

University Press, 2012); James Epstein, *Scandal of Colonial Rule: Power and Subversion in the British Atlantic during the Age of Revolution* (Cambridge: Cambridge University Press, 2012).

18 Julia Clancy-Smith and Frances Gouda (eds), *Domesticating the Empire: Race, Gender, and Family Life in French and Dutch Colonialism* (Charlottesville: University Press of Virginia, 1998); Elizabeth Buettner, *Empire Families: Britons and Late Imperial India* (Oxford: Oxford University Press, 2004); Durba Ghosh, 'Household Crimes and Domestic Order: Keeping the Peace in Colonial Calcutta, c. 1770–c. 1840', *Modern Asian Studies*, 38.03 (2004), 599–623; Emily J. Manktelow, *Missionary Families: Race, Gender and Generation on the Spiritual Frontier* (Manchester: Manchester University Press, 2016).

19 Ann Laura Stoler, *Carnal Knowledge and Imperial Power: Race and the Intimate in Colonial Rule* (Berkeley: University of California Press, 2002); Esme Cleall, Laura Ishiguro, and Emily J. Manktelow, 'Imperial Relations: Histories of Family in the British Empire', *Journal of Colonialism and Colonial History*, 14.1 (2013).

20 Michael Roper, 'Slipping Out of View: Subjectivity and Emotion in Gender History', *History Workshop Journal*, 59.1 (2005), 57–72; Cleall *et al.*, 'Imperial Relations'.

21 Damon Ieremia Salesa, *Racial Crossings: Race, Intermarriage, and the Victorian British Empire*, Oxford Historical Monographs (Oxford: Oxford University Press, 2011); T. J. Tallie, 'Queering Natal: Settler Logics and the Disruptive Challenge of Zulu Polygamy', *GLQ: A Journal of Lesbian and Gay Studies*, 19.2 (2013), 167–189; Mary A. Procida, *Married to the Empire: Gender, Politics and Imperialism in India, 1883–1947* (Manchester: Manchester University Press, 2017).

22 *Evening Telegraph*, 29 July 1893; *Singapore Free Press and Mercantile Advertiser (Weekly)*, 5 September 1893, 8.

23 K. A Ballhatchet, *Race, Sex and Class under the Raj: Imperial Attitudes and Policies and Their Critics, 1793–1905* (London: Weidenfeld and Nicholson, 1980).

24 Onni Gust, 'Mobility, Gender and Empire in Maria Graham's *Journal of a Residence in India* (1812)', *Gender & History*, 29.2 (2017), 273–291.

25 Homi Bhabha, 'Of Mimicry and Man: The Ambivalence of Colonial Discourse', *October*, 28 (1984), 125–133.

26 Mrs M. Chan-Toon, *A Marriage in Burmah: A Novel* (London: Greening and Co., 1909).

27 Accurate details of her publications can be found here, although the biographical details contain numerous errors: 'Chan-Toon, Mrs M.: Mabel Mary Agnes Cosgrove', in Sandra Kemp, Charlotte Mitchell, and David Trotter (eds), *The Oxford Companion to Edwardian Fiction* (Oxford: Oxford University Press, 2005).

28 *Evening News*, 20 February 1904, 2.

29 *Morning Post*, 13 October 1888, 3.

30 Chan-Toon, *A Marriage in Burmah*.

31 *Ibid.*, 286.
32 Radhika Mohanram, 'Dermographia Written on the Skin or, How the Irish Became White in India', *European Journal of English Studies*, 9.3 (2005), 251–270; Angela Woollacott, 'Whiteness and "the Imperial Turn"', in Leigh Boucher, Jane Carey, and Katherine Ellinghaus (eds), *Historicising Whiteness: Transnational Perspectives on the Construction of an Identity* (Melbourne: RMIT Publishing in association with the School of Historical Studies, University of Melbourne, 2007), 7–15.
33 *Aberdeen Daily Journal*, 18 March 1912, 3.
34 Gregory Mackie, 'Forging Oscar Wilde: Mrs. Chan-Toon and *For Love of the King*', *English Literature in Transition, 1880–1920*, 54.3 (2011), 267–288.
35 *Evening Telegraph and Post*, 13 January 1926, 3; *Aberdeen Press and Journal*, 12 November 1926, 8.
36 Mackie, 'Forging Oscar Wilde'.
37 *New York Times*, 8 June 1907.
38 *Aberdeen Press and Journal*, 1 March 1924, 4.
39 Chan-Toon, *A Marriage in Burmah*.
40 Ajay Skaria, 'Shades of Wildness: Tribe, Caste, and Gender in Western India', *The Journal of Asian Studies*, 56.3 (1997), 726–745; Charu Gupta, 'Feminine, Criminal or Manly? Imaging Dalit Masculinities in Colonial North India', *The Indian Economic & Social History Review*, 47.3 (2010), 309–342; Avril A. Powell and Siobhan Lambert-Hurley (eds), *Rhetoric and Reality: Gender and the Colonial Experience in South Asia* (New Delhi: Oxford University Press, 2006); Prem Chowdhry, 'Militarized Masculinities: Shaped and Reshaped in Colonial South-East Punjab', *Modern Asian Studies*, 47.3 (2013), 713–750.
41 Tinzar Lwyn, 'Stories of Gender and Ethnicity: Discourses of Colonialism and Resistance in Burma', *Australian Journal of Anthropology*, 5.1–2 (1994), 60–85.
42 Chie Ikeya, 'The "Traditional" High Status of Women in Burma', *The Journal of Burma Studies*, 10 (2005), 51–81.
43 Jonathan Saha, 'The Male State: Colonialism, Corruption and Rape Investigations in the Irrawaddy Delta c.1900', *Indian Economic Social History Review*, 47.3 (2010), 343–376.
44 Deborah Deacon Boyer, 'Picturing the Other: Images of Burmans in Imperial Britain', *Victorian Periodicals Review*, 35.3 (2002), 214–226.
45 Jonathan Saha, 'Madness and the Making of a Colonial Order in Burma', *Modern Asian Studies*, 47.2 (2013), 406–435.
46 Frank Mort, *Dangerous Sexualities: Medico-Moral Politics in England since 1830*, 2nd edn (London: Routledge, 2000).
47 Lucy Delap, 'Uneven Orientalisms: Burmese Women and the Feminist Imagination', *Gender & History*, 24.2 (2012), 389–410; Shobna Nijhawan, 'At the Margins of Empire: Feminist-Nationalist Configurations of Burmese Society in the Hindi Public (1917–1920)', *The Journal of Asian Studies*, 71.4 (2012), 1013–1033.
48 Saha, 'The Male State'.

49 Jonathan Saha, 'Whiteness, Masculinity and the Ambivalent Embodiment of "British Justice" in Colonial Burma', *Cultural and Social History*, 14.4 (2017), 527–542.
50 Chan-Toon, *A Marriage in Burmah*.
51 Carol Ann Boshier, *Mapping Cultural Nationalism: The Scholars of the Burma Research Society, 1910–1935* (Copenhagen: NIAS Press, 2018).
52 Archibald Mackirdy and William Nicholas Willis, *The White Slave Market* (London: Stanley Paul & Co., 1912).
53 Ballhatchet, *Race, Sex and Class*; Jeremy Neill, '"This Is a Most Disgusting Case": Imperial Policy, Class and Gender in the "Rangoon Outrage" of 1899', *Journal of Colonialism and Colonial History*, 12.1 (2011); Saha, 'Whiteness, Masculinity and Ambivalent Embodiment'.
54 Jonathan Saha, 'Among the Beasts of Burma: Animals and the Politics of Colonial Sensibilities, c.1840–1950', *Journal of Social History*, 48.4 (2015), 933–955.
55 Jonathan Saha, 'Colonization, Criminalization and Complicity: Policing Gambling in Burma c.1880–1920', *South East Asia Research*, 21.4 (2013), 655–672; Ashley Wright, *Opium and Empire in Southeast Asia: Regulating Consumption in British Burma* (Basingstoke: Palgrave Macmillan, 2013).
56 Chan-Toon, *A Marriage in Burmah*, 52–60.
57 *Standard*, 18 December 1885, 3.
58 Jordan Carlyle Winfield, 'Buddhism and Insurrection in Burma, 1886–1890', *Journal of the Royal Asiatic Society*, 20.3 (2010), 345–367.
59 *Standard*, 18 December 1885, 3.
60 *Manchester Courier and Lancashire General Advertiser*, 19 January 1891, 5.
61 *Pall Mall Gazette*, 21 June 1888, 10; *Singapore Free Press and Mercantile Advertiser (Weekly)*, 3 March 1904, 134.
62 *Liverpool Mercury*, 22 June 1888, 5.
63 *Morning Post*, 13 November 1888, 3.
64 *Standard*, 12 June 1895, 5.
65 This position was not uniformly welcomed in the British press. The radical newspapers ridiculed his praise for the freedom and meritocracy of England. William Morris's Anarcho-Communist journal, *The Commonweal*, drew attention to Chan-Toon's father's successful rice merchant firm to cast him as an imperial stooge acquiring his legal skills to keep Burmese working classes in subjugation. *The Commonweal*, 21 July 1888, 228.
66 Ikeya, *Refiguring Women*.
67 *Pall Mall Gazette*, 19 October 1888, 6; *Daily News*, 3 May 1889, 3.
68 Chan-Toon, *The Nature and Value of Jurisprudence*, 2nd (enlarged) edn (London: Reeves and Turner, 1889), ix–xviii.
69 Ibid., 103–124.
70 *Graphic*, 14 November 1889, 330.
71 *Pall Mall Gazette*, 9 December 1889, 6.
72 *A Reprint of the Printed Judgments of the Court of the Judicial Commissioner, Lower Burma, and Special Court, for the Period Extending from 1893–1900*, 2nd edn (Rangoon: Office of the Supdt., Government Printing, 1905).

73 *Cambridge Independent Press*, 4 March 1892, 4.
74 E. M. Collingham, *Imperial Bodies: The Physical Experience of the Raj, c.1800–1947* (Cambridge: Polity Press, 2001).
75 Ann Laura Stoler, *Race and the Education of Desire: Foucault's History of Sexuality, and the Colonial Order of Things* (Durham, NC: Duke University Press, 1995).
76 Chan-Toon, *A Marriage in Burmah*.
77 Philippa Levine, 'States of Undress: Nakedness and the Colonial Imagination', *Victorian Studies*, 50.2 (2008), 189–219.
78 Cecil Champain Lowis, *The Machinations of the Myo-Ok* (London: Methuen, 1903); George Orwell, *Burmese Days* (London: Penguin, 1989).
79 Clare Anderson, *Legible Bodies: Race, Criminality and Colonialism in South Asia* (Oxford: Berg, 2004); Jordanna Bailkin, 'Making Faces: Tattooed Women and Colonial Regimes', *History Workshop Journal*, 59.1 (2005), 33–56.
80 Saha, 'Whiteness, Masculinity and Ambivalent Embodiment'.
81 Colin Tyler, 'Performativity and the Intellectual Historian's Re-enactment of Written Works', *Journal of the Philosophy of History*, 3.2 (2009), 167–186.
82 *Daily News*, 8 August 1890, 5.
83 Partha Chatterjee, *The Nation and Its Fragments: Colonial and Postcolonial Histories* (Delhi: Oxford University Press, 1994); Elizabeth Kolsky, 'Codification and the Rule of Colonial Difference: Criminal Procedure in British India', *Law and History Review*, 23.3 (2005), 631–683.
84 Ann Laura Stoler, *Along the Archival Grain: Epistemic Anxieties and Colonial Commonsense* (Princeton: Princeton University Press, 2009).
85 Michael Adas, *The Burma Delta: Economic Development and Social Change on an Asian Rice Frontier, 1852–1941* (Madison: University of Wisconsin Press, 1974); Peter A. Coclanis, 'Southeast Asia's Incorporation into the World Rice Market: A Revisionist View', *Journal of Southeast Asian Studies*, 24.2 (1993), 251–267; Ian Brown, *A Colonial Economy in Crisis: Burma's Rice Delta and the World Depression of the 1930s*, RoutledgeCurzon Studies in the Modern History of Asia, 28 (London: RoutledgeCurzon, 2005).
86 Angela Woollacott, '"All This Is the Empire, I Told Myself": Australian Women's Voyages "Home" and the Articulation of Colonial Whiteness', *American Historical Review*, 102.4 (1997), 1003–1029; Mohanram, 'Dermographia'; Woollacott, 'Whiteness'; Sara Ahmed, 'A Phenomenology of Whiteness', *Feminist Theory*, 8.2 (2007), 149–168.

3

'Crutches as weapons': Reading Blackness and the disabled soldier body in the First World War

Hilary Buxton

On 25 June 1952, John Demeritte, a Bahamian who had served in the British West Indies Regiment (BWIR) during the First World War, penned a petition to the Bahamas House of Assembly to stake his claim as a disabled Black ex-serviceman deserving of aid from the imperial government. Nineteen years old when he sailed with the First Bahamas Contingent in 1915, Demeritte was injured in Egypt and sent back to Nassau to recover. His 'urge to serve in His Majesty's forces' was so great, he testified, that he re-enlisted in the Eleventh BWIR Battalion and crossed the Atlantic again. In the trenches in France, he was badly frost-bitten and lost both of his legs. Thirty-four years later, Demeritte's appeal to the colonial government emphasised his honourable service, his attempt to maintain economic independence, and his physical limitations. He had supported his family as a messenger in the Immigration Department for nineteen years, yet his condition rendered him dependent in other ways. His only means of transport was a Ministry of Pensions-supplied wheelchair, which was 'now old and in a dilapidated condition, very difficult to propel by hand especially going over hills'. 'Friends assist me by pushing me up hill,' he noted. His other orthopaedic devices were similarly run-down: 'The artificial legs which I am now using are broken which makes it painful for me to get about and most uncomfortable.'[1] Demeritte's distress is visceral, even when mediated by the conventions of the formal petition.

What did it mean for Demeritte, a Black subject who served in a unit trained for combat yet restricted to non-combatant labour, to make these claims? In a manner that echoed the claims of disabled white Tommies in the metropole, service and corporeal loss added up to a debt that stretched far beyond the borders of the British Isles.[2] 'In view of the fact that I have lost both legs in the service of my King and Country, and that I am unable to work as a result, it is my earnest prayer', he entreated, 'that the Honourable House of Assembly will consider my case sympathetically and give to me some help which I feel that I justly merit.' This was one in a series of petitions Demeritte submitted to the assembly over the course of nearly forty years from 1923 to 1962. He concluded each with the same salute: 'And as in duty bound your humble servant will ever pray'. Demeritte's reference to his duty, taken up voluntarily and at the cost of great physical sacrifice, highlighted the enduring bond between ex-serviceman and state: duty bound him to the imperial government as much as the government was bound in debt to him.

This claim had to be made, his physical sacrifice asserted and detailed. For when Demeritte first appeared in the British press in 1918, he did so in a most unlikely role. News accounts cast him as the purported instigator of a violent riot against hospital staff and disabled white soldiers in a Liverpool military hospital. His own war wounds went unmentioned. The extraordinary choice by British newspapers to omit all references to his disablement obscured Demeritte's status as a soldier hero, commensurate with the white soldiers he healed alongside. How and why did the British press transform a disabled Black serviceman into a racially marked perpetrator of violence against white soldier patients? How do we understand contemporary representations of Black, disabled, martial masculinity against what little we can glean about the experiences of men like Demeritte, of labouring, soldiering, and healing side by side with white soldiers?

The experience of illness, injury, and disability is a focal point in studies of white British soldier masculinity. Scholarship about First World War servicemen illuminates a diverse range of masculinities that tap into the classic martial ideal of military stoicism and the soldier hero, while simultaneously accommodating challenges to or deviations from this model. From cultural and medical perspectives to social histories of the personal experience of disablement, these studies demonstrate how social discourse connected male wounding and disablement to national ideals of sacrifice and the need to reclaim masculinity.[3] Many parse disablement and its social aftermath to illustrate how disabled soldiers' bodies subverted masculine norms and revealed the soldier hero's fragility. At the same time, recent studies reveal how these subjects – or the rehabilitative programmes offered to them – sought to reclaim various aspects of the masculine ideal by re-establishing their social and gendered dominance in the household and society at large.[4] This included passing with prosthetics or returning to their former status as breadwinners. Examining the wartime intersections of masculinity and disability, Wendy Gagen argues that supposed 'emasculated' (e.g. disabled) men could display or support hegemonic (able-bodied) masculinity. This 'fluid' hegemonic masculinity added to its power by incorporating both disabled and non-disabled men into patriarchal masculine ideals. Nonetheless, this body of literature predominantly depicts British soldier masculinity as fundamentally constituted through white culture and experience. Joanna Bourke called attention to how ethnicity, specifically Irishness, mediated soldiers' treatment, yet this story remains exclusively white.[5]

Very few works consider how issues of race affected white soldiers' masculinity during the war. Those which do are largely limited to configuring non-white servicemen in the public imagination, or to thinking about how intimacy with racial others affected soldiers' male identity.

New attention to the global dynamics of the First World War, meanwhile, has prompted historians to consider the diverse range of soldier experiences in the British world. Global and imperial-oriented scholarship observes how racial ideologies and bias, as well as cultural exchange, conditioned the experiences of non-white colonised subjects at war.[6] Fewer have engaged with masculinity as a focal concept. Work on Black servicemen from the British West Indies is a notable exception. Richard Smith examines the ways in which wartime rhetoric about martial masculinity and citizenship mobilised Jamaican servicemen to fight for the empire, and later informed post-war nationalist activism. More recently, Anna Maguire has pieced together life writing and scattered testimonies from Black BWIR servicemen to illustrate how they tapped into and transformed familiar rhetoric around heroic service to validate their masculine identity, even as they were denied combat experience. Non-white soldiers' mobility and interaction with a diverse range of servicemen, and the discrimination they faced from both policymakers and individuals, fed into their transmuted understandings of martial masculinity. In contrast, historians of First World War masculinity trace the evolution of white soldiers' masculine identity to their environment, their dislocation, their experiences of camaraderie, food, and illness – virtually everything but their encounters with those who served alongside them, ferried ammunition and food to them, and dug the latrines they relieved themselves in. Literature on late imperial manliness argues that as hegemonic masculinity increasingly modelled itself on the trope of the brave imperial soldier, in many ways, it defined itself through racial ideals like 'the martial races'.[7] Studies of the relationship between raced encounters and white *wartime* male identity are far rarer.[8]

This division – between historical understanding of the multiracial, multicultural, and multi-religious facets of masculinity in the British world, and the dominant historical treatment of white wartime masculinities as discrete and apart from non-white masculinities – is reproduced in the largely white history of masculinity and wartime injury. Despite recent efforts to decolonise disability history, studies of gendered disability at war have yet to meet those of race. We still know very little about the Black experience of war injury and disablement.[9] Why were some disabled soldier bodies more visible than others? How did sudden injury and limb loss mediate the relationship between troops of different races and ethnicities? And what can the wounded Black soldier body, like that of Demeritte, tell us about the nexus of race and masculinity in the British Empire at war?

This chapter approaches these questions by examining the visual and discursive politics of martial and disabled masculinity and their relationship with race in the First World War. It focuses specifically on the photographic and written depictions of the African Caribbean soldier body in the wartime press on the front and in hospital. West Indian servicemen were often in close proximity to white British soldiers. They occupied a unique position within the martial and medical hierarchy. Recruited as volunteers, trained as soldiers, the War Office nonetheless assigned the BWIR to non-combatant labour and denied them the chance to fight in active combat. Their movements and interactions with other troops and local civilians were sharply curtailed. Yet West Indian troops' service repeatedly put them in danger. The First Battalion in Egypt served as ammunition carriers in forward areas, the Third and Fourth battalions in France on railway construction and later as ammunition carriers – all positions involving dangerous work close to or within the firing zone.[10] Many were wounded and lost limbs in service. Unlike many other non-white servicemen and labourers, West Indian troops did not have separate hospital facilities. They were frequently sent to and healed in hospitals alongside white troops.

What follows is a history of Black embodiment in the First World War that examines representations of disabled masculinity and their consequences. It enlists contemporary visual imagery to suggest ways of understanding the linkages between martial, raced, and disabled masculinity. First, it takes up how the British press configured Black martial bodies to analyse the threat posed by wounded Black servicemen to the white monopoly on the masculine rhetoric of voluntary sacrifice. The chapter turns to a rare moment in which Black disabled servicemen and multiracial rehabilitation came into view for the anglophone reading public: a so-called riot at the Belmont Road Auxiliary Hospital in Liverpool, where John Demeritte recovered from his double amputation. The heavily reported incident offers a way to understand the dynamics between wounded Black and white soldiers – their solidarities and hostilities – within the space of the hospital ward. The racially bound representations of disabled servicemen that came out of the affair both enabled and hindered soldiers from making concrete claims for care and assistance. Such representations mediated how Demeritte and other BWIR members asserted themselves as simultaneously Black, disabled, and heroic.

The white British Tommie was far from the only serviceman serving on the front line and laid up in hospital in the Great War. From West Indian troops in the West Indies Regiment and BWIR and labourers from South Africa, to Aboriginal Australians and Maori, and South Asian servicemen in the Indian Army and Labour Corps, the War Office relied on manpower from nearly every corner of the empire to shore up British strength in every front of war.[11] Segregation and integration differed from regiment to regiment and site to site. West Indian servicemen's separation from white British troops varied. Housed in separate barracks, they were fed the same rations as British servicemen and hospitalised both in facilities intended for white British troops and those for 'native labour'. The War Office unofficially banned African Caribbean servicemen from the social meeting sites of French-run *estaminet*s in early 1917; however, the West Indian Contingent Committee, an organisation set up to advocate for BWIR troops, successfully appealed this practice in 1918.[12]

West Indian military service was not a new development. The West India Regiments (WIR), established in 1795, had performed both garrison and active duty throughout the nineteenth century in the Caribbean and West Africa, though never, notably, in Britain or mainland Europe.[13] When war broke out in 1914, the WIR was assigned to garrison duty in Sierra Leone and the German Cameroons. Yet more and more West Indians agitated to participate in the global conflict. Despite their desperate need for manpower, the British military was initially extremely hesitant to involve Black West Indian subjects in a 'European war' on European soil – military recruiters and naval officers frequently cited the colour bar for enlistment and turned away early Black volunteers seeking their own passage to England.[14] The Colonial and War Offices finally approved a West Indian contingent on 10 May 1915, but though nearly all were given combat training, they were demarcated as 'native troops' and limited to labour corps duties.[15] The First, Second, and Fifth BWIR battalions, stationed with the Egyptian Expeditionary Force, saw small bouts of active service in Palestine against Turkish forces from July 1917 to 1918, but their designation as non-combatants never changed. Richard Smith and Glenford Howe illustrate how the War Office's decision to place BWIR battalions on non-combatant duty was intended to limit comparisons between white and Black men and ensure the endurance of imperial racial and gendered hierarchies. To this end, white officers led and oversaw Black servicemen. While scholarship has rightly identified this as an issue of race, this was also crucially an issue of British accountability – a damage control exercise not only in racial supremacy but in imperial responsibility and West Indian rights. In Britain, the experience of combat and 'honourably' obtained wounds were deeply tied to rhetoric about collective debt to the white soldier – and the varying amounts of medical, economic, and political boons that came with martial sacrifice.[16] Restricting African Caribbean servicemen to difficult and often lowly labour duties, from ammunition carrying to cooking and latrine digging, the War Office curbed them from performing soldier service and the status and claims attached to it.

The metropolitan press underscored the presumed differences justifying the varied restrictions on non-white troops, even as it celebrated their enlistment. In its war coverage, sporting journal the *Field* published numerous reports about imperial soldiery. One extended feature in 1917, 'Soldiers of Empire', discussed the Indian Army, BWIR, and settler dominion forces. Accompanying photographs depicted the dress of New Zealand, Australian, Canadian, and South African infantrymen, but none of non-white soldiers and labourers, despite praising their BWIR troops' 'cool nonchalant behaviour under shell fire', and South Asian soldiers' 'dash and pluck'.[17]

West Indian soldiers were the subject of considerable reporting throughout London and in assorted colonies. Accounts frequently painted them as jolly, good-natured sources of entertainment, simultaneously highlighting racial difference. One article accompanied by photos in the *Natal Witness* in 1916 headlined 'Happy Darkies at the Front: No Bad Teeth in that Lot!', and noted that their faces 'Bear a remarkable resemblance to the African type ... They are splendid soldiers; and all speak English fluently. They have taken with them to Europe the manners and customs of the plantations, and their merry dispositions make them great favourites.'[18] These media depictions mingled admiration and approbation while recycling familiar racial tropes. The *Field* featured BWIR troops in a July 1917 issue. The article included a photograph of a line of volunteers, 'Some stalwart Bahamians', with a white officer, Captain Cole, in the centre, 'Introduced for the sake of comparison ... himself over 6 feet high, and it will be seen that each of the men is taller than he is'.[19] One of the *Field*'s many puff pieces on grand imperial war spirit, the feature celebrates West Indian enlistment. Nonetheless, its visual imagery reinforces colonial tropes and status quos: Captain Cole's placement at the centre reminds readers that white officers led Black troops. While praising their eager dispositions and physicality, the display of Black muscular prowess played into the long practice of the commodification of Black male bodies and their labour power.[20] Photographs of strong Black bodies bore traces of earlier examples used to make racist claims in service of sustaining coerced and unfree labour. British media operated a visual politics of masculine soldierhood that differentiated by race even as it upheld the basic manliness of the soldier hero. Richard Smith identifies how the British 'popular imagination' reordered Black male bodies as a reservoir of simple yet vigorous masculine power – a foil to wounded and traumatised white masculine authority. Nonetheless, as the war came to an end, this trope gave way once again to traditional portrayals of Black masculinity as sexual, dangerous, and irrational.[21] One constant in this conceptualisation, however, is the whole-bodied nature of the West Indian serviceman. The West Indian bodies described and depicted in the mainstream British press were almost exclusively whole, never injured or disabled.

Images of disabled men typically proliferate after conflicts, whether produced for political, philanthropic, medical, or military use. This was particularly true in First World War Britain.²² Some fundraising for rehabilitation programmes depicted disabled soldiers as cripples or schoolboys. As Seth Koven has shown, rehabilitative programmes and hospitals like Chailey in Sussex fashioned both literal and rhetorical relationships between crippled children and disabled soldiers.²³ In other sites, Ana Carden-Coyne reveals how the British public saw increasingly less imagery of infantilisation, and more of transformation.²⁴ Wartime and interwar Britain was awash in images of white disabled men reasserting masculinity by illustrating their autonomy – most often through photography that showed them working machines or engaging in new crafts, as well as modelling new types of prostheses which remade their manly bodies. Notably, those producing and disseminating such images – the War Office, hospital gazettes, philanthropies, and the press, among others – did not represent all forms of wounding for public consumption. Certain injuries, notably facial mutilation, were absent from journalistic representation.²⁵ Disabled servicemen's visibility also fluctuated depending on context. Institutional publicity material may have placed such men in the public eye, Jessica Meyer argues, but they were absent from commemorative spaces.²⁶ Nonetheless, the figure of the disabled soldier body formed a crux of wartime recovery, both real and figurative. Imagery of the upbeat or productive wounded served to re-instantiate gendered norms of stoic masculinity and socio-economic patriarchy.

The British press spoke volumes about wounded non-white troops, but their subjects were from the subcontinent, not Africa or the Caribbean. The Indian Army's swift mobilisation was largely due to its reputation as a bastion of the 'martial races'. This pseudo-scientific theory held that certain ethnic and religious groups, predominantly from the north of India, Nepal, and the Northwest Frontier Province, were biologically and socially inclined to fighting.²⁷ Unlike BWIR servicemen, Indian combatants and non-combatants were accommodated in Indian-only general hospitals, field ambulances, and hospital ships. The War and India Office readily photographed and publicised the healing of disabled Indian servicemen to underscore imperial benevolence. These accounts focused exclusively on combatant soldiers of the 'martial races', emphasising both their gallant stoicism and their foreignness. Meanwhile, the injuries and illness of South Asian non-combatants went virtually unseen. Of all the Indian medical facilities, Nash's faux-oriental Royal Pavilion in Brighton was the subject of a truly spectacular propaganda effort. Convalescent soldiers were pictured on automobile rides to local monuments and tourist sites, handbooks and photo albums of the hospital complex were distributed in the United Kingdom and India, and the entire operation was documented to the fullest.²⁸ The *Birmingham Gazette* placed a photograph of wounded

Indians at Brighton, entitled 'Sons of Empire', on the front page of their 16 December 1914 issue. 'These men have fought bravely for the maintenance of the Empire,' the *Gazette* affirmed: 'They bear their wounds with remarkable stoicism and their honours with calm dignity.'[29] The wounded Indian Army soldier, therefore, was the true counterpart of his unwounded self: a fighter who bore his injuries with the same stoicism ascribed to martial race soldiers in battle. Lauded as heroic warriors, their status as esteemed combatants validated their sacrifices for the empire.

Why, in contrast, were there few analogous images of other disabled non-white servicemen like those in the BWIR? This lack of representation may in large part be due to demographics. By the end of the war, the BWIR encompassed a total of 15,200 men – a small figure compared to the 5 million British men, or 1.4 million Indian servicemen, who served over the course of the conflict.[30] Though many were wounded on numerous fronts, they constituted a small portion of the hospitalised population. However, there is reason to believe that there were considerable disincentives for the War Office and the metropolitan press to photograph or feature disabled West Indian troops. Showing such images would have powerfully validated BWIR servicemen's physical sacrifice, their status as wounded heroes, and their ability to make claims for rights and welfare based on that status.

This absence was tied to a longer colonial history. In contrast to the widely circulated photographs of violently disabled Black amputees in the Belgian Congo, similar representations of the debilitated subject body in *British* colonies did not circulate in the Edwardian metropole. The photographic erasure of the debilitated or disabled colonial body from the British press had a long history, one that continued through the colonial upheavals of the 1920s and 1930s.[31] The Black *soldier* body, however, carried different anxieties, simultaneously raced, gendered, and martial. In limiting Black servicemen from combatant roles, the British state sought to contain what it owed them. Without combat experience or wounds, West Indian servicemen could claim neither the status of soldier hero nor the benefits, however meagre, of the 'heroic cripple'.[32] But BWIR servicemen *were* injured and disabled, as were many other non-combatants in British forces. The lack of representations of Black disablement in the anglophone press tallies with the ethos behind BWIR battalions' assignment to non-combatant duties. Even when restricted to non-combatant –and ostensibly safer – labour duty, wounds conferred martial masculinity on Black subjects. Not photographing such injuries short-circuited the logic of bodily sacrifice and with it, the claims attached to such sacrifice.

Readers of British papers likely had little idea that West Indians were grievously wounded in the course of their service, or that they were treated alongside white soldiers. In late 1918 Liverpool, however, this changed. The integrated nature of many wartime hospitals – and the visual politics of the wounded soldier body – came to light with an eruption of violence in a space of caregiving. The little scholarship that mentions the 'Belmont Affair' places it in the wider history of Black disenfranchisement and discrimination faced by African Caribbean servicemen.[33] A comparative exploration of the mainstream and Black press's treatment of the incident, however, illuminates a far more complex politics of race, masculinity, and debility. Disabled masculinity was not produced in racial silos. It was constructed in spaces where servicemen of different races healed and came to terms with disability. These spaces brought racial and colonial politics to the fore of disabled masculinity. At the same time, they could foster masculine solidarity regardless of racial identity.

In September 1918, only two months before the signing of the Armistice, readers of the London *Times* opened their papers to news of a riot. 'Coloured men' at the Belmont Road Auxiliary Hospital, *The Times* reported, had overstayed the time allowed to them out of the hospital. William Henry Taylor, the officer in charge, responded by doubling the military police guard and disciplining the soldiers in question – all African Caribbean troops from the BWIR. Yet when guards stopped a West Indian sergeant from leaving the hospital a few days later on 8 September, *The Times* relayed, he reacted violently. The sergeant 'Demetrius' – otherwise known as John Demeritte – 'immediately drew a razor and slashed wildly with it' before guards disarmed and placed him in a cell. Several other BWIR servicemen, hearing the commotion, refused to go to their wards and 'became very abusive'. When guards attempted to remove them to the cells, *The Times* alleged that '50 other West Indians' joined and took possession of the police lodge. Meanwhile, 400 wounded British soldiers in a concert at the hospital's hall 'came to the rescue of the military police'. The ensuing fracas, as *The Times* reported it, was a veritable caricature in which a place of healing transformed into a raced revolt: 'There was a struggle, in which crutches and sticks were freely used, and pots and pans were flying about.' With the help of the maimed Britons, 'order was restored'. In its depiction of the 'Belmont Hospital Affair', *The Times* failed to mention a crucial fact – that many of the soldiers in the hospital, both white and Black, were single or double amputees. They had not yet been fitted with artificial limbs or surgical devices. Most could no more terrorise guards with a razor than they could venture far from the hospital out of hours.

The Times story is one of normative soldier and racial roles upended. Rather than grateful and passive recipients of the care offered by the British, the thankless, violent West Indian soldiers turn against their benevolent healers and unreasonably demand independence (in this case, in the form of free movement outside the hospital). Their actions interrupted the convalescence of white British soldiers taking in a concert, just as they disrupted what Ana Carden-Coyne has termed 'the myth of the "happy hospital"', in which patients were supposed to be cheery and compliant.[34]

The raced parameters of the metropolitan press's reporting extended to gendered interactions. Though there were no fatalities, *The Times* article highlighted the death of a Nurse McShane four days later. *The Times* reported that she was 'carried off her feet' and 'knocked down' by the brawlers, and 'suffered from shock' in the aftermath.[35] At a hearing of medical evidence, the article noted, the jury returned a verdict of 'death through misadventure' – though McShane died from pneumonia. In their titling and subtitling, the reporter linked the two events and implicitly judged the BWIR wounded guilty: 'Disturbance by Black Troops: Army Nurse's Death'. By directly connecting the death of a white British woman with a seemingly Black-instigated colonial disturbance, the article recalled popular anxieties concerning the purported dangers of miscegenation and interracial interactions. These fears were echoed in the reporter's charge that West Indian troops had spent too much time outside hospital grounds. They disruptively entered public spaces that the hospital administration tried to isolate them from.

The Times and other regional papers' coverage is notable for erasing Black servicemen's disability. Reports similar to *The Times* piece appeared across the British press on the same day. 'Melee at a Military Hospital: Brave Nurse Met Her Death' reported the *Derby Daily Telegraph* and the *Aberdeen Evening Express*. The *Liverpool Echo* testified of 'A Nurse Victim'. Others were more explicit about who was to blame: the *People* reported 'Riotous Negroes', the Huddersfield *Daily Examiner* a 'Coloured Soldiers' Riot'. The *Western Daily Press* was unique among its peers. Its headline, 'Crutches as Weapons', called attention to yet elided West Indian servicemen's wounds by rendering their impaired state a source of masculine, martial aggression.[36] Rather than graciously accepting the healing technologies of the imperial motherland, they had turned their crutches into tools of rebellion. British coverage of the event described the BWIR convalescents as 'West Indians' or 'coloured men'. They were never identified as 'wounded' or 'soldiers'. In contrast, the papers labelled those alleged to have come to the guards' aid as 'wounded British soldiers who … came to the rescue of the military police'.[37] Despite their common status as injured servicemen, the press did not disclose African Caribbean troops' status of soldier hero and disabled veteran. Instead, it suggested that while Black troops might be healed alongside white, their wounds were fundamentally different.

In contrast to the British press's vision of a Black-instigated riot, the Afrocentric press saw an altogether different event: a provoked protestation of historic maltreatment that was not defined by racial boundaries. The *African Telegraph*, a pan-Africanist paper edited by John Eldred Taylor and Felix Hercules, devoted a two-page spread in its December issue to the 'Belmont Hospital Affair'. Begun in 1914 by Sierra Leonean journalist Taylor, the paper had a short run and was revived in 1918. The chairman of the Society of Peoples of African Origin (SPAO), Taylor recruited the Trinidadian Hercules as his successor to edit the paper, which ran until 1919, when Taylor was charged with libel and the paper was forced to close.[38] Hercules himself later became general secretary of the SPAO, and toured the West Indies on its behalf during the 1919 race riots.[39] By and large, the *African Telegraph* muted its criticism of British policy in Africa during the war. It covered both the conflict as well as news across Africa and the British West Indies. Long supportive of Black soldiers, however, the paper took a special interest in the reporting of the Belmont incident.

The *African Telegraph* emphasised that this was not a Black versus white disturbance. Of the 2,000 men being treated at Belmont Road, 'the best of friendship existed between the white and black' soldiers. Tensions at the hospital only began, the paper reported, with the arrival of a new group of patients. These soldiers were from South Africa, Canada, and places 'where black people are badly treated and receive scant justice'. The paper's coverage placed the September incident in a longer history of discrimination and inequality at the Liverpool hospital, touched off by dominion soldiers' presence. Within days of dominion troops entering the hospital, BWIR servicemen suffered increasing verbal and physical abuse. When one individual ridiculed West Indian soldiers in the hospital's concert room, a Black soldier 'knocked their tormentor down with his crutch' – an act which prompted the superintendent to ban all Black soldiers from attending concerts. On 8 September, hearing that they would once again be allowed to participate in hospital events, the wounded West Indians sent Sergeant John Demeritte to confirm their attendance.[40] The double amputee 'crawl[ed]' towards the guard at the gates of his ward, who happened to be one of their previous abusers. The guard abruptly 'pounced upon' Demeritte and threw him into a cell. When a group of BWIR amputees approached the guard, they were ordered to return to their wards. Upon resisting, some white soldiers in the concert room rushed to the guard's assistance, prompting a 'melee ... in which pots, pans, bottles, etc. ... crutches and sticks' were wielded by a combination of about 400 to 500 white soldiers and 50 West Indian convalescents, all of whom were recovering from serious wounds.

Unlike the metropolitan press, the *African Telegraph* identified the 'affair' simultaneously as a site of racially motivated violence and interracial solidarity: some white soldiers came to the aid of the West Indians. The *African Telegraph* attributed their actions to the 'English love of fair play'.

'We solemnly assert', the report claimed, 'that it is impossible to find a body of Englishmen in the Colonies or elsewhere who would all consent with one accord to perpetrate the same crime at the same time against the natives [i.e. BWIR men].' The paper could have limited its commentary on this act, sarcastically lambasting the humane liberalism which defined the British imperial ethos. The shared experiences of war and wounding deepened cross-racial bonds of solidarity: some of those 'who had fought side by side' with West Indians in the trenches 'took sides with the coloured soldiers'. By the time the provost marshal arrived on site, 'there were many white soldiers seen standing over crippled black limbless soldiers, and protecting them with their sticks and crutches from the furious onslaught of the other white soldiers until order was restored. All honour to them!' The experience of serving together, the reporter suggested, created a mutual sense of duty and protection amongst the patients. This feeling crossed racial boundaries, defining itself through a masculine camaraderie that centred on the multiracial nature of war service.

A War Office enquiry supported the *African Telegraph*'s version of events. The West Indian Contingent Committee confirmed that officials had found that, contrary to *The Times's* reporting, 'the whole affair had been exaggerated. There had been no "razor cutting" and no blame had been cast upon the West Indian men.'[41] At the same time, the enquiry also denied that any blame had been cast on the West Indian men for the disturbance. In an effort to rehabilitate the BWIR's reputation, the committee submitted a note to the British press encouraging it to redact its version of events – though none was printed. This biased reporting foreclosed other opportunities for cross-racial exchange and aid for Black troops. The 'circulation of bad reports', the *African Telegraph* claimed, had discouraged philanthropically minded Liverpudlians from visiting the troops. 'Many of the charitable people who used to call at the hospitals and wheel these limbless coloured men out, have refrained from doing so through fear of public opinion' – now, Black patients were 'more or less neglected'. Many West Indian patients were removed from Belmont to another convalescent hospital on Windsor Street.[42] The *African Telegraph* suggested that if the British Army's medical system was unable to house BWIR troops with dignity, they should dedicate resources to a separate hospital for 'black fighters' staffed by 'trained coloured nurses'. Disabled West Indian troops, the paper argued, were 'brave warriors' who deserved the same respect and honour given to disabled white Tommies.

The British press and the *African Telegraph* alike selectively mobilised the language of disablement to characterise the conflict. The innocent were 'patients', 'amputees', 'wounded soldiers', and 'limbless', while the perpetrators were merely 'soldiers' or 'West Indians'. At the same time, none of the wounded were figured as passive or pitiable – despite their convalescent status. Wounded and disabled troops of all races rally to self-defence and the defence of others – in *The Times*'s version, the wounded white soldier rallies to the guards; in the *Telegraph*'s, the wounded on both sides combat *and* aid each other. Yet where *The Times* and local British papers erased West Indian wounds, the *Telegraph* highlighted them. In the wards, the 'coloured limbless soldiers … crawled toward the guard at the gate as best they could'. Missing limbs, the BWIR servicemen are referred to as men, soldiers, and 'wary warriors' who sought access to the same spaces open to the white wounded. The *African Telegraph*'s coverage exonerated British West Indian servicemen and recovered the episode as an opportunity to mobilise an alternative disabled masculinity, one defined by both a reassertion of wounded West Indians' masculine heroism, and critical indignation at the racism and unequal treatment which BWIR patients experienced in a British site of healing.

Two photographs in the *African Telegraph* furthered this goal. In the first, Sergeant Demeritte sits alone in his hospital blues. In the second, he is accompanied by two other double amputees as well as 'two coloured friends', a Black serviceman without a visible injury and a woman, who are unnamed. Perhaps the woman was one of the many locals who regularly visited the hospital to attend to and provide some diversion for the wounded. Where the *African Telegraph* reported how regular white visitors abandoned the BWIR wounded after the onslaught of bad press post-riot, her presence testifies to the continued support of Liverpool's Black community for West Indian soldiers' welfare. In both images, Demeritte and other wounded soldiers sit cross-legged, the stumps of their amputated feet and lower legs bandaged and openly displayed. With the local woman's supportive, motherly hands on their shoulders, the centrality of the disabled servicemen in the frame draws attention to their martial manhood *and* their bodily injury.

These photographs constitute some of the scant visual documentation of disabled African Caribbean troops during the war.[43] They resemble several well-known photographs of limbless white soldiers at Roehampton.[44] In one of these images, single and double amputees sit in an orderly row in wheelchairs. Like the West Indians photographed for the *African Telegraph*, they wear their hospital blues. Joanna Bourke has described these men, 'tidily dressed … with calm smiles', as illustrative of 'the height of pathos and denial' surrounding the crisis of disability in the First World War.[45] For Bourke, the Roehampton wounded appear complacent about their injuries: they (or their outfitters and photographer) papered over their injured masculinity with biotechnical devices and the veneer of respectable masculinity.

Unlike the white troops depicted in these images, the three BWIR amputees are emphatically *not* in denial. Instead, their disablement serves as a testament that reaffirms, rather than detracts from, their masculinity. It is visual evidence of their maiming in the service of the empire, and, through the bias-driven riot at Belmont, evidence of their maiming *by* the empire. This representation is made possible by rejecting, rather than embracing, the crutch and the imperial hands that crafted it. It is no mistake that the *African Telegraph* chose to photograph the soldiers involved in the riot seated and without crutches or other mobility aids. Like the rest of the Belmont wounded, they had yet to be fitted with prostheses. The soldiers' defiant stances and unabashed display of their severely wounded bodies affirmed their lack of, and independence from, imperial technologies that could maim as well as heal. The image of Demeritte and his counterparts in their hospital blues reinforces their status as soldier heroes. As Jeffrey Reznick observes, the convalescent uniform was a conflicted, yet essential, symbol of wounded men's heroic sacrifices, marking them out from the public.[46] Neither whole-bodied, primitive, and violent men, nor the pitiable wounded, the article painted Demeritte and his counterparts as 'brave warriors' who retained their manhood and gendered authority even after their disablement. Unlike the white ex-serviceman, however, the *African Telegraph* pairs their reaffirmed masculinity with an indictment of British colonial policy and racial feeling. Their disablement is inseparable both from their gendered and raced identity and is tied to both their reasserted masculinity and their sense of raced injustice. This representation of disabled Black soldiery served a critical rhetorical purpose. By resituating Demeritte and his counterparts as the valiant war wounded, the *African Telegraph* rehabilitated the position from which they could make concrete claims for the care and respect that their designation as non-combatants sought to deny them.

The contrasting representations of raced masculinity arising out of the Belmont Affair do not provide much insight into how patients at Belmont Road understood their disabled subjectivity. Despite this lack of firsthand testimonies, the *African Telegraph*'s coverage suggests how to begin to think about the constellation of relationships formed between disabled masculine subjects across the empire. Scholarship on war disability in Britain recognises how the space of the hospital could offer limbless Tommies the chance to establish shared identity.[47] The anthropological concept of biosociality – in which individuals with the same condition form a shared identity around that condition – provides a way to understand how these relationships formed across racial boundaries. In Paul Rabinow's configuration of biosociality, biosocial relationships – formed between those with the same conditions, diseases, or disorders – efface the differences of race, class, and environment by emphasising mutual experience around the body.[48] Nonetheless, these new sources of identity could also be the source of new inequalities.

Originally developed as a counterpoint to the spectre of (eugenic) geneticism in sociobiology, Rabinow used biosociality to explore how communities might emerge out of new developments in genetics. Molecular genetics, he argued, would reshape society by producing new networks of identity. People would develop social collectives around mutual genetic conditions, in ways that moved beyond other forms of identity. More recently, critical disability scholars have moved beyond genetics and suggested biosociality as a way to characterise the formation of disabled communities.[49] Yet where biosociality highlights the shared 'condition' as the ultimate determinant of communal identity, the convalescents at Belmont were simultaneously tied by their status as male servicemen wounded in the course of war – an ultimate expression of masculinity (even as the divide between combatants and non-combatants remained). In the Belmont Hospital wards, then, biosociality – formed around the shared experience of amputation and disablement – melded with martial cultures of homosociality.

Military hospitals like Belmont Road were not entirely homosocial spaces. Nurses held positions of power, and charity-minded women visitors interrupted patient bonding. Nonetheless, the wards were marked spaces for male socialisation in which many men shared the experience of recovering from amputation. Rachel Moss has recently called for the treatment of homosociality as a complex framework determined by 'networks of socially codified relationships that maintain mainstream power structures' – not a natural process of mutual association, but one that required maintenance and energy.[50] At the Belmont Hospital, homosociality, like biosociality, may have served as markers of solidarity and community, but they never existed in a vacuum of gender or health-based identities.

Indeed, however present aspects of identity- and community-building bio- and homosociality may have been in the Belmont's wards, racialised understandings of difference during the war checked this process. It is essential to observe how these phenomena coexisted alongside persistent racism and degrading bias, on the part of the military, the state, and the individual. White Dominion troops imbued with notions of racial hierarchy may have opposed the presence of West Indian servicemen in the hospital, understanding it as an insult to their sacrifice. They rearticulated their white masculinity by verbally or physically attacking Black troops, using racial aggression to bolster their masculine superiority and efface their disabled masculine selves. On the other hand, wounded white troops also aided, protected, or fought with the West Indian convalescents. These patients could have been spurred to help through a paternalistic sense of morality.

Alternately, their common experiences at war, and mutual disablement, may have engendered a biosocial identification with and concern for their fellow wounded soldiers from the British West Indies. Seeing each other across hospital wards, with similar amputations and permanent injuries, servicemen of different races may have seen their new selves reflected in the bodies of those around them. This recognition triggered both violence and solidarity. In either case, war disablement opened up spaces in which patients could rearticulate and renegotiate their masculinity through exchanges that crossed racial and colonial borders.

In this light, the *African Telegraph*'s revisionist imagery attempted to contain racial tension by using tropes of amity to challenge the prevailing Belmont narrative. Adopting a conciliatory yet indignant tone, and focusing on the bonds between soldiers of different races, the paper drew on the long practice of colonised people performing protestations of goodwill as a precursor to airing grievances. Back in the Bahamas, John Demeritte's string of petitions employed the same technique, echoing the language of sacrifice and duty that infused rhetoric about the deservingness of the wounded British Tommie. None referenced the non-combatant labour to which Demeritte and his fellow West Indians had been relegated. Instead, Demeritte's accounts highlighted his will to serve and the physical price he had paid in the course of that service. Over time, they increasingly emphasised his elected service and bodily losses at war. In 1923, aged twenty-seven, he described himself as 'an Ex-Soldier' who 'joined the Forces of the British West Indies Regiment ... and served therein until he was discharged as physically unfit', noting that he was unable 'to obtain work of a nature suited to his physical condition'. By 1962, at age sixty-five, he self-identified as 'one of the "Gallant 30" Bahamaians who served with the British Forces', a loyal 'British subject' who 'lost both of my legs in the trenches in France' and was 'unable to make ends meet'.[51]

Demeritte's 1952 petition got the result he had long sought. The assembly resolved to grant him £450 for the fitting and purchase of new artificial legs and a motorised wheelchair – a monumental sum for a man whose annual disability pension was merely £72.[52] Noting that he had first unsuccessfully petitioned the colonial secretary, Demeritte, like many other soldiers, strategically shifted the case for his heroic service and sacrifice to local authorities. This was a case Demeritte had to make over and over again in his forty years of petitioning. He was, he insisted, a 'humble servant', 'duty bound' by the nature of his service to the empire to claim a position that the British state sometimes acknowledged, but more often denied him: that of a disabled Black soldier.

The Belmont Affair and the *African Telegraph*'s coverage of it reveal an embodied politics of masculinity centring on the labour, valour, and claims to rights of West Indian servicemen. This colonial politics of the body could be used to criticise the inadequacies of state provision, insisting on the soldier hero status of disabled Black servicemen. It radically emphasised the bonds and connections between the African Caribbean wounded and their white British counterparts, while simultaneously calling attention to their disablement at the hands of an empire whose military structure configured hierarchies of martial masculinity. The War Office's decision to keep BWIR men from combat, and the resulting depiction of them in the British media, sought to limit the extent to which Black servicemen could identify as soldier heroes and war wounded. The *African Telegraph* photographs, in contrast, insisted that it was possible to be simultaneously Black, disabled, and a soldier hero. They performed a critique of the systems that would deny West Indian servicemen those rights – both of state military policy on the ground, and of the system of representation that excluded them from it. This visual and rhetorical representation of disabled Black manhood – and of a fraternity of disabled manhood in the global empire – crucially helps to explain how such soldiers negotiated with the British public and state in the war's aftermath. At the same time, their visual exclusion from that fraternity is echoed in the continuing struggles of Black veterans to be included in centennial conversations and the global narrative of First World War legacies.

These representations of masculinity also offer a glimpse of the social relationships between disabled soldiers of different races. Their interactions and co-developed identities as men wounded in war offer a starting point for work that takes up the colonial and racial facets of British wartime masculinity. Many troops, both the unimpaired and wounded, continued to espouse dominant white masculinity that reinforced its normativity through an articulation of racial superiority. These sites also afforded Black servicemen the opportunity to rearticulate their masculine selves by asserting their equal status to the white soldier hero. West Indians' impairment could be a wellspring through which they articulated a martial critique or a manly reaffirmation of their dedication to empire. It frequently occupied ground in between these two poles. The experience of disability in multiracial wards generated both silent recognition and palpable solidarity. But these raced negotiations of masculine selfhood did not end with one's discharge from the hospital. Disabled ex-servicemen carried these understandings from the small confines of the Liverpudlian medical ward back to the British countryside, Johannesburg, and Nassau. Though their contact with one another often terminated with the Armistice, their raced experience of disability stayed with them through the process of repatriation and social reintegration. Their narrative should prompt new questions about the ways in which race intertwines with moments of change and contestation in the history of British masculinity (both in Britain and the empire, before and after the collapse of colonialism). This history was produced out of raced encounters in war and peace, and it must expand to include the complex masculine selves that both embraced and strained against one another and their shared bodily experiences.

Notes

1 John Demeritte to the House of Assembly, 25 June 1952, in *Votes of the Honourable House of Assembly of the Bahama Islands* (Nassau: Publishers Limited, 1952), 492–493.
2 On the petitions of British ex-servicemen, see Deborah Cohen, *The War Come Home: Disabled Veterans in Britain and Germany, 1914–1939* (Berkeley: University of California Press, 2001), 51–55, 107–115. See also the forthcoming database and work from Jessica Meyer and Alexia Moncrieff with the Men, Women and Care project at the University of Leeds.
3 Joanna Bourke, *Dismembering the Male: Men's Bodies, Britain, and the Great War* (London: Reaktion, 1994); Seth Koven, 'Remembering and Dismemberment: Crippled Children, Wounded Soldiers, and the Great War in Great Britain', *American Historical Review*, 99:4 (1994), 1167–1202; Julie Anderson, *War, Disability, and Rehabilitation in Britain: 'Soul of a Nation'* (Manchester: Manchester University Press, 2011); Jeffrey Reznick, *Healing the Nation: Soldiers and the Culture of Caregiving in Britain during the Great War* (Manchester: Manchester University Press, 2004). As regards able-bodied wartime masculinity, an exciting set of new works over the past decade has focused on neglected sites and subjects, frequently embracing plural and alternative masculinities, from male caregivers and conscientious objectors to non-combatants and those outside the well-parsed Western Front. See Jessica Meyer, *An Equal Burden: The Men of the Royal Army Medical Corps in the First World War* (Oxford: Oxford University Press, 2019); Lois Bibbings, *Telling Tales about Men: Conceptions of Conscientious Objectors to Military Service during the First World War* (Manchester: Manchester University Press, 2010); Justin Fantauzzo and Robert L. Nelson, 'A Most Unmanly War: British Military Masculinity in Macedonia, Mesopotamia and Palestine, 1914–18', *Gender & History*, 28:3 (2016), 587–603.
4 Wendy Gagen, 'Remastering the Body, Renegotiating Gender: Physical Disability and Masculinity during the First World War, the case of J. B. Middlebrook', *European Review of History*, 14:4 (2007), 525–541; Jessica Meyer, 'Wounded in a Mentionable Place: The (In)visibility of the Disabled Ex-serviceman in Interwar Britain', in David Swift and Oliver Wilkinson (eds), *Veterans of the First World War: Ex-servicemen and Ex-servicewomen in Post-war Britain and Ireland* (London: Routledge, 2019), 158–171.
5 Joanna Bourke, 'Effeminacy, Ethnicity and the End of Trauma: The Sufferings of "Shell-Shocked" Men in Great Britain and Ireland, 1914–39', *Journal of*

Contemporary History, 35:1 (2000), 57–69. See also Michael Robinson, *Shell-Shocked British Army Veterans in Ireland, 1918–1939* (Manchester: Manchester University Press, 2020).

6 Anna Maguire, '"I Felt like a Man": West Indian Troops Under Fire during the First World War', *Slavery and Abolition*, 39:3 (2018), 602–621; Richard Smith, *Jamaican Volunteers in the First World War: Race, Masculinity and the Development of National Consciousness* (Manchester: Manchester University Press, 2004); Glenford D. Howe, 'Military-Civilian Intercourse, Prostitution and Venereal Disease among Black West Indian Soldiers during World War I', *Journal of Caribbean History*, 31:1 (1997), 88–102; Santanu Das (ed.), *Race, Empire, and the First World War* (Cambridge: Cambridge University Press, 2011). On the Indian Army, see Santanu Das, *India, Empire, and First World War Culture: Writings, Images, and Songs* (Cambridge: Cambridge University Press, 2018), 70, 185, 334–335; and Kate Imy, *Faithful Fighters: Identity and Power in the British Indian Army* (Stanford: Stanford University Press, 2019).

7 Heather Streets, *Martial Races: The Military, Race, and Masculinity in British Imperial Culture, 1857–1914* (Manchester: Manchester University Press, 2004); Kate Imy, 'Queering the Martial Races: Masculinity, Sex and Circumcision in the Twentieth-Century British Indian Army', *Gender & History*, 27:2 (2015), 374–396. On the imperial soldier hero, see Graham Dawson, *Soldier Heroes: British Adventure, Empire and the Imagining of Masculinities* (London: Routledge, 1994).

8 Though few delve into the relationships between white soldiers and non-white servicemen, several works cover crucial ground in considering the relationship between race and wartime masculinity. Marco Ruiz examines how cross-imperial interactions in Egypt both underpinned and complicated British standards of masculinity. Richard Smith's work illuminates ideas about the Black body in the (public) white imagination. Finally, several works consider how colonial servicemen and subjects became sites of sexual anxiety. Mario M. Ruiz, 'Manly Spectacles and Imperial Soldiers in Wartime Egypt, 1914–19', *Middle Eastern Studies*, 45:3 (2009), 351–371; Richard Smith, 'The Black Male Body in the White Imagination during the First World War', in Paul Cornish and Nicholas J. Saunders (eds), *Bodies in Conflict: Corporeality, Materiality, and Transformation* (London: Routledge, 2014), 39–52; Mark Harrison, 'The British Army and the Problem of Venereal Disease in France and Egypt during the First World War', *Medical History*, 39 (1995), 133–158; Philippa Levine, 'Battle Colors: Race, Sex, and Colonial Soldiery in World War I', *Journal of Women's History*, 9:4 (1998), 104–130; Howe, 'Military-Civilian Intercourse'.

9 A notable exception is Gregory Mann's study of West African veterans in the French Empire. Gregory Mann, *Native Sons: West African Veterans and France in the Twentieth Century* (Durham, NC: Duke University Press, 2006). More work on the subject in the British imperial world has been conducted on the Second World War. Timothy Parsons, 'No Country Fit for Heroes: The Plight of Disabled Kenyan Veterans', in Judith Byfield, Carolyn Brown,

Timothy Parsons, Ahmad Sikainga (eds), *Africa and World War II* (Cambridge: Cambridge University Press, 2015), 127–143.

10 On the politics of where BWIR soldiers were deployed, see Robin Wallace Kilson, 'Calling Up the Empire: The British Military Use of Non-white Labor in France, 1916–1920' (PhD diss., Harvard University, 1990), 233–235.

11 On the presence and raced experiences of servicemen from the West Indies, see Smith, *Jamaican Volunteers in the First World War*; Glenford Howe, *Race, War, and Nationalism: A Social History of West Indians in the First World War* (Kingston, Jamaica: Ian Randle Publishers, 2002); Howe, 'Military-Civilian Intercourse'; and Maguire, '"I Felt like a Man"'. On Black servicemen, see Ray Costello, *Black Tommies: British Soldiers of African Descent in the First World War* (Liverpool: Liverpool University Press, 2015).

12 The National Archives, Kew (hereafter TNA), WO 95/83, War Diary of Director of Labour, 13 February 1917; Imperial War Museum, London (hereafter IWM), LBY EX. 349, West Indian Contingent Committee, 'Report for the Six Months Ended June 20th, 1918'.

13 The WIR was stationed for two years on garrison duty in Gibraltar in 1817. Roger Norman Buckley, *Slaves in Red Coats: The British West India Regiments, 1795–1815* (New Haven: Yale University Press, 1979); Brian Dyde, *The Empty Sleeve: The Story of the West India Regiments of the British Army* (Antigua: Hansib, 1997).

14 Howe, *Race, War, and Nationalism*, 32.

15 Kilson, 'Calling Up the Empire', 232–234.

16 Jessica Meyer, *Men of War: Masculinity and the First World War in Britain* (Basingstoke: Palgrave Macmillan, 2009), 100–102.

17 'Soldiers of Empire', *Field*, 7 July 1917, 6–8.

18 'Happy Darkies at the Front', *Natal Witness*, 25 January 1916. See also 'From the Plantation to the Battlefield', *War Budget*, 28 October 1918.

19 Institute for Commonwealth Studies, London (hereafter ICS), File 96/2/3, 'Some Stalwart Bahamians: Each of These Men Is over 6 Feet in Height', attributed to the *Field*, 7 July 1917.

20 See e.g. commentary on Louis Agassiz's photographs. Suzanne Schneider, 'Louis Agassiz and the American School of Ethnoeroticism: Polygenesis, Pornography, and Other "Perfidious Influences"', in Maurice O. Wallace and Shawn Michelle Smith (eds), *Pictures and Progress: Early Photography and the Making of African American Identity* (Durham, NC: Duke University Press, 2012), 211–243.

21 Smith, 'The Black Male Body'.

22 Ana Carden-Coyne, *Reconstructing the Body: Classicism, Modernism, and the First World War* (Oxford: Oxford University Press, 2009), chs 2–4; and Ana Carden-Coyne, *The Politics of Wounds: Military Patients and Medical Power in the First World War* (Oxford: Oxford University Press, 2014), 277–279; Bourke, *Dismembering the Male*, 56–58; Gabriel Koureas, *Memory, Masculinity and National Identity in British Visual Culture, 1914–1930: A Study of 'Unconquerable Manhood'* (Aldershot: Ashgate, 2007).

23 Koven, 'Remembering and Dismemberment'.

24 Transformation imagery increased in prominence as 'body culture' and physical fitness expanded throughout interwar Britain. Carden-Coyne, *Reconstructing the Body*, 183–185, 202–203.
25 Suzanna Biernoff, 'The Rhetoric of Disfigurement in First World War Britain', *Social History of Medicine*, 24:3 (2011), 666–685.
26 Meyer, 'Wounded in a Mentionable Place', 159.
27 Streets, *Martial Races*.
28 'Wounded Indian Soldiers at Play', *Birmingham Daily Gazette*, 16 September 1915, 6; 'Wounded Indian Soldiers in England', *Daily Mirror*, 7 November 1914, 7; 'King and Queen Visit Wounded Indian Soldiers in Hospital', *People*, 10 January 1915, 11; 'Wounded Indians in France and England', *Sphere*, 26 February 1916, 24; Wounded Turbaned Warriors', *Daily Record*, 9 November 1914, 8.
29 'Sons of the Empire Who Have Fought Bravely', *Birmingham Gazette*, 16 December 1914, 1.
30 *Statistics of the Military Effort of the British Empire during the Great War* (London: HMSO, 1922), 384.
31 On atrocity in the Belgian Congo and the power of photography, see Dean Pavlakis, *British Humanitarianism and the Congo Reform Movement, 1896–1913* (London: Routledge, 2016), 184–200; and Kevin Grant, *A Civilised Savagery: Britain and the New Slaveries in Africa, 1884–1926* (London: Routledge, 2005), 40. On photography and the debilitated body in the British Empire, see Timothy Pratt and James Vernon, '"Appeal from This Fiery Bed ...": The Colonial Politics of Gandhi's Fasts and Their Metropolitan Reception', *Journal of British Studies*, 44:1 (2005), 103–104.
32 Meyer, *Men of War*, 102.
33 Peter Fryer mentions the Belmont Affair in his landmark history *Staying Power: The History of Black People in Britain* (London: Pluto Press, 1984), 297; Howe, *Race, War, and Nationalism*, 167–168.
34 Carden-Coyne, *The Politics of Wounds*, 277–278.
35 'Disturbance by Black Troops, Army Nurse's Death', *The Times*, 26 September 1918, 3.
36 Among many reports, see 'Melee at a Military Hospital – Brave Nurse Met Her Death', *Derby Daily Telegraph*, 26 September 1918, 4; 'Crutches as Weapons', *Western Daily Express*, 26 September 1918, 4; 'A Nurse Victim', *Liverpool Echo*, 25 September 1918, 4; 'Riotous Negroes: Melee in a Hospital', *People*, 29 September 1918.
37 'Coloured Soldiers' Riot', *Huddersfield Daily Examiner*, 26 September 1918, 3; 'Hospital Melee: Nurse Fatally Injured in Fight with Blacks', *Leeds Mercury*, 26 September 1918, 6; 'Sad Fate of an Irish Nurse', *Belfast News-Letter*, 27 September 1918, 4.
38 After publishing supportive coverage of British policy, Taylor printed a series of articles protesting the use of flogging on African women in northern Nigeria. The British resident sued Taylor and the *African Telegraph*'s publisher. Though the suit was successful and the paper forced to close, the trial

was a media sensation, bringing further awareness to harsh judicial practices in British-controlled Nigeria. Jonathan Derrick, *Africa, Empire and Fleet Street: Albert Cartwright and the African Magazine* (Oxford: Oxford University Press, 2018), 152–156.

39 Hercules was born in Venezuela but raised in Trinidad. He received his BA at London University, where he met Eldred Taylor. On Hercules' editorship and activism, see Robert A. Hill (ed.), *Marcus Garvey and the Universal Negro Improvement Association Papers*, vol. 2 (Berkeley: University of California Press, 1983), 212, nn. 11–13.

40 The *African Telegraph* named the sergeant 'John Demerette'. BWIR medal rolls, however, list no 'Demerette', only two John Demer*ittes*, one of whom was an acting sergeant. I have thus referred to Demeritte throughout using his name at enlistment. TNA, WO 372/5/242313, Medal Card of John Demeritte; 'The Belmont Hospital Affair', *African Telegraph*, December 1918, 94–95.

41 ICS, West India Committee Records, File 97 1/6/1, West Indian Contingent Committee Minute Book, Meeting Minutes for 1 November 1918.

42 'The Belmont Hospital Affair', 95.

43 To date, they remain two of only three photographs of amputee BWIR servicemen I have located.

44 IWM, Q108161, Unknown Photographer, 'Servicemen with Missing Limbs in Wheelchairs at Roehampton Military Hospital', *c.* 1914–1918.

45 Bourke, *Dismembering the Male*, 58–59.

46 Reznick, *Healing the Nation*, 99–115.

47 Julie Anderson, '"Jumpy Stump": Amputation and Trauma in the First World War', *First World War Studies*, 6:1 (2015), 9–19.

48 Various fields have since built an umbrella of concepts out of biosociality – biological citizenship, genetic citizenship, bioidentity, etc. – to explore how the Foucauldian concept of biopower changes when applied to individual and collective identities. Paul Rabinow, *Essays on the Anthropology of Reason* (Princeton: Princeton University Press, 1996), 102–103; Sahra Gibbon and Carlos Novas, *Biosocialities, Genetics and the Social Sciences: Making Biologies and Identities* (London: Routledge, 2008).

49 Michele Friedner, 'Biopower, Biosociality, and Community Formation: How Biopower Is Constitutive of the Deaf Community', *Sign Language Studies*, 10:3 (2010), 336–347; Kelly Fritsch, 'Blood Functions: Disability, Biosociality, and Facts of the Body', *Journal of Literary and Cultural Disability Studies*, 10:3 (2016), 341–356.

50 Eve Sedgwick, *Between Men: English Literature and Male Homosocial Desire* (New York: Columbia University Press, 1985); Rachel Moss, '"And Much More I Am Soryat for My Good Knyghts": Fainting, Homosociality, and Elite Male Cultures in Middle English Romance', *Historical Reflections*, 42:1 (2016), 103; Rachel Moss, 'Ready to Disport with You: Homosocial Culture amongst the Wool Merchants of Fifteenth-Century Calais', *History Workshop Journal*, 86 (2018), 1–21.

51 Demeritte to the House of Assembly, 11 April 1923, in *Votes of the Honourable House of Assembly of the Bahama Islands* (1923), 226; Demeritte to the House of Assembly, 15 March 1962, in *Votes of the Honourable House of Assembly of the Bahama Islands* (1962), 164.
52 Demeritte to the House of Assembly, 25 June 1952.

Reflection: Male historians explain things to me: Masculinity, expertise, and the academy

Charlotte Lydia Riley

When I think about male historians explaining things to me, one moment stands out. I was giving a paper at a seminar, at which I had been invited to speak. I finished my paper and we opened the floor to questions: queries, suggestions, have-you-looked-at, do-you-think. It was pleasant, and I started to wonder why I had been nervous. Then a man asked me a question, a factual question about a date, or a name, or something (it really wasn't important) and I wasn't sure about the answer. I said I didn't know. A man in the audience did know the answer, and he supplied it: I thanked him.

The man in the audience knew the answer to the next question, too, and after my own response, he helpfully added an explanatory comment. After the following question, he didn't wait for me to speak. Turning around in his chair, he addressed the questioner directly, and explained the answer (the wrong answer) before I had opened my mouth. Once I had wrestled control of my own Q & A session back from the floor, the next man began his question by explaining that I had made a silly claim in my paper. When I interjected that I had not actually said this, and quoted the relevant part of the paper back to him, he conceded that I was right. He then proceeded to explain to me, at some length, what he *would* have said *if* I had said what he said I had said – even though, as he conceded, I had not. (It was at this point that I started to laugh.)

There is a moment when a male historian begins to explain your own research to you when you have a choice: do you try to interject, or do you let it wash over you? The first is tempting, but exhausting, and often pointless in any case. The fixed smile of the female historian who is suffering an explanation from a male historian of something she knows well is a common sight at conference drinks receptions. Male historians might choose to explain a basic aspect of your research to you ('if you are interested in class, perhaps you should read E. P. Thompson') or they might choose to explain why you are wrong about something ('Your archival sources might seem to show this, but surely that isn't quite correct') or they might want to explain why the very basis of your research is in fact flawed ('But were there, really, any influential women in the Labour Party at all?').

When I read Rebecca Solnit's 2008 essay 'Men Explain Things to Me', then, I was primed to understand it. The piece was reprinted in 2012 with a new introduction, in which Solnit placed her work within the context of 'the battle for women to be treated like human beings with rights to life, liberty, and the pursuit of involvement in cultural and political arenas'.[1]

Solnit framed her original essay around going to a party, at which a man reacted to her saying she had written a book on Eadweard Muybridge by telling her at length about the *very important* book on Muybridge that had come out that year. Of course, this book turns out to be Solnit's own, although her female friend has to interject to say 'that's her book' several times before the man acknowledges and then believes her.

This essay took a little part of the world by storm, not least because it led to the birth of the term 'mansplaining'. A lot of men do not like the term 'mansplaining'. Not all men, they point out, do this. (Two sentences ago, I was careful to type 'a lot'.) Mansplaining as a term is blurry, as all conceptual terms are, and it has been misappropriated, as all conceptual terms are eventually. We often think of it merely as a synonym for explaining, perhaps with a little too much force or enthusiasm. But this is to chip away at the specificity of the term.

Mansplaining describes the specific moment when a man assumes ignorance of a topic by a woman who is actually at least as knowledgeable, if not more knowledgeable, about the topic. In Solnit's words, 'men explain things to me, and other women, whether or not they know what they're talking about'. Whether most men know what they are talking about or not, the point is that *most* men assume themselves to be more knowledgeable about *most* topics than *most* women, even topics in which the woman might be reasonably expected to have as much or more expertise than the male speaker. In Solnit's case, the subject of her own book. Hers is the quintessential mansplaining experience: not just having men explain things to you, but having men explain your own ideas back to you, glossed with the confident patina of male authority. (If you point out that they are repeating your ideas, they will mostly just assume that *you* have copied *them*.)

As Solnit writes, in the essay:

> Every woman knows what I'm talking about. It's the presumption that makes it hard, at times, for any woman in any field; that keeps women from speaking up and from being heard when they dare; that crushes young women into silence by indicating, the way harassment on the street does, that this is not their world. It trains us in self-doubt and limitation just as it exercises men's unsupported overconfidence.[2]

Re-reading this essay, I was reminded of Carolyn Steedman, narrating another story of talking at a party about a book:

> I read a woman's book, meet such a woman at a party (a woman, now, like me) and think quite deliberately as we talk: we are divided. A hundred years ago I'd have been cleaning your shoes. I know this and you don't.[3]

These two parties and these two books point up different experiences. First, the experience of not having your expertise taken seriously, because you are a woman, and a man has therefore assumed that your expertise cannot possibly compare to his. Second, the experience of feeling out of place, of knowing that it is only an accident of social mobility that has ended up with you in this room talking about your expertise, and the constant, gripping anxiety that you might one day be found out. And so, women from working class backgrounds suffer from two related maladies. Men explain things to us, even things that we know well, even things in which we are experts, without embarrassment and without holding back. And our own instinct is to let these men explain these things, because deep down we are anxious that maybe, really, they do know more than us, and that we might soon be exposed as frauds.

Once you start to watch out for it, as a woman, you notice men explaining all sorts of different things to you. Doctors explain how you feel pain, and how much; taxi drivers explain the way to your own house; men that you meet at parties explain how universities work, despite not having stepped onto a campus in twenty years. And so male historians explain things to me, all the time, without even realising that they are doing it, or that their faces have assumed – as Solnit describes – 'that smug look I know so well in a man holding forth, eyes fixed on the fuzzy far horizon of his own authority'.[4]

As a woman from a working-class background, it would be easy here to list the places and the events at which I have had things explained to me by male historians (conferences, workshops, classrooms, archives, restaurants, bars). It would be easy to think of specific topics where male historians really enjoy holding forth: some predictable, some unusual, some surprisingly brave. (The time a man explained to me that my definition of second-wave feminism was wrong, and that he knew this because he 'took a class once', in a conversation about the class that I *teach* about second-wave feminism, remains a particular favourite.)

I am a contemporary British historian who works on the Labour Party, among other things, and so it is not only male historians who like to explain things to me. Political scientists, economists, sociologists, politicians, journalists, the man on the street, or on Twitter, who votes Labour, or doesn't. My experience of mansplaining is truly interdisciplinary. (Perhaps there is a grant I could apply for.) But as a historian by training, it is the male historians who are the biggest irritant. There are men, of course, in every field whose propensity for this behaviour (and, indeed, other unsavoury behaviours) is shared among women like a currency of belonging. I'm not going to name names here. This is about structures, not individuals.

The two identities available to a female historian, when male historians explain things, are the ingénue or the harridan. If you let male historians hold forth, they will never respect you as an expert. If you try to challenge them, they will continue to think that they hold more expertise than you, and also resent you for the interruption. If you draw attention to the gendered dynamic which allows them to do this explaining – and especially if you ever utter the word 'mansplaining' – you will be labelled 'intimidating' or 'difficult' or 'scary', even by men who are very senior to you, even by men who hold power over your career. Siri Hustvedt has written about the way that women are taught to be nice, and the penalties paid by women who refuse this niceness, including in academic settings. The woman she writes about who is described as 'really mean' attracts this label because she tries three times to ask a question at an academic paper without interruption by men; when she eventually makes a 'forceful, aggressive critique' in order to be heard, she is punished for allowing her expertise to override her niceness.[5] Letting male historians explain things to you is part of the emotional labour of being *nice*.

Of course, male historians do not limit themselves to explaining only historical topics. One of the things that male historians have explained to me, repeatedly, is how hard it is to be a male historian. Or rather: they have elaborated the different ways in which it is hard for each of them to be a male historian. (It should be pointed out that I have never asked about this. Perhaps I have a sympathetic face.)

This has usually come down to some perceived outsider status; male historians enjoy exploring the ways in which they do not fit into the academy. Sometimes they like to defend other men; I rarely share with male historians tales of male historians explaining things to me, because it means sitting through an explanation of why this might have occurred. This almost always comes down to some version of outsider status: the male historian is insecure! He is shy! He has, himself, been treated poorly in the past by other men! He is intimidated by me, or by women generally! Or perhaps the male historian will empathise by telling me a moment that *he* had something explained to *him*; this, of course, is not so much explanation as exoneration ('Silly woman, did you think this was about gender? Let me show you how you are mistaken.')

Of course, the academy is an ivory tower, a closed shop, and it can be a very hostile space for anyone who does not fit into the traditional framework of what it means to be an academic. Despite its liberal image and its notions of itself as a tolerant and diverse space, gender, class, race and sexual orientation can all be barriers to an academic career and to feeling accepted and included within academia's hallowed walls. But what should be noted – indeed, what has been noted, by every female historian that I have spoken to about this – is the enthusiasm with which white male historians like to talk about, elaborate, analyse, and bemoan their own outsider status. This usually and most conspicuously comes down to social class, or rather a notion of social class that they cling to, regardless of their current tastes, economies, or politics. In some cases, it revolves entirely around their relationship to Oxbridge or Ivy League institutions. But if Ginger Rogers had to do everything that Fred Astaire did, but backwards and in high heels, I sometimes feel like snapping that yes, we are all outsiders, but some of us are outsiders with a 15 per cent pay gap.[6]

This performance of outsider status also often serves to excuse questionable behaviour on the part of these men, who use their blurring of professional lines as further evidence that they are not traditional academics (although, in reality, nothing could be more traditional in academia than questionable behaviour by powerful men). One of the things that numerous male historians have explained to me is the terrible effect that professionalisation has had on the academy, forgetting (or perhaps remembering) that it is professionalisation that enables women to do things like take maternity leave, or raise a complaint about sexual harassment with HR.

Despite this, male historians also enjoy explaining what excellent allies they are to female historians. Male historians have often explained to me what wonderful feminists they are; how important feminism is; how terrible it is, of course, that there is still such gender inequality within the academy; how much we need to work to overcome this. This explanation is, often, the limit to their solidarity. An important part of male academic feminism is the ability to explain to women why, in any *particular* case under discussion, the problem is not gender. They accept that there are many problems in this world faced distinctly and specifically by women: they are self-professed feminists, after all! But this *specific* issue is not about gender: we, the women, are mistaken.

Sometimes they cannot let this issue go: they send us emails, after our discussion, to reiterate once again just how mistaken we are. The edited collection with only one token female contributor looks bad, of course: but all the women said no, or don't work on the topic, or just aren't senior enough to be taken seriously. The state-of-the-field panel had a female chair, and anyway women aren't as interested in these Big Questions, and they did *want* to take female contributions from the audience but women speak so quietly. Whether it is about our treatment by students, the reception of our work within our field, or the expectation of the performance of emotional labour with students or colleagues, male historians love to explain the many and varied factors in these topics that mean that gender is – surprise! – not relevant.

And, of course, male historians like to explain what history actually is. When E. H. Carr asked and answered this question, he did so by crafting a discipline populated entirely by men: 'The historian is of *his* own age, and is bound to it by the conditions of human existence ... the use of language forbids *him* to be neutral.'[7] Carr was himself of his own age, and male historians now concede that female historians exist, at least theoretically. But their citation practices often do not. Male historians explain their fields and their topics, often, through reference to other men; they are less willing, or able, to do so by citing women. As Sara Ahmed has written, citation is both a scholarly and a political act: 'Citation is how we acknowledge our debt to those who came before,' and citations can thus sustain or undermine structures and 'institutions of patriarchal whiteness'.[8] And when male historians choose to explain topics, or concepts, or whole fields, through reference only to other (white) men, that exclusion is an intensely political act. Adrienne Rich wrote about the moment of 'psychic disequilibrium' that comes when someone with authority 'describes the world and you are not in it'.[9] This psychic disequilibrium has been experienced by many women, who have found their work written out in the explanations of male historians.

This can be especially cutting when male historians explain the ways in which their own work is ground-breaking and original: the gaps that they identify in the field are, often, merely the spaces where women's work goes unseen. Lucy Robinson has written about the difficulty of being a feminist historian who is committed to kindness and collaboration, but working in a wider discipline that does not value these things, which leads to the jarring experience of listening to other historians describing a 'hole' in the existing research that is, in fact, the space in which you know your own work sits.[10] Many a female historian has been surprised to hear a male historian explaining his invention of a field, in which she has been working for some time, perhaps her whole career.

There is no conclusion, really, to an essay of this nature (perhaps I should have asked a male historian to explain how he would finish it). As Ahmed has written, there is the danger that 'to give the problem a name can be experienced as *magnifying the problem*'; as she points out, 'you can become a problem by naming a problem'.[11] But she also urges us to continue to name these problems: to insist that change is necessary. The 'exhaustion of having to keep struggling to transform disciplines' is real, but worthwhile.[12] As Solnit argued in her original essay, 'Most women fight wars on two fronts, one for whatever the putative topic is and one simply for the right to speak, to have ideas, to be acknowledged to be in possession of facts and truths, to have value, to be a human being.'[13] Male historians will never stop explaining things. Female historians might, one day, stop listening.

Notes

Ben Mechen and Jack Saunders listened to me talk about this piece at length without ever protesting that not ALL male historians. Chris Cook offered helpful, precise suggestions, and general enthusiastic support, while resisting the urge to explain anything at all. This essay is for Emily Baughan, Anna Bocking-Welch, Tehila Sasson, and Eve Colpus, with whom I have sat, open-mouthed, as men explain things to us: I hope to continue dissecting this behaviour and laughing at these men with you for many years to come.

1 Rebecca Solnit, 'Men Explain Things to Me', Guernica, 20 August 2012, www.guernicamag.com/rebecca-solnit-men-explain-things-to-me/ (accessed 29 August 2019).
2 *Ibid.*
3 Carolyn Steedman, *A Landscape for a Good Woman* (London: Virago, 1996), 2.
4 Solnit, 'Men Explain Things to Me'.
5 Siri Hustvedt, 'Knausgaard Writes like a Woman', Literary Hub, 10 December 2015, https://lithub.com/knausgaard-writes-like-a-woman/ (accessed 29 August 2019).
6 Clara Guiberg, 'Big University Gender Pay Gap Revealed', BBC News, 29 March 2019, www.bbc.co.uk/news/business-47723950 (accessed 29 August 2019). This pay gap is considerably worse for women of colour.
7 E. H. Carr, *What Is History?* (London: Penguin, 1990), 24–25 (emphasis added).
8 Sara Ahmed, *Living a Feminist Life* (Durham, NC: Duke University Press, 2015), 17.
9 Adrienne Rich, 'Invisibility in Academe', in *Blood, Bread and Poetry: Selected Prose, 1979–1985* (London: Virago, 1987), 199.
10 In her piece, Robinson thanks Florence Sutcliffe-Braithwaite for reminding the room of her work – 'she footnoted me in her question' – which highlights the work done by informal networks of feminist solidarity in resisting the explanations of male historians. Lucy Robinson, 'Referencing Sisterhood: Ego, Guilt and Being Kind', Now That's What I Call History, 21 September 2018, https://proflrobinson.com/2018/09/21/referencing-sisterhood-ego-guilt-and-being-kind/#more-1764 (accessed 29 August 2019).
11 Sara Ahmed, 'Introduction: Sexism – A Problem with a Name', *New Formations: A Journal of Culture/Theory/Politics*, 86 (2015), 8–9.
12 *Ibid.*, 6.
13 Solnit, 'Men Explain Things to Me'.

Part II

Histories

4

'Formal qualifications for full masculine status'? Challenging the fragmentation of the male life cycle through the First World War pension archives

Jessica Meyer

On 25 April 1959, C. H. Mardon, registrar in the district of Kent (subdistrict Maidstone), registered the death of LA1, age sixty-six, licensed victualler.[1] LA1 had died at home of carcinoma of the lung, certified by his doctor; the registrar had been informed of his death by LA1's son. This information, a matter of public record, can be found not only in the official records of death, but also in LA1's personal pension file relating to his disability from the First World War, one of 22,829 such files held in the PIN 26 section of the National Archives (London). LA1's death certificate, with its wealth of personal information, including residential address, profession, the fact that he had a son, and that his son lived at the same address, was required, along with a raft of other paperwork, for the official closure of the file because, since 29 August 1919, LA1 had been in receipt of a weekly pension, awarded for life. A gunshot wound to his right arm, which he had received at Arras in 1917, was deemed by ministry medical officials on 29 August 1923 to permanently incapacitate him at a rate of 25 per cent,[2] entitling him to a pension of 10s 10d a week for life.[3]

The process by which this final level of disablement was arrived at can be traced through medical cards and treatment records dating from the point of LA1's first wounding, as well as through the regular reports of medical inspections conducted by the Ministry of Pensions between his discharge from the military and the date of his final award. These contain extensive details of his physical condition over nearly seven years. The file also contains records of LA1's mobility, most notably from a non-commercial address in Maidstone to the pub he appears to have run until his retirement, and his military discharge records, which include his enlistment records, detailing his place of birth and pre-war occupation.

LA1's pension records, therefore, give insight into his life from birth to death. Nor is he unusual. Not all PIN 26 files contain a death certificate, as many men received a pension for illnesses and wounds deemed to have ultimately incapacitated them at a rate less than 20 per cent, meaning that they were eventually awarded a final, fixed-period terminal pension or terminal gratuity, or a combination of the two. Nonetheless, all the personal pension files held in the PIN 26 section of the archives contain material providing medical and demographic information, as well as details of military service. Many also contain additional information about marriages and marriage failures, children born and raised, work opportunities taken and missed, and, in a significant number of cases, the voices of the men themselves and their families, arguing and advocating with the ministry through personal correspondence. They thus form a rich resource for historians of masculinity interested in the quotidian lives of men in twentieth-century Britain.

The scale of the material held in the archive, however, combined with structural issues around the cataloguing of this material, which has tended to focus on the interests of family historians, has often made use of this resource problematic for historians examining broader socio-cultural questions. This chapter draws on material from a database of the demographic information contained in these files, created by the Men, Women and Care project, to consider how such data might be used by historians of twentieth-century British masculinities.[4] In particular, it examines how the longer term trajectory of the life records of individual men recorded in the files directs us to think about masculinity in terms of life cycles rather than periodisations, usually defined in the twentieth century by wars and global conflicts. It considers how applying approaches used by women's historians, early modernists, and historians of disability in relation to gender, temporality, and the life cycle may help to address recent challenges raised to rethinking our approach to the study of modern British masculinities.

The clearest articulation of such a challenge has come from John Tosh in 'The History of Masculinity: An Outdated Concept?'. Arguing that in the history of masculinity, 'questions of behaviour and agency have ... been sidetracked by a historical practice dominated by questions of meaning and representation',[5] Tosh calls instead for a renewed focus on individual agency and experience as a way of developing a 'culturally inflected social history which keeps its moorings in social experience'.[6] Such criticisms have a clear relevance for histories of First World War impairment in Britain, the field in which the PIN 26 files have had the most to contribute to date. Such histories have often focused on the interpretation of texts and images representing war-disabled masculinities in ways which run the risk of writing the historical actors themselves out of the record. The works of Ana Carden-Coyne and Gabriel Koureas on the disabled body in the memorial cultures of war demonstrates some of the ways in which post-war British society enabled the social and political marginalisation of disabled men without necessarily giving voice to men's experiences of this exclusion.[7] Deborah Cohen, Fiona Reid, Julie Anderson, and Seth Koven have all explored how such marginalisation functioned at an institutional rather than a personal, level, exposing some of the power dynamics which shaped the lives of war-disabled men.[8] Yet the comparative richness of these institutional archival records risks obscuring the subjectivities of these men. We enlarge our understanding into how society positioned and treated them without necessarily gaining insight into how they themselves experienced such treatment.

One way of addressing these concerns is to use gender as a lens through which to explore disability and war-attributable impairment. Nicoletta Gullace's analysis of the white feather campaign, for example, integrates analysis of historically contextualised symbols of cowardice with the lived experiences of men to discuss the gendered wartime relationships of power which policed both the bodies of men and the sexualities of women. Yet in exposing the retrospective nature of men's memories of the white feather campaign, Gullace's work, which itself relies, as she points out, on retrospective memories of gender shaming through white feathers, returns us to the problem of how historians can access historical subjectivities unmediated by representation, whether through language, visual imagery, or other forms of expression.[9] Even in the case of immediately contemporaneous source material, such as the letters of J. B. Middlebrook examined by Wendy Gagen,[10] the language analysed is inevitably shaped by Middlebrook's socio-cultural location as an articulate, educated member of the middle classes. The understanding of his lived experience is, at one level, only available to us through our reading and interpretation of the texts which he has left behind, texts which only cover the (albeit long) period of his hospitalisation. There does not appear to be an equivalent record of his life as an amputee after his discharge from both hospital and the military, with most of his public biography focusing on his career in the Methodist Church. As a result, Middlebrook, like the men discussed by Gullace, is defined in the historical record almost entirely as a disabled *soldier* of the First World War rather than as a disabled *man*.

Personal records of the sort created by Middlebrook are vital to our understanding of male subjectivities. Such material can be interpreted both in terms of the construction of subjective gender identities as relational through the construction of relationships in writing practices,[11] and as representations of an individual's personal negotiation of socio-cultural gender norms through the employment of generic conventions.[12] Yet the official records of the state and its institutions also have a significant part to play in our analysis if we are to arrive at the sort of social history Tosh argues for. This can be seen in Bruce Scates's work on the repatriation files of the Australian Imperial Force which have been digitised by the National Archives of Australia as part of the Project Albany initiative. These records contain three file types, those relating to military service, those relating to clinical or hospital treatment, and those relating to pension provision.[13] The range of information they contain allows the historian, according to Scates, to 'bridge what has long been a historical hiatus between wartime service and postwar experience'. He uses several case studies to demonstrate how such analysis can enable a reinterpretation of the lived experience of twentieth-century veteran identity and physical disability, including that of Bertram Byrnes. Byrnes suffered serious disfigurement by a gunshot wound which left him 'Permanently and Totally Incapacitated', with difficult swallowing, which caused digestive problems, as well as severe headaches and partial blindness. He survived until 1965, most of that time with no income other than his pension. While these records make, as Scates writes, 'for confronting reading', they also challenge historical understandings of facial disfigurements as stigmatising in interwar anglophone society. Not only did Byrnes marry, thereby fulfilling one of the central requirements of mature normative masculinity, he also 'never expressed shame at [his] injury. To the contrary, he saw himself as a returned man who had "done his bit" – a strong sense of moral economy informed his tireless petitioning. His status, then, was that of a veteran rather than a victim. He would march and wear his medals on Anzac Day.'[14]

Scates's analysis demonstrates how official records help to bridge Byrnes's wartime and post-war experiences, although in ways which continue to locate his identity almost entirely within his wartime service, as 'a man marred by war'.[15] This is unsurprising in an analysis located in war and archival studies rather than the history of masculinity. Yet the contents of the repatriation files, like the pension files, are suggestive of contributions to other histories and historical approaches. Byrnes mobilised his disabled body in his petitioning in ways which provide insight into his experience of the social and political economies of post-war Australia. Similarly, LA1's records reflect the (re)construction of disabled masculinity across the changing social landscape of twentieth-century England, not simply in but through time. There is thus great potential in approaching these records from the perspective of cultural history and the history of masculinity in particular.

PIN 26

It is the potential richness of the material held in PIN 26 files for providing insight into the lives of ordinary men and their families that prompted the creation of a database of information by the Men, Women and Care project.

While the surviving 22,829 files that form the project's corpus represent only approximately 2 per cent of all such files created in relation to this conflict,[16] they have, to date, proved complex to access for social and cultural historians due to the way in which they have been regarded and consequently catalogued. Deemed at one point of no historical value, and nearly destroyed entirely,[17] the only searchable metadata attached to them in the Discovery catalogue of the National Archives is the name, rank, regiment, and disability of the individual, the last of these relying on the language of the original diagnosis. The terms used are often highly subjective, reliant on an individual doctor's perspective at a given place and time, and regularly fail to reflect changes in condition or diagnosis that occurred over time. The case of EC2 is instructive here. Having initially been pensioned for a gunshot wound and disorder action of the heart (DAH) in 1919, his final pension of £2 a week for life was for the chronic nephritis that resulted from his original injury and which was listed as his cause of death in 1925.[18] The structural limits of the catalogue have meant that systematic analysis around analytic categories pertinent to social and cultural history has been extremely laborious. While the records have been used by historians through close readings of individual files, analysis of the sample as a whole has been impossible, while the selection of files for analysis has rarely been subject to robust sampling methodology. The Men, Women and Care project began the process of creating a searchable database of demographic information and a wider range of metadata related to these files to enable more systematic sampling, for instance, by region, date of birth, or need for hospital treatment. Information about file contents can also be used to identify files potentially useful to future researchers as sources for close reading, providing added value to the current catalogue.

The database is thus intended to make it easier for historians to interrogate this material more effectively, both qualitatively and quantitatively. Yet each file in and of itself contains, as Alexia Moncrieff has noted, only a snapshot of the lives lived by these men.[19] In LA1's case, the period between 1923 and 1959 is almost entirely blank. His marriage in 1919 is noted as is the death of his wife in 1952, but not the birth of his children, although at least one survived him. His listing at death as a retired licensed victualler would seem to indicate that he remained a pub landlord, although not whether of the same pub throughout nor when he retired. In comparison to the information provided on his life as a soldier during the four and a half years of his service, that relating to his life as a disabled ex-serviceman, husband, father, worker, taxpayer, and head of household in Britain in the first half of the twentieth century is limited.

The archive, for all its richness, is therefore not unproblematic. It does present the opportunity for exploring the lived experiences of men from a range of backgrounds who served in the First World War, but these experiences are episodic and uneven across both the sample and individual lives. However, this very unevenness provides an important opportunity to bridge the divide between men's wartime and post-war lives in ways which challenge the historiographic tendency to categorise experience by period. By hiving off experiences into discrete, periodised categories, historians of masculinity risk failing to fully access male agency across time and to appreciate both the importance of the life cycle to modern masculinities and the potentialities of alternative temporalities in reading male life experience. The history of war disability, through its bridging of periods in individual lives, provides an opportunity, yet to be fully exploited, to rethink twentieth-century British masculinities in these terms in ways which complicate our understanding not only of the gendered legacy of wars across the century but also of changing normative constructions of masculinity. Drawing on approaches already employed by historians of women, as well as early modernists and historians of disability, we may start to develop a practice that acknowledges the agency of men as problematic historical actors in their own right and across time, rather than as representations of the generically male subject at a given moment in time.

Challenging periodisation

The discrete definition of male roles within limited periods is, perhaps, a particular problem for twentieth-century European histories of masculinity. The tendency to periodise the history of the century through its wars, both hot and cold, has led to historical practices which focus on men's experiences either during or between conflicts, without necessarily acknowledging the extent to which periods could overlap or how individual lives encompassed multiple periods. The literature on generational transfer, such as Joel Morley's work on the relationships between veterans of the First World War and combatants of the Second, suggests one way to approach continuities and discontinuities in understandings of masculinity across the period.[20] Scope remains, however, for examining how men's lives and their sense of self as gendered social actors was shaped by shifting social meanings across periods in relation to peace as well as war.

Here I would suggest that the field has much to learn from the approaches taken by women's history and early modernists. In the former field, the work of social historians such as Selina Todd and Pamela Cox shows how women's identities and status as economic and gendered actors changed across time in response not only to socio-political contexts but also their position in the life cycle.[21] This life cycle approach has, in turn, been used by a new generation of historians such as Claire Martin, who has applied it to women's knowledge of sex and sexuality in early twentieth-century Britain. The focus on women's lived experience of sexual health and knowledge across the life cycle, from learning about sex through menstruation, pregnancy, and childbirth to the menopause, illuminates the shifting social and political contexts in which women lived their lives, rather than being defined by these contexts.[22]

To a certain extent, Tosh has himself pioneered this approach in his work on young men's coming of age in the middle-class home of the nineteenth century,[23] as well as his argument, in 'Hegemonic Masculinity and the History of Gender', that cultural history 'prioritises the current "moment" over a longer term perspective'.[24] However, Tosh's own foregrounding of a particular moment in the male life cycle – namely fatherhood – across his period of analysis risks obscuring the social, cultural, and political changes across time that individual men would encounter as they moved from boyhood to young manhood to masculine maturity, with each stage nuanced by its own set of complex and contingent power relations. This is not to suggest that the shifting social significance of fathers across time is not vital to our understanding of the history of gender and gender relations.[25] This approach does, however, point more clearly to continuity and change across time in relation to our understanding of masculinities, rather than exposing the depths of complexity of those masculinities at any given point in time.

Here the intricate constructions of masculine hierarchies based on age and position within the life cycle in the early modern period, as discussed by Alexandra Shepard, are instructive.[26] While never as clearly articulated in the twentieth century, the schemas of male aging that she outlines have relevance for a range of social and political changes in the period, from welfare provision to military conscription, from educational policy to periodic moral panics over youth gangs and drug use. Understanding how men experienced multiple stages of manhood *across* periods of pre-war, wartime, interwar, and post-war, rather than simply in relation to either a single period or a fixed stage in their life cycle, has the potential to shift analytic focus towards the more culturally inflected social histories called for by Tosh.

In addition, the work of historians of disability such as Joshua St. Pierre offers ways of thinking about how men experience time itself as both disabled and gendered actors. Drawing on feminist and queer theory, St. Pierre uses the experience of stuttering as a case study to argue that consideration of 'bodily temporalities', as exposed through queer/crip readings of time, enables a questioning, even a subversion, of 'straight-male' future-directed linearity in our interpretations of lives and life cycles. Such distinctions provide scope for questioning how disabled ex-servicemen's expectations of the male life cycle were disrupted and changed in the face of their new experiences of bodily time, now out of sync with those they might have held prior to illness or injury. In particular, the challenges of such disabled bodies to reproductive and familial time, 'where futures are in question, cut short, unable to be projected into domestic (heteronormative) bliss',[27] resonate throughout the pension files. How men negotiated these challenges across their lives can provide insight into both how normative expectations of appropriate masculinity altered across time and life stage, and how such social expectations interacted with subjective individual experience.

Rethinking temporalities

How, then, can we use the material in the PIN 26 archives to shift our analytic focus away from periodisation and other hegemonic temporalities? In the first instance, the longevity of many of the files provides insight into individual lives across a protracted period of time. While many of the files were subject to four-year closure assessments under the 1921 War Pensions Act,[28] and thus end in 1922 or 1923, a significant number span much of the twentieth century, with the last file closing in 1987. These long-opened files reflect one of two scenarios. Either, like LA1, the pensioner had been awarded a pension for life, or else the pensioner objected to some aspect of how his pension was assessed, whether the diagnosis of his disability, the amount awarded, or the treatment offered, and remained in contact with the ministry through appeals and letters of complaint.[29] In the first case, the files can have large gaps, where contact between the ministry and the pension was minimal, although they continue to reflect changes in political management and the national economy through modifications to the amount of the weekly award and the way it was paid out. Additionally, as in LA1's case, social details of a particular moment – that of the pensioner's death – are also captured, allowing for the, albeit fragmentary and partial, reconstruction of a life.

In the second case, more detail of the shape of individual lives across the entire period can be gleaned from the personal correspondence, statements of case, and letters of support written by advocates that form part of the appeals process. The work of Moncrieff on the pensions of men who emigrated overseas illustrates this. In her exploration of the impact of distance on state care provision, Moncrieff traces patterns of emigration among pensioners seeking work outside the difficult labour market which they faced in Britain through correspondence located in their pension files.[30] 'These letters', she notes, let slip the intimate details of people's lives, as individuals shared their circumstances with bureaucrats, and provide insight into the ways families interacted with state and imperial administrations. At the same time as the individual's voice can be heard in this archive – as they petition the Ministry and shape their stories to engender sympathy from officials – this archive also divulges how these narratives were received, understood and judged. The cases discussed in ... highlight the politics of respectability as they reveal both its performance and how that performance was interpreted.[31]

Tracing lives in this way thus enables understanding of the intersections between masculinity, domesticity, and imperialism as all three categories of analysis were subjected to stresses and change.

Intersections with a fourth key category of analysis can also be discerned here, that of work. Required to work even within a pensions system which was designed to compensate for '"loss of amenity", not "loss of earning capacity"', the men studied by Moncrieff found it particularly hard to secure work in an economy where 'disabled soldiers are not over popular as candidates for jobs'.[32] The pensions records reveal the dominance of Canada and the Unites States as destinations for men seeking manual work, although Australia, New Zealand, and India all feature as significant alternatives, pointing to the practical as well as imaginative importance of empire to metropolitan British masculine identity in this period. These files thus provide source material for the exploration of the 'sense of personal attachment between metropole and colonies [which formed a] ... basis for pro-empire sentiment in Britain', which Tosh identifies as a significant area for further discussion by historians of twentieth-century British masculinities.[33]

As Tosh notes, however, such sources are 'no more transparent or authentic than any other personal sources. One has to be alert all the time to the distortions of self-making.'[34] Indeed, the nature of the appeal to or challenging of authority implicit in the type of material contained in correspondence with a government department lends itself to particular types of self-construction designed to elicit a favourable response.[35] However, through their very act of self-fashioning, such material exposes both the gendered values which shaped lived experience and the cultural imaginaries that influenced the ways in which such values and experience was articulated. EB1, for example, emigrated to Canada in an attempt to 'start in an outdoor way of business' with the support of his father-in-law. His struggles to do so were consistently articulated to the ministry in terms of economic independence and domestic support of his sons.[36] By contrast, the report on his condition in 1930, after he had returned to England where he worked as a pub landlord, emphasises the labour of his wife in caring for her husband and assisting in his work.[37] The geographic context in which

EB1 found himself had changed, but so too had his point in the life cycle. The sons who he struggled to provide for in Canada had left home, with his relationship to his wife becoming central to his struggles to live with his disability. The ways in which men negotiated their sense of impaired masculinity arising from disability over time can thus be seen to provide a space where men could articulate experiences of emigration in terms that draw on the cultural texts of both empire and gender.

Alongside, and deeply implicated in, the imperial narratives mobilised by the pensioner emigrants run stories of domestic strain and breakdown.[38] These illustrate Tosh's point that 'the largest category of emigrant men were husbands with children: men who had achieved the formal qualifications for full masculine status, but whose circumstances usually made a bitter mockery of it; one might call them casualties of the patriarchal order.'[39] Emigrants were, of course, by no means the only such casualties, particularly in interwar Britain. War disability, with its paradoxical power to rob men of their claims to or hopes for full masculine status through the performance of the ultimate hegemonically masculine role of good husband and father, created a section of the male population, within as well as beyond Britain, who might be classified as acknowledged casualties of patriarchy. What a more comprehensive examination of the pensions archive demonstrates is not just the extent to which war disability contributed to this category of masculinity in this period. Approaching the archive in this way also highlights the ways in which the hegemonically dominant identity of the soldier was not merely a temporary one for many men, but a contingent one during the years of war as well as after.[40] The discharge papers included in almost all files allow for a more robust and representative analysis of the number of men who enlisted with a less than A1 health classification, enlisted over or under age, or served a significant part of their service in non-combatant units behind the lines than has been undertaken to date. Such information illustrates how, even within the familiar periodisation of the war years, men's individual location within the life cycle shaped their subjective relationship to cultural constructions of the male ideal. Regular inclusion of military enquiry records, meanwhile, indicates the extent to which men were wounded accidentally rather than in the gender-appropriate context of the front line, challenging the hegemonic dominance of the identity of 'soldier'. Qualitative analysis of the sample thus helps to complicate our understanding of what it meant to be a British man during the First World War.

Yet by forcing us to look beyond the temporal limits of the war years, these files have an even more important role to play in nuancing our understanding of how masculinity was coded in terms of male hegemonies across the twentieth century. This data also allows us to identify not only the men within the sample who received allowances for spouses and dependents, but also those who did not, and thus did not achieve the 'formal qualifications for full masculine status' of marriage and, more particularly, children.[41] The dominance of fatherhood in the historiography of nineteenth- and twentieth-century British masculinities has tended to sideline men who did not have children, a reflection of the power of the sort of heteronormative male timeframes which St. Pierre identifies as controlling constructions of disabled masculinities. The challenge that disabled male bodies pose to these normative cultural constructions of time and life cycle suggests that childless men potentially form a highly significant category within the sample of the war disabled. Locating their experience in the historical record allows us additional insight into the lived experience of such marginalised forms of masculinity, as well as the opportunity to explore men's engagement with hegemonic ideals in their articulations of masculinity. In bringing the experiences of men as sons, brothers, and in-laws to the fore, it allows for the exploration of the functioning of complex family structures of care across time, encompassing the emotional, the physical, and the financial. Thus the support provided to AF1's wife by her siblings and in-laws, as discussed by Eilis Boyle, can be seen to divide along gender lines, with men providing financial support and advocacy, the women domestic aid and nursing care.[42] CE1's complaint that 'I am now living on my wife's people', due to the paucity of his pension, speaks not to his sense of failure as a masculine provider but also the ways in which the dependence of disability shaped generational relationships between parents and children.[43] In combination with Michael Roper's exploration of the experiences of children growing up with war-disabled fathers and Marina Larsson's work on the Anzac experience of war disability,[44] such analysis will enable further insight into the legacy of war on both families and British society more broadly in gendered terms. It also allows us to map the changing nature of gendered understandings of family structures, and men's place within it, across the twentieth century.

Conclusion

As episodic as the PIN 26 files are, therefore, they have an important role to play in shaping our understanding of masculinities in twentieth-century Britain and the significance of both war and peace to gender as a socio-cultural force in the period. Both as individual files to be explored qualitatively and as a sample to be explored quantitatively, these files offer insight into changing perceptions, individual and collective, of masculinity over time. The genesis of their creation may have been a particular war, and the exceptional and unexpected physical and mental damage caused by the length and violence of that war. The stories they allow us glimpses into, however, are those of men – and their families and associates – whose lives encompassed significant periods of peace and even other wars, with their own effects on the socio-cultural significance of gender and gender relations. As disabled men, and men whose disabilities were obtained at the point of or beyond the achievement of full masculine status through the life cycle markers of employment, marriage, and fatherhood, their stories, told across time, have the potential to challenge normative framings of masculinity in relation to both period and life cycle.

Approaching the men whose stories are at least partially told in these files thus helps us to see these men more clearly, in spite of archival fragmentation, as individuals whose gendered identities were shaped by all the stages in their life cycle, not just their four years of war service, however profound the impact of that war service may have been on their bodies and minds. By seeing them holistically as men rather than as facets of masculinity – as soldiers, fathers, workers – we can more fully appreciate the multiplicity of masculine constructions which combine to shape lived experiences of individuals as well as the society in which they live.

Notes

1 Death certificate, PIN 26/235, 25 April 1959, The National Archives, London (hereafter TNA). Throughout this chapter, pensioners and their family members named in the PIN 26 archives will be anonymised via unique alphanumeric codes. This is in line with the practice agreed in the Men, Women and Care project's ethical review, PVAR 14–065.
2 For details of the schedule of impairment used by the Ministry of Pensions to evaluate war disability, see Joanna Bourke, *Dismembering the Male: Men's Bodies, Britain and the Great War* (London: Reaktion Books, 1996), 65–68.
3 PIN 26/235, *passim.*
4 'Men, Women and Care: The Gendering of Formal and Informal Care-Giving in Interwar Britain', European Research Council Starting Grant Project Number 638694, ran at the University of Leeds from 2015 to 2020.
5 John Tosh, 'The History of Masculinity: An Outdated Concept?', in John H. Arnold and Sean Brady (eds), *What Is Masculinity: Historical Dynamics form Antiquity to the Contemporary World* (Basingstoke: Palgrave Macmillan, 2011), 18.
6 Tosh, 'The History of Masculinity', 31.
7 Ana Carden-Coyne, *Reconstructing the Body: Classicism, Modernism and the First World War* (Oxford: Oxford University Press, 2009); Gabriel Koureas, *Memory, Masculinity and National Identity in British Visual Culture, 1914–1930: A Study of 'Unconquerable Manhood'* (Aldershot: Ashgate, 2007).

8 Deborah Cohen, *The War Come Home: Disabled Veterans in Britain and Germany, 1914–1939* (Berkeley: University of California Press, 2001); Fiona Reid, *Broken Men: Shell Shock, Treatment and Recovery in Britain, 1914–1930* (London: Continuum, 2010); Julie Anderson, *War, Disability and Rehabilitation: 'Soul of a Nation'* (Manchester: Manchester University Press, 2011); Seth Koven, 'Remembering and Dismemberment: Crippled Children, Wounded Soldiers and the Great War in Britain', *American Historical Review*, 99 (1994), 1167–1202.

9 Michael Roper, 'Slipping Out of View: Subjectivity and Emotion in Gender History', *History Workshop Journal*, 59 (2005), 57–72; Graham Dawson, *Soldier Heroes: British Adventure, Empire and the Imagining of Masculinities* (London: Routledge, 1994), 3–5.

10 Wendy J. Gagen, 'Remastering the Body, Renegotiating Gender: Physical Disability and Masculinity during the First World War, the Case of J. B. Middlebrook', *European Review of History: Revue européenne d'histoire*, 14 (2007), 525–541.

11 Roper, 'Slipping Out of View', 63–65.

12 Jessica Meyer, *Men of War: Masculinity and the First World War in Britain* (Basingstoke: Palgrave Macmillan, 2009), 10–13.

13 Bruce Scates, 'How War Came Home: Reflections on the Digitisation of Australia's Repatriation Files', *History Australia*, 16:1 (2019), 191–192.

14 *Ibid.*, 199–202.

15 *Ibid.*, 201.

16 The remaining files were either badly damaged during the Second World War or culled from the archive in a space-saving exercise in the 1990s.

17 See 'Ministry of Pensions and Successors: Selected First World War Pensions Award Files', Discovery Catalogue, TNA, https://discovery.nationalarchives.gov.uk/details/r/C11539 (accessed 17 April 2019). Additional information on the sampling process was provided to the author in an email from Professor Jay Winter, 13 November 2001.

18 PIN 26/273.

19 Alexia Moncrieff, 'Imperial Pensioners, Domestic Violence and the British Ministry of Pensions: State Involvement in Family Life', paper delivered at the No End to the War: Cultures of Violence and Care in the Aftermath of the First World War Conference, University of Manchester, 24 January 2019.

20 J. M. Morley, '"Dad Never Said Much but …": Young Men and Great War Veterans in Day-to-Day Life in Inter-war Britain', *Twentieth Century British History*, 29 (2018), 199–224.

21 Selina Todd, *Young Women, Work and Family in England 1918–1950* (Oxford: Oxford University Press, 2005); Pamela Cox, Heather Shore, Zoe Alker, and Barry Godfrey, 'Tracking the Gendered Life Courses of Care Leavers in 19th-Century Britain', *Longitudinal and Life Course Studies*, 9:1 (2018), 115–128.

22 Claire Martin, 'Bodies of Knowledge: Science, Popular Culture, and Working-Class Women's Experiences of the Life Cycle in Yorkshire, c.1900–1940' (PhD diss., University of Leeds, 2018).

23 John Tosh, *A Man's Place: Masculinity and the Middle-Class Home in Victorian England* (New Haven: Yale University Press, 1999).
24 John Tosh, 'Hegemonic Masculinities and the History of Gender', in Stefan Dudink, Karen Hagemann, and John Tosh (eds), *Masculinities in Politics and War: Gendering Modern History* (Manchester: Manchester University Press, 2004), 52.
25 Julie-Marie Strange, *Fatherhood and the British Working Class, 1865–1914* (Cambridge: Cambridge University Press, 2015); Laura King, *Family Men: Fatherhood and Masculinity in Britain, 1914–1960* (Oxford: Oxford University Press, 2015).
26 Alexandra Shepard, *Meanings of Manhood in Early Modern England* (Oxford: Oxford University Press, 2003), 55.
27 Joshua St. Pierre, 'Distending Straight-Masculine Time: A Phenomenology of the Disabled Speaking Body', *Hypatia*, 3 (2015), 54.
28 Helen Bettinson, '"Lost Souls in the House of Restoration"? British Ex-servicemen and War Disability Pensions, 1914–1930' (PhD diss., University of East Anglia, 2002), 74–78.
29 *Ibid.*, 4.
30 Alexia Moncrieff, 'Gendered Respectability and the Maintenance of Imperial Order: Family Breakdown and the Ministry of Pensions after the First World War' (unpublished paper, 2018). On the employment difficulties faced by disabled ex-servicemen in Britain, see Meyer, *Men of War*, 107.
31 Moncrieff, 'Gendered Respectability', 4–5.
32 JL1, Letter to the Secretary, Ministry of Pensions, 16 July 1924, PIN 26/19942, TNA.
33 Tosh, 'The History of Masculinity', 27.
34 *Ibid.*
35 Bettinson, '"Lost Souls in the House of Restoration"', 9.
36 This association of Canada with the outdoors chimes with the narrative of Canadian muscular masculinity in this period identified by David B. Marshall, '"A Canoe, a Tent and God's Great Out-of-Doors": Muscular Christianity and the Flight from Domesticity, 1880s–1930s', in Heather Ellis and Jessica Meyer (eds), *Masculinity and the Other: Historical Perspectives* (Newcastle upon Tyne: Cambridge Scholars Publishing, 2009), 23–42.
37 PIN 26/21230, TNA, *passim*.
38 Alexia Moncrieff, 'Assessing Respectability: Disabled British Veterans, Family Breakdown and the State after the First World War', *Australian Journal of Politics and History*, forthcoming.
39 Tosh, 'The History of Masculinity', 27.
40 Helen McCartney, *Citizen Soldiers: The Liverpool Territorials in the First World War* (Cambridge: Cambridge University Press, 2005), 2–3.
41 Tosh, 'The History of Masculinity', 27.
42 Eilis Boyle, 'Gender and Care in Interwar Britain: An Examination of the Care Provision and Experiences of Care for Facially-Wounded and War-Neurotic Ex-servicemen' (PhD diss., University of Leeds, 2020).

43 CE1, Letter to the Ministry of Pensions, 9 April 1920, PIN 26/21580, TNA.
44 Michael Roper, *Afterlives of War: A Descendants' History* (Manchester: Manchester University Press, 2023). Marina Larsson, *Shattered Anzacs: Living with the Scars of War* (Sydney: University of New South Wales Press, 2009).

5

Reimagining working-class masculinities in the twentieth century

Helen Smith

This chapter argues that region and work have had the greatest impact on how men lived and conceptualised their sense of self in twentieth-century Britain. In developing this idea, it shows how the historical production of masculinities can be mapped and understood outside of traditional narratives of war and crisis. These narratives have focused the historical understanding of masculinities on perceived moments of change, and anomalies to broader patterns of continuity, rather than longer and deeper continuations of experience. Set alongside the importance of differences of class, focusing on work and region thus allows for a new engagement with 'ordinary' masculinities and the way that these operated within everyday life. It also allows us to shift attention from metropolitan or elite masculinities and to give due consideration to the experiences of provincial and working-class men who have often been marginalised within historical scholarship.[1]

Work is an experience that most men, regardless of marital status, sexuality, or lifestyle, had in common during the twentieth century, while individual industries, and workplaces, in different regions made men's experiences specific. This juxtaposition between the shared and quotidian and the unique and exceptional emphasises the importance of work and the workplace as sites of both collective and individual identity: men could make their masculine identity in relation to work as well as to engage with more collective identities based around class and politics. Not only is work crucial to understanding 'ordinary' working-class masculinities, but it is also crucial to a working-class history of modern and contemporary British society.

Because of the primacy of work and the influence of place (particularly non-metropolitan) working-class masculinities remained remarkably stable in the face of the big military, political, and social events often credited with precipitating crisis. I argue that it was only when the policies of the 1970s and 1980s exacerbated the end of industry in Britain that these masculinities finally fractured and were remade. This chapter thus offers an alternative theoretical and geographical framework for the history of masculinities in modern Britain through the lens of work and regionality. It foregrounds the importance of late twentieth-century deindustrialisation in disrupting and re-emphasising notions of masculine power, dominance, and social position. Throughout much of the twentieth century, 'ordinary' masculinity could include behaviours, identities, sexual experiences, and values that came to be perceived as unacceptable after the collapse of industry forced many men into unemployment, unskilled, or white-collar work; thereby destabilising long-held notions of masculine identity.[2] The stability of masculinity tied to industrial work was lost, and men found different, often more destructive ways to reinforce their masculine identity. These could include violence, binge drinking, drug-taking, casual sex and misogyny, and criminal activities.[3] Of course, working-class men had engaged in these behaviours throughout the twentieth century, but what had been marginalised and regulated by traditional communities (often linked to an industry) became normalised when those communities collapsed.[4] The effect of this can still be felt today in the unstable, insecure, and often toxic masculinity which has come to dominate in the era of Trump and #MeToo.

Particularly when the field first emerged, histories of masculinity in Britain often focused on the middle and upper classes, all male institutions such as the public school, or gentleman's club, wartime experiences, and experiences of, and attitudes towards, domesticity and family life.[5] The growing body of literature on working-class masculinities during the twentieth century has often been rooted in men's lives outside of work, particularly around questions of leisure and unemployment.[6] Exceptions include excellent studies of the impact of work on working-class masculinity at war,[7] men's health,[8] men's responses to industrial welfare,[9] and men's domestic status in post-war Liverpool.[10] I argue here that, alongside this literature, a more sustained study of how the experience of work and workplace relationships shaped masculine identity would add nuance to the breadwinner model. Long accepted as a convincing way of understanding how men of all classes viewed their identity throughout the nineteenth and twentieth centuries, this model is focused on the outcome of work: a wage that allowed a man to provide a home and lifestyle for himself and his family. Despite its compelling nature, it does little to address the cultures and identities linked to the practice and experience of work itself. It also prioritises a heteronormative model of manhood: what about queer men, single men, and men who did not want or were unable to have a family? A focus on the cultures and experiences of work provides a way to address these gaps.

The most dominant theory that has either informed or been challenged by historians of masculinity is that of hegemonic masculinity, as popularised by R. W. Connell in the 1990s. Although, as Ben Griffin has recently argued, power relations between masculinities remain important to histories of masculinity, this theory needs rethinking to take into account the intersectionality of gender with other identities, and the myriad ways in which men actually experienced and performed their masculinity on a daily basis.[11] There is a tension here between theory and experience, which can often be the case when testing out such ideas against more traditional social history techniques, which place lived experience at the heart of analysis. A theoretical approach which has more space for the intricacies of human experience is that of 'everyday life' or 'the everyday'. Although more problematic, and less transparent than, according to Highmore, many social historians assume, the practice of analysing and questioning the ordinary, the overlooked, and the day to day 'can both hide and make vivid a range of social differences', and 'make the invisible, visible'.[12] In this way, the repetition of behaviours and actions, combined with the ways in which individuals move through the familiar spaces or 'micro cultures' of their lives can illuminate how they experienced their various identities, including gender.[13]

Work and the workplace proves a useful way to approach this idea as, historically, for most people, work provided both a regular daily routine and the arena in which they spent most of their lives, allowing for analysis of continuity as much as change. Both the steelworks magazines and the oral history interviews analysed in this chapter allow for privileged access to the day-to-day realities of working in Sheffield's steelworks, their 'micro cultures', and the daily, often mundane, reinforcements and performances of ordinary, working-class masculinity. It then becomes possible to see that if daily life at work changed little for much of the twentieth century, then neither did the masculinity rooted so firmly in such work. Within the steelworks, shift patterns and daily tasks remained similar until the modernisation of the industry began in the mid-1960s. Even then, many men were unaffected by this in their day-to-day jobs, which remained physically demanding.[14] For men in the works, every shift involved potential danger and the need to perform tasks well to be able to hand over to the next set of men clocking on.[15] Peers did not tolerate sloppy work, and 'lazy' men lost status.[16] Alongside this, the daily interactions with workmates on the same journey into work, the same shift pattern, the repetition of workplace stories, and reliance on other men for safety and guidance all helped to form the blueprint of what it meant to be a man.[17] Men bonded over and located their masculinity within their everyday working experiences, and this kept their masculinity stable in the face of macro-historical change – until that change fundamentally altered their everyday experience.

In this chapter, then, to access the day-to day life of men at work, I utilise two sets of material that have been under-used by academic historians: the company magazines of steelworks and the 'Songs of Steel' oral history collection.[18] Business and media historians have studied company magazines, but they are also a rich source for the social and cultural history of working-class men.[19] The contributors to works magazines were often the workers themselves and, largely, workers dictated the content. Sam Smith, an oral historian, conducted the interviews during 2009–2010, as the centrepiece of the HLF-funded project 'Songs of Steel'.[20] As documented by numerous historians, there are myriad problems and benefits to working with oral histories, and to using an archived collection, rather than conducting interviews specific to a project, but they are often vital for insight into lives that have been traditionally marginalised by the historical record.[21] The Songs of Steel interviews provide an in-depth account into the day-to-day life of both the works itself and the men and women who worked there, including the minutiae of their jobs, their relationships, and the social and cultural life associated with work – all crucial to understanding the nexus of working-class masculinity in the area.

South Yorkshire and the steel industry

For working-class men, work was often not just a way of earning money or supporting a family; it provided a framework for how to be a man, and how to engage with class, regional, and political identities. The culture of the workplace could offer opportunities to prove physical toughness, but also opened a space to build affectionate friendships, to access education, and to develop an identity that was influenced by the positive role models of older, more experienced men.[22] In heavy industry, this culture often spilled out of the works to influence the local area. As this chapter demonstrates, a close study of the tangible practicalities of work, alongside the more intangible culture, identities, and emotions associated with it, give an insight both into working-class masculinity outside of the framework of crisis and reaction, and working-class history more broadly. This approach could be used in any region, and with any type of work, but here, the steel industry will be analysed.

Throughout the twentieth century, there were hundreds of workplaces relating to the steel industry in South Yorkshire, ranging from small, artisanal cutlery workshops employing just a few men, to huge, heavy works employing over 10,000. At the industry's peak, over 100,000 people were employed in the Don Valley basin, which straddles the border between Rotherham and Sheffield.[23] Each of these works had their own culture and customs, but they also shared a commonality rooted in the culture of the steel industry, and a clear attachment to and central place within the local area.[24] Large firms such as Hadfields in Sheffield, and Steel, Peech & Tozer (known locally as Steelos) in Rotherham not only employed over 10,000 people on one site, they also provided a framework for leisure time that workers and their families could engage with as deeply or as sporadically as they wished – they were a culture in themselves, and were viewed by locals as a town within a town.[25] Steel towns and cities make an enlightening case study because, while they provide an as yet unexamined window into working-class life, they differ from the more widely analysed mining communities, which have been characterised by contemporaries and historians as distinct and isolated cultures, which did not reflect wider social experience and change.[26] Although steelworks provided a distinct sense of community and identity for their workers and their families, they were not isolated from the wider local culture, and, as will be seen, were sites of pride, leisure, and socialisation for the town, city, and county in which they stood. In this way, there was a reflexive relationship between work, place, and masculinity that adds to our current understandings of how men experienced their lives in the twentieth century.

It took the drastic process of deindustrialisation, which for the steel industry took place during the late 1970s and 1980s, to irrevocably rupture the deep-rooted identities forged in such a culture. As well as taking away the continuation (or prospect) of obtaining skilled, high-status work from men, it physically altered the landscapes of the places in which they and their families lived. Although the works could be enormous, dirty, and forbidding places, which dominated the local landscape, they were also sites of pride, both in terms of the men who worked there and the area itself. As these physical reminders were demolished, layers of history and tradition were stripped from the city, and the hierarchy of work and masculine identity began to change. The meaning of high status is locally specific, which is why regional studies are so vital to histories of gender and class. Here, skilled work in a well-respected firm like Steelos or Hadfields carried higher status for working-class men than that of a white-collar worker such as an accountant or lawyer, despite the potential differential in salary. The loss of such work forced a change in structure. This of course was different elsewhere, and masculinities tied to other regions and industries had different fracture points. Mapping these differences is crucial to help build a picture of the multiple working-class masculinities experienced throughout the century.

Emotional communities and emotional masculinity

Working-class community has long been a contested notion, both by contemporary theorists and historians. The very notion of community itself has been challenged by theorists from many disciplines, and memories of working-class community have been perceived as 'rose-tinted images of the past' that prove problematic for historical interpretation.[27] Nostalgia suffuses many working-class autobiographies and oral testimonies, including the Songs of Steel interviews, but that does not simply make them problematic. This offers a window into the hidden histories of identity and emotion, which scholars have begun to analyse.[28] In much of this work, community has been understood in the geographical sense; for example, the slums cleared to make way for council housing. However, I argue that community in relation to the steelworks of South Yorkshire was, by the post-war period, as much emotional as geographic. Barbara Rosenwein argues that emotional communities are largely the same as social communities, such as, in this case, the workplace and the neighbourhood, but that they also take into account affective bonds and 'systems of feeling', which, I argue, are crucial to understanding the intersectional identities of class and gender.[29]

Before the Second World War, many steelworkers lived in houses that were in close physical proximity to the works, and people lived their lives to the soundtrack of the forges and steel hammers. The only time that there was, for most people, an unsettling sense of quiet was during the summer shutdown weeks when the works closed for repairs, and workers went on their holidays.[30] However, from the 1930s, but the 1950s in earnest, new council estates were built in Sheffield and Rotherham, with a view that they would act as satellite estates for the big works. One of the largest, Kimberworth Park in Rotherham, was built during the early 1950s. Although only around three miles from Steelos, the new estate was entirely separate from the workplace, and boasted views of rural areas rather than of the melting shop and rolling mill. Although the physical communities of housing had been broken up, the emotional communities of the works remained in place. Even when people moved away from the shadow of the works, they provided a template for such a community, and the rhythms of the work and leisure calendar stayed the same, remarkably, from the 1920s right up to the late 1970s. Working-class masculinity opened the doors to this emotional community. In this sense, men's work was not just about breadwinning; it was also a coveted point of access to the pride in and benefits of a big works that offered a sense of meaning to individuals and the local community itself. Here, local identity and working-class masculinity were inextricably linked, and stable enough to weather the breaking up of more traditionally understood communities linked to housing, and close physical proximity to the workplace.

The Songs of Steel interviews are dominated by a sense of the works providing a way of life and of workmates providing solace when the work and routine proved tough. This began before a shift even started:

> I remember getting up on early days once and it was an horrible morning in the middle of winter. I remember thinking I don't like the idea of doing this for the rest of my life. And when I got off the bus in town and walked across the square to the Templeborough bus stop within five minutes I was laughing me head off because of the people in the queue … We'd get to work, once we got into the cabin everybody started cracking jokes and it was just so funny. And during the shift depending on how busy we were you'd just virtually laugh your way through the shift. And then when you went home it sort of quietened down again. And the next day you'd think hark at this weather, ah I don't really want to do this then you'd get to work and start laughing again. It was just incredible.[31]

Here, Richard Poole's participation in the emotional community of Steelos allowed him to weather the practical difficulties of a manual job in freezing weather. Even though he became more financially successful, after redundancy allowed him to start his own business, Richard organised yearly reunions for ex-employees, and felt that he has never enjoyed work as much, or been as connected to his work since Steelos.[32] This emotional attachment to the work itself and the workplace, rather than a work-based masculinity simply linked to breadwinning or physical toughness, is the reason why this version of working-class masculinity proved so resilient to change until the governments of the 1970s and 1980s destroyed the physical base of those emotional communities.

Masculinity and the social and cultural life of the works

The social life of the steelworks was crucial in melding working-class masculinity and local culture and ensuring the lasting success of the emotional communities discussed above. The prosperity of a whole town or city could be linked to either a particular works or to an industry more broadly. Large works provided full calendars of leisure activities, sports clubs, days out, theatricals, dances, medical care (extending to physiotherapy for injured workers), provisions for pensioners, and access to education for their staff. While such links between work, leisure, and employer are most commonly associated with the period before the welfare state, this went on at the steelworks well into the 1970s.[33] The 1960s were the high point of productivity and affluence for South Yorkshire, wages were good, and people were able to pick and choose their jobs and leisure activities. That they still chose to engage with the works and all they had to offer shows that there was a pride involved and attached to the identity of both steelworker and steelworker's family. The works were at the heart of the local area, just as the work itself was at the heart of working-class masculinity.

The chronicle of this social life was the works magazines. Through these it is possible to trace the social and cultural life of each works, and more broadly both the rhythm of life in the workplace and in the local area on an intimate, yearly basis. Despite the fact that the magazines varied in price and intention, they show a remarkably stable culture that weathered war, economic depression, and significant social change.[34] In the 1920s and 1930s, the yearly calendar was set, and did not alter until the mass, permanent redundancies from the industry of the late 1970s and 1980s. Sports clubs and teams played their seasons, and there were company dances in the summer and at Christmas, with departmental dances more regularly, day trips, and holidays (some abroad from the late 1950s onwards) in summer, a July family sports day, and days out and trips throughout the year.[35] During the 1950s, many of the works built modern sports grounds and leisure facilities, which were available to hire out when not being used by employees, and Steelos had the only golf club in the area aimed at working-class men.[36] The biggest works like Steelos and Edgar Allen held theatrical performances in central locations, and provided private cinema screenings for employees. It is not surprising that people engaged with these events before the Second World War when leisure options for working-class people in the area were more limited, but the fact that this engagement continued, and even increased during the 1950s and 1960s, high points of affluence in the area, show the social and cultural value that employees and their families placed on the works.

Alongside large-scale events, men were actively encouraged to pursue their interests, and the works would pay to facilitate many of their activities, 'anything you wanted to try out you could go to the education department and they were into anything like that'.[37] The wide variety of clubs that sprang up this way reflects the wide-ranging interests of working-class men in the period, a group all too easy to homogenise. These included caving, chess, climbing, boxing, swimming, archery, fishing, photography, dancing, amateur dramatics, gramophone, cinema, and book clubs.[38] Such variety also allowed for an acceptance of individuality, which sat within the more communal identity linked to work. Engagement with these social and cultural activities was widespread, as all the interviewees fondly remembered this aspect of working at Steelos, and mentioned joining clubs, socialising with workmates in the pub, and attending dances, regardless of the period they had worked there. Barry Jackson was hired as the photographer for the new weekly *Phoenix Gazette* in 1962, and remembered a hectic five years running between all these clubs, performances, and dances to document them for the magazine, which regularly sold out its run to thousands of workers.[39]

While the magazines promoted the works as cutting-edge technological spaces and players on an international business stage, individuals remembered a more visceral response to the scale and environment of the steel industry. British steelworks, particularly those in Sheffield, led the world for much of the twentieth century. It is easy to see why this would instill pride in the workers, and the wider local population. However, it was the physicality of the space that most impressed many boys and young men. Brian Rosling was advised to get into the steel industry, despite coming from a mining background in a small mining village.[40] On his way to Steelos to enquire about a job, he saw what a steelworks was like for the first time:

> In those days all the gates were open and you could look into the steelworks and see what was happening. I'll always remember walking past the ten-and-fourteen-inch mill and I could hear the rolling going off and the bashing of steel in there. And up towards what I now know as the slope canteen and bar mill was the forge, drop hammer forge and you could actually look through the gate into the forge where they were forging railway wheels, etc. I stood there for ten to fifteen minutes watching because it fascinated me, big hammer drop forging red hot stuff, guys walking about wi' flat caps on towels in their mouth and that sort of stuff. You couldn't see the full operation but enough to get you interested.[41]

Until stricter health and safety laws in the 1970s, works gates remained open onto the road, and passersby were able to see the scale and danger of the shop floor. When newly forged steel was left out to cool, people could feel the heat through the windows of passing buses.[42] There was something alluring about the near apocalyptic conditions of the shop floor: the elemental nature of the work, fire, noise, and sheer size of the operation was like a siren song for young men who wanted to test their mettle. The most common descriptions of conditions compared them to 'hell', or 'Dante's Inferno', but this was always said with a laugh or pride audible in the interviewee's voices.[43] Rather than being a reason to stay away from the works, the conditions were precisely the reason why some men wanted to work there.

From that point on, Brian became determined to work amongst the noise and heat of the shop floor, and despite undergoing a full training programme, and being offered a staff job in metallurgy, he refused this for a 'sexy' job in the melting shop.[44] The use of the word 'sexy' is telling here, and speaks to the high status of skilled, blue-collar work in the area. Skilled and dangerous jobs on the shop floor were desirable, and young men like Brian saw them as exciting and representative of a masculinity that they wanted to emulate – this view remained fifty years later. Of all the areas in a steelworks, the melting shop was the most dangerous and most visually thrilling: men dealt with molten metal, sparks flew, and drop hammers made the earth shake as they shaped steel. For many men, it became emblematic of the works and what it meant to be a good worker and mate. Men valued the sense of camaraderie fostered by such a workplace, 'it looked like hell but at the same time was a great laugh',[45] and such extreme conditions could produce extreme bonds, especially in the worst circle of Dante's Inferno, the basements below the furnaces:

> Every one of them men down there were the best guys I've ever worked wi' in terms of being totally mental. They would have gone well in a Vietnam War film cos they were all of that ilk. We don't care, we're mental, we're a gang who's gonna ger us. They were great.[46]

In the slightly less punishing environment of the melting shop proper, young men looked up to their older workmates, and if they were good at their job, the hero worship could last a lifetime. This is shown by Brian's recollections of his first boss, Arthur, as 'probably [the] cleverest guy I ever met in my entre life. He were so cool, knew what he were doing.'[47] Arthur was physically small and 'roly poly', and another much admired man was 'a big fat bloke like a bear. Massive backside', but despite not conforming to a physical ideal, their prowess in the melting shop gave them celebrity status.[48]

Flexible masculinities, secure masculinities

As the basement gang show, some men at the works were hard and dangerous, but the most valued colleagues and comrades were men who cared: about their work, workmates, and animals. The apprenticeship schemes within large works consisted of a mixture of on-the-job training in all the different departments, and, in the post-war years, a course at a local college, which resulted in a City and Guilds qualification. Other men were responsible for trainees on the shop floor, and not only did they have to teach them the various jobs, they had to look after their safety in an environment where they could easily be killed. Brian remembered how well the men looked after the young apprentices, but this relationship of care outlasted that of apprentice or worker. Before the late 1960s, there were no specific heath and safety laws, so men looked after each other, and took accident prevention as part of their roles.[49] This could be through the official works fire and ambulance departments, or on a more ad hoc basis as accidents occurred. Richard Poole found this element of work crucial to his identity and experience. When asked about camaraderie on the shop floor, he replied, 'Fantastic. I think it's proof that we're still meeting after twenty-seven years at a reunion what we were like. We looked after each other, it was a pleasure to go to work and not many can say that, nah.'[50] Later in the interview, Richard summed up the tension between working in an objectively difficult job and his (and others') fond remembrances, 'The working man looked after each other and you know they made a bad job worthwhile going cos they just accepted it and got on with it.'[51] Caring for workmates was not only accepted, but it was vital to both men's sense of self and to the success of their work. This care, and even sentimentality, was also directed towards animals. The magazines published features on dog breeds and pet care, and readers sent in their cutest pet pictures, from the 1920s onwards.[52] Feral cats lived in the works, and the men took great care in looking after them, as well as rescuing the many wild animals that strayed on-site from the adjacent rivers and canals.[53] In cases such as these, softness was a sign of strength and was highly valued. This combination of hard and soft points to a version of Sonya Rose's theory of temperate masculinity, with the 'soldier hero' part of a man's identity replaced by that of industrial worker, further underlining the need to go beyond war to properly understand working-class masculinities.[54]

As I have argued above, and elsewhere, the physical and dangerous nature of the industrial workplace, and the secure masculinity that this engendered, also allowed for men to take part in less obviously masculine leisure pursuits without it affecting their masculinity.[55] This was cultivated by the steelwork's policies to encourage men to pursue their own interests and their prioritisation of education. Alongside the training that young men received, older men were encouraged to continue their education throughout their career via various training courses, lectures, workshops, and the use of the works library. This led to many men gaining the equivalent of a university-level education in a period when university was not an option for working-class men, and to men valuing educational and cultural pursuits, as both a signifier of achievement and part of day-to-day life. Such engagement was reflected by the magazines, which advertised lectures and classes about non-work-related topics, and published men's own literary efforts and book reviews.[56] These reviews covered popular fiction and technical and political texts, but also tackled modernism, and recommended Virginia Woolf.[57] In February 1959, E. N. S. published a glowing review of the new paperback edition of Havelock Ellis's 'masterpiece', *The Psychology of Sex*.[58] The author had possessed a copy since 1933, and thought that everyone, especially the young, should have access to 'competent instruction' about sex. He praised the 'tolerant, straight-forward, and refreshingly healthy manner' that the book addressed the biology of sex, youthful sexual impulses, marriage and sexual deviation, and was delighted that the book has the potential to get rid of 'false shame' and 'woeful ignorance'.[59] The magazines allowed men to discuss their own literary preferences and preoccupations while also opening them up to consideration by the thousands of readers who bought each copy. This engagement with literature and education only ended in the late 1970s, when the magazines turned to politics and crisis management for the failing industry.[60]

Alongside literary pursuits, amateur dramatics played a significant part in the life of the works. All the biggest companies had operatic and theatrical societies, and members put a considerable amount of time and effort into their productions.[61] Both firms took their productions seriously, particularly Steelos, whose performances were seen by around 10,000 people per run. In 1948, the Operatic Society did a run of *Hit the Deck*, a musical about sailors. The *Gazette* ran an extremely complimentary twelve-page review written in dialect.[62] Accompanying the review is a series of photographs, many of which are, by today's standards, extraordinarily camp: particularly the younger men in bell-bottomed navy uniforms, and '"T" Sergent bloke', who was captured, hand on hip, pointing into the distance.[63] Clearly, these pursuits were not typically masculine, but they were extremely popular, and carried high status within the works and wider community. Set against the narratives explored in post-deindustrialisation fiction, such as *Billy Elliott*, these examples show that performance, singing, dancing, and acting were all highly regarded, and men could take part without having their masculine status challenged, as long as it was located within the broader emotional community of the works.

As has been demonstrated, working-class masculinity within the emotional community of the steelworks was flexible and adaptable, but it was also extremely strong. This is reinforced by the ways in which steelworkers responded to military service. Wartime masculinity, and the idea of military masculinity as hegemonic during the world wars, has been firmly established.[64] However, this was not quite the case for all men. Linsey Robb has written about the masculinity of non-combatant men during the Second World War, including the male industrial worker; however, what about the men from traditional, reserved industries who chose to fight, or were conscripted?[65] In the works magazines from the war years, there were sections devoted to employees now fighting abroad.[66] Serving soldiers were sent copies of the magazines on a regular basis, and they wrote letters to them to keep themselves tied into the emotional community of the works. Members of the ex-servicemen's club, who had also fought in the Great War, wrote to keep friends up to date with their activities, to thank them for keeping them involved in the life of the works, and asked them to 'save a place at the [works] Victory Dinner'.[67] Younger men who had been involved in the sporting life of the works carried on these pursuits in the forces, and kept mates up to date about their successes. For example, Ronnie Lindlay, who had been a boxing champion at Steelos, was now fighting for Yorkshire in his army regiment.[68] It is clear that while these men were clearly now soldiers, sailors, or airmen, they saw themselves first and foremost as steelworkers and members of their particular works communities. The emotional roots of their masculinity remained in their local areas and alongside their mates, rather than with their branch of the armed forces. It is because of the emotional nature of these ties that they remained so strong. This relationship worked both ways: at Steelos, men and women donated money throughout the year to send 'spending money' to their 200 colleagues on active service, raising £150.[69] Such efforts were acknowledged by 'scores' of letters from grateful friends and colleagues, who were more grateful for being remembered and included, rather than the money itself.[70]

The same applied to national service, where young men retained and developed their position within the masculine world of work and mates, and within the emotional community of the works. Here, young men wrote letters as well as feature articles about their military training and their travels. The *Phoenix Gazette* had a monthly feature called 'Letters from the Forces' that ran throughout the period of national service. Men used this to send messages to their workmates, to reinforce shared memories of the workplace, and to ensure that they remained a part of the local culture. Examples from January 1954 are typical of content and included L. A. C. Tone Rosse, who had just arrived in the Canal Zone in the Middle East, did not like the heat, and was 'wondering if the men in Nos. 5 and 7 shops are still drinking as much tea!'.[71] Colin Jackson described his life in the RAF near Whitby and 'wished all his friends at S. P. and T. a Happy New Year'.[72] L. A. C. R. Douglas let his friends know that he would be demobbed in February and would 'Hot Foot it back to Rotherham for the Works Dance'.[73] This is a touching mixture of the quotidian and the exciting. For many of these men, national service would have provided their first opportunity to travel abroad, and for the older men in the works, this would be an opportunity for them to engage in new ways with the rest of the world. Alongside this is the kind of banal detail that underlies daily life at work: talk about drinking tea and the weather show men retaining their links to normality and home by discussing the everyday that underpinned their working life and friendships. Their masculinity remained rooted in their normal working lives, and military service was an interlude in this more stable identity.

If times of war and conscription have been heralded as crisis points for masculinity, so too have moments of acute social and cultural change such as during the interwar years and the 1960s. Traditional working-class identity and masculinity has been presented as incompatible with moments of social and cultural change during the twentieth century. Shifts in fashion, behaviours, and moral standards, often triggered by war, have been viewed as crisis points in terms of both gender and class identities.[74] For example, in the interwar period, 'modern' masculinities were positioned against traditional, old-fashioned ones – the Bright Young Man, or the young man aping his Hollywood favourite as opposed to the flat caps and clogs of the steelworker or miner. During the late 1950s and 1960s, young, affluent masculinity became the cultural fashion, and this was set in direct opposition to older forms of work-based masculinity.[75] In this sense, the traditional and the new were presented as incompatible, and fundamentally at odds. However, for many men in the works, this proved a false dichotomy, and instead, they were able to find a middle ground that embraced fashion and the new, while grounding themselves in their long-standing emotional community.

From the interwar period the magazines regularly published pictures taken at company dances. In 1928, over 1,200 employees attended the Firth Thomas Christmas dance, and the pictures from the event show an extremely fashionable group of people. The women are wearing the drop waist, short dresses, beads, and shingled hair ubiquitous of the flapper, and the men are wearing fashionable suits or tuxedos, with the slicked back hair and clean-shaven faces of the matinee idol.[76] Working men were entrenched in the tradition of the workplace, while also embracing new fashions and pastimes, which their high wages allowed them to enjoy. A further melding of tradition and modernity occurs later in the same issue with the publication of the wedding pictures of two young couples, who met at the works. Both young couples were firmly embedded within the life of the works, as well as being involved in the local temperance movement, scouts and cubs troops, yet both presented themselves as the epitome of late 1920s glamour.[77] In this way traditional principles and identities blended with an engagement with the new and the modern of the period. Similarly, this can be seen as the century matured, and fashions reflected the subcultures of the 1950s, 1960s, and 1970s.

At Steelos, during the 1960s, many of the younger men on the shop floor were bikers and set up their own 'informal club'. Older men had motorbikes and sidecars that they used as family transport, and younger men without families 'had plenty of money' and therefore big bikes, which they used to socialise out of work.[78] Keith Hopkins remembered that 'we had some scooter lads, but not many' and that there was a mods and rockers 'thing' in the works, with rockers obviously dominant.[79] Subcultures have been viewed as a challenge to the dominant system, or as a way for young people to separate themselves from their parents' generation, and to forge a new identity for themselves. In this example, young men were entering into a biking and rocker subculture, both as a way to establish themselves as an affluent group within the works, but also to bond with their older workmates. They were not using the rocker subculture as an escape from the culture of the works, but as a way to blend their own interests with work, and a work culture that they enjoyed and respected. Photographs of works social events from the period show many young men with either the long hair or the American-style quiffs associated with the subculture, enjoying the less 'cool' activities on offer. These young men employed a reflexive masculinity that equally engaged with more traditional workplace cultures and more affluent ideals tied to music, material goods, and fashion.

Conclusion

Participation in the emotional community of the steelworks gave men a masculine identity that was both extremely strong and adaptable. It weathered widely agreed upon moments of crisis and change, such as war and working-class affluence, because it was grounded in the day-to-day rhythms of life and leisure in the steelworks. The study of masculinity through the lens of work, and region, allows for 'ordinary' masculinity to be mapped and understood alongside moments of crisis, conflict, and theories about flights to and from domesticity, and the changing meanings of hegemony. For the men represented in this chapter, there was only one real moment of crisis for their masculinity, and that was the demise of the steel industry. This irrevocably altered the physical landscape of their world, as well as the emotional communities in which they, and in many cases, their fathers and grandfathers had lived. Men lost their high-status work, security, and structure, and areas like Rotherham and Sheffield moved from affluence to post-industrial wastelands.[80] Richard Poole remembered the final days at Steelos:

> A few of old men were crying ... 'cos that was it, their life virtually finished from then on. They never worked ever again, they couldn't get any jobs, and at fifty odd who wants them at that age? At that time you know, that were it finished, and I know the number one bed man who used to run the show, a chap called Roy Naylor, he didn't last long ... He died within a few years, very very ... upsetting. He never come out of the house for a number of years just that depressed.[81]

Whether or not this was apocryphal, the idea that men died as a result of what they had lost in terms of work, and therefore their masculinity, remains strong in the area. In less dramatic terms, even those men who moved on successfully into a new career mourned the loss of the culture and camaraderie of their old work, and were never able to regain the same strong sense of self that came with being a steelworker.

The Songs of Steel collection highlights the emotional roots of working-class masculinity. It was not just the repetition of everyday actions that defined a man's selfhood, but it was also rooted in an emotional romanticism, which becomes clear in memory. As well as the physical toughness of the work and the masculine environment, camaraderie played a part in allowing the men to romanticise their jobs and the men around them as more than simple work colleagues, and as more than a way to collect a weekly pay packet. Both of these elements became entwined in a way of life and a masculine identity that has often been written off as nostalgia. Doing so misses the point that such 'nostalgic' recollections foreground working-class masculinity just as much as an emotional response as an analytical category. But what does this emotional connection to work mean to men excluded from such work by market forces and economic policy? This romanticisation of work and the kind of masculinity it represented could be dangerous in that it may lead to anger in young men coming of age in a world with different and potentially fewer opportunities. The shift from a clear potential pathway into work, friendship, and respect to unemployment at worse, or employment in low-status work at best, precipitated a clear crisis in masculinity in areas such as South Yorkshire.

Denied access to the emotional communities discussed in this chapter, the masculinity of young working-class men fractured, and they became unmoored, perceived as a social problem, and a subject of sociological, psychological, and cultural study.[82] The route to becoming a man no longer centred on skilled work, but could include drug-taking, binge drinking, fighting, and criminality of varying degrees of severity.[83] Because men no longer acquired their masculinity and sense of self through work, they performed it on the streets, and in the pubs and clubs, and this unstable and insecure identity had no place for the cultures of care and self-betterment valued by the steelworkers. The void left by work-centred masculinity was filled by anger at a loss of prospects and a way of life that, for some, morphed into a bigotry which was epitomised by the narrow-minded undertones of the majority Brexit vote in old industrial areas in 2016, and the success of the Brexit Party in the 2019 local elections.[84] This sense of anger and betrayal has, for some men, melded with feelings of inadequacy linked to the hard-won and still inadequate equalities of women, people of colour, and the LGBTQ community to inform one of the most pressing social concerns of the present: toxic masculinity. I argue, then, that the roots of toxic masculinity lay within the process of deindustrialisation and the way that governments mismanaged it – thousands of men were set adrift, and society, and those men, are still paying the price for it.

Notes

1 On the predominance of metropolitan and elite masculinities see e.g. John Tosh, 'The History of Masculinity: An Outdated Concept?', in John H. Arnold and

Sean Brady (eds), *What Is Masculinity? Historical Dynamics from Antiquity to the Contemporary World* (Basingstoke: Palgrave Macmillan, 2011), 24; Ben Griffin, 'Hegemonic Masculinity as a Historical Problem', *Gender & History*, 30:2 (2018), 378, 383, 387–388; Karen Harvey and Alexandra Shepard, 'What Have Historians Done with Masculinity? Reflections on Five Centuries of British History, circa 1500–1950', *Journal of British Studies*, 44 (2005), 274–280. For exceptions, see Pat Ayres, 'Work, Culture and Gender: The Making of Masculinities in Post-war Liverpool', *Labour History Review*, 69:2 (2004), 153–167; Nick Hayes, 'Heritage, Craft, and Identity: Twisthands and Their Machinery in What Is Left of the British Lace Industry', *Labour History Review*, 83:2 (2018), 147–177; Helen Smith, *Masculinity, Class and Same-Sex Desire in Industrial England, 1895–1957* (Basingstoke: Palgrave Macmillan, 2015); 'Working-Class Ideas and Experiences of Sexuality in Twentieth-Century Britain: Regionalism as a Category of Analysis', *Twentieth Century British History*, 29:1 (2018), 58–78; Angela Turner and Arthur McIvor, '"Bottom Dog Men": Disability, Social Welfare and Advocacy in the Scottish Coalfields in the Interwar Years, 1918–1939', *Scottish Historical Review*, 96:2 (2017), 187–213.
2 For examples of what ordinary masculinity could include, see Smith, *Masculinity, Class and Same-Sex Desire*.
3 Geoffrey Beattie, *Survivors of Steel City: A Portrait of Sheffield* (London: Chatto & Windus, 1986); Linda McDowell, *Redundant Masculinities? Employment Change and White Working-Class Youth* (Malden, MA: Blackwell, 2003); Anoop Nyak, 'Displaced Masculinities: Chavs, Youth and Class in the Post-industrial City', *Sociology*, 40:5 (2006), 813–831.
4 For examples of such regulation, see Smith, *Masculinity, Class and Same-Sex Desire*, 93–124.
5 For example, see Laura King, *Family Men: Fatherhood and Masculinity in Britain, 1914–1960* (Oxford: Oxford University Press, 2015); Jessica Meyer, *Men of War: Masculinity and the First World War in Britain* (Basingstoke: Palgrave Macmillan, 2009); Amy Milne Smith, 'A Flight to Domesticity? Making a Home in the Gentlemen's Clubs of London, 1880–1914', *Journal of British Studies*, 45:4 (2006), 796–818; John Tosh, *A Man's Place: Masculinity and the Middle-Class Home in Victorian England* (New Haven: Yale University Press, 1999).
6 For examples of masculinity and leisure, see Brad Beavan, *Leisure, Citizenship and Working-Class Men in Britain, 1850–1940* (Manchester: Manchester University Press, 2005); Andrew Davies, *Leisure, Gender and Poverty: Working-Class Culture in Salford and Manchester, 1900–1939* (Buckingham: Open University Press, 1992); Andrew Davies, 'Youth Gangs, Masculinity and Violence in Late Victorian Manchester and Salford', *Journal of Social History*, 32:2 (1998), 349–369; Richard Hall, 'Being a Man, Being a Member: Masculinity and Community in Britain's Working Men's Clubs, 1945–1960', *Cultural and Social History*, 14:1 (2017), 73–88; Martin Johnes, 'Pigeon Racing and Working-Class Culture in Britain, c. 1870–1950', *Cultural and Social*

History, 4:3 (2007) 361–383; Melanie Tebbutt, *Being Boys: Youth, Leisure and Identity in the Inter-war Years* (Manchester: Manchester University Press, 2012); Melanie Tebbutt, 'Rambling and Manly Identity in Derbyshire's Dark Peak, 1880s–1920s', *The Historical Journal*, 49:4 (2006), 1125–1153. For examples of masculinity and unemployment, see Marjorie Levine-Clark, 'The Politics of Preference: Masculinity, Marital Status and Unemployment Relief in Post-First World War Britain', *Cultural and Social History*, 7:2 (2010), 233–252; Marjorie Levine-Clark, *Unemployment, Welfare, and Masculine Citizenship: So Much Honest Poverty in Britain, 1870–1930* (Basingstoke: Palgrave Macmillan, 2015); Neil Penlington, 'Masculinity and Domesticity in 1930s South Wales: Did Unemployment Change the Domestic Division of Labour?', *Twentieth Century British History*, 21:3 (2010), 281–299; Stephanie Ward, *Unemployment and the State in Britain: The Means Test and Protest in 1930s South Wales and North-East England* (Manchester: Manchester University Press, 2013).

7 Arthur McIvor, 'Rebuilding "Real Men": Work and Working-Class Male Civilian Bodies in Wartime', in Linsey Robb and Juliette Pattinson (eds), *Men, Masculinities and Male Culture in the Second World War* (Basingstoke: Palgrave Macmillan, 2017); Linsey Robb, *Men at Work: The Working Man in British Culture, 1939–1945* (Basingstoke: Palgrave Macmillan, 2015).

8 Ronnie Johnston and Arthur McIvor, 'Dangerous Work, Hard Men and Broken Bodies: Masculinity in the Clydeside Heavy Industries, c. 1930–1970s', *Labour History Review*, 69:2 (2004), 135–152.

9 Nick Hayes, 'Did Manual Workers Want Industrial Welfare? Canteens, Latrines and Masculinity on British Building Sites 1918–1970', *Journal of Social History*, 35:3 (2002), 637–658.

10 Ayres, 'Work, Culture and Gender'.

11 Griffin, 'Hegemonic Masculinity', 395.

12 Ben Highmore, *Everyday Life and Cultural Theory: An Introduction* (London: Routledge, 2002), 1–3.

13 *Ibid.*, 16.

14 Derek Hickling, interviewer Sam Smith, 29/09/09, SOSOHP13, *Rotherham Archives*.

15 Brian Rosling, SOHP16 interviewer Sam Smith, 28/08/09, *Rotherham Archives*.

16 Brian Rosling.

17 Brian Rosling, Derek Hickling, and Richard Poole, interviewer Sam Smith, 9/9/09, SOSOH08, *Rotherham Archives*.

18 *Edgar Allen Magazine 1919–1966*, and *Works and Sports Magazine 1920–1931* 052.74 SQ; *Firth Brown News 1957–1978* 052.74 S and SQ; *Hadfield Group Staff Society 'New Era' 1964–1968* 052.74 SQ; *Hadfield News 1978–1982* 052.74 SQ; *Osborn News, 'The Hand and Heart Magazine' 1920, 53–78* 052.74 S and SF; *Steel Peech & Tozer Social Services Gazette 1932–1969* 052.74 S; Thomas Firth and Sons Company Magazine *'The Bombshell' 1917–1932* 052.74S, *Sheffield Local Studies Library*; 'Songs of Steel' Collection, SOSOHP1–30, *Rotherham Archives*. I have analysed the magazines of five of the largest works in the area, and these, with gaps in the archive, cover the years

1917–1982. The interviews cover the war years, until 2010, with the majority focusing on the late 1950s onwards.

19 John Griffiths, 'Exploring Corporate Culture: The Potential of Company Magazines for the Business Historian', *Business Archives: Sources and History*, 78 (1999), 27–37; Michael Heller, 'British Company Magazines, 1878–1939: The Origins and Functions of House Journals in Large-Scale Organisations', *Media History*, 15:2 (2009), 143–166.

20 Sam conducted twenty-six interviews with ex-Steelos employees, and he trained interviewees to conduct four more, making a total of thirty. The aim of the project was to create a legacy for what has, since the collapse of the industry, become a troubled and deprived area: www.joinedupheritagesheffield.org.uk/content/project/songs-of-steel (accessed 2 July 2019).

21 On oral history methodologies and uses, see Penny Summerfield, *Histories of the Self: Personal Narratives and Historical Practice* (London: Routledge, 2018), 106–134. For issues with memory and the construction of identity, see Penny Summerfield, 'Culture and Composure: Creating Narratives of the Gendered Self in Oral History Interviews', *Cultural and Social History*, 1:1 (2004), 65–93. On using archived collections, see April Gallwey, 'The Rewards of Using Archived Oral Histories in Research: The Case of the Millennium Memory Bank', *Oral History*, 41:1 (2013), 37–50.

22 This toughness was rooted in the ability to perform difficult work and withstand harsh conditions rather than that linked to violence; see Davies, 'Youth Gangs Masculinity and Violence'.

23 Geoffrey Tweedale, 'The Business and Technology of Sheffield Steelmaking', in Clyde Binfield *et al.* (eds), *The History of the City of Sheffield 1843–1993, vol. 2: Society* (Sheffield: Sheffield Academic Press, 1993), 167.

24 For a close study of a non-industrial workplace, see Danielle Sprecher, 'Fashion for the High Street: The Design and Making of Menswear in Leeds 1945–1980' (PhD diss., University of Leeds, 2016).

25 Barry Jackson, interviewer Sam Smith, 10/09/09, SOSOHP09, *Rotherham Archives*.

26 For example, see Norman Dennis, Fernando Henriques, and Clifford Slaughter, *Coal Is Our Life: An Analysis of a Yorkshire Mining Community* (London: Tavistock Publications, 1956); Keith Gildart, 'Mining Memories: Reading Coalfield Autobiographies', *Labor History*, 50:2 (2009), 139–161.

27 Anne Baldwin *et al.*, 'Introduction', in Anne Baldwin *et al.* (eds), *Class, Culture and Community: New Perspectives in Nineteenth and Twentieth Century British Labour History* (Newcastle upon Tyne: Cambridge Scholars Publishing, 2012), 2; Joanna Bourke, *Working-Class Cultures in Britain 1890–1960: Gender, Class and Ethnicity* (London: Routledge, 1994), 136–137.

28 Ben Jones, 'The Uses of Nostalgia: Autobiography, Community Publishing and Working-Class Neighbourhoods in Post-war England', *Cultural and Social History*, 7:3 (201), 355–374; Chris Waters, 'Representations of Everyday Life: L. S. Lowry and the Landscape of Memory in Postwar Britain', *Representations*, 65 (1999), 121–150.

29 Barbara Rosenwein, *Emotional Communities in the Early Middle Ages* (Ithaca: Cornell University Press, 2006); Barbara Rosenwein, 'Problems and Methods in the History of Emotions', *Passions in Context I*, 1 (2010), 11.
30 John Heaps interviewer Sam Smith, 22/09/09, SOSOHP14, *Rotherham Archives*.
31 Richard Poole.
32 *Ibid.*
33 For example, see Simon Phillips, 'Industrial Welfare and Recreation at Boots Pure Drug Company, 1883–1945' (PhD diss., Nottingham Trent University, 2003).
34 For example, by the early 1980s, Hadfields' magazines were free and looked like they were printed off by staff in the works themselves, while the *Bombshell* cost 4d in 1917 and was professionally printed.
35 *Edgar Allen Works and Sports Magazine*, June and July 1920–1921, January and September 1922–1931; *Edgar Allen Magazine* March and December 1947–1966; *The Bombshell*, January and July 1917–1932; *Firth Brown News* Summer and Autumn 1957–1978; *Hadfield News* 1978–1982; *Hand and Heart* March and July 1953–1967; *Steel Peech and Tozer Social Services Gazette*, 1938–1946; *The Pheonix Gazette* 1946–1969.
36 Keith Hopkins SOSOHP01 interviewer Sam Smith 25/08/09, *Rotherham Archives*; Barry Jackson.
37 Keith Hopkins.
38 For example, the *Edgar Allen Works and Sports Magazine* of January 1925 has examples of these hobbies, as does the *Edgar Allen Magazine*, Spring 1965, with the gramophone replaced by records.
39 Barry Jackson.
40 Brian Rosling.
41 *Ibid.*
42 Barry Jackson.
43 *Ibid.*; Brian Rosling; Malcolm Salter, SOHP04 interviewer Sam Smith 03/09/09, *Rotherham Archives*.
44 Brian Rosling.
45 Barry Jackson.
46 Brian Rosling.
47 *Ibid.*
48 *Ibid.*
49 Keith Hopkins; Richard Poole.
50 Richard Poole.
51 *Ibid.*
52 For a particularly adorable Pekinese, see *Edgar Allen Work and Sports Magazine*, August 1921, 14.
53 Barry Jackson.
54 Sonya O. Rose, *Which People's War? National Identity and Citizenship in Britain 1939–1945* (Oxford: Oxford University Press, 2003), 153, 160–161.
55 Smith, *Masculinity, Class and Same-Sex Desire*.

56 For example, the Edgar Allen Literary, Social, and Dramatic Society arranged a series of lectures, including ones on 'Humour in Music' and 'Carlyle', *Edgar Allen Works and Sports Magazine*, June 1920, 9.
57 In the *SP&T SS Gazette*, December 1938 edition, books as diverse as light romance, Elsa Lanchester's autobiography, a biography of Lenin, and the political writings of Brice Lockhart were recommended as gifts. Virginia Woolf's *Between the Acts* was commended as a work of genius and recommended to all readers in the December 1941 issue.
58 *Edgar Allen News*, February 1959, 443.
59 Ibid.
60 By 1979 *Hadfield News* was dominated by the Thatcherite threat to the steel industry, the possibility of industrial action, and financial problems, with a few sections on sports, trips, etc. and nothing on education and culture.
61 *Edgar Allen Magazine,* March 1949, 87.
62 *Phoenix Gazette*, February 1948, 33.
63 Ibid., 28, 33.
64 Graham Dawson, *Soldier Heroes: British Adventure, Empire and the Imagining of Masculinities* (London: Routledge, 1994).
65 Robb, *Men at Work*, 40–76.
66 For example, 'Men Serving with the Forces', *SP&T Gazette*, October 1940, 42.
67 *SP&T Gazette*, February 1940, 11.
68 Ibid., June 1940, 7.
69 *SP&T SS Gazette*, January 1944, 21.
70 Ibid.
71 *Phoenix Gazette*, 22:1, January 1954, 30.
72 Ibid.
73 Ibid.
74 Adrian Bingham, *Gender, Modernity, and the Popular Press in Inter-war Britain* (Oxford: Oxford University Press, 2004), 2; Joanna Bourke, *Dismembering the Male: Men's Bodies, Britain and the Great War* (London: Reaktion Books, 1996), 13; Alison Oram, *Her Husband Was a Woman! Women's Gender-Crossing in Modern British Popular Culture* (London: Routledge, 2007), 17.
75 This idea was most keenly promoted by the 'Angry Young Men' literary movement in texts such as Alan Sillitoe, *Saturday Night and Sunday Morning* (London: W. H. Allen & Co., 1958).
76 *Bombshell*, 3:1, January 1929, 2, 6, 40.
77 Ibid., 29.
78 Keith Hopkins.
79 Ibid.
80 Beattie, *Survivors of Steel City*.
81 Richard Poole.
82 For example, see Stuart Hall and Tony Jefferson, 'Once More around *Resistance through Rituals*', in Stuart Hall and Tony Jefferson, *Resistance through Rituals: Youth Cultures in Post-war Britain*, 2nd edn (London: Routledge, 2006), vii–xxxii; McDowell, *Redundant Masculinities?*; Nyak, 'Displaced Masculinities';

Sara Willott and Christine Griffin, '"Wham Bam, Am I a Man?": Unemployed Men Talk about Masculinities', *Feminism & Psychology* 7 (1997), 107–128.
83 Beattie, *Survivors of Steel City*; McDowell, *Redundant Masculinities?*; Nyak, 'Displaced Masculinities'.
84 EU Referendum, 'Local Results', BBC News, www.bbc.co.uk/news/politics/eu_referendum/results/local/b (accessed 13 September 2019); Angelique Chrisafis, '"Swept Up on a Tide": Disaffected Voters Flock to Brexit Party across North-West', *Guardian*, 24 May 2019, www.theguardian.com/uk-news/2019/may/24/disaffected-voters-boost-brexit-party-across-north-west (accessed 13 September 2019).

6

Perceptions of crisis in the history of masculinity: Power and change in modern Britain

Ben Griffin

Masculinity, commentators frequently tell us, is in crisis; and diagnoses of this crisis have become a commonplace of journalistic, political, and academic debate.[1] Historians have learned to be sceptical of such claims, for the simple reason that masculinity appears always to have been in crisis, no matter which period in the past has been under investigation. Early research on the history of masculinity identified crises of masculinity at the end of the nineteenth century, during the First World War, and during the interwar period, while sociological studies of Britain since 1945 have likewise identified multiple instances of manhood in crisis.[2] Faced with this picture of men 'interminably in crisis', the very notion of crisis seems superfluous: masculinity appears always and everywhere to have been uneasy and uncertain.[3] Moreover, given how resilient male social and political dominance has been, talk of masculinity in crisis seems preposterously overstated. Now that historians have largely abandoned the concept, however, it might be worth pausing to reflect on *why* diagnoses of crisis have haunted the history of masculinity. What might this indicate about the subject that historians are trying to describe and the intellectual apparatuses that have been brought to bear on the study of the past? Why, in short, has it been so easy for historians of any period to claim that masculinity is in crisis?

Crisis rhetoric usually involves a synecdoche: to say that there is a crisis of masculinity is usually to make a claim about an unsettling of a broader set of power relations within which masculinity is situated – a crisis of the gender order rather than one of its parts. This rhetoric also treats 'masculinity' as a synonym for the position of men within that structure, thereby failing to acknowledge either that there are multiple masculinities in any society, or that gender refers to the cultural interpretation of sexual difference rather than 'men'. John Tosh has identified three separate anxieties about social change underpinning much of the talk about crisis: a concern that men are losing power and status relative to women, fears about the effects of changes in the labour market, and changes in sexual politics – most importantly gay liberation; others would add changes in the family, like increasing numbers of divorces and single-parent families. The effects of these changes are then registered in distressing statistics about male mental health, educational attainment, and incarceration.[4] This chapter will not engage with these transformations; instead, it will argue that there is another set of structural changes capable of generating crisis talk that has been neglected in the current literature – changes in the relationships of power that exist between masculinities. Understanding these dynamics will allow us to understand why it has proved so easy to argue that masculinity was in crisis, when in practice the gender order has proved remarkably resilient.[5]

The creation of power relations between masculinities can be understood as a four-fold operation.[6] First, there is the process of cultural contestation whereby some models of masculinity are privileged over others. Second, the techniques, mechanisms, or opportunities that allow men to identify themselves with those models are not available to all men equally. Third, there is the process by which the performance of a particular masculinity is accorded recognition by others. Fourth, individuals recognised as performing particular masculinities are positioned in relation to sets of institutional practices, rewards, and sanctions. The argument of this chapter is that disruption to any one of these operations might generate a diagnosis that masculinity was in crisis, without that disruption necessarily impacting on any of the other three or prompting a wider reconfiguration of the gender order. In other words, diagnoses of crisis might be lumping together different kinds of phenomena: teasing these apart allows us to see different kinds of change shaping the history of masculinities in modern Britain.

Contesting cultural stereotypes

Following the pioneering work of R. W. Connell, gender historians are now familiar with the idea that there are hierarchies between masculinities, with some achieving a normative or 'hegemonic' status, while others are subordinated, marginalised, or moved into positions of either complicity or resistance relative to the normative model.[7] These hierarchies are constructed by shifting sets of cultural norms relating to (among other things) sexuality and intimacy, physique and bodily capacity, and emotional control. These qualities are articulated through repertoires of cultural models that constitute recognised ways of being a man.[8] One of the most important in modern British history has been the figure of the 'gentleman' – a model of masculinity characterised not just by a class position, but by distinctive aesthetics, dispositions, and deportment.[9] Twentieth-century Britain has seen the rise and fall of many such models. These include: teddy boys, yuppies,[10] respectable artisans/tradesmen,[11] the family man, the working-class 'good husband',[12] the masher,[13] the swell, the spiv,[14] the businessman, the manager,[15] the organisation man,[16] the clerk, Rastafarians, punks,[17] goths, mods, rockers, hippies, new romantics, skinheads, rude boys, bikers, farmers, hard men,[18] new men, the 'honest poor';[19] in universities, the reading man, the aesthete, the athlete and the sporting man;[20] leather boys, queans,[21] bears,[22] and clones;[23] 'scuttlers',[24] 'corner lads',[25] chavs, tramps, intellectuals, young fogeys, football hooligans, hipsters, dandies, 'new lads',[26] dirty old men in long macs, the white van man, the soldier,[27] the flyer,[28] the non-conformist preacher, the heroic missionary, the trendy vicar, and the jet-setting international playboy. Each of these types offered a model for how to be a man, but they must be studied as cultural models, not as descriptions of actual men. This is because individual men could perform more than one of these models over the course of the life cycle, or even over the course of a single day: the good husband and the football hooligan, the businessman and the biker, could be descriptions of the same man.[29]

The meanings of these various models, the status accorded to them, and their popularity all changed over time, although few have been subjected to the same kind of historical attention as the eighteenth-century macaroni or 'polite' gentleman.[30] The first operation of power to discuss, then, concerns the cultural contests that created hierarchies between models of masculinity. This kind of cultural politics can be seen in Josiah Wedgewood's 1927 suggestion that American films provided good role models for men:

> The he-man is the essence of the American film. He is the self-made man who struggles to the top. He is a type that we want more of and a wholly good example to set before our young people. Let us have that sort of hero rather than the dude who never works but spends his time horse-racing, hunting and dallying in dance halls.[31]

We have a large historical literature on contests of this kind. For example, the literature on the rise, fall, and re-emergence of domestic ideals of middle-class masculinity in the century before the Second World War, or Linsey Robb's study of how hierarchies between types of masculinity were reconfigured during the Second World War.[32] The emergence of new models could at all times prove disorienting for men, but it is important not to misidentify the routine process of cultural contestation as symptoms of a crisis. When, in 1931, S. F. Hatton complained about young men 'who are more given to the softer delights of the cinema and the dance hall, than the more vigorous and manly sporting instincts of boxing, football, and suchlike pastimes', this was simply the ordinary work of the gender order, not a symptom of a deeper dislocation.[33]

But within what kind of social formation does a particular cultural model of masculinity attain normative status? Rather than attempt to generalise about 'Britain' as a whole, a more useful approach is to use Simon Szreter's concept of 'communication communities'.[34] These are social formations characterised by people who share sets of norms because they participate in the same networks, institutions, and practices that generate those norms. For example, in the nineteenth century, middle-class men in different parts of the country belonged to the same communication community because they went to the same sorts of schools and read the same newspapers, whereas working-class communication communities tended to be more localised, with dialect literature and local schools, street corners, and workplaces producing regionally diverse community norms. It was in these communication communities that boys learned what it meant to be men. As a result, we can see how, well into the twentieth century, different communication communities demonstrated substantial variation in their beliefs and practices regarding sex, intimacy, and child-rearing.[35] As Helen Smith argues, '[a]cceptable behaviour could be defined street by street, never mind county by county, and this reflected what locals in an area valued'.[36] Other communities were less geographically bounded, as we can see from the distinctive cultures into which men were socialised when they joined the medical or legal professions, or the Brigade of Guards.[37] The cultural politics that established hierarchies between models and norms of masculinity were carried out within these communication communities. This work was done in large part by what we might call 'authorising institutions', such as the Church, schools, the press, the medical profession, or governing bodies within professions.

Seen from this perspective, the history of modern Britain becomes a history of multiple social formations existing side by side with one another (and sometimes overlapping or nested inside one another), each with its own authorising institutions. Thus, Lucy Delap's study of Anglican masculinities has found that 'In determining which models were adopted by individuals ... contests over hierarchies and authority within particular parishes or church institutions seem more influential than broader social changes such as war and economic depression.'[38] An implication of this analysis is that the masculine qualities prized in one communication community might be valued differently in another, and consequently the hierarchies between various masculinities might differ. In the 1950s, for example, Michael Young and Peter Willmott found that manual workers in East London differed sharply from 'experts' in the social status that they accorded to different occupations, a substantial proportion regarding non-manual commercial or clerical occupations as of lower status than agricultural or dock labour.[39] Since men might belong to multiple communication communities simultaneously, individuals might have to negotiate potentially conflicting identities, loyalties, and values. For example, Michael Roper's study of British business management since 1945 describes the culture clash that occurred between middle-class managers and men on the shop floor. One senior manager felt that 'if you weren't running around hitting bits of iron with hammers or wielding a spanner, then you weren't a man'.[40] Similarly, Robb has identified tensions during the Second World War between the 'hard man' masculinity valued by NCOs (Non-Commissioned Officers) from working-class communities and the 'seemingly effete notion of manly duty espoused by many conscientious objectors' from different backgrounds.[41] It seems a plausible hypothesis that certain features of Britain's modernity – increases in geographical and absolute social mobility, changing occupational structures, the growth of leisure, and the dislocations of war – meant that men needed to navigate between multiple communication communities more frequently than before. One might therefore suggest that modernity required more complex gender performances.

With this in mind, we can identify a number of possible changes in this cultural politics that might be taken to constitute a crisis of masculinity. The first of these would be a sudden shift in the relative positions of different models of masculinity. Modern British history has seen no change as dramatic as the sudden privileging of Western modes of dress and behaviour among social elites in Japan after the Meiji restoration, or the attacks on clerical masculinities that followed the French Revolution. Certainly, particular cultural models have suddenly lost prestige: the figure of the 'country gentleman' was far less central to political culture in the twentieth century than it had been in the nineteenth. Similarly, some have suggested that the shift away from militaristic models of masculinity after the First World War constituted a 'crisis of masculinity'.[42] While such changes may have been disorienting, they scarcely seem to constitute a crisis, for two reasons. First, when certain models of masculinity declined in popularity or status, other forms embodying desirable traits were usually available.[43] So, for example, Adrian Bingham has shown how, after 1918, sporting heroes provided new models of masculinity that embodied those qualities of courage, endurance, and physical strength that had previously been modelled by military heroes.[44] Secondly, and most importantly, since the relative hierarchies between masculinities were specific to particular communication communities, change in the cultural organisation of masculinities within one community would not necessarily be replicated in others. To put it another way: the rise of the yuppie in the 1980s might have displaced the figure of the urbane city gent, but this shift had little impact outside the communication community within which it was located.[45] Disruption within a single communication community, in other words, would not necessarily lead to a more general crisis. For this reason, sweeping arguments about challenges to 'hegemonic masculinity' in Britain are rarely sustainable.

A different form of crisis might conceivably involve a radical restructuring of communication communities, in such a way that men originally socialised in one community might find themselves unexpectedly located in another with different norms, values, and expectations. One can see how this might have followed the development of more numerous *national* communication communities which overlaid older ones, as a result of compulsory schooling from 1880 and the development of mass media technologies. Laura King, for example, has argued that in the twentieth century the expansion of the press led to the emergence of a more homogeneous national culture which supplanted the regionally diverse cultures of parenting described by Siân Pooley.[46] It seems safer to say that new national communities did not displace existing localised cultures as much as provide a mutual frame of reference for actors who participated in both.[47] Current anxieties about the impact of social media are another example of this kind of change.

More important for our purposes was the post-war transformation of the authorising institutions within communication communities. The declining authority of the churches, and the growing authority of the medical profession, for example, are two of the most important stories in modern gender history.[48] They accompanied a fundamental reconceptualisation of the role of the state in authorising or censuring gender performances: a change often described as the move to a 'permissive society'. 'Permissiveness' was a response to the fracturing of a Victorian moral consensus that had endured well into the twentieth century (and it is worth remembering that the last generation to have left school before Queen Victoria died were still only in their fifties in the 1940s). By the 1930s the confident certainties that had characterised the public doctrines of the Victorian generation were giving way to a rather uneasy ethical pluralism in which there was much less agreement about what constituted a good life.[49] Now that public moralists no longer spoke with one voice, the state was prompted to distinguish more sharply between 'public' morality that legitimately remained within its purview, and 'private' matters that did not. The Wolfenden Report of 1957 set out this new vision when it proclaimed that 'It is not, in our view, the function of the law to intervene in the private lives of citizens, or to seek to enforce any particular pattern of behaviour.'[50] In other words, the state began to limit its role in the cultural battles to authorise or to proscribe certain forms of masculinity. At the same time, however, new institutions were emerging which claimed authority to pass judgement on what was really 'masculine' behaviour. Increasingly, judges, doctors, teachers, clergymen, and politicians had to compete with advertisers, sociologists, psychologists, charities, consumer groups, social workers, relationship counsellors, newspaper agony aunts, moral entrepreneurs, pop groups, filmmakers, celebrities, lifestyle magazines, stylists, social media 'influencers', and the full panoply of 'experts'.

These changes created the conditions which made possible the rapid expansion of the available repertoire of cultural models of masculinity. It is striking how many of the cultural stereotypes listed at the start of this section developed in the post-war years, driven by affluence, technological change, and especially by new kinds of advertising and marketing firms eager to promote new cultural stereotypes for young men.[51] The multiplication of authorising institutions and the breakdown of older public doctrines not only promoted the multiplication of cultural models, it also made it harder to establish hierarchies between them, because competing models aspiring to normative status could claim support from rival institutions. In this discursive landscape, men who pushed prams could claim authority for their gender performances as easily as their opponents.[52] Likewise, although their parents may not have approved, mods, rockers, punks, and goths could all find magazines, films, and commentators to validate their choices in a way that has no nineteenth-century equivalent. For this reason, some of the anxieties identified as symptoms of a contemporary crisis of masculinity might be better described in terms of a crisis of institutional authority. Anxious masculinities have been the product not simply of the profusion of cultural models of masculinity, but an inability to establish some preferred models or characteristics as more legitimate than others.

A further dimension of this change has been the growing influence of women in authorising institutions – notably the judiciary, parliament, the clergy, the medical profession, and the press – which had for years resisted their admission.[53] The expanding number of authorising institutions further amplified women's voices in contests over masculine norms. Not the least significant feminist achievement has been the creation by women of new forums that have allowed women to participate in these contests, from the feminist periodicals of the 1970s to the Everyday Sexism Project website and the use of social media in the #MeToo movement. As a result, the term 'toxic masculinity' has entered common parlance; this is an important intervention in the cultural contests over norms of male behaviour.

For this reason, contemporary 'men's rights' activists are keen to blame their perceived ills on authorising institutions that they believe have been 'corrupted' by feminism, such as universities and the family law division of the High Court.[54] The fact that, in 2013, the organiser of a petition asking that more women's faces appear on banknotes received threats of murder and rape is a further symptom of this. The absurd headline on the front page of the *Sun* in 1998, which asked 'Are we being run by a gay mafia?', likewise indicates concerns about the composition of authorising institutions.[55] This presents a different kind of 'crisis' sensibility than those encountered earlier in the century, when the principal anxieties were the product of men increasingly needing to navigate between communities with different gender norms, or by changes in the status accorded to particular masculinities within any given community.

Performing masculinities

Studying this cultural politics, however, tells us nothing about how these masculinities were performed by flesh and blood individuals. This requires us to consider the historically specific opportunities, mechanisms, or techniques that enabled men to identify themselves with particular types of masculinity. For example, to pass as a 'gentleman' required a man to wear the right clothes, adopt the correct body language, and display appropriate manners.[56] The same is true of those who wished to identify as skinheads, bikers, or businessmen. These qualities could be learned or acquired: *How to Shine in Society* (1860) reassured its readers that the culture and refinement expected of gentlemen 'are within the reach of every man who chooses to make the necessary effort to acquire them'.[57] In the 1930s, the magazine *Men Only* played a similar role, advising its readers on how to perform desirable masculinities.[58] But access to the necessary mechanisms, techniques, and opportunities were not available to all.[59] Different levels of material and cultural capital, and different bodily capacities, meant that some men were better placed to associate themselves with normative masculinities than others. Not everyone could afford the clothes or education required to perform certain forms of masculinity; fathers unable to support their families' financial needs were unable to lay claim to the prestige attached to the male breadwinner; and physical frailty, deafness, or failing eyesight placed limits on the repertoire of masculinities that a man could perform. In short, an individual's ability to undertake a particular gender performance required access not only to the relevant script, but also access to the correct costume and props, and the requisite bodily capacities.[60]

Attending to this point allows us to bridge the gap between cultural and social history. For example, since courage was valued as a desirable quality in men, we can ask what means were available to men to establish that they were brave. Young men could join street gangs 'to prove themselves through displays of aggression and fighting prowess'.[61] Labourers could take unnecessary risks at the workplace.[62] During wartime a different set of opportunities became available, and Roper has identified 'a belief among the post-war generation [of] men that they were superior *men*' by virtue of their military experience.[63] But later generations had to find different ways of identifying themselves with 'heroic' forms of masculinity, which might explain the curious increase in macho and militaristic language in political discourse in the late 1960s and 1970s.[64] One might similarly chart the ways in which the history of mass consumerism affected men's ability to perform certain masculinities. Interwar retailers, for example, marketed affordable menswear by targeting the consumer who wanted to be a gentleman 'but who had previously been excluded from his wardrobe'.[65]

An implication of the argument so far is that it would have been advantageous for men to have the capacity to perform multiple masculinities: this was an adaptive capacity that facilitated social mobility. The early generations of Labour MPs were persistently handicapped by the limited repertoire of masculinities available for them to perform. It was not easy for working-class men to perform the gentlemanly masculinities valued in the House of Commons, and some of the characteristics that working-class men usually exhibited to prove their 'manliness' – like manual skill, the ability to provide financially for a family, physical toughness, or negotiating skill – could not easily be demonstrated on the floor of the House. It is no surprise that so many trade unionist MPs found the Commons intimidating: it was by no means clear how they could be a man in that space.[66] Movement within communication communities was as important as movement between them, and in particular the need to perform multiple masculinities over the course of the life cycle deserves more attention than it has received. Youth culture tends to be studied in isolation, which leaves unexplored the question of how teenage punks became middle-aged estate agents. If we accept the hypothesis that modernity required men to be able to move between communication communities more frequently than before, then this would presumably have intensified the political struggles over the allocation of the mechanisms, techniques, and opportunities needed to perform masculinities.

How might this help us to refine the notion of a crisis of masculinity? Seen in these terms, a crisis of masculinity might occur when a group of men face a sudden loss of access to the mechanisms that allow them to identify themselves as particular kinds of men. Mass disablement after the First World War would clearly count as a crisis in these terms.[67] A second example would be the onset of mass unemployment. Consider the speech that the Labour MP James O'Grady made in 1911.

> Take a typical case of a skilled workman out of employment. He walks about from factory to factory, knowing his own skill, but driven away every time because his labour is not wanted. The wife has probably gone into the factory. Think of the degradation of the man's manhood that his own wife should become the breadwinner instead of himself![68]

There is a lot of evidence that during the mass unemployment of the 1920s and 1980s, men experienced unemployment as emasculating.[69] That is because regular work and the role of breadwinner were considered essential for men if they were to access the most prestigious forms of masculinity in working-class communities.[70] An economic crisis was also experienced, in part, as a crisis of gender identity. This kind of sudden change must be distinguished from the more routine deprivations of class.[71] The inequitable distribution of resources means that the usual condition of the lower middle and working classes has been precarious access to the means that would enable them to perform masculinities that they considered desirable.[72] As Leonore Davidoff and Catherine Hall put it, 'consciousness of class always takes a gendered form'.[73] This can also be seen in the anxiety that some middle-class men experienced in the 1940s and 1950s as a result of rationing, which meant that they were unable to access the clothes, food, and petrol that they used to perform their preferred masculinities.[74] Crises of this kind may be quite rare. Few cultural models are reliant on just one technique or mechanism to enable their performance, so that men might lose one but retain access to others. And men have been very creative in finding substitutes: unemployed men in the 1930s, for example, preserved their self-respect by maintaining their status in the home, or by promoting new cultural models of 'honest poverty'.[75]

This does not mean that men have greeted such moments with equanimity. We can interpret many moments of conflict in modern gender politics as moments of anxiety that men might be about to lose access to mechanisms or techniques that have been important to their gender performances. Access to education and to professional qualifications has been particularly fought over.[76] The University of Cambridge, for example, refused to grant women degrees until 1948, precisely because its members valued an all-male environment as a forum in which distinctive styles of elite masculinity could be cultivated. In 1897, one student objected to admitting women on the grounds that 'Cambridge exists not for mere erudition, but for the education of the male youth of England – education of body, mind, feelings; and its object is to make a man a finished gentleman.'[77] Feelings ran so high that votes on whether to admit women were accompanied by less than gentlemanly rioting.[78] Studying at Cambridge was a way of claiming gentlemanliness, but if women could study there too then that undermined one's ability to claim gentlemanliness by virtue of having studied there. As an article from *Men Only* in 1935 put it, women's presence in the professions and seats of learning was 'merely an emasculating one'.[79] For working-class men during the First World War, opposition to women workers doing the same jobs as male workers was a symptom of similar anxieties. Alternatively, worries might be generated at moments when new groups of men gained access to mechanisms, techniques, or opportunities that had previously been restricted. This lay at the root of concerns that all of those who had received commissions during the First World War ought to be treated as gentlemen after demobilisation, even though, as one public school-educated observer remarked, 'Many of them came from the lower middle-class and had no manners, including table manners, of any kind.'[80] It is easy to see how the men involved in these battles over who had access to the means of performing masculinity may have perceived a crisis, even if in retrospect the diagnosis seems overstated.

Audience recognition

Even if an individual has access to the necessary scripts, props, and costumes required to perform a particular kind of masculinity, that does not mean that the performance will necessarily be recognised as authentic by those viewing it. Men who joined the Volunteers in the second half of the nineteenth century, or the Home Guard in the 1940s, may have hoped that this was a way to perform prestigious military masculinities that demonstrated bravery, physical strength, and self-control, but in fact they were repeatedly mocked by onlookers for 'playing at soldiers'.[81] What is at stake here is not whether some models of masculinity are valued above others, but whether an individual is performing that model correctly. Women have been particularly important as judges of male gender performances. In South Wales in the 1930s, for example, 'strike-breakers and those in the "scab" unions were derided by women for not being real men'; while in the First World War women took it upon themselves to hand out white feathers to men they deemed to be shirking their gendered responsibilities by refusing to fight.[82] This ability to validate particular gender performances by conferring or withholding recognition should be understood as a third kind of power-creating hierarchies between men.

In this sense communication communities also function as sites of interpretation. Unless a man's performance can be identified as one of an acknowledged repertoire of masculinities then his social status will remain uncertain at best. At this stage, considerations of ethnicity frequently become important. Communities have often refused to acknowledge the legitimacy of performances of high-status masculinities by immigrant or non-white men. Those same men might enjoy high status within another communication community. This kind of power is particularly pressing for trans politics: an individual who is biologically female, and identifies with a particular masculinity, might find that their gender performance is not recognised as legitimate by the audiences that individual encounters.[83]

This provides a model for a third type of crisis of masculinity: a moment when communities suddenly refuse to recognise as legitimate the gender performances of large numbers of men. That moment when large numbers of men were suddenly deemed physically substandard as they volunteered to fight in the Second Boer War might offer an example; another might be sudden changes in attitudes towards promiscuity during the AIDS crisis. In modern British history it is feminism that has created the most acute male anxieties about the legitimacy of their gender performances. Feminist campaigns against domestic abuse or sexual incontinence in the late nineteenth century were rarely interested in challenging hierarchies between types of masculinity; instead, activists tended to accuse men of failing to live up to the role of the loving, self-controlled breadwinner.[84] More recently, anxieties about 'political correctness' – a term which refers to informal policing of public address in the pursuit of respectful treatment of minority groups and women – reflect concerns that familiar forms of male performance are being actively repudiated by women. This of course runs in tandem with women's participation in contests over cultural norms described above. Thus, a study of online reactions to a feminist campaign in 2013 urging retailers to stop selling 'lads' mags' found that men responded by depicting men and masculinity variously as 'under threat', 'attacked', 'victimised', or 'demonised' so that 'men are not allowed to be men'.[85] The hostility to women passing judgement on men is dramatised by the term adopted by some radicalised misogynists online – 'incel' – which is a portmanteau term meaning 'involuntary celibate'.[86] Their diagnosis of a crisis of masculinity, although nonsensical in many respects, draws attention to the fact that successful performances of gender depend on an audience's power to confer or withhold recognition of that performance's legitimacy.

Institutional rewards and sanctions

The last of our four operations of power describes the processes whereby individuals are positioned in relation to sets of institutional practices, rewards, and sanctions once their gender performances have been recognised as either legitimate or illegitimate. Men who were acknowledged to be good husbands and providers, for example, were said to be more likely to rise up the ranks of trade unions in the mid-twentieth century.[87] Alternatively, men who are not recognised as good providers for their families can become targeted by agents of the state including social workers and the Child Support Agency. Perhaps the best example of the state rewarding or penalising masculinities can be seen in how it enfranchised some men but not others.[88] The electoral reforms of the late nineteenth century deliberately set out to enfranchise fathers of families with a settled residence who were economically independent: recipients of poor relief and men without a settled residence of their own were ineligible to vote, and during the First World War conscientious objectors were also stripped of the franchise. State-sponsored rewards and sanctions multiplied in the late nineteenth century as new forms of liberal social science encouraged politicians to believe that the morals of the poor could be reformed by legislation – prompting new restrictions on leisure practices, alcohol consumption, and domestic violence as well as increases to women's rights.[89] This liberal optimism may later have waned, but identifying and regulating 'problematic' masculinities has remained central to the activities of the modern state.

But were there any changes in the distribution of institutional rewards such as might constitute a crisis of masculinity? The Terror during the French Revolution and the histories of modern dictatorships might furnish examples, but modern British history furnishes nothing comparable. The closest contender is possibly the flurry of measures passed by the Whig governments of the 1830s, which destabilised traditional patterns of political, social, and religious authority, placed new restrictions on female and child labour, and which (in the form of new police forces, attacks on trade unions, and the New Poor Law) threatened multiple aspects of working-class masculinity.[90] Twentieth-century reforms have been far less sweeping in their effects, although often consequential for particular communities (particularly in relation to interwar unemployment). The decriminalisation of male homosexuality in 1967 (in England and Wales), 1980 (in Scotland), and 1982 (in Northern Ireland), and the introduction of gay marriage in 2013, stand out as important moments, but they cannot be said to have precipitated a crisis in any but the cultural sense.

Conclusion

So why has it been so easy for historians and commentators to identify 'crises of masculinity'? The argument of this chapter has been that, in addition to changing relations between men and women, and changes in the structures of the family and labour market, relations of power between masculinities have also been in flux. I have identified four different kinds of power relations, each of which might be disrupted or reconfigured in such a way that produced perceptions of crisis.

This is not to say that those perceptions have been accurate: change has been easier to find than crisis. This is what one would expect, given the turn against 'crisis talk' amongst historians. But one advantage of distinguishing between the various kinds of power relationships described above is that it helps us to understand *why* change has not amounted to crisis. In the first place, I have argued that the cultural processes that give meaning to gender operate in discrete communication communities, each with their own structures and hierarchies. As such, crises of cultural authority or of recognition are likely to be localised within communities, and rarely capable of disrupting the broader gender order. This remains true despite the spread of mass communications. Secondly, it will be apparent that change in one of our four operations of power will not necessarily lead to change in any of the others. This offers a way of explaining why, despite repeated observations that masculinity was changing or in crisis, patterns of sexual inequality have proved so durable.

What this study of crisis leads us to, then, is a clearer sense of what kinds of change have been important to the history of masculinity, and this provides an agenda for future research. Accounts of cultural change, sensitive to the variety of communication communities, need to attend to the expansion of the available repertoire of masculinities, their changing meanings, and the ways in which their status was contested by an expanding range of institutions claiming authority to determine appropriate norms. We also need a deeper understanding of how men performed multiple masculinities, and how the resources needed to perform particular masculinities were distributed inequitably: that takes us to the heart not only of histories of class, but also disability and ageing. We need a better appreciation of the conditions in which audiences refused to acknowledge gender performances as legitimate: that will provide a clearer understanding of phenomena like racism. And finally, a deeper understanding of patterns of institutional rewards and sanctions will allow us to see how organisations, businesses, and the state have contributed to those inequalities between men that are part of the warp and weft of the gender order. What kinds of periodisation might this produce? Caught between visions of masculinity perpetually in crisis and the blunt reality of persistent sexual inequality, we need an approach that allows us to reconcile the two – one that can explain how shifting power relationships between men have contributed to the broader gender order. Disaggregating the forms of power that exist between men, and tracing their distinct trajectories, will allow us to explain why masculinities always appear to have been troubled and uncertain, without losing our ability to make meaningful generalisations about change over time.

Notes

1 For example, Isabel Hardman, 'Save the Male! Britain's Crisis of Masculinity', *Spectator*, 3 May 2014; Pankaj Mishra, 'The Crisis in Modern Masculinity',

Guardian, 17 March 2018; Anthony Clare, *On Men: Masculinity in Crisis* (London: Cornerstone Digital, 2000); Anthony Clare, 'Masculinity in Crisis', *World Today*, 73:6 (2017–2018). For a significant political intervention, see Diane Abbott's 2013 Demos lecture 'Britain's Crisis of Masculinity', 16 May 2013, www.dianeabbott.org.uk/news/news/articles/item915 (accessed 24 April 2023).

2 A useful guide to the early historical literature on crises of masculinity can be found in Frank Mort, *Cultures of Consumption: Masculinities and Social Space in Late Twentieth-Century Britain* (London: Routledge, 1996), 212, n. 34. See also Tracey Loughran, 'A Crisis of Masculinity? Re-writing the History of Shell-Shock and Gender in First World War Britain', *History Compass*, 11:9 (2013), 728. Important accounts include Elaine Showalter, *Sexual Anarchy: Gender and Culture at the Fin de Diècle* (London: Virago, 1991); Susan Kingsley Kent, *Making Peace: The Reconstruction of Gender in Interwar Britain* (Princeton: Princeton University Press, 1993); Lynne Segal, *Slow Motion: Changing Masculinities, Changing Men*, 3rd edn (Basingstoke: Palgrave Macmillan, 2007), xviii–xx. Although John Tosh is sometimes cited as having identified a crisis of masculinity in the late nineteenth century, he explicitly denied this interpretation: John Tosh, *A Man's Place: Masculinity and the Middle-Class Home in Victorian England* (New Haven: Yale University Press, 1999), 160. Useful introductions to the sociological literature are Tim Edwards, *Cultures of Masculinity* (London: Routledge, 2006), ch. 1; David Morgan, 'The Crisis in Masculinity', in Kathy Davis, Mary Evans, and Judith Lorber (eds), *The Handbook of Gender and Women's Studies* (London: SAGE, 2012), 109–123; Steven Roberts (ed.), *Debating Modern Masculinities: Change, Continuity, Crisis?* (Basingstoke: Palgrave Macmillan, 2014).

3 Judith Allen, 'Men Interminably in Crisis?', *Radical History Review*, 82 (2002), 191–207.

4 John Tosh, *Manliness and Masculinities in Nineteenth-Century Britain: Essays on Gender, Family and Empire* (Harlow: Pearson Longman, 2005), 19; Morgan, 'The Crisis in Masculinity', 111–115.

5 Regrettably, there is not space here to consider Ireland's distinctive dynamics.

6 This analytical framework is set out fully in Ben Griffin, 'Hegemonic Masculinity as a Historical Problem', *Gender & History*, 30:2 (2018), 377–400.

7 R. W. Connell and J. W. Messerschmidt, 'Hegemonic Masculinity: Rethinking the Concept', *Gender and Society*, 19 (2005), 829–859. For a critical account, see Griffin, 'Hegemonic Masculinity'.

8 My thinking on this point has been strongly influenced by Henry French and Mark Rothery, *Man's Estate: Landed Gentry Masculinities, 1660–1900* (Oxford: Oxford University Press, 2012).

9 Ben Griffin, 'Masculinities and Parliamentary Culture in Modern Britain', in Sean Brady *et al.* (eds), *The Palgrave Handbook of Masculinity and Political Culture in Europe* (Basingstoke: Palgrave Macmillan, 2018), 408–409, 418–22.

10 Mort, *Cultures of Consumption*, 171–173.

11 Keith McClelland, 'Masculinity and the "Representative Artisan" in Britain, 1850–1880', in Michael Roper and John Tosh (eds), *Manful Assertions: Masculinities in Britain since 1800* (London: Routledge, 1991).
12 Andrew Davies, *Leisure, Gender and Poverty: Working-Class Culture in Salford and Manchester, 1900–1939* (Buckingham: Open University Press, 1992), 49–50; Simon Szreter and Kate Fisher, *Sex before the Sexual Revolution: Intimate Life in England 1918–1963* (Cambridge: Cambridge University Press, 2010), ch. 5.
13 Brent Shannon, *The Cut of His Coat: Men, Dress, and Consumer Culture in Britain, 1860–1914* (Athens: Ohio University Press, 2006), 139.
14 Mark Roodhouse, *Black Market Britain: 1939–1955* (Oxford: Oxford University Press, 2013).
15 Mike Savage, 'Affluence and Social Change in the Making of Technocratic Middle-Class Identities: Britain, 1939–55', *Contemporary British History*, 22:4 (2008), 457–476.
16 Michael Roper, *Masculinity and the British Organisation Man since 1945* (Oxford: Oxford University Press, 1994).
17 Matthew Worley, *No Future: Punk, Politics and British Youth Culture, 1976–1984* (Cambridge: Cambridge University Press, 2017), ch. 7.
18 Ronnie Johnson and Arthur McIvor, 'Dangerous Work, Hard Men and Broken Bodies: Masculinity in the Clydeside Heavy Industries, c. 1930–1970s', *Labour History Review*, 69:2 (2004), 135–152; Andrew Davies, 'Youth Gangs, Masculinity and Violence in Late Victorian Manchester and Salford', *Journal of Social History*, 32:2 (1998), 353; Nick Hayes, 'Did Manual Workers Want Industrial Welfare? Canteens, Latrines and Masculinity on British Building Sites 1918–1970', *Journal of Social History*, 35:3 (2002), 637–658.
19 Marjorie Levine-Clark, *Unemployment, Welfare, and Masculine Citizenship: 'So Much Honest Poverty' in Britain, 1870–1930* (Basingstoke: Palgrave Macmillan, 2015).
20 Paul Deslandes, *Oxbridge Men: British Masculinity and the Undergraduate Experience, 1850–1920* (Bloomington: Indiana University Press, 2005), 72.
21 Matt Houlbrook, *Queer London: Perils and Pleasures in the Sexual Metropolis, 1918–1957* (Chicago: University of Chicago Press, 2005), 141–149.
22 For an American sociological study, see Peter Hennen, 'Bear Bodies, Bear Masculinity: Recuperation, Resistance, or Retreat?', *Gender and Society*, 19:1 (2005), 25–43.
23 Mort, *Cultures of Consumption*, 175–176.
24 Davies, 'Youth Gangs', *passim*.
25 Davies, *Leisure, Gender and Poverty*, 97.
26 Laura García-Favaro and Rosalind Gill, '"Emasculation Nation Has Arrived": Sexism Rearticulated in Online Responses to Lose the Lads' Mags Campaign', *Feminist Media Studies*, 16:3 (2016), 382.
27 Graham Dawson, *Soldier Heroes: British Adventure, Empire and the Imagining of Masculinities* (London: Routledge, 1994).
28 Martin Francis, *The Flyer: British Culture and the Royal Air Force, 1939–1945* (Oxford: Oxford University Press, 2009).

29 Griffin, 'Hegemonic Masculinity', 384. The con man provides an extreme case: Matt Houlbrook, *The Prince of Tricksters: The Incredible True Story of Netley Lucas, Gentleman Crook* (Chicago: University of Chicago Press, 2016), 58–60.
30 Peter McNeil, 'Macaroni Masculinities', *Fashion Theory*, 4:4 (2000), 373–403; Philip Carter, *Men and the Emergence of Polite Society, Britain 1660–1800* (London: Routledge, 2001); Michèle Cohen, '"Manners" Make the Man: Politeness, Chivalry, and the Construction of Masculinity, 1750–1830', *Journal of British Studies*, 44 (2005), 312–329.
31 Quoted in James Nott, *Going to the Palais: A Social and Cultural History of Dancing and Dance Halls in Britain, 1918–1960* (Oxford: Oxford University Press, 2015), 242.
32 Martin Francis, 'The Domestication of the Male? Recent Research on Nineteenth and Twentieth-Century British Masculinity', *Historical Journal*, 45 (2002), 637–652; John Tosh, 'Home and Away: The Flight from Domesticity in Late-Nineteenth-Century England Re-visited', *Gender & History*, 27:3 (2015), 561–575. Linsey Robb, *Men at Work: The Working Man in British Culture, 1939–1945* (Basingstoke: Palgrave Macmillan, 2015).
33 Quoted in Nott, *Going to the Palais*, 241; see 243 on similar anxieties in the 1950s.
34 Simon Szreter, *Fertility, Class and Gender in Britain 1860–1940* (Cambridge: Cambridge University Press, 1995), 546–549.
35 *Ibid.*, 488–503; Szreter and Fisher, *Sex before the Sexual Revolution*; Siân Pooley, 'Child Care and Neglect: A Comparative Local Study of Late Nineteenth Century Parental Authority', in Lucy Delap, Ben Griffin, and Abigail Wills (eds), *The Politics of Domestic Authority in Britain, 1800–2000* (Basingstoke: Palgrave Macmillan, 2009), 223–242; Siân Pooley, '"All We Parents Want Is That Our Children's Health and Lives Should Be Regarded": Child Health and Parental Concern in England, c.1860–1910', *Social History of Medicine*, 23:3 (2010), 528–548; Pat Ayers, 'The Making of Men: Masculinities in Interwar Liverpool', in Margaret Walsh (ed.), *Working Out Gender: Perspectives from Labour History* (London: Routledge, 1999), 68–83.
36 Helen Smith, 'Working-Class Ideas and Experiences of Sexuality in Twentieth-Century Britain: Regionalism as a Category of Analysis', *Twentieth Century British History*, 29:1 (2018), 75.
37 Matt Houlbrook, 'Soldier Heroes and Rent Boys: Homosex, Masculinities, and Britishness in the Brigade of Guards, circa 1900–1960', *Journal of British Studies*, 42:3 (2003), 351–388.
38 Lucy Delap, '"Be Strong and Play the Man": Anglican Masculinities in the Twentieth Century', in Lucy Delap and Sue Morgan (eds), *Men, Masculinities and Religious Change in Twentieth-Century Britain* (Basingstoke: Palgrave Macmillan, 2013), 138.
39 Michael Young and Peter Willmott, 'Social Grading by Manual Workers', *British Journal of Sociology*, 7:4 (1956), 341; Jon Lawrence, 'Class, "Affluence" and the Study of Everyday Life in Britain, c.1930–64', *Cultural and Social History*, 10:2 (2013), 281.

40 Roper, *Masculinity and the British Organisation Man*, 105.
41 Linsey Robb, 'The "Conchie Corps": Conflict, Compromise and Conscientious Objection in the British Army, 1940–1945', *Twentieth Century British History*, 29:3 (2018), 424.
42 Jill Greenfield, Sean O'Connell, and Chris Reid, 'Fashioning Masculinity: *Men Only*, Consumption and the Development of Marketing in the 1930s', *Twentieth Century British History*, 10:4 (1999), 459, 465.
43 In French and Rothery's model, this would be expressed as the persistence of 'core' values of masculinity articulated through a changing array of conjunctural forms. French and Rothery, *Man's Estate*.
44 Adrian Bingham, *Gender, Modernity, and the Popular Press in Inter-war Britain* (Oxford: Oxford University Press, 2004), 222.
45 Mort, *Cultures of Consumption*, 171.
46 Laura King, *Family Men: Fatherhood and Masculinity in Britain, 1914–1960* (Oxford: Oxford University Press, 2015), 122, 194–195; it should be noted that King's sources are not such as would reveal continuing regional variation. For Pooley's work, see n. 35.
47 Daniel LeMahieu, *A Culture for Democracy: Mass Communication and the Cultivated Mind in Britain between the Wars* (Oxford: Oxford University Press, 1988), 59, 232.
48 On religion, see Ben Griffin, *The Politics of Gender: Masculinity, Political Culture and the Struggle for Women's Rights* (Cambridge: Cambridge University Press, 2012), ch. 4; Delap and Morgan, *Men, Masculinities and Religious change*. On the medical profession, see Frank Mort, *Dangerous Sexualities: Medico-social Politics in England since 1830*, 2nd edn (London: Routledge, 2000).
49 Stefan Collini, *Public Moralists: Political Thought and Intellectual Life in Britain, 1850–1930* (Oxford: Oxford University Press, 1991), ch. 2; Peter Mandler and Susan Pedersen, 'Introduction: The British Intelligentsia after the Victorians', in Peter Mandler and Susan Pedersen (eds), *After the Victorians: Private Conscience and Public Duty in Modern Britain* (London: Routledge, 1994); Jose Harris, *Private Lives, Public Spirit: Britain, 1870–1914* (London: Penguin, 1993), 252–253. On the fracturing of this consensus, see Frank Mort, 'Love in a Cold Climate: Letters, Public Opinion and Monarchy in the 1936 Abdication Crisis', *Twentieth Century British History*, 25:1 (2014), 30–62.
50 Quoted in Frank Mort, *Capital Affairs: London and the Making of the Permissive Society* (New Haven: Yale University Press 2010), 141.
51 Mort, *Cultures of Consumption*, 142 and *passim*.
52 Laura King, '"Now You See a Great Many Men Pushing Their Pram Proudly": Family-Orientated Masculinity Represented and Experienced in Mid-Twentieth-Century Britain', *Cultural and Social History*, 10:4 (2013), 599–617.
53 Ulrike Schultz and Gisela Shaw (eds), *Women in the World's Legal Professions* (Oxford: Oxford University Press, 2003); Brian Harrison, 'Women in a Man's House', *Historical Journal*, 29 (1986), 623–654; Brian Heeney, *The Women's Movement in the Church of England, 1850–1930* (Oxford: Oxford University Press, 1988); Susan

Dowell and Jane Williams, *Bread, Wine and Women: The Ordination Debate in the Church of England* (London: Virago, 1994); Suzanne Franks, *Women and Journalism* (London: I.B. Tauris, 2013), 9–12.
54 For example, the group that calls itself 'Justice for Men and Boys'; *Guardian*, 18 January 2015.
55 *Sun*, 9 November 1998.
56 Griffin, 'Masculinities and Parliamentary Culture', 407–418.
57 Anon, *How to Shine in Society* (Glasgow: G. Watson, 1860), 10.
58 Greenfield *et al.*, 'Fashioning Masculinity', 466.
59 Michael S. Kimmel, 'Masculinity as Homophobia: Fear, Shame and Silence in the Construction of Gender Identity', in Harry Brod and Michael Kaufman (eds), *Theorizing Masculinities* (London: SAGE, 1994), 125.
60 Christopher E. Forth, *Masculinity in the Modern West: Gender, Civilization and the Body* (Basingstoke: Palgrave Macmillan, 2008), 55.
61 Davies, 'Youth Gangs', 363.
62 Johnson and McIvor, 'Dangerous Work'; Hayes, 'Did Manual Workers Want Industrial Welfare?'.
63 Roper, *Masculinity and the British Organisation Man*, 112.
64 Griffin, 'Masculinities and Parliamentary Culture', 406.
65 Bronwen Edwards, 'A Man's World? Masculinity and Metropolitan Modernity at Simpson Piccadilly', in David Gilbert, David Matless, and Brian Short (eds), *Geographies of British Modernity: Space and Society in the Twentieth Century* (Oxford: Oxford University Press, 2003), 161; Mort, *Cultures of Consumption*, 137.
66 Griffin, 'Masculinities and Parliamentary Culture', 412–413.
67 Joanna Bourke, *Dismembering the Male: Men's Bodies, Britain and the Great War* (London: Reaktion Books, 1996); Jessica Meyer, *Men of War: Masculinity and the First World War in Britain* (Basingstoke: Palgrave Macmillan, 2009), ch. 4.
68 *Hansard*, vol. 21, col. 589 (10 February 1911); quoted in Levine-Clark, *Unemployment, Welfare, and Masculine Citizenship*, 86.
69 Tosh, *Manliness and Masculinities*, 20.
70 Joanna Bourke, *Working-Class Cultures in Britain 1890–1960: Gender, Class and Ethnicity* (London: Routledge, 1994), 130–131; Bingham, *Gender, Modernity, and the Popular Press*, 229–236.
71 Tosh, *Manliness and Masculinities*, 21.
72 Gregory Anderson, *Victorian Clerks* (Manchester: Manchester University Press, 1976), 68–71. This point was anticipated by Roper and Tosh (eds), *Manful Assertions*, 19.
73 Leonore Davidoff and Catherine Hall, *Family Fortunes: Men and Women of the Middle Class, 1780–1850* (London: Routledge, 1987), 13.
74 David Kynaston, *Austerity Britain, 1945–51: Smoke in the Valley* (London: Bloomsbury, 2007), 260.
75 Neil Penlington, 'Masculinity and Domesticity in 1930s South Wales: Did Unemployment Change the Domestic Division of Labour?', *Twentieth Century*

British History, 21:3 (2010), 281–299; Levine-Clark, *Unemployment, Welfare, and Masculine Citizenship.*
76 Penny Summerfield (ed.), *Women, Education and the Professions* (Leicester: History of Education Society, 1987); Rosemary Auchmuty, 'Whatever Happened to Miss Bebb? *Bebb v The Law Society* and Women's Legal History', *Legal Studies*, 31:2 (2011), 199–230; Carol Dyhouse, *No Distinction of Sex? Women in British Universities 1870–1939* (London: UCL Press, 1995); Carol Dyhouse, *Students: A Gendered History* (London: Routledge, 2005); Deslandes, *Oxbridge Men.*
77 *Granta*, 15 May 1897, 324.
78 Rita McWilliams Tullberg, *Women at Cambridge*, 2nd edn (Cambridge: Cambridge University Press, 1998), 116–117, 165–167.
79 Greenfield *et al.*, 'Fashioning Masculinity', 467.
80 Martin Petter, '"Temporary Gentlemen" in the Aftermath of the Great War: Rank, Status and the Ex-officer Problem', *Historical Journal*, 37:1 (1994), 141.
81 Hugh Cunningham, *The Volunteer Force: A Social and Political History, 1859–1908* (Hamden: Archon Books, 1975); Penny Summerfield and Corinna Peniston-Bird, *Contesting Home Defence: Men, Women and the Home Guard in the Second World War* (Manchester: Manchester University Press, 2007), 126.
82 Penlington, 'Masculinity and Domesticity', 289; Nicoletta Gullace, *'The Blood of Our Sons': Men, Women and the Renegotiation of Citizenship during the Great War* (Basingstoke: Palgrave Macmillan, 2002), ch. 4.
83 Alison Oram, *Her Husband Was a Woman! Women's Gender-Crossing in Modern British Popular Culture* (London: Routledge, 2007); Jack Halberstam, *Female Masculinity* (Durham, NC: Duke University Press, 1998).
84 Griffin, *The Politics of Gender*, ch. 3.
85 García-Favaro and Gill, '"Emasculation Nation Has Arrived"', 380, 388.
86 Zoe Williams, '"Raw Hatred": Why the "Incel" Movement Targets and Terrorises Women', *Guardian*, 25 April 2018.
87 Penlington, 'Masculinity and Domesticity', 285.
88 Anna Clark, 'Gender, Class and the Nation: Franchise Reform in England, 1832–1928', in James Vernon (ed.), *Re-reading the Constitution: New Narratives in the Political History of England's Long Nineteenth Century* (Cambridge: Cambridge University Press, 1996), 62–88; Griffin, *The Politics of Gender*, pt. 3.
89 Griffin, *The Politics of Gender*, ch. 3.
90 For example, the speech by Rev. J. R. Stephens, *Northern Star*, 17 November 1838, 6; Anna Clark, *The Struggle for the Breeches: Gender and the Making of the British Working Class* (Berkeley: University of California Press, 1995).

Reflection: Masculinities and history for the present

John Tosh

The history of masculinities has been a growing concern in Britain since the early 1990s. Given the lapse of a generation, one might ask how useful it is to measure an established branch of historical scholarship against the aspirations which informed its beginning. In this case the exercise is particularly suspect, since I was one of the handful of scholars who participated in its early development, and I must admit to a measure of retrospective pride on that account. The reason why academic recall serves a useful purpose lies in the continuing relevance of the cultural politics of that time. In the 1990s left politics was deeply imprinted with feminism and gay liberation. Radical scholars from this background asserted the claims of their disciplines to social and political relevance. Men's reactions to the women's movement spanned the entire spectrum from a defensive masculinism to an anti-sexist men's movement which strongly supported women's emancipation. But the impact of these alignments on historical research into men was still comparatively low-key in 1991 when Michael Roper and I published *Manful Assertions*.[1] The book did not of course start with a clean slate. Our theoretical debts to Lynne Segal and R. W. Connell were evident.[2] Historically we were inspired and informed by Leonore Davidoff and Catherine Hall's work on the English middle class.[3]

Manful Assertions was the first attempt to explore the implications of gender theory for the history of masculinity, and to exemplify it in a variety of topics. The book was the outcome of an informal study group beginning in 1988. It had no institutional standing and met in the home of one of the editors. Such informality was characteristic of radical initiatives during this period: one of the best known and most enduring was the London Feminist History Group.[4] Almost by definition, participants in such groups were on the margins of the academic profession, if not completely outside it. In our case we started with a very provisional notion of what we were about. The name of the group evolved from the Men's History Group to the acronym HOMME (history of men, masculinity, etc.).[5] To begin with we focused on readings, mostly culled from other disciplines, with contributions from members growing over time. The idea of producing a collective volume only emerged after more than a year of discussions. Eight members of the group – three women and five men – were featured in the book. Defining the field in the editorial introduction was anything but straightforward. We drew on socialist feminism, sociology, and cultural studies. The arguments that we pursued with most energy then have long since become common wisdom – the separation of men from masculinity; the plurality of masculinity; its capacity for change; and above all its investment in power over women, both material and symbolic. This theoretical position was what most distinguished our book from previous historical work on masculinity in Britain.[6] It occurred to none of us that thirty years on our efforts would be hailed in some quarters as the foundational text of a burgeoning field.

In the 1980s there was still plenty of life in the notion – originating in the 1960s – that the boundaries of academic discourse should be broken open to popular access. Women's history and gay history offered persuasive examples. But *Manful Assertions* was relatively conservative in approach. The reviewer for *Achilles Heel* was probably alone in saluting the book as 'a means to gauge the prospects for a more liberated future'.[7] *Manful Assertions* addressed two constituencies: the historical profession and our intellectual neighbours (sociology and cultural studies). It did not attempt to reach a lay readership. Nor, with the exception of Peter Lewis's memoir on all-male institutions, did it extend the boundaries of academic discourse.[8] All the other contributors were either established historians or aspirants to the profession, and they framed their chapters accordingly. This approach certainly enhanced the likelihood of a respectful hearing from other historians, but it also placed limits on the social reach of our scholarship. The book was a step towards the full gendering of historical practice rather than an engagement with the concerns of the present.

Thirty years on, the relationship of academic scholarship to the present-focused reader continues to prompt reflection. Thus Jorma Kalela calls for a 'history-in-society';[9] while Alix Green champions 'history with public purpose'.[10] But in the present regulatory climate relevance is at risk of being subsumed under the anodyne heading of 'impact'. We need a more focused – and more politically sophisticated – point of address. This explains the recent recourse to Michel Foucault's 'history of the present'. The phrase sometimes denotes little more than a nod at the ideological conjuncture in which a particular history is composed. But Foucault had something more radical in mind. History, he believed, should begin with 'a diagnostic of the present'. Its aim was to understand the fault lines of the present. Foucault did not propose a naïve projection of today's preoccupations backwards in time. Instead the clue to understanding today's crises lay in the always different world of the past. In this way, he believed, history tells us what we are today. The 'history of the present' prioritises the most insistent crisis points in the present and looks for their antecedents in the past.[11]

The aspiration to write history of the present sometimes produces only oblique results. But Foucault's contribution has an obvious relevance for historians of masculinity, if only because crises of masculinity have framed much of our discussion. In 1991 that way of thinking about masculinity was widely current among gender specialists. In the introduction to *Manful Assertions* we described the book as 'a symptom of masculinity in crisis',[12] but it was more than that. The plurality of masculinities documented in the book showed that existing patterns of masculinity were subject to change, not cast in stone. It followed that the changes which were causing such angst in the present were not so much a crisis as part of an ongoing pattern of adaptation. If I have a reservation about the history of the present, it is its confinement within academic discourse. Foucault did not consider how work under this banner might make a difference by reaching a lay readership, and this has been an almost non-existent priority among subsequent practitioners of history of the present. My suggestion is that 'history of the present' could usefully be relabelled as 'history *for* the present'. The change of preposition implies not only a more compelling prioritisation of topicality, but an active public to whom some at least of our work can speak directly.

How that public might actually be reached is a continuing conundrum for the practice of a democratic history. Not many historical works of an explanatory and critical kind have made their mark in the marketplace. So far the most effective response to the demand of topicality is the History and Policy website (historyandpolicy.org.uk). Policy papers by Jeffrey Weeks, Lucy Delap, and Laura King take their place in a field dominated by political and economic subject matter. It is hard to measure the impact of History and Policy, but unacknowledged use by journalists probably accounts for most of its impact. In a world flooded by the written word, broadcasting is a critical medium: not so much television, but radio, which can accommodate talks and discussions not bound by the three-minute attention span. Radio 3 and Radio 4 have an honourable record of in-depth historical enquiries.

But achieving access to the wider public depends on more than choosing the right medium. It raises the issue of what historical register we adopt in our published work. Too often historians have been inhibited from adapting the historical frameworks which prevail outside the academic world for fear of 'dumbing down', the assumption being that a more direct engagement with the public must conflict with the tenets of the discipline. One such historical framework is analogy: a means of orientation which people habitually apply to the past as well as the present. Historical analogy is often equated with repetition, a profoundly ahistorical approach which academics rightly disparage. But the real value of pursuing an analogical approach is that it reveals the differences between the chosen historical moments, as well as what appears to be the same.

The interpretative value of the tension between congruence and divergence is demonstrated by the way historians approach the crisis of masculinity. Some media comment altogether denies history a role. According to this view nothing in the past bears comparison with the present crisis, which makes the experience of crisis all the more overwhelming and portentous. The alternative view is that today is a re-run of the 'sexual anarchy' of the *fin de siècle*, launched on its public path in 1990 by Elaine Showalter's book of that title. Recent historical scholarship leaves no doubt of the upheaval in relations between the sexes in the *fin de siècle*. On the other hand, closer examination reveals only a limited convergence. This is particularly clear with regard to men's responses to the perception of crisis. At the close of the nineteenth century the dominant reaction to both the feminist offensive and the enhanced visibility of homosexuality was to narrow the definition of manliness so that any suspicion of the feminine was excluded. Today there is a broader spectrum of response. The extremes of violence and exploitation which go under the name of toxic masculinity are cause for alarm, but against them must be set the relative freedom of sexual expression and the social acceptability of shared domestic roles. Analogical analysis shows that the complexity of gender relations today is formed partly by deep continuities, partly by genuine innovation, and partly by paths not taken in earlier crises.[13]

In one of the foundational texts of our study, Joan Scott wrote, 'I assume that history's representations of the past help construct gender for the present.'[14] More than an assumption is required to bring historical enquiry into a productive engagement with the present. If our starting point as historians of masculinity is to be the priorities of a lay audience, the direction of our scholarship may need to be reset. Here I give two examples – not accomplished cases of history for the present, but some indication of what such a history might look like. Both document major constituents of masculine identity whose disappearance helps to explain some of the current agonising about masculinity: the collapse of the twentieth-century model of male working-class employment, based on relative job security, pride in skill, and homosocial solidarity; and the impact on masculinity of the effective disappearance of the expectation of military service.

Historians may not be the first experts people turn to for an understanding of men's experience of the labour market in modern Britain, but they have an illuminating narrative to tell. Unemployment has taken the limelight,[15] but the history of the male working class during the twentieth century is about not only the ravages of unemployment but the changing nature of work itself. As Helen Smith shows in her chapter above, during the first two thirds of the twentieth century the workplace held a pivotal place in the culture of the English working man. Unless put out of work, there was a reasonable prospect of stable employment during which close ties developed with fellow workers. This was most obviously true of skilled workers, but it also applied to many in manual or semi-skilled work, notwithstanding the onerous nature of much employment.[16] In many occupations, notably mining, shipbuilding, and engineering, the labour process was based on the team, evoking strong values of mutual aid and solidarity, often carried over into leisure time. Occupational communities like these were the foundation of a confident masculine identity. Progression from apprenticeship to experienced worker was the gateway to full masculine status, validated by the peer group. As the radical trade unionist Jimmy Reid remarked in 1971, 'We didn't only build ships on the Clyde, we built men.'[17]

From a gender perspective the culture of the shop floor was flawed: the men were uncompromising in their affirmation of their superiority over women, and often content to limit themselves to the margins of domestic life.[18] But the value to men of a homosocial work culture was undeniable. It not only made their working lives more endurable; it conferred standing in the wider community. The dignity of labour was the precondition of a respectful treatment in the culture at large. It was emblematic of the labour movement. The steady erosion of that shop floor culture since the 1970s therefore entailed more than the loss of reliable employment.[19] The time is surely ripe for a reappraisal of that vanished world in the light of the prevalent conditions of employment today.

Even less thought has been given to my second suggestion: to address the ways in which masculine identities have been modified by the much reduced prospect of participation in military conflict. The winding up of national service in 1962 ended a period of fifty years in which most British men could expect to fight at some point in their lives. National defence became subsumed in the nuclear deterrent which appeared to negate the need for conventional forces. Britain has been called a 'post-military' society, not because the state's military capacity has been significantly reduced, but because an increasingly technologised army has retreated to the margins of society.[20] A future demand for universal conscription is almost inconceivable. As a realistic expectation, the prospect of military service has retreated to near vanishing point.

These are changes not only in the status of the armed services, but in the content of masculinity, especially its hegemonic forms. At issue here is not the realities of military service (which for the vast majority of national servicemen did not extend to actual combat), but what the military obligation meant to the generality of men. The military dimension of masculinity has been an almost permanent fixture because in most societies men must shoulder the burden of defence and be prepared to place their lives at risk. Historically one of the prime functions of codes of masculinity was to overcome men's reluctance to put themselves on the line by defining manhood in militarised terms – hence the emphasis on physical courage, stoical endurance, the suppression of emotion, and an absolute distinction from women.[21] The past generation has seen a progressive undermining of martial masculinity. In her illuminating study of the Falklands War, Helen Parr predicts that the ways in which manhood has been linked to the responsibility of military service will seem 'dated, perhaps even absurd'.[22] That erosion is already under way. Martial masculinity retains much of it appeal as fantasy, in boys' play and in gaming, but it seems to have forfeited its authority as a code for living. The change is implicit in historical accounts of the post-war turn towards male domesticity, and in contemporary challenges to binary sexual difference. But the ramifications of the decline of martial masculinity are more extensive and are a prime candidate for a fully contextualised study of the twentieth century.

To these two perspectives I would add a theme which has much less popular resonance but which potentially offers a significant adjustment to the framing of masculine identity: the development and popularisation of the concept of 'masculinity' itself. In a telling theoretical intervention ten years ago Jeanne Boydston warned against essentialising the gender terms embedded in our own culture and imposing them on the societies we study in the past.[23] Though historians of masculinity may be as guilty as the generality of gender historians, they have a respectable track record in this respect: thus Victorian manly precepts are generally distinguished from their contemporary equivalents.[24] But what we have *not* done is to explain the historical processes by which masculinity came to prevail. The popularisation of 'masculinity' marked a significant change in the way men (and women) thought about men's gender. 'Manliness' was an external measure; it foregrounded demeanour and action, as validated in the estimation of one's peers. 'Masculinity', on the other hand, is both a psychic and a social category: it brings together the physical, emotional, and sexual, as facets of a whole identity. It is not just a code of conduct but expresses the 'authentic' self.[25]

Naming men's gender as 'masculinity' has had consequences. The notion of masculinity as an integrated identity makes any encroachment on it seem all the more threatening. Male unemployment and an assertive women's movement threaten not just particular areas of life but the integrity of masculinity itself. Anxiety about masculinity as a personal attribute can make men more vulnerable to self doubt and enhance the appeal of hypermasculine behaviour as a compensatory strategy. In so far as recent decades have witnessed a crisis of masculinity, the language in which men's experience is characterised (both by men and by women) tends to inflate rather than minimise the sense of loss and failure. How men have come to own masculinity is thus an historical issue of considerable moment. Relevant factors include the popularisation of Freudian psychology, which elevated the priority given to interiority, and second-wave feminism, which employed 'masculinity' as a convenient label under which to analyse men's stake in the oppression of women. But a coherent narrative has yet to materialise. It is perhaps the most surprising void in historical scholarship. We could better interpret men's condition today if we understood how masculinity acquired its conceptual hegemony.

Shortly after *Manful Assertions* appeared, R. W. Connell complained that historical work on themes of masculinity was 'extremely rare'.[26] Connell contrasted the poverty of academic scholarship with the beguiling image of a golden age so popular with masculinist groups of the right.[27] In Connell's view what was lacking was a history of masculinity across the ages which tracked the development of hegemonic forms of masculinity to the present day. Few scholars took their lead from Connell's bold preliminary sketch.[28] In planning *Manful Assertions* it was no part of our intention to address that need. One of the few attempts to grapple with the problem was made in a symposium in the *Journal of British Studies* in 2005. The editors, Karen Harvey and Alexandra Shepard, aimed to establish long-term narratives of British masculinity, but the strength of the symposium lay in the individual contributions, none of which spanned more than a century or so.[29]

There are several reasons for this historiographical imbalance. The revolution in gender studies established that masculinity is everywhere in culture, politics, and society, but that very universality militates against a coherent linear narrative. It is also hard to abstract masculinity from the vast extent of historical writing which traditionally has been the history of men in all but name. In *Manful Assertions* we favoured a case-study approach for a different reason. We maintained that this was the only way to do justice to what we took to be the defining character of masculinity: the tension between structure and subjectivity. Extended linear history was likely to be weighted towards power and precept, at the expense of interiority. For all these reasons a high priority has therefore been attached to realising a particular conjuncture in fully contextualised form. This is why the historiography of masculinity has been more dependent than most on collections of case studies, at the expense of overviews in depth.[30]

At first glance this hardly looks like an effective way of addressing the needs of the present. From the vantage point of advocates of 'the big picture' – Connell's phrase – case studies are beside the point: what counts is the linear logic of history over extended time. But work on that scale is not the only way of registering the needs of the present. History connects with wider audiences not only by time depth, but also by studies confined within a specific historical moment. Such studies are a rich source of thinking by analogy. The particularities of person and circumstance may not convey the direction of travel, but they can bring into focus continuities and ruptures which serve to define the present moment more clearly and to identify alternative routes to the future. From that perspective *Manful Assertions* and the present volume are recognisably phases of the same endeavour.

Notes

1 Michael Roper and John Tosh (eds), *Manful Assertions: Masculinities in Britain since 1800* (London: Routledge, 1991).
2 Lynne Segal, *Slow Motion: Changing Masculinities, Changing Men* (London: Virago, 1990), R. W. Connell, *Gender and Power: Society, the Person, and Sexual Politics* (Cambridge: Polity Press, 1987).
3 Leonore Davidoff and Catherine Hall, *Family Fortunes: Men and Women of the English Middle Class, 17870–1850* (London: Routledge, 1987).
4 London Feminist History Group, *The Sexual Dynamics of History: Men's Power, Women's Resistance* (London: Pluto Press, 1983).
5 To my knowledge this name was only once taken up in print. Graham Dawson, *Soldier Heroes: British Adventure, Empire and the Imagining of Masculinities* (London: Routledge, 1994), xi.
6 We particularly had in mind J. A. Mangan and James Walvin (eds), *Manliness and Morality: Middle-Class Masculinity in Britain and America, 1800–1940* (Manchester: Manchester University Press, 1987), which confined its attention to precept and considered its male subjects in isolation from women.
7 Gini Whitehead, review of *Manful Assertions*, *Achilles Heel*, autumn 1991.
8 Peter M. Lewis, 'Mummy, Matron and the Maids: Feminine Presence and Absence in Male Institutions, 1934–63', in Roper and Tosh (eds), *Manful Assertions*, 168–189.
9 Jorma Kalela, *Making History: The Historian and Uses of the Past* (Basingstoke: Palgrave Macmillan, 2012), 146.
10 Alix R. Green, *History, Policy and Public Purpose: Historians and Historical Thinking in Government* (London: Palgrave Macmillan, 2016), 6.
11 Michel Foucault, *Discipline and Punish: The Birth of the Prison*, trans. Alan Sheridan (New York: Vintage Books, 1995), 30–31.
12 Michael Roper and John Tosh, 'Introduction: Historians and the Politics of Masculinity', in Roper and Tosh (eds), *Manful Assertions*, 19. This perception was shared in Frank Mort's review: 'Crisis Points: Masculinities in History and Social Theory', *Gender and History*, 6:1 (1994), 124–130.
13 For a brief survey of work in progress, see John Tosh, *Why History Matters* (London: Red Globe Press, 2019), 66–69.

14 Joan Wallach Scott, *Gender and the Politics of History* (New York: Columbia University Press, 1988), 2.
15 An excellent recent example is Marjorie Levine-Clark, *Unemployment, Welfare, and Masculine Citizenship: 'So Much Honest Poverty' in Britain, 1870–1930* (Basingstoke: Palgrave Macmillan, 2015).
16 Paul Willis, 'Shop-Floor Culture, Masculinity and the Wage Form', in John Clarke, Chas Critcher, and Richard Johnson (eds), *Working Class Culture: Studies in History and Theory* (London: Hutchinson, 1979), 196.
17 Quoted in Ronnie Johnston and Arthur McIvor, 'Dangerous Work, Hard Men and Broken Bodies: Masculinity and the Clydeside Heavy Industries, c. 1930–1970s', *Labour History Review*, 69:2 (2004), 138.
18 Norman Dennis, Fernando Henriques, and Clifford Slaughter, *Coal Is Our Life: An Analysis of a Yorkshire Mining Community* (London: Tavistock Publications, 1956), 226, 243; Cynthia Cockburn, *Brothers: Male Dominance and Technological Change* (London: Pluto Press, 1983), 133–134.
19 The classic treatment of this theme is Susan Faludi, *Stiffed: The Betrayal of Modern Man* (New York: W. Morrow and Co., 1999).
20 Martin Shaw, *Post-military Society: Militarism, Demilitarization, and War at the End of the Twentieth Century* (Cambridge: Polity Press, 1991).
21 Joshua S. Goldstein, *War and Gender: How Gender Shapes the War System and Vice Versa* (Cambridge: Cambridge University Press, 2001), 282–290.
22 Helen Parr, *Our Boys: The Story of a Paratrooper* (London: Penguin, 2018), 290.
23 Jeanne Boydston, 'Gender as a Question of Historical Analysis', *Gender and History*, 20:3 (2008), 558–583.
24 John Tosh, *Manliness and Masculinities in Nineteenth-Century Britain: Essays on Gender, Family and Empire* (Harlow: Pearson Longman, 2005), 2–4, 61–82.
25 Michael Roper, 'Between Manliness and Masculinity: The "War Generation" and the Psychology of Fear in Britain, 1914–1950', *Journal of British Studies*, 44:2 (2005), 350, 361.
26 R. W. Connell, 'The Big Picture: Masculinities in Recent World History', *Theory and Society*, 22 (1993), 606.
27 R. W. Connell, *The Men and the Boys* (Cambridge: Polity Press, 2000), 5–6.
28 Connell, 'The Big Picture', 603–614.
29 Special feature on masculinities, *Journal of British Studies*, 44:2 (2005).
30 Other examples of the case-study genre are Heather Ellis and Jessica Meyer (eds), *Masculinity and the Other: Historical Perspectives* (Newcastle upon Tyne: Cambridge Scholars Publishing, 2009); and John H. Arnold and Sean Brady (eds), *What Is Masculinity? Historical Dynamics from Antiquity to the Contemporary World* (Basingstoke: Palgrave Macmillan, 2011).

Part III

Everyday lives

7

Gender, locality, and culture: Revisiting masculinities in the Liverpool docklands, 1900–1939

Pat Ayers

This chapter arises out of a long-standing preoccupation with dockland family economies in interwar Liverpool. Initial work highlighted household tensions around money and the extent to which both men and women colluded to maintain the status and domestic prerogatives afforded men as providers, even in situations where they did not provide.[1] A desire to understand and explain *behaviour* beyond the rather simplistic 'men oppressing women' model diverted attention to an exploration of the construction and expression of masculinity in the North End of Liverpool. The extent to which masculine identities have varied historically, culturally, and spatially has long been recognised.[2] Numerous case studies highlighting the significance of factors such as class, locality, and industrial setting have added measurably to our understanding of the complex mix of factors and influences that shaped gendered identities and relationships in the decades before the Second World War and demonstrate the value of a spatially focused approach.[3]

Analysis of Liverpool's North End communities showed that although understandings of manhood did not take a common form, the key collective identity in northern dockland Liverpool was gender rather than class.[4] Even while writing, though, the limitations of what was being argued were only too clear; crucially that the masculinities described and the processes by which they were fashioned were particular to that area of the city which was the focus of the study. John Tosh has shown the value of 'exploring the social and cultural meanings of masculinity in specific historical conjunctures, where other identities and other structuring principles are also in play'.[5] What follows shifts attention to a different dockland setting to highlight the continued importance of the local study in understanding the influences that contribute to the shaping of a masculine sense of self and, as Doreen Massey has argued, the infinite adaptability of patriarchy to accommodate different developmental forms to ensure the endurance of male power.[6]

Context

Pre-war dockland Liverpool comprised chains of residential areas from Bootle in the north to Garston some eight miles to the south. These localities housed many thousands of men, women, and children who shared space with warehouses, mills, shipyards, and hundreds of port-related industries and services. However, whatever the commonalities of experience linking those lived along the waterfront – most obviously poverty – there were clear differences that created diverse arenas within which local masculinities were constructed and played out. Significantly, in the South End docklands, the presence of a long-established Black community and the emergence of a significant Anglo-Chinese enclave in the latter part of the nineteenth century means that exploration of the construction of individual and collective identities within those localities – whatever their origins for those with either brown *or* white skin – must be contextualised relative to racism and ethnic prejudice.[7] In terms of this chapter's return to Liverpool masculinities, though, the existence of a series of interviews with men and women who had grown up in Garston in the decades before the Second World War made this locality the most obvious starting point.[8]

Garston was only incorporated into Liverpool in 1902. In arguing for the city's expansion, the area was portrayed as 'a little local district governed by a clique'.[9] Those campaigning for the continuance of self-government were understandably outraged by this sort of dismissive rhetoric. By the beginning of the twentieth century, the area surrounding Garston Docks had already become an important centre of commerce and industry. Unlike Liverpool, Garston Docks were constructed and developed by railway companies keen to facilitate fast and competitively priced transmission of imports and exports. Investment in hydraulic cranes and other technology facilitated the movement of heavy tonnage such as timber, coal, iron ore, and perishable imports. Miles of railway sidings and warehouses made the dock estate attractive to carriers. In addition to those directly employed on the railways, all associated services undertaken by stevedores, dock labourers, porters, and warehousemen were under the control of the railway company,[10] giving Garston 'so distinct an individuality'.[11]

Several important industries were also located in Garston, offering alternative employment to local men and women. Some were technologically sophisticated with relatively small workforces but others, such as copper processing, the gas works, and Morton's iron and engineering works, employed large numbers of skilled and unskilled workers. Smaller firms including Rawlinson's Sawmill and the bottle works were collectively significant. Although several companies employed women, the local labour market overall was highly sex-segmented and in common with other

Liverpool firms, the marriage bar was firmly in place. However, at the turn of the century, the introduction of a new area of production challenged the status quo in a number of ways. This relative latecomer to Garston industry made a cultural impact that stretched beyond the factory gates, infusing mill town attitudes into the Garston labour market. Wilson's, which manufactured bobbins and shuttles, originated in Todmorden, a mill town on the Lancashire/Yorkshire border. The company, which imported timber through Garston Docks, opened a local branch in 1892. Within five years, the works had expanded and many departments relocated to the new premises. By 1930, all production was undertaken at Garston.[12]

Large numbers of workers from the original Cornholme site accompanied the firm, swelling the local community and filtering textile area culture into the existing dockland setting. Most obviously, the firm employed large numbers of women and had no marriage bar. We can only speculate about the motivation and process by which change happened but by the time Bryant & May opened their match works in Garston in 1922, with women making up two thirds of the workforce, the new factory was the only one in the area that still obliged women employees to leave when they wed. Of course, the employment of women to replace men during the First World War might have been significant in influencing this shift in practice but throughout the rest of the city, men temporarily displaced by war regained their jobs on return and there is no evidence that traditional attitudes to the 'proper' place of married women in the labour market were affected by the experience of war, even in new 'sunrise' firms of the 1930s.

However, change in employment practice did not necessarily imply change in employee behaviour. Traditional notions of respectability and the association of married women with unpaid domestic work within the home meant that many women still left work upon marriage and of those who did stay on, relatively few remained once children came along. Crucially, women had some choice in the matter and the opportunity to engage in paid employment on their own behalf offered options if husbands did not/could not live up to expectations with regard to household support.

Furthermore, interviews with local men and women often revealed very different attitudes and experiences than were to be found in other parts of Liverpool. Some male interviewees sought to distance themselves from the rough culture of neighbours, emphasising the importance of living 'respectably'. Several spoke reflectively about setting up home for the first time, their emotions and sometimes romantic expectations of girlfriends and wives, which were perhaps initially fuelled by the cinema and other forms of popular culture but reflected, for some men at least, a sense of manhood that accommodated attitudes and responsibilities that elsewhere in the city, if overtly expressed, would have diluted masculine credibility.[13] While popular culture might have inspired more idealised romantic models of masculinity for local men to aspire to, the socio-economic environment had to encourage, or at least tolerate, such expressions of gender identity.[14] Albeit not representative of anything other than those who were sharing their memories, the testimony was beguiling. In particular, the gendered division of household chores, especially those related to childcare, was less acute than elsewhere in the city.

Laura King has identified the rise of 'a family-orientated masculinity' in British working-class communities following the First World War. She argues that while this did not necessarily challenge traditional understandings about gendered areas of responsibility within households, popular press promotion of positive images of fatherhood validated men's relationship with their children and offered an additional dimension to masculine ideals that some men embraced.[15] The expansion in discourse King notes might actually, however, have reflected as much as initiated broader expectations associated with fatherhood as a facet of masculinity. It is always difficult to disentangle cause and effect but influences are rarely one way. Certainly, the presence of 'lovely dads' whose role as fathers carried real meaning was evident in many parts of Liverpool. What set Garston apart was that without prompting, men spoke about their relationships with children as something natural and part of everyday experience, public expression of which did not compromise their manhood.

When Tanyard worker Bill J. and his wife were planning to marry, for example, they went each week to the local pawnbroker and bought unredeemed household goods. There was pride in his voice when he said, 'We had everything we needed, right down to salt and pepper.' He was clearly untroubled by potential public exposure as a doting dad: 'I always took the babies out … I used to take them for miles. Pushing the old pram.'[16] Asked about shopping, John P. recalled that 'always and ever, I brought in the salt fish for Sundays'.[17] Mary L. remembers, 'On Sundays, *after* the pubs had shut the dads would turn the rope for us, in the street, while we all queued up for our turn.'[18] There were many men to the north of the river whose commitment to wives and families was absolute, who regarded fatherhood as a joy as well as a responsibility, who sat up with sick children, bathed babies, and shared their food with sons and daughters but their involvement tended to be confined to the home.[19]

Interestingly, several census forms completed by Garston husbands recorded the occupations of their wives as, for example, 'Looking after the family' and 'Domestic Service. At Home'. Peter O., father of two young children whose wife was a borer in the Bobbin Works, recorded his mother-in-law's occupation as 'Househelp'.[20] This practice was still unusual but suggestive of a recognised value placed on housework, not found in a similar sample for the North End.

Of course, attitudes implied by these examples have no universal application and whatever the extent of men's 'help', it was still women who had primary responsibility for childcare and domestic tasks. Moreover, as elsewhere in the city, a family's disposable income was contingent on how much the man turned over to his wife for 'housekeeping'. Sean O'Connell has highlighted the extent to which a woman's choice of a husband dictated the extent to which she struggled to keep house.[21] Although in Garston some married women undertook paid work outside the home and others took in lodgers, what they earned seems primarily to have been used for family support, while men's wages were theirs to share or to keep – distribution was in their gift. As Valerie Burton has shown for seafarers, while marriage and fatherhood increasingly 'became key reference points in the definition of masculinity' and men's role as breadwinners was actually used as leverage in wage bargaining, they retained an absolute right to decide on the destiny of the wage they secured.[22]

Married women who worked and had families were usually reliant on the work of other women to enable them to do so. Also, it is not clear whether their earnings dramatically increased the standard of living of the family or simply subsidised their husbands' leisure. As in other industrial settings, untangling the complex web of internal family finance defies generalisation. It is clear, though, even if the implications of this for individual households cannot be assumed, that cultural expectations of men's right to personal spending was the norm along the length of the waterfront. Visible differences in the attitudes and behaviour of Garston men and women did not necessarily imply change in gendered experience and outcomes. Male authority persisted; the ability of masculinity to remake itself to accommodate cultural and structural differences without damaging men's understanding of themselves as true men ensured the continued prioritisation of male privileges, just as it did in northern riverside communities – something returned to below.[23]

Factors that impacted on alternative understandings of masculinity in Garston variously included availability of regular employment, the paid work of women, and attachment to a moral economy historically fashioned in very differently structured labour markets. In part, this self-conscious fashioning of a particular set of values and aspirations derived from the diverse origins of local people – while Irish residents were to be found and Catholic/Protestant bigotry certainly had a presence in Garston, the area was less segregated than North End communities. While men proud to march with the Irish Foresters or Orange Lodge, in manly displays of sectarian allegiance, were prepared to fight to protect marching rights over particular spaces and processions often ended in violent confrontations,[24] sectarian affiliation was not universal. The presence of white incomers – from Lancashire,

Wales, Shropshire, Cornwall, and Yorkshire – tempered the emotional cleavages that were so significant in the North End. In addition, Garston offered more varied opportunities for riverside employment than were to be found elsewhere along the waterfront. In particular, access to regular, paid employment was much greater than in other dockland enclaves. Although notions of masculinity were consolidated in other arenas, work and the workplace were central to the fashioning of masculinity in the area around Garston Docks.

Employment and masculinity

The loading and unloading of ships comprised the single most significant area of employment for local men. Even after the registration of dockers under the Liverpool Dock Scheme of 1921, Garston Docks remained independent and labour continued to be 'engaged on an unrestricted casual basis'.[25] However, Garston's dockers were more likely to be regularly employed than those seeking work along the rest of the Mersey and, indeed, in other British ports.[26] There were several reasons for this, but essentially the Docks Union branch of the Transport and General Workers Union exerted a degree of control over the size of the casual labour pool at Garston Docks. New membership of the union – a prerequisite of employment – was confined to the sons of dockers. Union official Jack Jones explained, 'Restricting the number available for work, and ensuring a degree of loyalty through family connections, was regarded as essential protection against the job being swamped and a defence against the use of scabs by employers.'[27] Thus, casual dock labourers competed for available work but in the knowledge that they were part of a wider, agreed group of insiders whose numbers were regulated by the union. Moreover, the way in which the work was organised with loading/unloading on a piecework or tonnage basis 'paid to gangs rather than individuals' with earnings shared relative to hours worked, consolidated male relationships, and made the gang 'something like a family'.[28] This allowed concessions to be made to older and/or less able men but pressure to work fast to maximise wages, allied to poor safety regulation, made hazardous work even more dangerous and serious accidents were common.[29]

There were always more men chasing work than work available – a situation exacerbated by trade dislocations and economic depression. However, Garston dockers had more opportunity to maintain a basic income than was usual elsewhere along the river. Competition for work at Garston Docks was diluted by the presence of other local industries and services which offered the possibility of regular employment and side opportunities for casual and seasonal work when extra labour was needed – the gas industry, for example, employed extra workers through the winter. Also, although the housing conditions many families subsisted in were appalling and the air people breathed was heavy with smoke and noxious fumes from surrounding industry, unlike in the North End, where not so much as a blade of grass grew between the cobblestones, local people had access to the countryside and the shore. Proximity to the river and the woods and farms just a short walk away offered men opportunities not easily accessible elsewhere in the city. Two men earned their living by shrimp casting on the beach.[30] Potato and fruit picking offered adults and children seasonal opportunities for paid work and poaching, while risky, gave some men access to 'free' food for their families, offering an extra dimension to the role of breadwinner, or to sell on.[31]

Outside the docks, the availability of industrial work for men also had implications for their understandings of themselves as men. Most obviously, perhaps, as in Manchester and Salford, industrial diversity offered boys and young men 'diverse role models' they might aspire to.[32] Johnston and McIvor have shown that work in the Clydeside metal industries 'hardened boys up, de-sensitizing them to danger and socialising them into a competitive, *macho* environment'.[33] In the mid-1930s, at the height of the depression, more than 700 local men were regularly employed in metal production and many others were engaged in equally dangerous and physically demanding areas of employment.[34] Work in these industries was heavy, gruelling, and hazardous and men employed in them had to look out for each other – especially important when workmates were also kin or friends beyond the factory gates. Employers favoured personal recommendation as their main recruitment strategy, believing that it would guarantee them a more amenable workforce. Of course, drawing on existing community networks in this way offered opportunities to subvert workplace discipline[35] and reinforced the trusting interdependence necessary in hellish work conditions. The experience of toil and the bonds of shared peril strengthened male family and neighbourhood networks creating solidarities that crossed factory/community divides and contributed to the mirroring of a masculine self that was mutually fortifying, often made visible in the behaviour of the hard men of Garston but able to accommodate different, acceptable modes of male identity.[36]

Men may perform different roles in different settings – the tough fella at work and play and the indulgent papa at home were not necessarily mutually exclusive. The stereotyped 'hard man' was not the only identity available to workers. Johnston and McIvor remind us that alternative identities were available even in the most brutal of industries; that the reality was more 'fluid than the dominant *machismo* discourse' and there was a 'divide ... between rough and respectable masculinity' that was often linked to skill.[37] The skilled/unskilled divide was clearly relevant in Garston but the area's historical development, especially the significance of the railway as a key employer of local labour, provided the backdrop to the emergence of a community where trades unionism and an awareness of collective capacities informed the perspective of local men.[38]

However, although layered onto pre-existing structural differences that set Garston apart from communities to the north of the river, it was the arrival of the Bobbin Works which shaped Garston into a locality that had more in common with Salford Docks than comparable areas elsewhere in Liverpool.[39] In so doing, the infusion of attitudes and experiences associated with traditional textile communities into Garston's existing socio-cultural milieu, combined with the expansion of opportunities for regular employment for both men and women, contributed to the making of a particular sort of Garston masculinity that persisted.

The Bobbin Works

In the decade before the First World War with more than 2,000 workers, the Bobbin Mill was the largest single employer in the area and remained important to the local economy up to the Second World War. The company provided employment for large numbers of women and, significantly, did not distinguish between those married and unmarried. This is not to say that women necessarily stayed on in paid work after they married. Census evidence for 1911 shows that relatively few married women were engaged in full-time paid work, although this does not of course mean that they were not paid for some of the work they did. Many more households than in the north of the city had lodgers living within them and, as Miriam Glucksmann found for Salford, some undertook paid domestic work to enable other women to go out to work.[40] Those women who continued in the Bobbin Works after marriage and/or children seem to have had someone else within the household who was able to deputise for them.[41] Seafarer's wives had the opportunity to earn regular wages while their men were away and there is also evidence that women returned to work if abandoned or widowed.[42]

More than this, evidence suggests that the mill worker background of men and women, imbued as it was with the experience of labour organisation, workers' rights, and collective challenges to the power of employers, made local workers more conscious of their potential and thus receptive to industrial action. In 1912, employees walked out in a dispute that lived long in the collective memory of Garston people. George B., his father, and two brothers joined the strike, 'We all went out for more money and less working hours. Seventeen weeks and ... no pay ... It was hard times. No hope.'⁴³ More significantly, the bussing in of scab labour to replace strikers resulted in huge demonstrations and violent clashes with police, involving men and women, not all of whom worked in the mill. Many of those making formal complaints of police brutality sought to increase the credibility of their statements by offering evidence of their non-partisanship.⁴⁴ Protestants and Catholics set aside their usual bitter sectarian tribalism to march together in support of striking workers and to protest at police actions.⁴⁵ Hardship collections in support of strikers attracted contributions from shopkeepers, local pubs and clubs, and from workers in other industries.⁴⁶ In part this reflected the mood of the moment, coming as it did in the wake of the 1911 Liverpool general transport strike but the tangible sense of class solidarity evident in Garston in the summer of 1912 persisted, made visible in community resistance, membership of trades unions and mutual societies, the presence of the Co-operative Women's Guild, and electoral support for the Labour Party.

Resistance and masculinity

Across North End dockland communities chronic casualism, sectarianism, and the weakness of trade unionism militated against the development of a united class perspective.⁴⁷ Garston seemed to offer more potential for the emergence of self-conscious, class solidarities. Throughout the interwar years, despite high levels of unemployment, confrontations between employers and workers over wages, conditions, hours, and in defence of jobs were common across local industry. Tensions were not simply confined to employer/employee relations. In April 1914, the potential of neighbourhood solidarity evident during the bobbin dispute had echoes in community response to an organised attempt by local landlords to increase the rents of tenants living in the enclave's crowded, insanitary, bug-, rat-, and cockroach-infested, terraced streets.⁴⁸

> My dad said, 'Never, not a penny more until that fireplace is sorted.' There was a crack in chimney breast where the smoke came through and mother was always complaining that the fire didn't draw properly. Every week the rent was there and the rent collector said you're sixpence short and mother told him there'd be no extra sixpences until the work was done.⁴⁹

Tenants approached the local Labour Party for help. It quickly responded by calling a meeting and appointing a Vigilance Committee to investigate housing conditions and monitor property owners' reactions to resistance. Enraged landlords said that Labour was only supporting the action as a vote catcher.[50] Whatever the motivation, the party was clearly regarded as a potential advocate. Whether this translated into electoral support that reflected or contributed to the making of male identity is, however, as shown below, questionable.

Although revealing, the sort of resistance described above was exceptional – workplace disputes were much more common. Even during depressed trade conditions, port employers were anxious to avoid confrontations and Garston dockers were relatively powerful. In November 1925, for example, dock workers refused to unload a ship because four of the crew were not members of a trade union. The ship owners wanted to bring in their own labour, but the employers refused because the importation of outside labour implied a strike that would have closed the whole port.[51] When dockers in other parts of the city returned to work following the general strike, those in Garston remained out.[52]

Successful collective bargaining of this sort strengthened workers' view of themselves as powerful. Of course, the power was often illusionary and at best, relative. Low pay, long hours, and hazardous work conditions on the docks and across other industries were the norm and there were always more seeking work than employed. Victories often implied costs. Despite assurances, several of those who led the 1912 dispute lost their jobs when the strike ended.[53] The Secretary of the Vigilance Committee had to resign this position when his employers, under pressure from the landlords, said he would lose his job if he did not.[54] In 1933, 1,100 men brought the port to a standstill insisting that foremen who were salaried workers for London, Midland and Scottish Railway (LMS) became union members. This unofficial strike was ultimately successful,[55] but an upturn in activity at the port and the desire to avoid a costly dispute was perhaps as influential as the demands themselves. Although in November 1934 dock workers successfully won a partial reinstatement of wage cuts made in 1931, they had not been strong enough to resist their imposition in the first place.[56]

Nevertheless, it was the *perception* of agency that was crucial. Strikes and the achievement of concessions specific to highly sex-segmented local industries and the Garston waterfront empowered workers as men.[57] It might be argued that action to improve status, conditions, and wages or to defend existing rights shaped male solidarities that represented working-class challenges to capital. However, involvement in workplace confrontations did not necessarily imply a collectivist, much less a socialist, perspective. For many, involvement was passive or pragmatic in nature. Layered into notions of manliness associated with heavy, dangerous work and/or the possession of skills, trade union membership contributed to the shaping of masculinity all those who had work could relate to, but which might not have meaning outside the factory or dock gates. Jones writes that some men paid union dues reluctantly and suggested that the key attraction might have been 'cheap beer and billiards'.[58] The Protestant Workingmen's Conservative Club, an 'avenue for the political expression of [working-class] Toryism', was well supported.[59] Garston was a Labour stronghold but Davies says the local party was distinctive and was criticised for acting independently of Liverpool Labour.[60] Fred Christopher, Protestant, trade unionist, and member of the Labour Party, offered his own explanation of local political identity, 'The sickest memories I've got is the political ones ... Everybody that was Protestant voted Tory and everybody that was Catholic voted Labour. That's the way Garston was.'[61]

James Cronin writes of the 'myriad layers of working-class life that intervene between the demographic formation of class and the articulation of class interests in politics'.[62] Clearly, the Garston labour market was structurally more favourable to the emergence of formal workplace capacities than to the north of the river. However, agency of this sort had no necessary connection to wider political visions or aspirations. Tony Lane paints a persuasive portrait of Liverpool men and women made 'assertive and defiant' as a result of a seafaring mentality which imposed itself on the self-image of those who lived in the port. It was the traditions and practises of seafaring which infused the Liverpool docklands with a population characterised by pride, independence, and defiance in the face of authority.[63] However, for many, political ideals were inseparable from the religious allegiance of Catholic and Protestant men.

Moreover, defiant assertiveness was also bolstered, even for those who had little or no direct contact with Black or Chinese Liverpudlians, by the sense of ascendency and entitlement associated with white skin. Dockland communities were infused with racist ideology fuelled, in the wake of the First World War, by the seamen's unions' campaign to protect the jobs of white seafarers. Racist rhetoric, the imposition of a 'colour bar', and race riots involving attacks on Black men were widely reported and served to emphasise white male solidarities even in the face of divisions such as age, skill, occupation, religion, and ethnicity.[64]

In Garston, while the historic influence of seafaring was woven into the collective mentality of the local community, settlers who had grown up in very different socio-cultural environments may well have found some manifestations of the Liverpudlian characteristics Lane describes as alienating. Face-to-face interactions with neighbours or workmates could have countered feelings like these but we have to look beyond the workplace to see the fashioning of threads that united local people in a common pursuit of justice, albeit temporarily – outrage at police violence, for example, or an unjustified increase in rent. Moments like this cut across individual and community divisions including gender. Men *and* women challenged what were perceived to be unjust incursions into their lives but challenges were goal-focused, transient, and implied no long-term, collective emergence of political ambition.

For the most part, outside the workplace, men's validation as real men was made visible in their position as family providers. Marriage, fatherhood, and the associated role of breadwinner offered evidence of masculine maturity irrespective of whether individual men were able or willing to fulfil associated responsibilities or, indeed, the contribution of others. In Garston, unlike the North End of the city, the visible employment of married women in formal work situations compromised neither the respectability of their families nor the masculinity of their husbands.[65] Here, as in other parts of Liverpool, women's love, the desire to maintain the illusion of possessing a 'good' husband, and/or the threat of domestic violence meant women prioritised the welfare of husbands and in addition to men's personal spending allowance, granted them the lion's share of limited subsistence resources, thus shoring up and legitimising male identity associated with breadwinning, irrespective of how much bread men provided. In so doing, they enabled men to access exclusively male spaces outside the workplace. Whatever their focus, unchallenged rights to engagement with male cultural pursuits were an important component in the construction of male identity.

Masculinity and leisure

A strong associational culture was central to the infrastructure of North End communities. This was essentially parish based and had Roman Catholicism at its heart. In those areas where parish was synonymous with community, the church was important in a secular sense, providing spaces where men and boys could socialise with each other.[66] Religious identity was one of the cornerstones of masculinity even among those who did not actually attend church. While overt displays were usually saved for particular days, religious affiliation was woven into the fabric of individual and collective identity. Those able to vote, for the most part, voted along sectarian lines.[67]

Although sectarian identity was not as collectively significant in Garston, neighbours who had migrated from other localities could be bewildered or alienated by religious divisions. 'Mother didn't like it. They [Catholics and Protestants] used to be always fighting. Not like in Todmorden.'[68] Further, religious allegiance was not simply a choice of Catholic/Protestant. The diverse origins of the local inhabitants supported the establishment of a variety of non-conformist chapels that offered opportunities for social contact and cultural affirmation away from pubs and clubs where alcohol was served. In addition to services, the Welsh chapel held Sunday schools, Bible study, and Welsh language classes and ran a scout troop that included Catholic boys who were not expected to attend services and, astonishingly, were there with the approval of the local Catholic priest – a situation unthinkable in North End parishes.[69]

In Garston, the potential for making connections across the sectarian divide in work, neighbourhood, and leisure diluted the ties of religious partisanship and provided a more positive environment for the development of alternative identities. Work relationships were extended into the community via a variety of social activities organised through firms. Several local industries had football teams with matches supported by large numbers of local men and boys. The Liverpool Works Bowls League included teams from Wilson's, the Tannery, LMS, and Garston Docks. Successes at billiards were regularly reported in the local press.

Pigeon racing was a Sunday morning preoccupation for many local men. Those without their own lofts rented space in Stanton Brothers' 'famous York Street lofts'. Club subscriptions supported prizes and competition was fierce. Award-winning pigeons were a great source of pride and could attract high prices when sold. The hobby was relatively expensive, though, and fanciers belonging to Garston Working Men's Club were forced to sell 600 birds because they had been 'hard hit' by the general strike and could not afford to maintain them.[70] Davies has shown the extent to which gambling was embedded in working-class culture.[71] Many local men and women 'had the betting habit' – something that preoccupied police anxious to disrupt activity of this sort.[72] Gambling also brought men together in informal gatherings. In June 1933, twenty men were arrested following a police raid on the foreshore. Several others escaped, two by jumping in the river. Three of those caught were too young to prosecute but the rest were ultimately found guilty of 'gaming while playing Banker'.[73]

For many men, drinking together outside the workplace was an integral part of the male bonding experienced. As Jack Jones recalled, 'You worked together in gangs, you knew each other very well and got friendly and very close. The community of work and the community of the streets was cemented in the pubs and the clubs.' Garston had no shortage of clubs – all exclusively male spaces. Jones himself went out several evenings a week and always on Saturday nights.[74] However, although as Beaven argues such spaces emphasised the work/non-work dichotomy and contributed to the development of a '"consciousness" of leisure time' for men, the partisan nature of many Garston venues made them less effective in shaping and consolidating class identity.[75]

The Royal Antidiluvian Order of Buffaloes, or the Buffs, as it was known, was a mutual aid society modelled on freemasonry of a type more frequently associated with textile districts. There were two branches in Garston. Rules outlawed gambling and any discussion of religion or politics – very different to the Orange Lodge Victoria Social Club. The Workingmen's Conservative Club was Protestant and 'composed of respectable artisans'.[76] The LMS railway company had donated the Railway Institute as a social club for its male workers. In September 1925, the club applied for an extension of its licence until 10.30 p.m., explaining that many of the men scheduled to work until 10 p.m. were leaving at 9.30 p.m. to get a drink before closing, 'something detrimental to both the company and the men'. In addition to venues such as these, virtually every street had a pub on its corner. Jones recalls these as 'full even in times of abject poverty because they were the social centres of the working man outside the home'.[77]

Of course, any crude assumption of collective masculine selfishness in the securing of a proportion of limited family income for personal spending is of little assistance in understanding the multitude of factors and priorities that shaped individual men's sense of self in Garston at this time. While alcohol dependency accounted for some men's commitment to pub/club culture, the pull of male company outside work, masculine banter – 'sport, sex, beer and ... the job' – was also alluring.[78]

It is important also to note that involvement in the sort of masculine pursuits outlined above was not universal. Behaviour could vary without this necessarily compromising personal or perceived notions of manhood. As Griffin argues, historians need to acknowledge that 'different men in the same society might have different, equally valid, understandings of masculinity'.[79] There were men 'who preferred to keep themselves to themselves' or who found fulfilment and male friendship outside the home in scouting, cycling, or rambling.[80] Diverse performances of masculinity were accommodated or at least tolerated in communities where familiarity was unavoidable and social networks overlapped. Male bonding in a locality where boys schooled together and lived in close proximity began in childhood and persisted. Relationships such as these were valued as repositories of shared experience, mutual validation, and practical support, albeit not explicitly acknowledged because 'real men' did not speak about such things. What matters is that as in other dockland communities, whatever form it took, men's right to leisure was regarded as absolute and not contingent on whether they had paid work or the implications for disposable family income.[81]

Conclusion

The nature of the local labour market and the network of socio-cultural relationships that connected work and community supported a self-conscious awareness of personal and collective agency that manifested itself in a variety of ways and helped to shape male identity in Garston, in the first half of the twentieth century. However, the emergence and maintenance of alternative masculinities that incorporated the pursuit of economic justice and an idealised family life took place without compromising men's sense of themselves as real men nor, indeed, yielding any of the privileges attached to a male identity.

Patriarchy is fluid, pragmatic, and normalises women's subordination in very different socio-economic environments. Whatever the dominant features of the local labour market, whatever the specific gendered relationships, the *choice* about the responsibilities and behaviour of men remained with men. As in other settings, patriarchy adapted to an evolving milieu to ensure the maintenance of male authority. The ability of masculinity to remake itself to accommodate change without damaging men's understandings of themselves as true men ensured the continued prioritisation of male privileges. In Garston, the parameters of both male and female identity shifted to avoid sacrificing any of the perceived prerequisites integral to manliness.

Notes

1 Pat Ayers and Jan Lambertz, 'Marriage, Money and Domestic Violence in Working-Class Liverpool, 1919–1939', in Jane Lewis (ed.), *Labour and Love: Women's Experience of Home and Family, 1850–1940* (Oxford: Basil Blackwell, 1986); Pat Ayers, 'The Hidden Economy of Dockland Families: Liverpool in the 1930s', in Pat Hudson and Robert Lee (eds), *Women's Work and the Family Economy in Historical Perspective* (Manchester: Manchester University Press, 1991).

2 Michael Roper and John Tosh, 'Introduction', in Michael Roper and John Tosh (eds), *Manful Assertions: Masculinities in Britain since 1800* (London: Routledge, 1991); David Morgan, *Discovering Men* (London: Routledge, 1992).

3 Jerry White, *The Worst Street in North London: Campbell Bunk, Islington, between the Wars* (London: Routledge & Kegan Paul, 1986); Andrew Davies, *Leisure, Gender and Poverty: Working-Class Culture in Salford and Manchester, 1900–1939* (Buckingham: Open University Press, 1992); Ellen Ross, *Love and Toil: Motherhood in Outcast London, 1870–1918* (Oxford: Oxford University Press, 1993); Sean O'Connell, 'Violence and Social Memory in Twentieth-Century Belfast: Stories of Buck Alec Robinson', *Journal of British Studies*, 53:3 (2014), 734–756.

4 Pat Ayers, 'The Making of Men: Masculinities in Interwar Liverpool', in Margaret Walsh (ed.), *Working Out Gender: Perspectives from Labour History* (Aldershot: Ashgate, 1999).

5 John Tosh, *Manliness and Masculinities in Nineteenth-Century Britain: Essays on Gender, Family and Empire* (Harlow: Pearson Longman, 2005). See also Melanie Tebbutt, *Being Boys: Youth, Leisure and Identity in the Inter-war Years* (Manchester: Manchester University Press, 2012).
6 Doreen Massey, *Space, Place and Gender* (Cambridge: Polity Press, 1991), 191–192.
7 See Ray Costello, *Black Liverpool: The Early History of Britain's Oldest Black Community, 1730–1918* (Birkenhead: Picton Press, 2001); Andrea Murphy, *From the Empire to the Rialto: Racism and Reaction in Liverpool, 1918–1948* (Birkenhead: Liver Press, 1995); Maria Lin Wong, *Chinese Liverpudlians: A History of the Chinese Community in Liverpool* (Birkenhead: Liver Press, 1989). There remains much work still to be undertaken around the formation of gender and class identities in the racist and prejudiced context of local communities.
8 Interviews were undertaken as part of the Leverhulme-funded Docklands History Project, University of Liverpool, 1985–1990.
9 J. M. Swift, *The Story of Garston and Its Church* (Garston: A.M. Proffit, 1937), 153.
10 Swift, *Story of Garston*, 165–168.
11 David Caradog Jones (ed.), *The Social Survey of Merseyside: Volume I* (Liverpool: University Press of Liverpool, 1934), 348.
12 Swift, *Story of Garston*, 190–191.
13 Tebbutt, *Being Boys*, ch. 4.
14 This is not to say that such views and behaviour were absent in the North End, but incorporated into ideas about respectability and the significance of gendered identity in social and economic survival were regarded as private and rarely publicly shared or shown.
15 Laura King, 'Hidden Fathers? The Significance of Fatherhood in Mid-Twentieth-Century Britain', *Contemporary British History*, 26:1 (2012), 26–31.
16 Interview 9 May 1988: B. J., born 1921.
17 Interview 19 July 1988: J. P., born 1917.
18 Interview 6 July 1988: M. L., born 1928.
19 Ayers, 'Making of Men', 73–74.
20 A detailed survey of the 1911 census returns for fifteen streets was undertaken; respectively, H. E., 21 Brunswick St.; W. T., 43 Cellar Canterbury St.; P. O., 29 Derby St. Most of the examples found were entered by men who had come to Liverpool from Todmorden or Yorkshire.
21 Sean O'Connell, *Credit and Community: Working-Class Debt in the UK since 1880* (Oxford: Oxford University Press, 2009), 20.
22 Valerie Burton, 'The Myth of Bachelor Jack: Masculinity, Patriarchy and Seafaring Labour', in Colin Howell and Richard Twomey (eds), *Seafaring World: Essays in the History of Maritime Life and Labour* (Halifax: Acadiensis Press, 1991), 187. See also E. Mahler and E. F. Rathbone, *Payment of Seamen: The Present System: How the Wives Suffer* (Liverpool: Liverpool Women's Council, 1911). There has been no space here to discuss the particular situation of Garston's seafarers' wives.

23 This process is evident in other industrial settings. Penlington found that despite the impact of unemployment on men's role as breadwinners in South Wales during the 1930s, they were able to maintain authority in their homes. Neil Penlington, 'Masculinity and Domesticity in 1930s South Wales: Did Unemployment Change the Domestic Division of Labour?', *Twentieth Century British History*, 21:3 (2010), 281–299.
24 Interview 14 July 1988: J. P., born 1921; Jack Jones, 'A Liverpool Socialist Education', *History Workshop*, 18 (1984), 93.
25 Caradog Jones (ed.), *Social Survey*, 129.
26 For a summary of the impact of the scheme in other ports, see National Joint Council for Dock Labour, *Report of the Advisory Committee on Registration and Decasualisation* (London: NJCDL, 1937).
27 Jack Jones, *Union Man: The Autobiography of Jack* (London: Collins, 1986), 29. When work was short, Garston dockers could join the ranks of others along the South End waterfront where their union membership advantaged them in the twice daily competition for work. See *ibid.*, 28.
28 *Ibid.*, 31.
29 *Ibid.*, 31–32. The *Liverpool Echo* frequently reported injuries and deaths associated with dock work and other areas of local employment that were no less hazardous. See, for example, 'Liverpool Man Falls from Mast', 14 December 1938; 'Garston Man Injured', 6 November 1936; 'Explosion in Scrap Metal Yard', 25 May 1934.
30 Interview 17 May 1988: F. C., born 1910.
31 Interview 15 August 1988: T. D., born 1908.
32 Andrew Davies, 'Youth Gangs, Masculinity and Violence in Late Victorian Manchester and Salford', *Journal of Social History*, 32:2 (1996), 351.
33 Ronnie Johnston and Arthur McIvor, 'Dangerous Work: Hard Men and Broken Bodies: Masculinity in the Clydeside Heavy Industries, c. 1930–1970s', *Labour History Review*, 69:2 (2004), 138.
34 Swift, *Story of Garston*, 165–168.
35 Although perhaps less essential to maintaining a collective sense of control than among the casually employed. Ayers, 'Making of Men', 68–70.
36 The 1911 census returns for fifteen streets within the dockland enclave are suggestive, with adult family members working in the same places together with additional workers – recorded as lodgers – who might or might not be extended kin but who almost certainly had connections based on place of birth. Returns sometimes also showed similar connections across different households.
37 Johnston and McIvor, 'Dangerous Work', 143.
38 Dock workers, as railway employees, were expected to be union members. See David Howell, *Respectable Radicals: Studies in the Politics of Railway Trade Unionism* (London: Routledge, 1999).
39 See Davies, *Leisure*, 12; Miriam Glucksmann, *Cottons and Casuals: The Gendered Organisation of Time and Space* (Durham: Sociology Press, 2000); and T. S. Simey (ed.), *The Dock Worker* (Liverpool: Liverpool University Press, 1956).
40 Glucksmann, *Cottons*, 23.

41 Typically, Annie Williams, aged twenty-seven of 3 Leeming St., had three children, the oldest of whom was six. She and her husband worked in the Mill. They had three lodgers: two men who also worked in the Bobbin Works and Mary Anne Cooke, aged fifty-seven, who had no work outside the home and presumably looked after the home and children so Annie did not have to.
42 Interview 17 May 1988: F. C., born 1910. His father was a foreman in the Bobbin Works where Fred himself worked.
43 Interview 21 October 1988: G. B., born 1891.
44 See Liverpool Central Library, Depositions of Witnesses, 331/TRA/5/8/3.
45 Philip Waller, *Democracy and Sectarianism: A Political and Social History of Liverpool 1868–1939* (Liverpool: Liverpool University Press, 1981), 262.
46 Mike Axworthy, 'The Garston Riots', *Nerve 25*, Autumn 2006.
47 See Eric Taplin, *The Dockers' Union: A Study of the National Union of Dock Labourers, 1889–1922* (Leicester: Leicester University Press, 1986). On the implications of this for masculinity, see Ayers, 'Making of Men'.
48 A. Thomas, *Chapel Road Garston: A Short History of the Welsh Chapel in Garston* (Liverpool: A. Thomas, c.1936), 2; interview 15 August 1988: T. D., born 1908.
49 Interview 11 August 1988: E. R., born 1906.
50 'Raising the Rent', *Liverpool Echo*, 28 March 1914.
51 *Liverpool Echo*, 30 November 1925.
52 'Work on the Ships', *Liverpool Echo*, 14 May 1926.
53 Interview 17 May 1988: F. C., born 1910; interview 21 October 1988: G. B., born 1891.
54 'Against High Rents', *Liverpool Echo*, 24 April 1914.
55 'Dock Dispute Ends', *Liverpool Echo*, 17 July 1933.
56 'Dockers' Wage Increase', *Liverpool Echo*, 9 November 1934; Jones, *Union Man*, 41.
57 Although examples offered here focus on the docks, disputes in other industries were often reported. For example, 'Garston Copper Workers Strike', *Liverpool Echo*, 14 June 1924; 'Garston Strike: Settlement Denied', *Liverpool Echo*, 11 April 1930. The latter dispute was between LMS and TGWU.
58 Jones, *Union Man*, 50.
59 Sam Davies, *Liverpool Labour: Social and Political Influences on the Development of the Labour Party in Liverpool, 1900–1939* (Keele: Keele University Press, 1996), 227.
60 Davies, *Liverpool Labour*, 99.
61 Interview 17 May 1988: F. C., born 1910.
62 James Cronin, *Labour and Society in Britain, 1918–1979* (New York: Schocken, 1984).
63 Tony Lane, *Liverpool: Gateway of Empire* (London: Lawrence and Wishart, 1987), is still the most perceptive and engaging introduction to the city's history.
64 Diane Frost (ed.), *Ethnic Labour and British Imperial Trade: A History of Ethnic Seafarers in the UK* (London: Frank Cass, 1995), 59–88; Michael Rowe, 'Sex, "Race", and Riot in Liverpool, 1919', *Immigrants & Minorities*, 19:2 (2000), 53–70.

65 Ayers, 'Hidden Economy'.
66 For an explanation of the significance of this for the making of gendered identities, see Ayers, 'Making of Men', 75–79.
67 Lane, *Liverpool*, ch. 4; Greg Quiery, *In Hardship and Hope: A History of the Liverpool Irish* (Liverpool: G&K Publishing, 2017).
68 Interview 29 Ocotober 1988: G. B., born 1891; spoken in a broad Yorkshire accent eighty-nine years after moving to Garston from the Lancashire/Yorkshire border.
69 Thomas, *Chapel Road*, 7–9.
70 'Championship Bird', *Liverpool Echo*, 14 August 1926.
71 Andrew Davies, 'The Police and the People: Gambling in Salford, 1900–1939', *Historical Journal*, 34:1 (1991), 87–115.
72 Pilgrim Trust, *Men without Work* (London: Pilgrim Trust, 1938), 99.
73 'Jumped in River to Escape Police', *Liverpool Echo*, 12 June 1933. Those brought to court were aged between sixteen and forty-six.
74 Jack Jones, 'A Liverpool Socialist Education', *History Workshop Journal*, 18 (1984), 99. This club had been founded by wood-cutting and boilermen trades unionists, following the 1912 strike at the Bobbin Works.
75 Brad Beaven, *Leisure, Citizenship and Working-Class Men in Britain, 1850–1945* (Manchester: Manchester University Press, 2005), 5.
76 Waller, *Democracy*, 202.
77 Jones, 'Socialist Education', 93.
78 Jones, *Union Man*, 41.
79 Ben Griffin, 'Hegemonic Masculinity as a Historical Problem', *Gender & History*, 30:2 (2018), 377.
80 Jones, *Union Man*, 50; Thomas, *Chapel Road*; S. G. Jones, *Workers at Play: A Social and Economic History of Leisure, 1918–1939* (London: Routledge & Kegan Paul, 1986); Melanie Tebbutt, 'Rambling and Manly Identity in Derbyshire's Dark Peak, 1880s–1920s', *Historical Journal*, 49:4 (2006), 1125–1153.
81 In port communities there might well be a perceived, rational need for men to participate in cultural pursuits of the sort described here. See Ayers, 'Making of Men'.

8

Struggling 'heroes': Everyday masculine encounters in the public library, 1890s–1920s

Michelle Johansen

Introduction

In March 1897, a long letter from the chief librarian of Lewisham public library in London appeared in a weekly paper devoted to municipal affairs. Charles Goss objected to the content and tone of a new training manual that aimed to provide guidance for librarians on topics such as shelving arrangements and cataloguing. Goss was especially annoyed that the manual's author directed negative comments towards systems introduced by the men in charge of Britain's free libraries in the second half of the nineteenth century. The Lewisham librarian believed pioneer figures of the rate-assisted movement stood beyond reproach for the valuable work they had carried out in the nation's first publicly funded libraries 'without models of any kind' to guide their efforts.[1]

At one point in the *London* letter, Goss launched into a detailed defence of the workplace methods favoured by William Haggerston of Newcastle public library. During this passage, the Lewisham librarian referred to his one-time manager in north-east England as a 'struggling "hero"' – a complex term which provides the conceptual framework for the chapter that follows.[2] The 'struggling' element reflects subjects' shared experiences as embattled underdogs at the start of the period under scrutiny. Notwithstanding their privileged male gender, the senior librarians who form the focus of this study were not advantaged in terms of class background and professional status. Here were self-educated men from mainly working-class homes outside the metropolitan core fighting to establish themselves in middle-class occupational worlds in London at the end of the long nineteenth century. What does their struggle tell us about how masculinity was felt and expressed by upwardly mobile individuals? How does the hero designation offer insight into their subjective experiences, both in personal and professional terms? And what was the gendered significance of the quote marks placed by the Lewisham librarian around the word 'hero' in his 'struggling hero' designation?

These questions are addressed through the richly reconstructed lives of a research sample consisting of more than 130 male senior rate-assisted librarians, all of whom worked in London libraries during the period under scrutiny.[3] The entire city is covered. Subjects managed buildings in leafy suburban areas like Penge and Chiswick, newer industrial suburbs such as West Ham and Erith, crowded inner-city districts like Shoreditch and Whitechapel, affluent residential localities such as Hampstead and Chelsea, and dockside areas such as Canning Town and Rotherhithe. Informed by the methodology of the genealogist and the classifications used in prosopography, a family history was constructed for each subject using census data and birth, marriage, and death records.[4] These private findings were mapped onto public experiences, recovered through workplace correspondence, press cuttings, ephemera and reports, professional journals, societal minutes, subjects' published writings, and on the pages of the contemporary library media. Aside from occasional heated debates in library journals surrounding the value or otherwise of recruiting female librarians, these sources are silent on the subject of gender. The topic of manliness stimulated no discussion in the public library world during the period covered by this study. The assertion that masculinity is 'everywhere and nowhere' in the historical record therefore holds true, too, for the library historical record.[5]

This chapter is divided into four parts. The first part describes the gendered character of library work and subjects' retrospective 'struggle' to be recognised as self-directed masculine figures. The second revisits the moment at which my cohort took charge of a new wave of rate-supported libraries in London, to demonstrate the manly aspects embedded within their shared occupational experiences. The third examines heroism through the understated (and somewhat neglected) prism of masculine self-forgetting, recognising the potential for small-scale acts of 'heroic' selflessness practised by subjects in everyday encounters both behind the library desk and in domestic settings. This part also explains how second-generation public librarians were influenced by Great Men predecessors such as Peter Cowell of Liverpool and John Mullins of Birmingham. The final part examines heroism stripped of its quotation marks. It identifies manly influences beyond the library walls before indicating how the socio-political dimension intrinsic to library work (particularly in less affluent urban districts) might confer a heroic status of sorts upon the senior municipal librarian at the end of the long nineteenth century.

Struggling

Nineteenth-century public librarianship in London at senior level was a masculine form of labour. All the candidates recruited to manage the city's first free libraries from the late 1880s were men.[6] At junior level, too, male assistants were the norm.[7] When girls and women were appointed, it was either to oversee what were viewed as feminine spheres of activity such as the ladies' reading room or it was because their recruitment was regarded as a means of cutting costs and raising workplace standards (college-educated women could be obtained for salaries considerably lower than those needed to attract their male graduate counterparts to junior posts).[8] Leaving aside the progressive hiring systems implemented at Clerkenwell and Manchester, it remained usual to appoint male candidates in metropolitan rate-assisted libraries up to the middle of the First World War.

The introduction of conscription in 1916 altered gendered recruitment patterns virtually overnight. At the start of the war, every assistant role in Croydon library was held by a man. Following the expansion of the call-up to include both unmarried and married men in May 1916, thirteen women were recruited to fill positions vacated by male librarians departing for national service.[9] Although many men did return to their previous roles after the war – both at Croydon and elsewhere – public librarianship was never again so clearly a man's world as it had been when my subjects entered the profession in the late nineteenth century. Across the middle decades of the twentieth century, the library profession became increasingly viewed as peculiarly suited to women. By the turn of the twenty-first century Black accurately concluded that the public librarian role had become 'virtually synonymous with a feminine stereotype'.[10]

Public library services have witnessed a decline in value since the expansive developmental phase under scrutiny in this account, which has had an impact on how their early managers have been represented beyond their lifetimes.[11] Negative depictions of male public librarians, in particular, are present in every cultural form across the second half of the twentieth century. In literary and popular fiction, library staffs are numerically dominated by women, but men occupy the top positions. These men are portrayed as emasculated, prurient types. Senior librarians in novels are physically unprepossessing. They are awkward in the presence of the opposite sex. They are in thrall to domineering mothers. They are subject to ridicule from their mainly female junior colleagues – colleagues who are generally presented as sympathetic characters. Intellectually and professionally unfulfilled, fictional chief librarians vent their private frustrations by jealously guarding their collections and making it as difficult as possible for readers to access and enjoy the materials on the shelves in their institutions.[12]

In general histories, literary autobiographies, and studies of the reading lives of working men and women, senior librarians appear censorious or condescending.[13] In working-class memoir, depicting public librarians as intimidating is a short-hand method of highlighting the harsh socio-cultural terrain out of which a working-class autodidact has flourished against the odds.[14] These unfavourable assessments of municipal librarians reflect a growing ambivalence towards librarianship across the second half of the twentieth century.[15] Librarians were themselves aware that their profession was not held in high regard, so they headed off criticism through defensive statements that insisted upon the value of library work notwithstanding its old-fashioned, vocational character.[16] Once librarian-historians began selecting subjects for biographical study from the 1960s, the tendency was to overlook the broad mass of nineteenth-century library managers (with their earnest, Victorian approach to their duties) and focus instead upon a small, unrepresentative fraction of iconoclasts within the profession who possessed 'extraordinary' personalities more in keeping with late twentieth-century values.[17]

When senior public librarians were assessed as an undifferentiated cohort, the emphasis was on their strict or patronising attitudes towards readers and junior staff.[18] Otherwise, accounts highlighted the amateur quality of their occupational experience. Library historians agreed that an identifiable public library profession only started to emerge after 1900 and that the process of professionalisation occurred at a leisurely pace.[19] Munford depicted Victorian chief librarians as 'the inadequately qualified, under-paid and over-worked drudges of dominating Library Committees'.[20] Kelly described them as poorly paid and lacking in status: 'nowhere was the librarian regarded as a professional man: he was merely the servant of the library committee.'[21] The status preoccupation was apparent even in revisionist assessments. Black put forward a range of factors to explain the nineteenth-century public librarian's lowly standing, including the long hours worked, the relatively low salaries offered, and the absence of formal professional training. His gatekeeper role was also highlighted.[22]

Assessed as part of a wider classed cohort, public librarians fall within a 'constrained and emasculated' black-coat grouping that includes shopworkers, low-level clerks, and unqualified school teachers.[23] Popular and scholarly sources recounting these forms of white-collar work have accentuated its unmanly nature, even (or especially) when that work is performed by men.[24] Twentieth-century narratives have depicted disempowered lower-middle subjects undertaking menial, repetitive duties in cramped environs.[25] Even revisionist scholars portrayed the male black-coat experience as intrinsically non-heroic.[26] Both within and without the library walls, then, subjects have 'struggled' to be recognised as self-directed masculine figures.

Because the biographical aspect of the public library story has been generally overlooked – and librarian historians have not marked clear distinctions between different phases and places of free library development – the manly potential of public librarianship at senior level at the start of my period has passed unnoticed. Suggestions of amateur conduct might be relevant in accounts describing the establishing decades of the free library movement outside the metropolitan core from the 1850s to the 1880s; allegations of a gatekeeper approach were arguably apposite during the period of consolidation that took place from the 1930s to the 1960s; but such assessments were not appropriate for the moment of 'buoyancy and hopefulness' that occurred from the late 1880s in London.[27] This was the point at which the majority of subjects relocated from Newcastle, Birmingham, Edinburgh, Liverpool, and elsewhere to take charge of a new generation of rate-assisted libraries opening across the city to considerable fanfare and tremendous popular interest.

'Struggling'

The 1850 Public Libraries Act gave local governing bodies in England and Wales the power to use money from the rates to fund free libraries for public use. The first large urban centre to react to the terms of the act was Manchester. Other towns and cities followed Manchester's example, including Liverpool, Norwich, and Sunderland, but in London the response was unenthusiastic. Two rate-supported institutions opened in Westminster in 1857 and 1858 before progress stalled altogether for almost three decades. From the mid-1880s a combination of factors caused London's library movement dramatically to accelerate and by the early twentieth century there were over 100 rate-assisted libraries in the city.[28]

Many of these libraries were purpose built to a high specification using funds donated by library supporters such as John Passmore Edwards, Henry Tate, and Andrew Carnegie.[29] The idea of the Great Man was incorporated into the fabric of these civic spaces. Everyday encounters with statues of male literary giants positioned in niches over the entrances to their places of work (as at Hammersmith) or busts of male library benefactors (as at Manor Park) or aphorisms and mottoes almost uniquely written by men and carved into reading room walls (as at West Ham) acted as inspiring memorials to manly achievement in literary endeavour, civic progress, and self-help or self-sacrifice.[30] As others of their generation, my male subjects unthinkingly accepted these concrete affirmations that privileged them over their female counterparts in the public realm – notwithstanding their comparatively lowly social position.

According to income and the non-manual character of their profession, subjects shared a lower-middle-class status in the 1890s. This location typically represented an upwards shift from class status at birth, in some cases a significant shift. Almost two thirds of my sample emerged from working-class backgrounds, having grown up in homes where the main breadwinner earned a living as a skilled or unskilled labourer or artisan.[31] For the studious son of a plasterer, a carpenter, a coal miner, or a labourer, securing a junior role in the local free library on leaving school at the age of thirteen or fourteen was viewed positively. Apart from the opportunity to continue his education and indulge a nascent love of literature in a workplace setting, a career in public librarianship offered the chance to make real and unlooked-for material gains for a bright young candidate from a non-privileged background.[32] Through hard work, focus, flexibility, an interest in books, a degree of ability in areas such as cataloguing, and a touch of good fortune, subjects were able to ascend a hierarchal professional ladder at a time when practical know-how was prized over formal qualifications in the library world.

From the late 1880s, advertisements started to appear in the local, national, and specialist press seeking candidates to manage the new rate-assisted institutions springing up across London. With substantial hands-on experience of public librarianship gained outside the capital, my subjects were strong contenders for these competitive roles.[33] Their understanding of like-for-like workplace systems ensured they were not only shortlisted for interview but also made a positive impression face to face. Thus, with four years' experience at Rotherham in Yorkshire and five years at Leek in Staffordshire, William Hall was appointed the first chief librarian of Croydon in 1889; with seven years' experience at Birmingham in the Midlands, five years at Newcastle in the north-east, and three years at Darlington (also in the north-east), Frank Burgoyne was recruited as Lambeth's first chief librarian in 1887; with ten years' experience at South Shields library in the north-east and seven years at Halifax in Yorkshire, Joseph Reed Welch was taken on as the first chief librarian at Clapham in 1889; and so on.

The businessmen, literary gentlemen, philanthropists, and government officials sitting on the committees overseeing London's first libraries did not possess an equivalent understanding of the nuts and bolts of the profession, relative to the knowledgeable regional candidates they had recruited to run their library services. This was an unprecedented (and never repeated) occupational moment that meant subjects enjoyed opportunities for self-realisation, dominion, and decision-making behind the metropolitan library desk. From the first, candidates like Hall, Burgoyne, and Welch provided informed leadership on key areas, including staff recruitment, systems development, and the purchase of books.³⁴ Taking charge from the beginning generated a feeling of ownership that reinforced senior librarians' sense of manhood.³⁵ This proprietorial aspect of librarianship (augmented by the living-in convention which saw roughly half of subjects occupying a library house or flat for at least some of their tenure) also encouraged extended periods of service of between twenty and forty years behind the London library desk.³⁶

My all-male cohort took charge of their metropolitan public libraries at the *fin de siècle*, amid gendered fears of degeneration and anxieties around androgyny.³⁷ As this section has suggested, the 'myriad masculine anxieties' troubling the late Victorian middle and upper classes were likely not shared by this set of men.³⁸ Rather, here were respected authority figures who operated against a manly architectural backdrop in the late nineteenth century. Notwithstanding their fluid regional identities, their uncertain social status, and the feminine character of their white-collar profession, subjects did not struggle to assert or express their masculinity in a workplace setting. Instead, it appeared that the first senior London librarians held non-negotiable expectations of manhood, expectations reinforced by the behaviours of male 'heroes' they encountered in the workplace as impressionable young men from the late 1870s.

'Heroes'

Historians agree that studying objects of popular worship in the past sheds light on wider socio-cultural patterns.³⁹ It has been noted that socially and geographically mobile subjects were particularly likely to seek out role models outside their birth families.⁴⁰ Recent scholarship has expanded our understanding of heroism by interrogating heroic behaviours beyond socially elite groupings. Price bypassed military success on far-flung battlefields, for example, to document everyday acts of bravery carried out closer to home by otherwise ordinary men and women. Heroism remained associated with physical valour, however, and occurred only during exceptional incidents (shipwrecks, house fires, skating accidents) that posed an immediate threat to life.⁴¹ During subjects' formative years, heroism was more broadly understood than even Price's fresh interpretation allows. According to the expansive terms of Samuel Smiles' mid-Victorian self-improvement project, everybody possessed heroic potential.⁴² Thomas Carlyle's influential interpretation of heroism was similarly capacious: 'If Hero mean [*sic*] *sincere man*, why may not every one of us be a Hero?'⁴³

Including ethical attributes such as sincerity, perseverance, and moral courage alongside physical prowess suggested that greatness stood within everyone's reach – more accurately, within every man's reach – during the second half of the nineteenth century. Nevertheless, the Lewisham librarian elected to place quotation marks around the word 'hero' in his 1897 *London* letter. Charles Goss was sensitive to the humble character of public librarianship in the eyes of those positioned on the higher rungs of a hierarchical occupational ladder. He understood that, relative to the academic librarian, the private librarian and the literary gentlemen who dominated the meetings and committees of the Library Association of the United Kingdom (a powerful professional grouping established in 1877), the typical rate-assisted library manager was not held in high regard.[44] His use of quote marks around the word 'hero' therefore aimed at puncturing suggestions of unmanly self-importance. Significantly, elsewhere in the letter, Goss made dismissive references to the conceit, vanity, and narcissism of the author of the training manual he had written to criticise.[45]

Goss's explicit distaste for self-regard reminds us of the central importance of humility to masculine self-identity in the long nineteenth century. Men may have dominated the Victorian public sphere, but cultural norms demanded that displays of arrogance were suppressed in the British male subject. True manliness was attained by placing the needs of others first through a process described as self-forgetting or 'ignoring self'.[46] Self-forgetting might be elevated to heroic status at the start of my period, particularly among the lower middle and middle classes; it entailed the regulation of energy and emotion, which in turn required strenuous physical and psychological effort.[47] This form of erasure demanded that subjects valiantly '*fought back* emotion' during times of happiness, disappointment, or loss.[48] Following bereavement, public librarians articulated grief through non-verbal gestures (such as standing in silence) that brought a reassuring sense of order at moments of distress.[49] Here we can identify a connection between the rise of professionalism, the expansion of the black-coat sector, and shifting norms of masculinity: as men moved from jobs requiring physical exertion and strength into careers demanding mental labour, so the currency of emotional effort and the struggle towards self-command rose on the metaphorical stock exchange of masculinity.[50]

In the domestic sphere, self-forgetting entailed prioritising the well-being of dependent family members, most notably wives and children. All but seven subjects were married and none of their wives worked outside the home, reflecting contemporary classed expectations.[51] Women were in charge within the domestic sphere and men dominated without, with each man expected to bring in sufficient income to provide a measure of comfort and security for his family.[52] More than half of subjects' households included extended family members, usually as a short-term arrangement. Whether opening up their homes to accommodate widowed mothers or mothers-in-law (as James Ames of East Ham and John Rivers of

Hampstead), aged in-laws (as Harry Poulter of Walthamstow and William Taylor of Holborn), elderly fathers (as Anthony Gill of Twickenham), unmarried sisters or sisters-in-law (as Evan Rees of Westminster and Walter Williams of Whitechapel), or widowed sisters or aunts (as Charles Newcombe of Camberwell and James Seymour of Kilburn), public librarians took their roles as providers and protectors seriously.

Librarian marriages typically lasted a lifetime and were notable for their ritualised displays of respect and tenderness. The idea of 'affectionate' propriety is reminiscent of what Vincent identified as a 'bourgeois moral manliness' that emphasised 'self-restraint, self-improvement, stern propriety, and the support of, and consideration for, wives and children'.[53] Wives and other close family members attended professional gatherings, suggesting a keen interest in their partner's occupational activity and gesturing towards the companionate forms of marriage favoured by this cohort of men. In the interwar years, many subjects marked significant wedding anniversaries. A large party, which included the entire local library staff, gathered in Stepney for a whist drive and dance in 1920 to celebrate the silver wedding anniversary of chief librarian Albert Cawthorne. During the evening's speeches, junior assistants thanked their chief for securing improved pay and conditions for them. Cawthorne refused to accept credit for this, insisting he had only acted as others would have done in his position.[54]

In everyday encounters behind the library desk, manly self-forgetting of this type found expression through individual acts of kindliness that reflected the soft forms of patriarchy practised by subjects.[55] Senior librarians played the part of mentor to younger assistants to good effect, both within their institutions and without through active contributions to professional bodies that sought to empower or educate. Henry David Roberts of St Saviour's in Southwark was a driving force behind the Library Association Education Committee, the body responsible for establishing transparent and transferable standards of skills in librarianship from the late nineteenth century. Other subjects gave their time freely to facilitate the work of the Library Assistants' Association (LAA), a group that offered junior staff opportunities for social intercourse as well as a space for the sharing of workplace ideas and experiences. During the early 1900s, George Roebuck of St George in the East was LAA honorary secretary, George McCall of Limehouse and Herbert Jones of Kensington supplied illustrations for the LAA's monthly magazine, Alfred Cotgreave hosted training events for LAA members at his West Ham library, and James Duff Brown was an occasional high-profile attendee at informal LAA gatherings.[56] Such displays of 'kindly feeling' or 'fatherly oversight' were appreciated by up-and-coming assistants.[57]

Paternalistic modes of workplace behaviours were enshrined in emergent training guidelines from the late nineteenth century, the most influential of which were produced by John Mullins of Birmingham. Nine subjects trained under Mullins. The remainder read and re-read his lecture on the management of free libraries, which went through a number of reprints following publication in 1868. *Free Libraries and Newsrooms* confirmed the masculine potential of public library work at the start of my period. It was self-effacing in tone, with Mullins adding an appeal for 'some more competent person' to expand his incomplete introductory training principles.[58] The Birmingham chief also directed library committees not to employ 'flashy young swells' who might act dismissively towards less affluent borrowers.[59] He instructed library staff to offer a courteous welcome to all library visitors but added that an especially friendly welcome should be shown to the poorest users.[60] These inclusive principles were reinforced in *Public Library Staffs* (1893), a training manual produced by Peter Cowell of Liverpool. Four subjects started their careers under Cowell. Others knew and respected him from his presence on the pages of the library media or as a speaker at professional gatherings. My research cohort took on board his directive to cultivate an approachable demeanour that would encourage even the novice learner to feel comfortable seeking advice.[61] They also noted his warning to guard against self-importance.[62]

Through everyday encounters with first-generation librarian 'heroes' as up-and-coming assistants in the 1870s and 1880s, my second-generation librarian cohort discovered sympathetic masculine role models outside the home.[63] The practical, kindly support and guidance of workplace father figures such as Cowell, Haggerston, and Mullins, whether offered face to face or via the influential pages of standard training manuals, taught subjects to value masculine ideals of public service that (a) prioritised the needs of the less powerful or less privileged, and (b) were discharged without fanfare or self-congratulation. Senior public librarians gained manly satisfaction from offering help efficiently and unobtrusively in a congenial working environment. Such words as 'courteous' and 'obliging' were attached to them – in the late nineteenth century, these traits were gendered male and viewed as attractive to the opposite sex.[64] Senior librarians did not struggle to attract long-term partners as young men and their gendered sense of self was strengthened by their roles as providers to wives, children, and other family members. It was further reinforced by the heroes they looked to beyond the library walls.

Heroes

Edward Foskett's working-class background mirrored the majority of my subjects' non-privileged childhood experiences, but his career path was practically unique since he obtained a chief librarian role without ever having worked in a library. In 1889, he was appointed to take charge of the new Camberwell public library. This appointment came about partly because Foskett's pro-library campaigning work during the 1880s equipped him with an excellent abstract understanding of public librarianship. As a clerk with more than twenty years' experience of office work, he also possessed valuable administrative skills at a time when chief librarians were expected to fulfil a dual role as clerk and librarian to their offsite vestry managers. Finally, his reputation as a bookman, editor, and poet made him a competitive candidate, notwithstanding the fact that 220 applications were received for the Camberwell post.

Poetry was viewed as a feminine form of self-expression by the late nineteenth century, but Foskett's published works handled decidedly masculine topics.[65] His best-known composition was 'A Nation's Fame' (1876), which criticised instructions issued by the British Admiralty to ship captains to return runaway slaves to their masters. The poem was frequently quoted by opponents of the scheme during a successful campaign to force the government to withdraw the so-called fugitive slave circulars. 'A Nation's Fame' alerts us to the support for the underdog typically maintained by the struggling hero librarian type, in part because of his own classed experiences of social injustice growing up but also (in later years) because of the discrimination he faced as a low-status public servant in the wider library and literary world.[66]

Foskett's creative output otherwise placed the accent on the hero element of the struggling hero construct – in this context, stripped of its qualifying quotation marks. He used poetry as a means of expressing admiration for the deeds and virtues of eminent men, from literary icons like Shakespeare and Milton to political figures such as William Gladstone. In the spring of 1883, he wrote a sonnet in praise of the Liberal leader's speech-making in Parliament, which he transcribed and sent to the then prime minister. We cannot know if Gladstone personally read this tribute, but his secretary certainly cast an eye over it before providing a summary of the 'nicely written' content on the reverse of the page.[67] Underneath this summary, Gladstone instructed 'Thank', then added, 'I only wish he had a worthier subject to do his muse greater justice.'[68] That the prime minister sought to save time by scribbling only 'thank' (rather than 'thank the writer' or even 'send thanks') yet still felt obliged to express his own unworthiness in a private note to his secretary is further evidence of the importance of self-forgetting to middle- and upper-class masculine self-identity in the nineteenth century.

In the sonnet, Foskett used imagery suggestive of the battlefield to convey the heroic character of Gladstone's oratory in Westminster.[69] He was by no means alone among my subjects in his capacity to make masculine otherwise non-masculine activities or settings through the use of gendered terms and symbols. Whether consciously or unconsciously, chief librarians linguistically refashioned their professional lives to embed a practical manly element within their delivery. Most senior librarians had grown up in working-class homes where the male head of the house earned a living through physical labour which required bodily strength or manual dexterity to construct buildings, create objects, or extract materials that made a concrete, quantifiable difference to the lives of others. My subjects therefore instinctively held applied experience in high regard, as expressive of manliness, in adulthood. They presented librarianship as a 'craft', describing the reference works on their office shelves as their 'working tools' as if they laboured alongside grandfathers, fathers, uncles, or brothers in the workshop, at the coalface, or on the building site.[70]

They likewise made manly their own relatively inactive (otherwise, feminine) occupation by working energetically to meet the needs of staff and users, thus satisfying themselves that they were not falling short of the arduous (that is, masculine) workplace experiences of their childhood role models.[71] Outside the workplace, they prized robust good health of a type that was fostered through strenuous leisure pursuits. Energetic hobbies that included cricket, hiking, and cross-country running were used as a means of offsetting sedate, cerebral working lives. A few subjects chose spare-time activities that called for a greater degree of daring and technical know-how and the opportunity to acquire plenty of manly 'kit' (potholing, motorcycling, rally driving) – but, after hours, this cohort of men was most often to be found surrounded by books and papers, continuing into adulthood the diligent habits of self-education adopted in their youth.

Samuel Martin of Hammersmith had a fascination with Ancient Egypt; James Dyer Young of Greenwich was curious about European philosophical thought; Cecil Davis of Wandsworth was an expert in local history; Zebedee Moon of Leyton studied poetry and linguistics; Frank Burgoyne of Lambeth concentrated his attention on the Elizabethan period; Percy Farnborough of Edmonton was a keen zoologist; and so on. Their intellectual interests were not approached in a dilettante fashion. Nor were they indicative of morbid introspection. Despite being carried out in isolation (which might in any case be reframed as independent, therefore masculine) these interests had an outward-looking dimension. They aimed to contribute to what Ernest Callard of Wandsworth referred to as 'the common store of knowledge'.[72] Subjects' extra-curricular subaltern scholarly activity was intended for dissemination, either in print form or as public talks or lectures. Invariably, books and articles were accompanied by a 'self-forgetting' acknowledgement of the inadequate or incomplete character of the contribution to the field.[73]

These cerebral pursuits might comfortably be accommodated within a manly self-identity because of the cultural foundations sunk by Thomas Carlyle earlier in the century.[74] In reconfiguring intellectual activity as masculine, Carlyle complicated prevailing gendered interpretations that placed the accent on athleticism, muscular labour, skilled craftsmanship, and conventionally heroic deeds.[75] Carlyle's intervention did not altogether dislodge the physically strenuous aspects of manliness from their Victorian pedestal. Middle-class artists and writers – including Ruskin and, indeed, Gladstone – continued to envy what they viewed as untroubled forms of working-class masculinity founded on honest toil or labour.[76] From the 1850s, at least on a part-time basis, Gladstone refashioned himself as a simple workman through his performative pastime of wood-cutting in the grounds of his family home in north Wales.[77]

Nevertheless, Gladstone was afterwards to absorb and assimilate Carlyle's brain work thesis. As he set about arranging and listing his private collection of books and papers for public use from the late nineteenth century, he represented his library work as arduous physical labour.[78] He also made masculine the benefits of free library provision. Presiding over rate-supported library openings, the Liberal leader's muscular speeches employed the active language of factory processes and manual toil to ensure the 'intelligent growing lad' appreciated that a visit to the public library would enhance rather than diminish the 'metal' of his manhood.[79] From the highest societal level, and from a source worshipped as a hero by subjects, the labour of the public librarian was depicted as manly because it possessed a didactic dimension and the power to influence and uplift wider society.

As self-taught men from mainly working-class backgrounds, subjects were sensitive to this aspect of their work. They knew that they actively assisted in a broader self-improvement project that countered elitism and privilege.[80] London's first chief librarians conceptualised their institutions as polytechnics of the people because they appreciated that education did not begin and end in the school room.[81] My research cohort collaborated with national organisations (the University Extension Society, the Home Reading Union) or specialist regional bodies (natural history societies, literary groups, pupil teacher centres) to arrange opportunities for self-acculturation in their buildings. They did not simply target the enthusiastic autodidact seeking low-cost rational recreation opportunities in his or her leisure time, however. Before the introduction of labour exchanges, libraries supported those looking for work by posting job adverts from the local papers outside their institutions.[82] They shared reading materials with neighbouring workhouses, prisons, asylums, and hospitals; in short, every effort was made to ensure their offer was of practical use to the whole community.

In this way subjects might be positioned shoulder to shoulder with philanthropists, university settlement workers, and other social reformers, working collectively to tackle poverty and its causes in their metropolitan districts.[83] The manly impulse to improve the lives of those less fortunate might be viewed as another variant of the 'fairy godfather effect' identified by Tindall.[84] It resonates with Black's masculine reformer librarian type ('evangelical ... tied to the tenets of liberalism').[85] It also carries echoes of Snape's assessment of public librarianship as 'a missionary undertaking to the vast masses of ill-educated and unsophisticated working-class populations'.[86] Yet these appraisals overlook the vital fact that subjects were themselves part of the 'vast masses'. Judged according to their non-privileged backgrounds, the first generation of London librarians shared much in common with the men, women, and children whose lives they struggled to improve through everyday bookish encounters in their public library buildings. It was this aspect of their duties (duties discharged even-handedly, energetically, and with kindliness across a working lifetime) which shone an unexpectedly heroic light upon the seemingly non-heroic occupational lives of my male, white-collar subjects.

Conclusion

Late Victorian heterosexual masculinity was a complex construct that included such qualities as chivalry, authenticity, honesty, industry, tenacity, knowledge, athleticism, and 'manly reserve' in its broad embrace.[87] Senior public librarians displayed all of these qualities at different moments during their careers. Notwithstanding their marginal social position, their non-metropolitan origins, and their comparatively lowly rate-assisted status, the first senior librarians in London experienced no crisis of masculinity. They were able seamlessly to accommodate the 'muscular' forms of manliness practised by their working-class fathers growing up within the new 'white-collar' forms of masculinity they were required to rehearse behind the public library desk. In effecting this social transition, they took direction from heroic male role models inside and outside their institutions with Carlyle's recalibration of the hero as man of letters, in particular, enabling them to refashion their otherwise feminine bookish interests as masculine brain work. Within their own institutions, among their professional peers, inside the home, and across the communities they served, this generation of black-coat workers enjoyed a measure of authority, respect, esteem, and affection. As this chapter has sought to show, here were subaltern 'heroes' manfully striving to effect positive social change from their metropolitan library offices at the end of the long nineteenth century.

Notes

1 'To the Editor', *London*, 18 March 1897, 205. Within six months of writing this letter, Goss had left Lewisham to take charge of the Bishopsgate Institute Library near Liverpool Street Station. I am giving his affiliation as Lewisham because this was accurate at the time the letter was written. Elsewhere in the chapter, the convention is to cite the London affiliation held for the longest period of a subject's career. Subjects typically served at three or more institutions during their early careers. Adopting this convention avoids including irrelevant detail that would disrupt the narrative flow.
2 *Ibid*.
3 The focus on senior librarians is because their experiences are more fully documented than their junior counterparts.
4 Katharine Keats-Rohan, *Prosopography Approaches and Applications: A Handbook* (Oxford: Unit for Prosopographical Research, Lincare College, University of Oxford, 2007), 15–18.
5 John Tosh, *Manliness and Masculinities in Nineteenth-Century Britain: Essays on Gender, Family and Empire* (Harlow: Pearson Longman, 2005), 31; Harry Brod 'The Case for Men's Studies', in Harry Brod (ed.), *The Making of Masculinities: The New Men's Studies* (Boston: Allen & Unwin, 1987), 40–41; Alison Oram, *Women Teachers and Feminist Politics 1900–39* (Manchester: Manchester University Press, 1996), 172.
6 In 1858, Elizabeth Smith was taken on to oversee the Trevor Square branch building in the parish of St Margaret's in Westminster. The service operated out of two rooms in a cottage leased from her parents.
7 In 1900, there were over 200 male and 16 female assistants in the city's public libraries. B. L. Dyer and Joseph Lloyd, 'Women Librarians in England', *The Library Assistant*, 1 (January 1898–September 1899), 219–222.
8 Anon., 'Educated Women as Librarians', *The Library Assistant*, 1 (January 1898–September 1899), 103; or *The Library Assistant*, 5:41 (October 1905), 41.
9 'Croydon 27th Annual Report of the Libraries Committee', 1915–1916, 12, Croydon Museum and Archive Service.
10 Alistair Black, 'Man and Boy: Modifying Masculinities in Public Librarianship 1850–1950', in Evelyn Kerslake and Nickianne Moody (eds), *Gendering Library History* (Liverpool: Media Critical and Creative Arts, Liverpool John Moores University, 2000), 208.
11 A steep rise in the use of volunteer staff arguably devalues the expertise once held by public librarians. www.gov.uk/government/publications/libraries-deliver-ambition-for-public-libraries-in-england-2016-to-2021/libraries-deliver-ambition-for-public-libraries-in-england-2016-to-2021 (accessed 22 August 2017).
12 Examples can be found in Kingsley Amis, *That Uncertain Feeling* (London: New English Library, 1966 [1955]), 38, 149; Barbara Pym, *No Fond Return of Love* (London: Jonathan Cape, 1961), 52; Barbara Pym, *An Unsuitable Attachment* (London: Grafton Books, 1983 [1982]), 26–27, 73, 107, 192, 196; Elizabeth Taylor, *A View of the Harbour* (London: Virago, 2006 [1947]), 37, 237–238;

Mary Kelly, *March to the Gallows* (London: M. Joseph, 1964), 5, 83–84, 96–98, 118–119; Philip Larkin, *A Girl in Winter* (London: Faber and Faber, 1975 [1947]), 16.

13 Richard D. Altick, *Victorian People and Ideas* (London: Norton, 1973), 197; Juliet Gardiner, *The Thirties: An Intimate History* (London: HarperPress, 2011 [2010]), 133–134; Mary Hammond, *Reading, Publishing and the Formation of Literary Taste in England, 1880–1914* (Aldershot: Ashgate, 2006), 45–48; Ursula Howard, *Literacy and the Practice of Writing in the 19th Century: A Strange Blossoming of Spirit* (London: National Institute of Adult Continuing Education, 2012), 3–5, 113–117; Jonathan Rose, *Intellectual Life of the British Working Classes* (New Haven: Yale University Press, 2001), 43, 49, 189; Stanislaus Joyce, *My Brother's Keeper* (New York: Viking, 1958), 89–90.

14 Joseph Stamper, *So Long Ago* (London: Hutchinson, 1960), 168–171.

15 R. J. B. Morris, *Parliament and the Public Libraries* (London: Mansell, 1977), 12; Richard D. Altick, *Writers, Readers and Occasions: Selected Essays in Victorian Literature and Life* (Columbus: Ohio State University Press, 1989), 149–150, 218–219.

16 D. J. Foskett, *The Creed of a Librarian: No Politics, No Religion, No Morals* (London: Library Association, 1962).

17 Walter Fry and William Munford, *Louis Stanley Jast: A Biographical Sketch* (London: Library Association, 1966); William Munford, *James Duff Brown, 1862–1914: Portrait of a Library Pioneer* (London: Library Association, 1968); James G. Olle, *Ernest A. Savage: Librarian Extraordinary* (London: Library Association, 1977).

18 James G. Olle, 'A Librarian of No Importance', *Library Review*, 22:6 (1970), 294.

19 William Munford, 'Confessions of a Library Biographer', *Library Review*, 21:6 (1968), 293.

20 William Munford, *Penny Rate: Aspects of British Public Library History, 1850–1950* (London: Library Association, 1951), 83.

21 Thomas Kelly, *Early Public Libraries: A History of Public Libraries in Great Britain* (London: Library Association, 1973), 99.

22 Alistair Black, *A New History of the English Public Library: Social and Intellectual Contexts, 1850–1914* (London: Leicester University Press, 1996), 194–199.

23 Christopher Breward, 'Sartorial Spectacle: Clothing and Masculine Identities in the Imperial City, 1860–1914', in Felix Driver and David Gilbert (eds), *Imperial Cities: Landscape, Display and Identity* (Manchester: Manchester University Press, 1999), 250.

24 Teresa Davy, '"A Cissy Job for Men; a Nice Job for Girls": Women Shorthand Typists in London 1900–1939', in Leonore Davidoff and Belinda Westover (eds), *Our Work, Our Lives, Our Words: Women's History and Women's Work* (Basingstoke: Macmillan Education, 1986), 130. See also Jack Common, *Kiddar's Luck* (Newcastle upon Tyne: Bloodaxe, 1990 [1951]), 83.

25 Robert Gray, *The Labour Aristocracy in Victorian Edinburgh* (Oxford: Clarendon Press, 1976), 91, 95, 98–100, 143; Harold Perkin, *The Rise of Professional Society: England since 1880* (London: Routledge, 2002), 78–101.

26 Peter Bailey, 'White Collars, Gray Lives? The Lower Middle Class Revisited', *Journal of British Studies*, 38:3 (1999), 276, 281; A. James Hammerton, 'Pooterism or Partnership? Marriage and Masculine Identity in the Lower Middle Class, 1870–1920', *Journal of British Studies*, 38:3 (1999), 307, 319.

27 Thomas Greenwood, *Public Libraries: A History of the Movement and a Manual for the Organization and Management of Rate-Supported Libraries* (London: n.p., 1890), 287. See also Ernest Savage, *A Librarian's Memories: Portraits & Reflections* (London: Grafton, 1952), 64–65; and John J. Ogle, *The Free Library: Its History and Present Condition* (London: G. Allen, 1897), v.

28 Administrative reforms from the late 1880s ushered in an expansive mood of enterprise at local government level in London. Davis situates free library development alongside growth in other areas of civic activity in the final years of the nineteenth century, including the establishment of wash houses and technical schools. John Davis, *Reforming London: The London Government Problem, 1855–1900* (Oxford: Clarendon Press, 1988), 20–30, 156–164.

29 Dean Evans, *Funding the Ladder: The Passmore Edwards Legacy* (London: Francis Boutle Publishers, 2011), 128–150.

30 Black, *A New History*, 236–238.

31 For a full assessment of subjects' class location, see Michelle Johansen, '"The Supposed Paradise of Pen and Ink": Self-education and Social Mobility in the London Public Library (1880–1930)', *Cultural and Social History*, 16:1 (2019), 51–52.

32 Savage, *A Librarian's Memories*, 25.

33 Senior London jobs typically attracted 100–200 applicants, but some roles drew even greater levels of interest: in 1886, around 1,000 applications were received for the position of chief librarian at Wandsworth.

34 Commissioners for Public Libraries and Museums for the Parish of St Mary Battersea, 11 April 1888, 128. BP/1/13/1/1 Wandsworth Heritage Service (WHS).

35 Oram, *Women Teachers and Feminist Politics*, 1996), 45–46.

36 For an account of the living-in convention, see Michelle Johansen, '"The Father and Mother of the Place": Inhabiting London's Public Libraries, 1885–1940', in Jane Hamlett, Lesley Hoskins, and Rebecca Preston (eds), *Residential Institutions in Britain, 1725–1970: Inmates and Environments* (London: Routledge, 2013), 125–139.

37 George L. Mosse, *The Image of Man: The Creation of Modern Masculinity* (New York: Oxford University Press, 1996), 78–79, 83.

38 Herbert Sussman, *Victorian Masculinities: Manhood and Masculine Poetics in Early Victorian Literature* (Cambridge: Cambridge University Press, 1995), 37–38, at 37.

39 Raphael Samuel and Paul Thompson (eds), *The Myths We Live By* (London: Routledge, 1990), 7; John Price, *Everyday Heroism: Victorian Constructions of the Heroic Civilian* (London: Bloomsbury, 2014), 12.
40 Norma Clarke, 'Strenuous Idleness: Thomas Carlyle and the Man of Letters as Hero', in Michael Roper and John Tosh (eds), *Manful Assertions: Masculinities in Britain since 1800* (London: Routledge, 1991), 28, 30.
41 Price, *Everyday Heroism*.
42 Adrian Jarvis, *Samuel Smiles and the Construction of Victorian Values* (Stroud: Sutton, 1997), 59–60, 143; Samuel Smiles, *Self-Help* (London: J. Murray, 1859), ch. 1.
43 Thomas Carlyle, *On Heroes, Hero-Worship, and the Heroic in History* (1841), quoted in Juliette Atkinson, *Victorian Biography Reconsidered: A Study of Nineteenth-Century 'Hidden' Lives* (Oxford: Oxford University Press, 2010), 54; see also 48–55.
44 'Current Views', *The Library Association Record* (hereafter *LAR*), 14 February 1914, 3–4; Eric Leyland, *The Public Library* (London: Pitman, 1937), 14.
45 'To the Editor', *London*, 18 March 1897, 205.
46 'No Author Entered', Gladstone Papers, Vol. CCCXCV 703, MS44480, 261–262. The author was Edward Foskett (afterwards chief librarian of Camberwell library); see below.
47 Mosse, *The Image of Man*, 79; Trev Lynn Broughton, *Men of Letters, Writing Lives: Masculinity and Literary Audio/Biography in the Late-Victorian Period* (London: Routledge, 1999), 18–19, 25.
48 My italics: the martial metaphor mattered. 'Presentation to Mr Cawthorne', *East London Advertiser*, 27 June 1936, Tower Hamlets Local History Library and Archives (THLH); 'Obituary', *LAR*, Vol. III (1901), 541.
49 Julie-Marie Strange, '"Speechless with Grief": Bereavement and the Working-Class Father, c.1880–1914', in Trev Lynn Broughton and Helen Rogers (eds), *Gender and Fatherhood in the Nineteenth Century* (Basingstoke: Palgrave Macmillan, 2007), 141; 'Society of Public Librarians Minute Book', 4 October 1911, SPL/1-4, Bishopsgate Institute and Archive.
50 Sussman, *Victorian Masculinities*, 24–35, 44; Atkinson, *Victorian Biography*, 72.
51 'Female Suffrage: A Letter from the Right Hon. W. E. Gladstone, M. to Samuel Smith, M., London 1892', in 'Speeches and Writings, Vol.11', M34.9G/1, 5–8, Gladstone's Library (GL).
52 Martin Francis, 'The Domestication of the Male? Recent Research on Nineteenth- and Twentieth-Century British Masculinity', *The Historical Journal*, 45:3 (2002), 637–652; Michael Heller, *London Clerical Workers, 1880–1914: A Development of the Labour Market* (London: Pickering & Chatto, 2011), 82, 196–197.
53 David Vincent, *Bread, Knowledge and Freedom* (London: Europa, 1981), 53–56.
54 'Stepney Librarian's Silver Wedding', *East London Advertiser*, 11 September 1920, THLH.

55 William Plant to Master Yeulet, 26 August 1897, Letter Book 1897–1900, L/M 12, Hackney Archives.
56 *The Library Assistants' Association*, Vol. I, January 1898–September 1899; Vol. V, October 1905–September 1907.
57 British-born US librarian Lucie Stone unfavourably compared the discourteous conference behaviours of male and female senior American colleagues at a post-war professional conference with the kindly behaviour of their male British counterparts in the interwar years. Lucie R. Stone, 'A Professional Meeting in the U.S.A.', *The Assistant Librarian*, 48:2 (1955), 26. See also 'The Library Staff', *Library World*, June 1899.
58 John Mullins, *Free Libraries and Newsrooms: Their Foundation and Management* (London: H. Sotheran & Co., 1879 [1868]), preface.
59 *Ibid.*, 16; see also 13.
60 *Ibid.*, 12; see also 6–9, 16–17.
61 *Bromley and District Times*, 20 May 1898, 5; *LAR*, 26, 1924, 195; *Willesden Chronicle*, 24 January 1919; Edward T. Clarke, *Bermondsey: Its Historic Memories and Associations* (London: Elliot Stock, 1902), 258–259.
62 Peter Cowell, *Public Library Staffs* (London: Library Association, 1893), 8–9, at 9.
63 'Death of Mr W. J. Haggerston', 5 May 1894, Newcastle Library Cuttings, Vol. 1, 45, Newcastle City Library.
64 *Newcastle Weekly Chronicle*, 28 June 1879; W. Bullivant (Chairman of the Library Commissioners), 'Notes for Speech Made at the Opening of Poplar Library', 3 October 1894, in 'Description of the New Public Library for Poplar', THLH, LC12678, 850.20.
65 Carol T. Christ, '"The Hero as Man of Letters": Masculinity and Victorian Nonfiction Prose', in Thais E. Morgan (ed.), *Victorian Sages and Cultural Discourse: Renegotiating Gender and Power* (New Brunswick: Rutgers University Press, 1990), 23.
66 In 1895, together with Goss of Lewisham and John Frowde of Bermondsey, the Camberwell librarian founded the Society of Public Librarians (SPL) in part to address this issue. More than fifty subjects were involved in some capacity in SPL business. Almost thirty subjects were active society members, attending the monthly meetings for periods of between five and thirty-fifty years. Michelle Johansen, 'A Fault-Line in Library History: Charles Goss, the Society of Public Librarians and the "Battle of the Books" in the Late Nineteenth Century', *Library History*, 19 (2003), 76–91.
67 'No Author Entered', Gladstone Papers, 262.
68 *Ibid.*
69 *Ibid.*, 261.
70 John Brydon and Frank Burgoyne, 'Paper Read before RIBA, 20 February 1899', from Journal of RIBA, Vol. 6, Third Series, No. 8, 25 February 1899, in 'Cuttings from Professional Journals', IV/63/1/42 (4), 15, Lambeth Archives.
71 *LAR*, Fourth Series, Vol. 5, March 1938, 142; *LAR*, Fourth Series, Vol. 6, January 1939, 47; *LAR*, Fourth Series, Vol. 25, March 1958, 103.

72 *The Borough News*, 3 November 1933, 'The Ernest Callard Archive. Loose Items'. HOW/47, WHS.
73 Foskett prefaced his collected poems with a self-deprecating quotation from Byron ('What is writ, is writ – would it were worthier!'). Quoting a 'Great Man' of the literary world while playing down his own contribution to the field offers a tidy summation of the struggling 'hero' concept. Edward Foskett, *Poems* (London: Kegan Paul, 1886), preface.
74 Clarke, 'Strenuous Idleness', 40–41.
75 Ruth Clayton Windscheffel, *Reading Gladstone* (New York: Palgrave Macmillan, 2008), 197–198, 205–206; 'Lecture V. [Tuesday, 19 May 1840] The Hero as Man of Letters', in David R. Sorensen and Brent E. Kinser (eds), *On Heroes, Hero-Worship, and the Heroic in History* (New Haven: Yale University Press, 2013), 132–161.
76 David Bebbington, *The Mind of Gladstone: Religion, Homer, and Politics* (Oxford: Oxford University Press, 2004), 292.
77 In so doing he experienced a fresh surge of popularity, particularly among the labouring classes. Peter Sewter, 'Gladstone as Woodsman', in Roland Quinault, Roger Swift, and Ruth Clayton Windscheffel (eds), *William Gladstone: New Studies and Perspectives* (London: Routledge, 2012), 174–175.
78 William Gladstone, 'Books and the Housing of Them', in Speeches and Writings, Vol. 10 (1888–1891), M34.9G/1, 388, GL.
79 Greenwood, *Public Libraries*, xxiv.
80 Alexander Ireland, *Address on the Moral Influence of Free Libraries* (Manchester: Henry Blacklock & Co., 1892), 6.
81 Edward Foskett (ed.), *The Readers' Monthly*, 1:1 (1898), 5; Charles Welch, 'The Public Library Movement in London', *The Library*, 7 (1895), 97–109; Henry Calder Marshall, *The Public Libraries of London, Their Histories and Accounts* (London: Gee, 1890), 21.
82 Laurence Inkster of Battersea even provided notepaper and envelopes free of charge for the use of men and women seeking positions.
83 Henrietta Barnett, *Canon Barnett: His Life, Work, and Friends, Vol. II* (London: J. Murray, 1918), 11.
84 Gillian Tindall, *The Born Exile* (London: Temple Smith, 1974), 83; see also 78, 89.
85 Black, 'Man and Boy', 209.
86 Robert Snape, *Leisure and the Rise of the Public Library* (London: Library Association, 1995), 48.
87 G. R. Humphrey, 'The Reading of the Working Classes', *The Nineteenth Century*, 3 April 1893, 690–701, esp. 692; Broughton, *Men of Letters*, 19.

9

Fathers, sons, and 'normal', 'ordinary' family life, 1945–1974

Richard Hall

As a number of historians of masculinity have argued, despite calls for greater engagement with masculine subjectivities over the last thirty years, more work remains to be done if we are to understand how men and boys negotiated available social structures and cultural scripts at any given historical moment.[1] Such work demands that we look intimately at male emotional lives, that we concern ourselves less with elusive claims to representativeness and more with the particularity of individual responses to society and culture. In this way, not only do we gain insight into some of the richness, texture, and range of historical lived experience, but we also learn more about the viability of established socio-cultural themes and chronologies. The experiences of fathers and sons in the decades following the Second World War offer rich potential for engagement with these dynamics. As Frank Mort argued in his autobiographical reflection on a post-war father–son relationship, 'the narratives of the post-war years are so portentous and authoritative that they constantly threaten to engulf subjectivity'.[2] Drawing on father–son relationships in fourteen families from a range of social backgrounds, as they were narrated in oral history interviews, this chapter assesses how masculine selfhoods were reproduced intergenerationally by exploring adult men's memories of post-war family life.[3]

The stories of post-war socio-cultural change are well known. Most families lived healthier, longer lives, in improved homes, with more time and money to spend on leisure; there was a substantial shift from blue-collar to white-collar work and a dramatic increase in average incomes; access to education widened and secondary, further, and higher education was transformed; and the arrival of rock and roll, the seven-inch single, television, and mass consumerism created hitherto unknown cultural outlets for a new generation.[4] However, rather than the ensuing generational rupture described in some cultural accounts, Selina Todd and Hilary Young have argued that the opportunities wrought by post-war British society fostered continuities of classed solidarities across generations, as parents supported their children's newly available choices.⁵ This chapter intervenes in this debate, arguing that the social and emotional interplay of post-war father–son relationships is better characterised by ambiguity and ambivalence. Each man and boy was bound by available gendered cultural scripts within a changing social structure; but they also played their parts in particular, interpersonal familial dynamics. In doing so, fathers and sons alike evoked memories of 'normal' performances of boyhood and adult masculinity, drawing on ideas of the classic post-war nuclear family model. As their narrations show, the model was both idealised and unstable. As sons succeeded fathers as workers in a society marked by rising living standards, they contested the 'ordinary' family lives of their childhoods by telling self-reflective stories of individuality. James Hinton has argued that in mid-twentieth-century Britain, 'selfhood was not a given, but a quest';⁶ this chapter locates that quest between and across male generations in response to discourses of 'normal', 'ordinary' family life.

Oral history interviews with people in later life provide vantage points from which respondents can assess and contextualise their life trajectories. As Mary Jo Maynes has argued, life narratives 'provide access to individuals' claims about how their motivations and actions have been shaped by memories, emotions, imagination, and cumulative life experiences ... they thus offer a methodologically privileged location from which to view significant aspects of human agency'.⁷ Typically, having become fathers and grandfathers themselves, men in interviews were able to locate historic experiences of fatherhood and 'sonhood' against familial landmarks and socio-cultural timelines. Of course, their memories should be engaged with critically, probed for inconsistency, confusion of personal with cultural memories, or tendencies towards nostalgia, for example. However, these men were also self-critical.⁸ Often, they acknowledged uncertainty around particular memories, or expressed discomfort with continuities of feeling against changed cultural modes of acceptability. However imperfect their oral testimony, though, these men remained uniquely placed to tell intimate stories of their family relationships across the course of their lives.⁹ A focus on interviews with *pairs* of fathers and sons (roughly half of whom were interviewed together) revealed the essentially *inter*subjective dynamics of these relationships. Parenting was – and is – a multidirectional process, characterised by reciprocity as well as imposition.¹⁰ Drawing on upper-middle, middle, and working-class experiences, I also foreground the common lens of two-way intergenerational transmission, which cuts across class boundaries, in stories of both post-war social mobility and continuities of particular classed cultures.

Normality and the post-war gender order

The years following the end of the Second World War in Britain are often seen to have heralded a welcome return to 'normal family life'.[11] The creation of the welfare state in 1945 had provided family allowances for every child after the first and the security of free healthcare and comprehensive National Insurance.[12] The 1944 Education Act enshrined free secondary education for every child up to the age of fifteen.[13] Full employment and rising wages added to families' levels of confidence and security, which, for many parents, marked a significant change from their childhood experiences in the 1920s, 1930s, and early 1940s. The quality of home lives also improved, as the interwar migration to new towns and suburban areas continued.[14] However, as Pat Thane has argued, ideas of 'normality' in post-war British culture were in many respects both novel and precarious.[15] Two-children families were in fact a departure both from larger Victorian family sizes and smaller interwar ones, full employment created stable but atypical conditions for male breadwinning, and women's roles sat uneasily amid rising participation in the workforce and pressure to be full-time mothers and homemakers.[16] Enquiries into post-war family life have identified such precariousness from a range of perspectives. Claire Langhamer has described the 'emotional instability and subversion of established norms' in mid-century marriages.[17] Deborah Cohen has illuminated the tension between people's increasingly private family lives and their unburdening of family secrets to experts.[18] Lucy Delap has uncovered disclosures of child sexual abuse in the 1950s and 1960s that was routinely dismissed as evidence of 'normal' childhood sexuality.[19] Instances of sexual and domestic violence were similarly normalised.[20] Moreover, as Matt Houlbrook has argued, 'normal' might best be viewed as a fundamentally elusive social category.[21] Nonetheless, the desire to label post-war society as such was pressing – both contemporaneously, to mark a removal from the tumult of wartime, and retrospectively, to locate the 1950s and early 1960s as the settled midpoint between 1940s war and austerity, and the cultural upheaval of the later 1960s and 1970s.[22]

The lived experiences of young families after the war belied both the yearning to live 'normal' lives and the simultaneous acknowledgement that such lives were illusory. In all cases, however, notions of normality were tightly moored to the generational reproduction of the heterosexual nuclear family, which was to be emotionally harmonious and sanctified by marriage. Born in 1942, Alan Sorrell summed up his mother and father's hopes for him when he said, 'I suppose all parents are the same. They want you to grow up and be good, get married, have children and not the other way round, and just lead a good, normal life, I suppose.'[23] Post-war father

Henry Curd echoed these sentiments, thinking marriage to be a 'part of a normal way of life' and that 'the only thing what might have upset me, if they had boyfriends ... [but] they had a normal way of life, they had girlfriends and that sorta' thing'.[24] Interviewed in the mid-1980s, Alan and Henry reflected with satisfaction that their families had subscribed to 'normal' ideals. However, their respective qualifications about the potential for children out of wedlock and homosexual relationships betray underlying anxieties. Post-war secularisation was buffeted by the persistently pervasively custom of Christian marriage; at the same time, moral panics about same-sex relationships were commonplace in popular discourse.[25] As Frank Mort has illustrated, there was little space in dominant ideas about post-war family life for non-heteronormative masculine subjectivities.[26]

Peter Coverley, a father of four, was open to the different family structures available to his children's generation, but conscious that they represented a departure from the norm as he understood it:

> Well, after Mary died, I was up visiting them and I said to the children, 'Why don't you get married?' They just said, 'What for?' I said, 'Well, I suppose you've got something there' ... I must confess, I take a fairly tolerant view, although from my own point of view, I would marry. Because I had such a happy marriage. It's only occasionally that it suddenly dawns on me that lots of people haven't. I was lucky.[27]

Peter's evocation of a happy marriage resonates with the mid-century flourishing of romantic love that Claire Langhamer has identified, in which 'new models of selfhood ... prioritised self-fulfilment over self-control'.[28] But he also understood that the nature of self-fulfilment was changing for his children's generation. Late 1960s 'permissive' legislation saw a reduction to the age of marriage without parents' consent, divorces becoming easier to obtain, and the decriminalisation of homosexuality.[29] At the time of Peter's interview in the mid-1980s, cohabitation was also considered more common. The cultural legacy of heterosexual marriage continued to loom large in the psyches of all men across the late twentieth and early twenty-first centuries, even if its hegemony as the 'norm' was increasing contested by younger generations.

Central to the success of post-war normal family life were the gendered performances of breadwinning and homemaking. Laura King has argued that the 1950s witnessed the advent of a 'new, if fragile, family-oriented masculinity'.[30] But while post-war newspaper columnists, judges, and social scientists were keen to advance the case for modern, emotionally engaged fathers, in practice, as 1970s feminist critiques were quick to underline, the gender ordering of everyday family life changed little.[31] Even the more optimistic social studies concluded that men's domestic responsibilities remained partial and conditional. John Goldthorpe and his colleagues' findings were typical: there were a majority of 'affluent workers' involved with 'putting their children to bed', 'reading to children and telling stories', and 'taking out younger children and babies', but these were 'main responsibilities' for just 10 per cent, 22 per cent, and 7 per cent of the sample, respectively.[32] Most commonly, during a period of near full-male employment, men's family lives remained oriented around their hours of work.[33] As the post-war decades unfolded, the rising number of women in workplaces was beginning to influence gendered relationships of power in the home, but expectations of women's domestic obligations remained.[34] The best-selling parenting advice literature of the era only rubberstamped these conventions.[35] In the minds of mid-twentieth-century marriage reformers, the meaning of 'companionate marriage' had moved from Victorian notions of husbandly authority and wifely devotion to ideas of mutual sexual attraction, respect, and affection.[36] However, these modernising shifts sat uneasily with the persistence of traditional gender orderings of family life, at least until more visible challenges to the nuclear family ideal from the early 1970s.[37]

Kate Fisher and Simon Szreter emphasise couples' agency and pragmatism in their negotiations of each other's gendered contributions of breadwinning and homemaking, positing the overarching idea of 'caring and sharing' to describe their particular, tailored approaches.[38] Many postwar fathers and sons' testimonies broadly corroborated this notion, while emphasising the leading roles played by women. Fathers would not entirely exempt themselves from domestic activities, such as washing up, reading to children, or even bathing and clothing them, but these activities were always directed by mothers. Democratic structures of household organisation might also include children, once old enough; although, as had been the case before the war, the younger generation's weight of responsibility was often similarly unequally gendered.[39] For example, it was Andrew Coverley's sisters who would help their mother with the cooking, washing, and cleaning, while Andrew would join his father, Peter, to do the shopping every Saturday morning.[40] Peter's job was also to carry out repairs and undertake the 'heavy manual' work in the garden, while his wife was 'on flowers and general supervision'.[41] Andrew explained that it was 'all done as a unit', but that his mother was 'the great organising factor behind everything that was ever done by the family'.[42]

Men's side of the division of household labour was routinely characterised by the undertaking of home improvements. By the end of the 1960s, do-it-yourself (DIY) had found mass popularity, as families became more likely than not to own their homes, or rent them on a long-term basis from the council.[43] With some justification, DIY was championed contemporaneously as evidence of men's increasingly home-centred lives.[44] But such claims require qualification. Increasing numbers of men were engaging in home improvements in response to their improved material conditions, but their endeavours were routinely undertaken alone. DIY was inherently a home-centred activity, but though it doubtless improved the lives of families, it did not directly involve them. The craftsmanship involved was an important exemplar of adult masculinity for post-war children, but often not a site of direct generational transmission of skills and behaviour.[45] From the perspective of adulthood, sons had negotiated their gendered inheritances with various outcomes: from pleasure in having succeeded their fathers as practical men to feelings of shame and insecurity at having failed to live up to their example. As one son reflected, remembering a recent interchange with his father: 'I came around to borrow something – he was having a clear-out of his tools – and he said, "you don't do so much of the DIY do you?" [pause] I thought I did [laughs], but no, I don't do all the great building projects that he did.'[46] Post-war fathers practised DIY almost universally; their sons' engagements were more ambiguous and contested.

The post-war DIY boom provided an outlet for latent work-related skills of male craftsmanship and creativity, which were increasingly uncalled for whether on newly automated shop floors or in clerical and managerial professions.[47] However, where it was considered normal for men to perform work *inside* the home, women's work *outside* it signalled discomfort and transgression.[48] Like many post-war women, Phil and Fred Avery's mother waited until Phil (her youngest) was old enough to be left on his own before returning to work. Later in life, Phil lamented that 'she probably chose to do it a bit too soon. Because I can remember being on my own, left to my own devices.'[49] Bill Taylor, a motor mechanic, went so far as to change his son's nappies and dress him for school so his wife, Edith, could sleep after working the night shift as a nurse. However, he stopped short of helping with cooking or cleaning, as he explained: 'that's what women did in those days, how we kept them down!'[50] His remark was meant humorously, with one eye on Edith, who was also present for the interview; but the humour betrayed Bill's discomposure, illustrating how, from the perspective of later life, he found the historical inequity of their respective workloads difficult to justify. Nonetheless, speaking in 2015, Edith continued to cook and clean for them both; it was not unusual for normative gender roles, once established, to endure across life-courses.

As a consequence of his mother's shift work, Bill and Edith's son, John, remembered mournfully having to play quietly as a young child, so as not to wake her. He located his experience amid unsettling feelings about a lack of parental intimacy. His claim that his childhood had been 'normal' and 'happy' in this context could only be arrived at with recourse to humour and fantasy:

> I don't think we were a particularly close ... er, cuddly close. I don't remember ever being cuddled particularly ... I mean I'm sure I was occasionally, but I don't remember anything like that, it wasn't that kind of relationship. Erm ... we just ... happy, what I would call a happy, normal childhood ... or ... apart from when they locked me in the cupboard and whipped me! That's not true! Made that bit up! [big laugh][51]

John's joke allows him to regain 'composure' in his interview, in so far as he uses the language of culture (cupboards and whip) to process traumatic memories (not being cuddled) and normalise his experience.[52] His pathologisation of 'normal' as a signifier of emotional stability resonated with contemporary popular psychological discourse. In his influential parenting advice book, *The Child, the Family and the Outside World*, Donald Winnicott titled two chapters 'What Do We Mean by a Normal Child?' and 'Support for Normal Parents'.[53] Winnicott sought to underline the fact that his advice was intended for parents and children whose emotional development was expected to be normal; *abnormal* cases fell under the remit of the medical profession.[54] As Laura Tisdall has shown, the new 'child-centred' psychology – of which Winnicott was a leading proponent – proceeded from understanding the distinction between a 'normal childhood' and a 'normal adulthood', each of which were considered foundational to a healthy democratic citizenship.[55]

Such discourses over the post-war period formed part of a wider psychoanalytic move towards individual freedom of expression in therapeutic practices, and a focus on childhood experience in families to explain the psychological health of adults.[56] In this context, we can see how the processes of oral history and talking therapy interact, as middle-aged and older men negotiated their past subjectivities in the present.[57] What emerges most prominently is a desire to have participated in heteronormative nuclear family structures, with minimal emotional discord and common understandings of traditional gender roles – even though the insecurity of that desire was often laid bare.

Ordinariness and the generational reproduction of class, work, and political subjectivities

The terms 'normal' and 'ordinary' were sometimes used interchangeably by fathers and sons. Often, similar sentiments might be expressed with phrases such as 'like everybody else', or 'what everybody else was doing'.

However, if conceptions of normality tended towards descriptions of psychological health and the ordering of gender relationships *within families*, ordinariness, broadly conceived, tended towards conceptions of *families' positions in society*. Celebrations of ordinariness can be traced back to 'people's war' mythologies of classless national unity.[58] From the 1960s, such discourses collided with a growing trend towards the individual. In his secondary analysis of Goldthorpe's *Affluent Worker* studies, Mike Savage argues that the 'central claim that respondents sought to elaborate was their ordinariness and individuality'.[59] Post-war labourers were keen to retain universalising 'badges of respectability' associated with practical skill in the process of deindustrialisation, while managers celebrated the 'increasing embrace of merit, technique and skill' and the decline of inherited power.[60] Each made claims on ordinariness, while also resisting post-war forms of social classification. In subsequent decades, politicians preoccupied with 'ordinary people' or 'ordinary working people' met with a citizenship whose 'ordinariness' encompassed the individual freedom and self-determination to eschew party loyalty.[61] Families in which sons came of age in the 1960s and 1970s pivoted generationally on this shift from ordinariness to ordinariness and individuality. Oral testimony from the younger generation was more inclined towards narratives of self-fulfilment, reflecting the greater educational, economic, work, and socio-cultural opportunities that had been available to them.[62] But such narratives were ambivalent towards those of their fathers, which belied greater conformity to established social structures. Analysis of the two generations together reveals how dialogues with paternal inheritances produced both harmonious and contested dynamics, which were framed by shifting perspectives on class identity, work, and political subjectivities. Moreover, as Claire Langhamer has recently highlighted, discourses of ordinariness in post-war British society existed in constant tension with the agency and *extraordinariness* of people's lives.[63]

In working-class families across the period, childhood memories of the social order frequently alighted on the erstwhile working-class distinction between 'rough' and 'respectable'.[64] This was Martin Curd's memory. He explained that there were children in his community who were 'a rough lot ... they always got into fights and they used to walk around with knives ... but they're the ones who came out worst in the end 'cause they used to play around so much they didn't get on at all'.[65] 'Getting on' was the colloquial expression for self-improvement, which Martin explained in generational terms:

> Well, improve meself. [My parents] got to a certain standard, but they couldn't afford anymore ... What they used to think were extra luxuries – like

an automatic washing machine, colour television – they used to have the old black and white. We take 'em as normal things ... So really, we are better off than they were.[66]

It emerged that Martin was a proud advocate of 'getting on'. After initially failing his eleven-plus examination, he went on to pass the exam at thirteen, instigating a belated path through grammar school, then technical college, where he met 'all different people who've got all different jobs'.[67] He became interested in

> getting more money so you can get the better things in life. So, you're not working in a factory ... [instead] working in a job where you're maybe wearing a suit, as it used to be then. If you had a job with a suit, then you were a bit better than the chap working in a factory with a cloth cap.[68]

Interviewed in the 1980s, while in his mid-forties, Martin's feelings as an adult marked a change from his childhood self. Revering his father, Henry, who was a skilled manual worker (a pattern maker), Martin claimed to have deliberately failed his eleven-plus at the first attempt because, as he explained, 'at that time, I wanted to be the same as my dad'.[69] His subsequent interest in 'getting on' saw him go on to run his own heating engineering business. As sociologists Michael Young and Peter Willmott argued, social relations between post-war fathers and sons were especially affected by occupational mobility, because of the discomforting feelings engendered by different job statuses across generations.[70]

Martin had framed his childhood memories of *intra*-class difference – between 'rough' and 'respectable' – in terms of individual choice; unlike other members of his working-class peer group, he decided to change his circumstances for the better. He contrasted his feelings with his father's sense of *inter*-class distinction. Henry had explained to him that 'there was sort of "them and us".[71] There's them who've got all the money, and there's us poor beggars ... we were always sort of the lower ones, we were the working class.'[72] The intergenerational differences of perspective, thrown into relief by Martin's coming of age, were illuminated in the intersection of their respective work identities and classed subjectivities. However, it was their different political worldviews that prompted their most tempestuous arguments as adults. With heavy understatement, Martin admitted that he and his father now have 'a few little heated discussions'.[73] Remembering his switch from Labour to Conservative, Martin explained that 'with Labour it seemed ... that everybody's gotta have exactly the same. In a way, it's a bit like the Communists ... it's gotta be spread equally. You're not allowed to really get on.'[74] Henry, a long-standing trade unionist and son of a local Labour ward secretary, despaired of his son's outlook. Like Martin, though, he associated it with his broadened horizons as he came of age:

The only way I can explain it, is that [Martin] don't think. That anybody who's got a ha'pence of sense can figure that the situation that's in this country now, its gonna' get nowhere, it's gonna' get worse, unless you get some type of socialism ... Maybe because when he went to the grammar school or technical college, he's been with a different type of people to what I was with when I was at work.[75]

In fact, Henry went on to qualify his remarks. He was anti-Tory, but 'not such a socialist as I used to be'.[76] His views on class had changed too: 'I say: yes, I belong to the working class, because everybody must ... even a judge is working class ... but some people say working class stops at the navvy type, and above that are not working class, but I think anybody who works for a living is a working-class type.'[77] Henry's evolution from thinking in terms of 'us and them' towards a more ecumenical view of class identity resonates with the idea that notions of class distinction were gradually replaced by more universalising expressions of ordinariness across the late twentieth century.[78] Martin, however, believed his social ascent, born of individual will, had made him middle class.[79] Paradoxically, it is Labour-voting Henry's view that more closely echoes Margaret Thatcher's rhetorical move to reorient opinion away from languages of class and towards a collective understanding that 'we are all working people who basically want the same things'.[80] As Florence Sutcliffe-Braithwaite argues, however, such positions reflected the complexities and contradictions of popular attitudes to class in the 1980s, when both Henry and Martin were interviewed.[81]

Henry's and Martin's testimonies were typical of the intersubjective exchanges that unfolded between fathers and sons in relation to class, work, and politics; but they were not wholly representative. For example, father and son Harry and Steve Tillett, from the East Midlands, had many things in common with the Curds – the childhood memories of 'rough and respectable' families, the legacy of trade union membership, Harry's once trenchant working-class identity being supplanted by his contemplative reflection in old age that 'everybody has to work for a living'.[82] Like Martin Curd, Steve also followed his father in voting Labour before 'thinking for himself' and changing tack.[83] Unlike Martin, however, Steve led an itinerant life, with spells of work and dole interspersed with foreign travel, which prompted feelings of shame at not having inherited his father's and grandfather's work ethic. Despite his casual attitude to work, Steve was more closely wedded to his working-class identity than Martin, as he explained: 'I mean I could win the Pools tomorrow and win a million pounds, but it still wouldn't stop me being working-class.'[84] Another post-war son, Alan Sorrell, had similar feelings, declaring that 'if I was a millionaire I'd still class meself working class. I don't wanna' be an upper-class snob.'[85]

The fantastical *extraordinariness* of extreme wealth was commonly evoked as a counterpoint to the *ordinary* state of affairs, in which money was not so plentiful.[86] Steve's and Alan's proud assertions of their class identities, unaltered since childhood, show how the younger generation's tendency towards individualism and self-fulfilment were not always in conflict with their social and familial inheritances. John Taylor was another working-class son whose politics were in sympathy with his father's, but right wing, rather than left. He explained, 'I lived through the Harold Wilson years so, you know, from '63 to whenever it was, 1970 ... and they couldn't stand Harold Wilson ... and that definitely imprinted on me because it ... I've always ... made me a Conservative.'[87] Corroborating John's account, Bill proudly confirmed that 'all my sons are Conservative'.[88]

The period spanning the 1960s and early 1970s was a pivotal moment for the reproduction of masculinities in working-class families, whose material conditions were improving, workplace landscapes changing, and political subjectivities becoming less certain. Father–son narrations frequently alighted on intersubjective points of agreement and difference with regard to work, class identity, and political worldview, determined by life-course effects, personality, and in response to changing socio-political discourses. Though both generations engaged with universalising ideas of ordinariness, it was post-war sons whose narratives were most characterised by assertions of individual choice – whether their views cohered with, or departed from, those of their fathers.

Socially mobile fathers and middle-class families

As well as 'horizontal' patterns of generational change and continuity, in which a cohort of sons can be seen in dialogue with a cohort of fathers, families also experienced 'vertical' processes of generational change, in which parents' circumstances altered over the course of children's lives.[89] Such experiences were often framed by the effects of affluence. Norman Livingstone, the son of a miner, was born in Newcastle in 1935. He left school at fifteen to apprentice as a draughtsman at an engineering firm, where he was to meet his wife, Muriel. It was customary for couples in the 1950s to marry within their class, but Norman and Muriel crossed a social divide.[90] Norman remembered, 'going up their street, there was actually trees! And there was ... drives, gardens, that sort of thing ... well Wallsend didn't have that you see – it was quite low-key. And going up the street with the trees and what-have-you.'[91] After they were married, the young couple had to move to a small flat back in working-class Wallsend, where they had their son, Stephen, who was born in 1958. But by 1961, with

Norman's salary increasing, they were able to move to Monkseaton, to the sort of semi-detached house with a bathroom and garden that Muriel had been used to growing up. The change in circumstances delighted Norman's father so much, he used to make regular visits on his motorbike to tend to the garden and stay over when Norman and Muriel went away on holiday.

As a small child, Stephen found the move from the close-knit neighbourliness of Wallsend to the 'different world' of Monkseaton traumatic. Norman remembered that Stephen, aged three, would gaze out of the living room window saying he wanted to 'go home'.[92] From the perspective of an oral history interview in middle age, however, Stephen considered himself 'quite privileged' to have glimpsed the 'old world' and the transition he witnessed over the course of the 1960s.[93] Once his father became a manager, Stephen remembers how the gap between his grandparents' and his parents' lifestyles grew wider. Visiting Wallsend at weekends, 'it was grimy, you know. Coal dust and smut ... and cinder tracks', where their extended family would meet up at weekends, going 'from house to house, in the same street ... and you'd have a bit of a sing-song and that type of thing'.[94] Meanwhile, his mother and father had become 'quite a smart couple ... they went to dinner dances and my mum used to make long evening gowns, and my dad would have his suit and his dickie-bow every now and again'.[95] Nonetheless, Norman was quick to emphasise the ordinariness of his experiences. He remained 'the same person'; any change in lifestyle was merely accordant with 'the way of the country, the country has gone through a change'.[96] Similarly, while broadly supportive of his son's socio-cultural passage through education and work (Stephen had become an artist/teacher, having gone to art school, via spells as a punk and working in a kibbutz), Norman was keen to play down any hints of pretension. When Stephen described how a love of Tolstoy had helped him overcome difficulties reading aloud in class, Norman interjected 'that's a bit bragging Steve!'.[97] Norman was a socially mobile post-war father who nonetheless remained grounded in an ordinary working-class sensibility. Stephen was respectful, even reverential, of his family's class heritage, but was equally proud to have traced a more individualised path towards self-fulfilment.

Other intergenerational journeys through post-war affluence were more fraught. In Goldthorpe's critique of the embourgeoisement thesis, he maintained that the 'normative convergence' of class cultures has a twin focus: 'instrumental collectivism' and 'family-centredness'.[98] The former concerned a continuance of trade union engagement, and the latter referred to the tendency of working-class men to invest their new-found wealth – along with their leisure time – in the family home.[99] The Avery family experience complicated this theory. While it was true that Fred and Phil's father, Sid, appeared to show little signs of aspiration to middle-class values, he was, nonetheless, 'a little bit capitalistic', as Fred remembered, 'even though he was a bricklayer, a tradesman'.[100] In fact, the Avery brothers' childhood had unfolded in the shadow of a £400 loan that their father had taken on to fund a series of ill-advised renovation projects. Phil recalled that the money 'hung like a millstone round his neck for most of our childhood: servicing this £400'.[101] It was their mother that bore the brunt of his recklessness, though, living for long periods with unfit kitchen facilities, and being forced to juggle housework, childrearing, and paid work to bolster family finances. Eventually, the loan was paid off, and Jack established a profitable property investment company, in which the whole family were named as shareholders. For much of their childhoods, however, Jack Avery's high-risk form of provision both disrupted the normative breadwinner–homemaker family structure, and presented a complicated model of adult masculinity for his sons to negotiate.

In families for whom relative affluence was maintained across the period, there was more emphasis on intergenerational continuity, which, nonetheless, concealed particular and dynamic intersubjective experiences. As Savage argues, post-war middle-class claims on ordinariness were made in response to a society that placed value on the meritocratic accumulation of skill and ability (compared with pre-war deference to inherited wealth and position).[102] There were also, however, certain aspects of middle-class culture that spanned generations, such as work statuses, particular institutional affiliations, and forms of paternalistic altruism.[103] Such trappings were more overtly concerned with the intergenerational sustenance of social status and cultures of personal betterment than was the case for working-class families, for whom material improvements demanded social and emotional negotiations with a less affluent past. However, just like their working-class and socially mobile counterparts, middle-class boys were keen to emphasise their agency and individuality in negotiation with their paternal inheritances.

Remembering his middle-class upbringing in post-war Cheshire, Andrew Coverley, born in 1950, reflected on a contradiction underpinning his parents' social outlook:

> Being a teaching family we were definitely distinct from a lot of other people ... I think it was that 'we must help the disadvantaged' business. It is funny, isn't it, through sort of concern and so on you are actually reinforcing class barriers, because you are sort of admitting that there are [sic] lower class of people who need help.[104]

So alert was Andrew to this contradiction, he gave it a name: 'naïve snobbery'.[105] His parents had sought to alleviate inequality, on the one hand, while reinforcing a social hierarchy, on the other. Paradoxically, despite feeling 'distinct' from other families, Andrew also reflected on childhood claims of ordinariness. He remembered thinking that 'everybody was like us, I thought everybody shared the same opinions, we are all like this'.[106] His family was at once exemplary and universally replicated. Between birth and early adulthood, Andrew's family's material conditions and middle-class status had remained little changed. However, on becoming a sound engineer in the 1970s, he took on a job that was both relatively unusual and which signalled his social descent. Growing up, he had 'always envisaged [a] big rambling house [with] a big rambling garden' for his future family, but in adulthood had been limited to a small bungalow. His disappointment was mitigated both by his retrospective realisation of the instability of 'naïve snobbery' and his pleasure that his children – who were less geographically isolated than he had been as a child – had plenty of friends on their estate.

Post-war father Alan Birchwood, like his middle-class counterpart Peter Coverley, was a social liberal. He and his wife were involved in a number of middle-class associational activities designed to improve the lives of those less fortunate. Also like Peter, however, Alan wanted to preserve the social distinction inherent within those activities. His keenness on the preservation of social hierarchy emerged in a conversation about work. He explained:

> I mean, there's your status at work – the fact that you're recognised as, oh yeah, quite a good bloke, but also in society outside, to say that you were a chartered engineer does carry some weight. Not as much as we would like ... because everybody knows 'oh, engineer, you're the bloke that comes and reads the meter'. We've been fighting that for years, it's a lost cause I'm afraid.[107]

Alan's son, Mark, did not have the same misgivings about his parents' social outlook as Andrew Coverley. However, he bore the weight of his paternal inheritance ambivalently. As a Scout leader, Mark Birchwood was proud to have continued a long-standing intergenerational link with an altruistically minded middle-class association, but regretful that he had not achieved as much career success as his father.[108] As was the case in working-class families, among middle-class fathers and sons too, work identities, and perspectives on social status cast long intergenerational shadows.

Sutcliffe-Braithwaite has linked the ascent of ordinariness in the construction of late twentieth-century selfhoods with a decline of deference.[109] Most of the working- and middle-class fathers and sons interviewed would have agreed on the undesirability of class hierarchy, even if some of their narratives betrayed the instability of their subject positions. For one upper-middle-class father and son, however, the preservation of class hierarchy across generations was fundamental. As retired major general Norman Henry explained, 'I think if you get down to basics, if you have it you don't want to lose it; if you haven't got it, you want it. And that is really the social divide.'[110] Mindful that 'nothing could be worse than working for Ford's in Dagenham', he sent his son, Charlie, to an elite public school and personally secured him interviews at several City of London investment banks.[111] Yet, of course, it was inconceivable that Charlie would emerge in blue-collar work given his background. 'Ford's in Dagenham' was part of a rhetorical strategy that simultaneously presented the Henrys as connected and removed from the rest of society. Most prominent in their strategy was their use of understatement. Norman described his family as 'moderately comfortable middle class' and 'privileged financially to a certain extent'; never 'upper class', 'upper-middle class', or 'wealthy'.[112] Despite having five servants and a nanny during Charlie's childhood, they were only 'comparatively well-off';[113] and although they attended expensive public schools, Norman and Charlie described themselves as 'philistines', 'badly educated', and not 'very cultured'.[114] As Andrew Miles and Mike Savage have argued, such false modesty has underpinned the enduring cultural refrain of the 'gentlemanly ethic' despite the rise of technocratic meritocracy.[115] At this end of the social scale, claims of ordinariness are turned on their head; however, the Henrys' male intergenerational succession still demanded processes of intersubjective negotiation. Despite Norman's explicit interventions in his son's life to secure the family's long-term class status, Charlie was insistent that his career choice and Conservative Party support were born of personal inclination, not paternal influence.

Conclusion

It would be too simplistic to suggest that the extraordinariness of the Henrys' testimony only serves to reinforce the discourses of ordinariness drawn elsewhere. Ordinary was a fluid and capacious category, evoked to assert working-class pride, to reconcile processes of social mobility, and to defend participation in universalising human and social experiences, whether from working – or middle-class origins. It interacted with normality, which was used to underline commonly understood gender and generational roles, and to set parameters for the physical and psychological health of families at a time when *the family* as a social entity approached a precipice. In reflecting on their subjectivities across life-courses, fathers engaged in particular negotiations with their families' cultural, classed origins, as sons carved out life narratives characterised more by independence and individuality. Both generations remained bound by their ties to male breadwinning, during a period which saw sons afforded greater opportunities, but fathers also engaging with new industrial landscapes and the effects of rising affluence. Men's relationships with their work in these contexts was closely intertwined with their social and political perspectives, which created moments of intergenerational tension and harmony in the familial reproduction of masculine subjectivities. Post-war fathers and sons made different claims on 'normal', 'ordinary' family lives, told from the vantage points of later life. Viewed intimately, however, their narrations highlight the particularity of male experience in response to prominent discourses of post-war social change.

Notes

1 Ben Griffin, 'Hegemonic Masculinity as a Historical Problem', *Gender & History*, 30:2 (2018), 377–400; Michael Roper, 'Slipping Out of View: Subjectivity and Emotion in Gender History', *History Workshop Journal*, 59:1 (2005), 57–72; John Tosh, 'The History of Masculinity: An Outdated Concept?', in John H. Arnold and Sean Brady (eds), *What Is Masculinity? Historical Dynamics from Antiquity to the Contemporary World* (Basingstoke: Palgrave Macmillan, 2011), 17–34.
2 Frank Mort, 'Social and Symbolic Fathers and Sons in Postwar Britain', *Journal of British Studies*, 38:3 (1999), 383.
3 I conducted interviews with eighteen men between 2015 and 2017 as part of my doctoral research, 'The Emotional Lives and Legacies of Fathers and Sons in Britain, 1945–1974' (PhD diss., University of Cambridge, 2019). I also analysed existing interviews with a further ten men from Paul Thompson and Howard Newby, *Families, Social Mobility and Ageing: An Intergenerational Approach, 1900–1988* (Colchester: University of Essex, 1988). Each father became a parent and each son experienced childhood between 1945 and 1974. All interviewees were white British. I address the ethnic make-up of my research, including the particularity of immigrant experiences and ideas of 'whiteness' as racial category in my wider thesis.
4 See e.g. Derek Fraser, *The Evolution of the British Welfare State: A History of Social Policy since the Industrial Revolution* (Basingstoke: Palgrave Macmillan, 1984); Ian Gazeley, 'Manual Work and Pay, 1900–70', in Nicholas Craft, Ian Gazeley, and Andrew Newell (eds), *Work and Pay in 20th Century Britain* (Oxford: Oxford University Press, 2007), 55–79; Claire Langhamer, 'The Meanings of Home in Postwar Britain', *Journal of Contemporary History*, 40:2 (2005), https://doi.org/10.1177/0022009405051556; Peter Mandler, 'Educating the Nation I: Schools', *Transactions of the Royal Historical Society*, 25 (2014), 5–28; Bill Osgerby, *Youth in Britain since 1945* (Oxford: Blackwell, 1998).
5 Selina Todd and Hilary Young, 'Baby-Boomers to "Beanstalkers": Making the Modern Teenager in Post-War Britain', *Cultural and Social History*, 9:3 (2012), 451–467.
6 James Hinton, *Nine Wartime Lives: Mass-Observation and the Making of the Modern Self* (Oxford: Oxford University Press, 2010), 4.

7 Mary Jo Maynes, 'Age as a Category of Historical Analysis: History, Agency, and Narratives of Childhood', *Journal of the History of Childhood and Youth*, 1:1 (2008), 119.
8 On interviewees' conscious engagement with cultural scripts, see Anna Green, 'Individual Remembering and "Collective Memory": Theoretical Presuppositions and Contemporary Debates', *Oral History*, 32:2 (2004), 35–44.
9 I explore this dynamic in more detail in Richard Hall, 'Emotional Histories: Materiality, Temporality and Subjectivity in Oral History Interviews with Fathers and Sons', *Oral History*, 47:1 (2019), 61–70.
10 On multidirectional intergenerational transmission, see Siân Pooley and Kaveri Qureshi, 'Introduction', in Siân Pooley and Kaveri Qureshi (eds), *Parenthood between Generations: Transforming Reproductive Cultures* (New York: Berghahn Books, 2016), 1–42.
11 For example, Michael Peplar, *Family Matters: A History of Ideas about Family since 1945* (London: Longman, 2002), 26–28.
12 Fraser, *Evolution of the British Welfare State*, 270–286.
13 Mandler, 'Schools', 8.
14 Peter Mandler, 'New Towns for Old', in Becky Conekin, Frank Mort, and Chris Waters (eds), *Moments of Modernity: Reconstructing Britain, 1945–1964* (London: Rivers Oram Press, 1999), 208–227.
15 Pat Thane, 'Family Life and "Normality" in Post-war British Culture', in R. Bessel and D. Schumann (eds), *Life after Death: Approaches to a Cultural and Social History of Europe during the 1940s and 1950s* (Cambridge: Cambridge University Press, 2003), 193–210.
16 On this last point, see Dolly Smith Wilson, 'A New Look at the Affluent Worker: The Good Working Mother in Post-war Britain', *Twentieth Century British History*, 17:2 (2006), 206–229.
17 Claire Langhamer, *The English in Love: The Intimate Story of an Emotional Revolution* (Oxford: Oxford University Press, 2013), 7.
18 Deborah Cohen, *Family Secrets: Living with Shame from the Victorians to the Present Day* (London: Viking, 2013), 211.
19 Lucy Delap, '"Disgusting Details Which Are Best Forgotten": Disclosures of Child Sexual Abuse in Twentieth-Century Britain', *Journal of British Studies*, 57:1 (2018), 94.
20 Marcus Collins, *Modern Love: An Intimate History of Men and Women in Twentieth-Century Britain* (London: Atlantic, 2003), 106.
21 Matt Houlbrook, 'Thinking Queer: The Social and the Sexual in Interwar Britain', in Brian Lewis (ed.), *British Queer History: New Approaches and Perspectives* (Manchester: Manchester University Press, 2013), 134–164.
22 Nick Thomas, 'Will the Real 1950s Please Stand Up?', *Cultural and Social History*, 5:2 (2008), 227–235.
23 SN: 4938–1 Interview 133; Thompson and Newby, *Families*.
24 SN: 4938–1 Interview 042.
25 Callum Brown, *Religion and Society in Twentieth-Century Britain* (Harlow: Pearson Longman, 2006), 25–26; Chris Waters, 'Disorders of the Mind,

Disorders of the Body Social: Peter Wildeblood and the Making of the Modern Homosexual', in Conekin *et al.* (eds), *Moments of Modernity*, 134–151.
26 Mort, 'Social and Symbolic Fathers', 355.
27 SN: 4938-1 Interview 037.
28 Langhamer, *The English in Love*, 45–47; see also Martin Francis, 'Tears, Tantrums, and Bared Teeth: The Emotional Economy of Three Conservative Prime Ministers, 1951–1963', *Journal of British Studies*, 41:3 (2002), 382.
29 Langhamer, *The English in Love*, 175–176; Cohen, *Family Secrets*, 227; Waters, 'Disorders of the Mind', 136.
30 Laura King, *Family Men: Fatherhood and Masculinity in Britain, 1914–1960* (Oxford: Oxford University Press, 2015), 191.
31 On the promotion of 'modern' fathers, see e.g. King, *Family Men*, 116; and Elizabeth Newson and John Newson, *Patterns of Infant Care in an Urban Community* (Harmondsworth: Penguin, 1963), 139–140. On the continuance of the domestic gendered division of labour, see Angela Davis and Laura King, 'Gendered Perspectives on Men's Changing Familial Roles in Postwar England, c.1950–1990', *Gender & History*, 30:1 (2018), 71–72. On the feminist critique of post-war companionate marriage, see Hannah Gavron, *The Captive Wife* (London: Routledge, 1970); and Ann Oakley, *Housewife* (London: Allen Lane, 1974).
32 John H. Goldthorpe, *The Affluent Worker in the Class Structure* (Cambridge: Cambridge University Press, 1969), 105–106.
33 Gazeley, 'Manual Work and Pay', 62. In 1965, the average working week had reduced to 41.4 hours, but overtime was so routine that the amount men actually worked, on average, was 47.3 hours.
34 For contrasting perspectives on this tension, see Helen McCarthy, 'Women, Marriage and Paid Work in Post-war Britain', *Women's History Review*, 26:1 (2017), 46–61; Wilson, 'A New Look'.
35 Most notably, John Bowlby's 'attachment theory', which warned of the dangers of 'maternal deprivation'. John Bowlby, *Child Care and the Growth of Love* (London: Penguin, 1953).
36 Collins, *Modern Love*, 93; Langhamer, *The English in Love*, 47–50.
37 On the 1970s demise of the family, see e.g. Cohen, *Family Secrets*, 214.
38 Simon Szreter and Kate Fisher, *Sex before the Sexual Revolution: Intimate Life in England 1918–1963* (Cambridge: Cambridge University Press, 2010), 96–225.
39 Selina Todd, 'Flappers and Factory Lads: Youth and Youth Culture in Interwar Britain', *History Compass*, 4:4 (2006), 722.
40 SN: 4938-1 Interview 037; SN: 4938-1 Interview 038.
41 SN: 4938-1 Interview 038.
42 *Ibid.*
43 'Home Ownership in the UK, 2017', Resolution Foundation, www.resolutionfoundation.org/data/housing/ (accessed 1 October 2018). The numbers break down as follows: 16.2 per cent own outright; 19.5 per cent mortgage; 24.3 per cent council.

44 Michael Young and Peter Willmott, *Family and Class in a London Suburb* (London: Routledge & Kegan Paul, 1960), 25; Ferdynand Zweig, *The Worker in an Affluent Society: Family Life and Industry* (London: Heinemann, 1961), 96–100, 127.

45 Elizabeth Roberts, *Women and Families: An Oral History, 1940–1970* (Oxford: Blackwell, 1995), 40; Paul Thompson, 'Imagination and Passivity in Leisure: Coventry Car Workers and the Families from the 1920s to the 1990s', in David Thoms, Len Holden, and Tim Claydon (eds), *The Motor Car and Popular Culture in the 20th Century* (Aldershot: Ashgate, 1998), 266–267.

46 ELL05, *Mark Birchwood*, 26 April 2016.

47 Thompson, 'Imagination and Passivity in Leisure', 263; Michael Roper, 'Yesterday's Model: Product Fetishism and the British Company Man, 1945–85', in Michael Roper and John Tosh (eds), *Manful Assertions: Masculinities in Britain since 1800* (London: Routledge, 1991), 190–211.

48 On the capacity of post-war women's work to alter power dynamics in relationships, see McCarthy, 'Women, Marriage and Paid Work', 48.

49 ELL03, *Fred and Phil Avery*, 14 April 2016.

50 ELL02, *Bill Taylor*, October 2015.

51 ELL01, *John Taylor*, October 2015.

52 On composure, see Graham Dawson, *Soldier Heroes: British Adventure, Empire and the Imagining of Masculinities* (London: Routledge, 1994), 22; Alistair Thomson, 'Anzac Memories: Putting Popular Memory Theory into Practice in Australia', in Robert Perks and Alistair Thomson (eds), *The Oral History Reader* (London: Routledge, 1990), 300–301.

53 D. W. Winnicott, *The Child, the Family and the Outside World* (London: Penguin, 1964), chs 19 and 26.

54 *Ibid.*, 173.

55 Laura Tisdall, 'Education, Parenting and Concepts of Childhood in England, c.1945 to c.1979', *Contemporary British History*, 31:1 (2017), 27, 40.

56 Cohen, *Family Secrets*, 223–226; Francis, 'Tears', 381–383; Matthew Thomson, *Psychological Subjects: Identity, Culture, and Health in Twentieth-Century Britain* (Oxford: Oxford University Press, 2006), 266.

57 On the therapeutic qualities of oral history, see Joanna Bornat, 'Oral History as a Social Movement: Reminiscence and Older People', *Oral History*, 17:2 (1989), 16–24.

58 Sonya Rose, *Which People's War? National Identity and Citizenship in Britain, 1939–1945* (Oxford: Oxford University Press, 2003), 3.

59 Mike Savage, 'Working-Class Identities in the 1960s: Revisiting the Affluent Worker Study', *Sociology*, 39:5 (2005), 929.

60 Mike Savage, *Identities and Social Change in Britain since 1940: The Politics of Method* (Oxford: Oxford University Press, 2010), 235.

61 Emily Robinson *et al.*, 'Telling Stories about Post-war Britain: Popular Individualism and the "Crisis" of the 1970s', *Twentieth Century British History*, 28:2 (2017), 273; Florence Sutcliffe-Braithwaite, 'Discourses of "Class" in Britain in "New Times"', *Contemporary British History*, 31:2 (2017), 295–296.

62 See also Robinson *et al.*, 'Telling Stories', 273, 302.
63 Claire Langhamer, '"Who the Hell Are Ordinary People?" Ordinariness as a Category of Historical Analysis', *Transcations of the Royal Historical Society*, 28 (2018), 175–195.
64 On working-class respectability, see e.g. Beverley Skeggs, *Formations of Class and Gender: Becoming Respectable* (London: SAGE, 1997), ch. 3.
65 *Ibid.*
66 *Ibid.* See also Jon Lawrence, 'Class, "Affluence" and the Study of Everyday Life in Britain c.1930–64', *Cultural and Social History*, 10:2 (2013), 282–283, on the political and sociological obsession with aspirational men like Martin.
67 *Ibid.*
68 *Ibid.*
69 *Ibid.*
70 Young and Willmott, *Family and Class*, 84–85.
71 On the tendency of working-class men to adopt this characterisation, see Ross McKibbin, *Classes and Cultures: England, 1918–1951* (Oxford: Oxford University Press, 1998), 204–205.
72 SN: 4938–1 Interview 043.
73 *Ibid.*
74 *Ibid.*; David Butler and Richard Rose, *The British General Electon of 1959* (Basingstoke: Palgrave Macmillan, 1970), 15. Martin's worldview resonates with Butler and Rose's analysis of late 1950s working-class Conservatives, who were culturally working class but enjoying the material benefits of rising affluence.
75 SN: 4938–1 Interview 042.
76 *Ibid.*
77 *Ibid.*
78 See e.g. Matthew Hilton, Chris Moores, and Florence Sutcliffe-Braithwaite, 'New Times Revisited: Britain in the 1980s', *Contemporary British History*, 31:2 (2017), 145–165; Savage, 'Working-Class Identities'.
79 Martin's classed interpretation of 'getting on' corresponds with the popular contemporary sociological idea of embourgeoisement, in which conditions of affluence caused working-class people to aspire to middle-class needs and values. See e.g. Zweig, *The Worker*. Zweig's account was famously contested by John Goldthorpe in his series of Affluent Worker studies.
80 Quoted in Sutcliffe-Braithwaite, 'Discourses of "Class"', 295. Thatcher made this remark in 1988.
81 *Ibid.*, 301.
82 SN: 4938–1 Interview 140.
83 SN: 4938–1 Interview 141.
84 *Ibid.* Selina Todd makes a similar point in *The People: The Rise and Fall of the Working Class, 1910–2010* (London: John Murray, 2014), esp. 8–9.
85 SN: 4938–1 Interview 133.
86 On working-class gambling and wish fulfilment, see Richard Hoggart, *The Uses of Literacy: Aspects of Working-Class Life* (London: Penguin, 2009), 117–118.

87 ELL01, *John Taylor*, October 2015.
88 ELL02, *Bill Taylor*.
89 Pooley and Qureshi, 'Introduction', 15–17. Pooley and Qureshi identify three forms of generational change: vertical, in which experiences accumulate palimpsestuously; horizontal, in which individuals engage with a common culture in opposition to their parents; and 'linear', which refers to a contested teleology of ever greater 'modernisation'.
90 On the greater likelihood of people to marry within their class, see Langhamer, *The English in Love*, 57.
91 ELL13, *Norman and Stephen Livingstone*, March 2017.
92 *Ibid.*
93 *Ibid.*
94 *Ibid.*
95 *Ibid.*
96 *Ibid.*
97 *Ibid.*
98 Goldthorpe, *Affluent Worker*, 27.
99 *Ibid.*
100 ELL03, *Fred and Phil Avery*.
101 *Ibid.*
102 Savage, *Identities and Social Change*, 235.
103 For a sociological perspective on the middle-class tendency to cultivate these ties, see Young and Willmott, *Family and Class*, 87–98.
104 SN: 4938–1 Interview 038.
105 *Ibid.*
106 *Ibid.*
107 ELL04, *Alan Birchwood*.
108 *Ibid.* The Birchwoods' association with the Scouts dated back to Alan's grandfather attending a speech by Robert Baden-Powell in 1908. On the twentieth-century growth of middle-class professional associations and their social prestige, see Harold Perkin, *The Rise of Professional Society: England since 1880* (London: Routledge, 1989), 20.
109 Florence Sutcliffe-Braithwaite, *Class, Politics, and the Decline of Deference in England, 1968–2000* (Oxford: Oxford University Press, 2018).
110 ELL08, *Norman and Charlie Henry*, February 2017.
111 *Ibid.*
112 *Ibid.*
113 *Ibid.*
114 *Ibid.*
115 Andrew Miles and Mike Savage, 'The Strange Survival Story of the English Gentleman, 1945–2010', *Cultural and Social History*, 9:4 (2012), 595–612.

Reflection: Doing gender history and the history of masculinity

Michael Roper

My interest in the history of masculinity was sparked in October 1985, when I joined the gender history MA seminar at Essex led by Leonore Davidoff – it was at that point, I think, one of only two such courses in the UK. I had come to the sociology department to begin a PhD on the feminisation of clerical work, but inspired by the possibilities of gender history, by the end of 1985 my focus had shifted to the history of corporate masculinities in post-war Britain. The resulting PhD (awarded in 1989, the year that the journal *Gender & History* was launched) was a study of the 'organisation man', the practices that had sustained the male dominance of management in the mid-century, and the social and economic shifts in the 1980s that were destabilising this identity.

Family Fortunes (published in 1987) was in the final stages of preparation when I joined the seminar. We discussed draft chapters and met Cath Hall and other feminist historians. It was an exciting time but sometimes uncomfortable too. I was the only man in the group, and my presence sparked discussions about whether men should be admitted. Some felt that since women had initiated the field, often in the face of indifferent or hostile male colleagues, it would be a retrograde step to open the seminar to men. My presence was perceived as a form of entryism. Others saw the value in a man bringing a gender perspective to bear on a field like business history which, because it was ostensibly about the doings of men, had until then largely ignored women's and feminist history. These debates had wider echoes at the time, as feminists in the late 1980s pondered the tensions between women's history, feminist history, and gender history. There were concerns that while the study of gender might help to mainstream such approaches within the profession, it might also dilute the feminist emphasis on the oppression of women, and that a focus on the history of gender identities might blunt the structural analysis of patriarchy.[1]

I was unsure at the time if I counted myself, or wished to be counted, as a feminist. David Lockwood, the sociologist of class at Essex – Leonore's colleague, and her husband – tended to be critical of feminist sociology, describing it as a cause rather than a way of doing social science, too impassioned and lacking in rigour and distance. He once described me as a 'fellow traveller', and although he probably intended the comment as a put-down, in retrospect I am happy to embrace this description.

I have never been comfortable with the study of masculinity outside a relational framework – by 'relational', however, I don't just think of relations between men and women, but between different kinds of men and masculinities, between generations, across differences of ethnicity, class, and race, and across the life-course. This kind of approach, as Lucy suggests in the Conclusion, offered a way of doing historical work that is analogous to intersectional approaches today. Reading back over some of the debates in the late 1980s, there are certainly parallels. For me, gender has always been a relational concept, and I saw the discussions in the Men's History Group that met at John's home between 1988 and 1991 – and the volume that resulted from them – as the working through of a relatively new aspect of gender history. The project was well-supported by gender historians, and as I recall, Leonore Davidoff wrote a very positive report for Routledge on the manuscript of *Manful Assertions*.

Note

1 Judith M. Bennett, 'Feminism and History', *Gender & History*, 1:3 (1989), 251–272. For a commentary which seeks to integrate Bennett's emphasis on histories of women's oppression with the history of masculinity, see Karen Harvey, 'The History of Masculinity, circa 1650–1800', *Journal of British Studies*, 44 (2005), 296–311.

Part IV

Bodies

10

Dirty magazines, clean consciences: Men and pornography in the 1970s

Ben Mechen

On 22 September 1977, Mr James Birkett of South Kensington posted to the Home Office three closely written pages calling for reform of the country's strict obscenity laws. 'It must be admitted', he wrote, 'that illustrations of adult couples in the most intimate of loving situations are erotic, but can also be of great value.'[1] Far from dirty pictures, such images, like 'the ballet and other forms of dance', showed 'the full potential of human love and experience', and should therefore be subject to 'encouragement' rather than prohibition; made, as scholars of pornography would later frame this opposition, '*on*' rather than '*ob*'-scene.[2] To accept explicit, eroticised images of men and women in the nude or engaged in sexual activity as healthy, educational, sexy, even beautiful, would mark, Birkett argued, 'a positive advance of our standard of civilisation' and not, as others believed, a descent into debauchery or objectification.[3] Pornography, he claimed, could be good for you.

Mr Birkett was responding to an appeal – about an inch square – that he had read in *The Times* a few days before. It had been placed there (and in every other daily paper) by the Home Office's newly appointed Committee on Obscenity and Film Censorship, set up by the Labour Home Secretary Merlyn Rees and chaired by the Cambridge liberal philosopher Bernard Williams.[4] The committee sought expressions of public and expert opinion on the laws around 'obscenity, indecency and violence in publications, displays and entertainments in England and Wales'.[5] This was a broad remit. But the committee's energies, as documented by its final report published in 1979, came to focus on the trade in pornography, which the committee defined as books, poems, photographs, or films that combined an 'intention' to 'arouse [their] audience sexually' with 'explicit representations of sexual material', be they 'organs', 'postures', or 'activity'.[6]

The committee, many across the political spectrum felt, had good reason to exist. In 1959, the Obscene Publications Act had replaced old and unevenly applied common law proscriptions against obscenity by making it a clear criminal offence to publish materials that might 'tend to deprave and corrupt persons ... likely to ... read, see or hear' them. It had also provided a get-out clause for publishers of works serving a nebulously defined 'public good'.[7]

Since the successful use of this public good defence in the *Lady Chatterley* trial of 1960, however, eroticised representations of sex and nudity had become more and more widely available, and more and more widely consumed. Legal, cultural, and technological changes had together opened space for new entrepreneurs of sex and desire, as well as their customers. The difficulty of pinning down the 'depraving' or 'corrupting' tendencies of a given publication had confused the police and other authorities, who found other uses for their time.[8] And in court, juries and magistrates, as the *Chatterley* trial had shown, were increasingly reluctant to convict.

This gradual 'decensorship' of British literary and popular culture was one expression of a broader social and sexual liberalism from the 1950s to 1970s, carving out a limited zone of personal sexual privacy where it was 'not the law's business' to go – in the famous formulation of the 1957 'Wolfenden Report'.[9] Crucially, as Christopher Hilliard has recently argued by analysing a sample of letters to the Williams Committee, this new liberalism among lawmakers and intellectuals was supported by the 'neighbourly liberalism' of the public at large, who were becoming less interested in what others got up to behind closed doors.[10] In addition, important changes on the supply side were underway. As the trend for newspaper 'Sunday Supplements' was showing, colour print was becoming cheaper, and the mechanisms of production and distribution slicker. Across genres and audiences, including pornography, the 1970s were a very good time for magazines.

As a result, by the late 1970s, the porn business was flourishing at home and abroad. In the US, respectable men and women were queuing up to watch *Deep Throat* and respectable newspapers to review it: this was, as it became christened, the decade of 'porno chic'.[11] With British authorities continuing to hold the line against the free circulation of 'hard' depictions of sex, an aesthetic that mixed softcore 'sauciness' with the humour of old seaside postcards came to predominate. But the money rolled in – and the state-of-the-nation think-pieces of newspapers and political weeklies rolled out – just the same. Soho was the epicentre of the trade, home to 'porn barons' like Paul Raymond and David Sullivan, the Met's famous (and famously corrupt) Dirty Squad, the 'British Linda Lovelace', Mary Millington, and so-called private shops selling items catering to all known vices.

More significant in the committee's eyes, though, was the way figures like Raymond, Sullivan, and the American Bob Guccione had turned their magazines – *Penthouse*, *Men Only*, *Mayfair* – which usually combined strongly worded text with images of frontal nudity, and occasional suggestions of masturbation, into commodities available on newsagent top-shelves from Halifax to Harpenden. The committee discovered that magazines like *Penthouse*, launched in Britain in 1965, were shifting 250,000 copies per month by the late 1970s.[12] Add to this the illegal but apparently unstoppable traffic – mail-ordered, under-the-counter – in hardcore magazines and films from Europe, and especially Denmark, and it was clear that pornographic consumption was becoming a mainstream rather than fringe activity in Britain by the late 1970s.

The formation of the Williams Committee addressed itself to this shift; a need to work out the position of the law in a changing reality. In this sense, it was perhaps the last of the official – or, as often, unofficial – committees and commissions grappling with Britain's 'permissive' moment.[13] As Hilliard has demonstrated, the Williams Report's eventual call for a new statute that would focus on restricting the 'harmful' public display of 'offensive' material, rather than the consumer's ability to access this material by choice, fell victim to a change of government in 1979.[14] In its evidence-gathering stage, however, the committee had nonetheless been able to soak up a wide range of responses to pornography's growing availability, at a time when the claims to political relevance of 'ordinary' opinion remained high. As it was arguably as much the function of such bodies to prompt (and safely channel) debate on matters of controversy as it was to initiate reforms of public policy, the committee was therefore a success. Around 1,400 members of the public provided written evidence, along with around 150 interested organisations, from the Advertising Standards Agency and the Gay Christian Movement to the Royal College of Psychiatrists and the *Spare Rib* Collective.

Accordingly, the letters received by the Williams Committee are an invaluable source for the historian trying to understand what pornography meant to 'ordinary' people in post-war Britain. Aside from studies of a few well-known collectors, the history of pornography in Britain has to date mostly been a history of texts and their distribution and regulation rather than a history of pornographic consumption or consumers (or, importantly, of pornographic labour). The new interdisciplinary field of 'porn studies', though, has partly tried to find a route round seemingly intractable debates about the political and ethical status of pornography by refocusing attention on the complex set of relationships between pornography, agency, and subjectivity.[15]

As pornography has over time become increasingly a feature of popular culture, these relationships have arguably become tighter and more pluralised. Lisa Sigel and Jamie Stoops have shown Britain had a reasonably well-developed popular market in pictorial pornography by the Edwardian period at the latest.[16] By mid-century, this market had grown further, fuelled by texts that skirted the border between legitimate and illegitimate forms of sexual knowledge and representation, between legality and illegality.[17] But, as Marcus Collins has convincingly argued, the 1960s and 1970s were really the first decades of the age of *mass* pornographic reproduction and consumption in Britain.[18] As I have shown elsewhere, by the mid-1970s, with the rise of 'Readers' Wives' features, pornographic *participation* was being added to this mix too.[19] The Williams Committee letters therefore offer the historian insight into a moment when pornography was becoming a fact of life, a phenomenon of everyday experience, that everyone had to negotiate in their own way.[20] Letters like Birkett's, detailing his enjoyment of 'illustrations of adult couples in the most intimate of loving situations', emerge as important because they reveal to us something of how this transformation was lived, but also bought into and indeed pushed along not just by the 'porn barons' of tabloid lore but by hundreds of thousands of consumers and especially men. We can also begin to trace out the various gaps and connections between the masculinist (and frequently misogynist) gender and sexual politics of the top-shelf titles themselves – well documented by Collins – and what men made of these magazines as readers. We can begin to recover part of pornography's 'absent audience'.[21]

One real advantage of doing so is that we can move beyond simplistic assumptions about what pornography was, meant, or did, and that replay rather than document and contextualise the prevailing logics of the past. As mentioned earlier, at the heart of the 1959 Obscene Publications Act lay the causal notion that what made something potentially 'obscene' was its potential *effects*, its tendency to 'deprave and corrupt'. Countering this image of the depraved male reader, during the boom of the 1960s and 1970s, pornographic publishers instead constructed their audiences as sophisticated, affluent, and streetwise.[22]

By the time the Williams Committee began its work, however, a significant number of commentators and activist organisations, including some providing evidence, were renewing ideas of pornography as a threat to personal and social well-being by framing popular consumption as a crisis of masculinity. For socially conservative figures like Lord Longford and Mary Whitehouse – who had been goaded by the pornographer David Sullivan when he named a new top-shelf title, *Whitehouse*, after her – pornography's popularity indicated an unwelcome departure from the moral uprightness, and sturdy religiosity, of pre-permissive masculinities. It signalled a move towards a new world of sexual licence and corruptibility: a masculinity *in* crisis. For some feminists, meanwhile, particularly after the emergence of radical feminism from the later 1970s, pornography was argued as both violent and productive of violence against women. In a formulation implicit

Dirty magazines, clean consciences 257

in the naming of the 'Rape Crisis' movement and Robin Morgan's famous dictum that 'pornography is the theory, rape is the practice', this instead was masculinity *as* crisis. Porn encouraged men, as a leaflet circulated by the Leeds Revolutionary Feminists put it, 'to see women as bodies which exist solely for their pleasure ... to be leered at, groped, assaulted and raped – used and thrown away'.[23]

In each of these examples, from the 1959 Act to revolutionary feminism, a straight line was drawn between the act of reading or looking at pornography and a singular 'effect'; indeed, the media studies scholar Brian McNair has called this the 'effects paradigm' shaping most debate on pornography in contemporary society.[24] But using the contemporaneous letters of the Williams Committee to take broader stock of how consumers encountered these texts allows us, as historians of men and masculinity, to ask instead: how have pornographic representations of sex been placed alongside (or against) men's real-life sexual experiences and expectations? How has pornography actually been felt by men as a site of sexual and gender conformity and norm-setting, of bodily violence and moral decay, or else of transgression, self-realisation, and liberation – or of something else besides? How has pornography shaped men's attitudes towards women and other men? And what positions, drawing these questions together, has explicit sexual imagery occupied within men's overall organisation and experience of the sexual?

This chapter draws upon some of the 1,400 letters of the Williams Committee received in 1977 and 1978 to understand a particular set of these traversals and negotiations of the new pornographic landscape: those made and articulated by male consumers, pornography's core but (as the letters also reveal) not exclusive market at this time, about their generally positive relationship to what they were buying and seeing. (Another way of writing this chapter would have been to instead trace the paper trail of refusal, critique, and even disgust.) The men whose responses I analyse here wrote to the committee after seeing calls for evidence in the large circulation tabloid newspapers the *Daily Mirror* and the *Sun*, the mainstream broadsheet newspapers *The Times* and the *Guardian*, and the small circulation communist newspaper the *Morning Star*. We can surmise that the social and political locations of these respondents varied accordingly, and that the letters discussed in this chapter are therefore reasonably representative of 'ordinary' – if motivated – opinion. Letter-writers were of mixed sex and sexual orientation or identity (in so far as these are implied), and from across the UK and Northern Ireland. However, to avoid replicating the excellent study by Paul Deslandes of gay respondents to the committee, I have in this chapter focused on male respondents who framed themselves as basically straight or heterosexual.[25]

These letters, by moving us on from the sphere of expertise and cultural commentary about changing sexual mores towards what the committee termed 'ordinary people's views', or at least the views of some ordinary people, provide one way into gauging the relationship between pornographic discourse and gendered and sexual subjectivity in late twentieth-century Britain. In analysing them, this chapter joins a raft of recent work considering the 'Sexual Revolution' and 'permissiveness' as socially made and experienced.[26]

The letters of the Williams Committee show that, while men like James Birkett actually agreed with the Obscene Publications Act, social conservatives, and feminists that pornography had effects, they rejected the notion that these effects were, or at least were always, bad. Instead, they made the case for a more positive relationship between sexual explicitness and well-being, and particularly their own well-being as male sexual subjects, seeking, often from the grounds of experience, to turn the arguments of their opponents on their head. I now want to explore three of these formulations in turn, and in the process think about the ways they help us trace the growing importance in late twentieth-century Britain of a model, and a way, of expressing and inhabiting sexuality, which we can term that of the liberal sexual subject, as well as the building up of a new idea of normative masculinity around this: a masculine sexual subject that coded 'healthy' sexuality as embodying a particular conception of the sexual self (individualist, free of so-called hang-ups, and something to be grown into or realised as part of a 'sex life' and a 'sexual career', especially through processes of learning and experience); a particular embrace of sexual pleasure, to which the pornographic image, and more broadly practices of sexual looking, were central; and a particular relationship to the market (that is, one of sexualised consumption, including of pornography).

A number of male writers argued that pornography was a useful source of sexual knowledge, able to turn darkness into light. In their clarity of expression, such correspondents argued – in the very explicitness of their words and pictures – top-shelf magazines taught readers about sex and the sexual body with a precision that other potential sources of sexual knowledge refused. Such observations ask us to recognise that for some consumers of pornography – which usually combined nude or hardcore images with written accounts of sexual experience and instruction – explicit representations of sex existed on a continuum with the kinds of liberal, frank sex advice, highly popular in Britain in the 1970s, found in popular magazines like *Cosmopolitan* and manuals like Alex Comfort's million-selling *The Joy of Sex* and which counselled readers in the importance of thinking about sex not merely as something you did but as something you learnt about, worked at, and improved.[27] This could be started young.

In the words of Peter Gardner of Liverpool, pornography was thus 'a form of sex education', one cherished not only by himself but his teenage 'sons',[28] while for Richard Kirk Brown of Rochdale, another father, it was 'the most important source of information' available to young people otherwise kept in ignorance thanks to 'the timidity of parents' and 'the educational system', as confirmed a few years earlier by the infamous banning of Martin Cole's candid sex-education film, *Growing Up*.[29]

Pornography, in the views of men like Gardner and Brown, thus did not corrupt the young by tearing them out of a putative sexual innocence, as more conservative letter-writers frequently argued. It was not a 'bad' or 'faulty' form of sexual knowledge. Instead it instructed readers in the beauty of the body and the delights of sexual exploration, often for the first time, helping them develop an open approach to sexuality that would find its ultimate ends in the movement from solitary pleasures to meaningful connections or, in the words of Mr Knight of Derby, the formation of 'normal sexual relationships'.[30] It could also help more mature readers when these relationships foundered, reawakening desire, or providing the kinds of new sexual ideas that kept older couples in each other's thrall. Robert Hollings of Bristol, for example, explained to the committee that magazines like *Playbirds* and *Men Only*, his favourites, did not cleave couples apart, as some argued, but rather helped them 'increase their satisfaction', ensuring that their relationships did not 'deteriorate into routine or non-existent lovemaking'.[31] Peter Gardner of Liverpool, meanwhile – middle-aged and sharing a 'wonderful sex life' with his wife – praised pornography for keeping his and their desires fresh.[32] For these correspondents of the Williams Committee, pornography, contrary to what many of its critics believed, did not provide an unhealthy substitute for 'real', 'loving' sex, but rather complemented and encouraged it as a space of sexual learning and inspiration. Pornography, positioned in these men's letters as a technology of healthy sexual formation and ongoing sexual well-being – in the face of new critiques, in both popular women's magazines and feminist pamphlets, of men's ability to satisfy women's desires – helped relationships live and grow.[33]

A much larger proportion of the committee's male correspondents, though, were keen to draw a more direct connection between the consumption of pornography and the pursuit of sexual pleasure. In this formulation, sexually explicit material was framed not as an instrument of sexual learning, inspiration, and improvement but as an instrument for men's *individual* sexual arousal, even as direct references to masturbation remained uncommon. This formulation is, of course, unsurprising – it constitutes, and constituted then, the common-sense understanding of what pornography is and was for. What this large cache of letters can show us is the historically situated language in which the connection between pornography and individual pleasure-seeking was cast and the claims for its validity male consumers put forward. Many writers were firm in the belief that sexual pleasure, however arrived at, and the sexual body subjected to the male gaze, were worthy of celebration rather than censure whether viewed in person or in print: if the sexual liberalism of pornography had for the previous group of letter-writers turned on its possibilities for projects of self-improvement and self-realisation, this group was invested in pornography and the sexual liberalism it espied as a visual regime that normalised a presumptively male pornographic gaze – a pleasure-driven erotics of 'looking' – fixed most often upon the bodies of women. Mr Turnpenney of Pudsey, thirty-six years old and married with three children, told the committee that he found 'considerable enjoyment' in both softcore British magazines like *Whitehouse* and harder European titles like *Colour Climax*, as, he claimed, did his wife, and wanted to see an end to any censorship of 'sex between male and female, or two females'.[34] Richard Kirk Brown was more philosophical in his arguments, arguing that 'material of an intensely erotic nature can only do good by generating pleasure and satisfaction', demonstrating to viewers that 'erotic bonding ... generates the deepest happiness that we can know', a sentiment echoed by a Mr Eyre of Cowplain in Hampshire, who wrote simply that 'sex is bueatifull [sic], and apart from indulging in [it], we should be able to see it if we wish'.[35]

At the same time, correspondents like Brown and Eyre, again in a manner that accorded with the advice of contemporary 'sexperts' like Comfort, moved beyond a merely hedonistic evaluation of pornography. They drew a more encompassing and meaningful connection between sexual pleasure, whether masturbatory or mutual, and self-realisation, or the unashamed acceptance of oneself as a sexual, desiring being, or as Brown put it, echoing the best-selling claims of the pop zoologist Desmond Morris, a 'sexual animal'.[36] In a similar fashion, Mr and Mrs Whiting of Doncaster co-signed a letter in which they 'readily admit[ted] to reading "sexy" or "pornographic" magazines' for amusement and titillation, but firmly rejected the notion that such magazines could be deemed obscene, for 'what could be less obscene than the human body or natural (what is unnatural?) lovemaking between adults?'[37]

This idea that pornography could help consumers come to terms with and indeed *inhabit* their sexualities was put most radically, in the context of its time, by a number of male writers who identified themselves as homosexual, as Paul Deslandes has shown.[38] A Mr Colgate of Slough, for example, who described himself as a regular buyer of both 'soft' and 'hard' gay pornography, defended his right to 'enjoy' such material without feeling 'a menace to the public', a label to which he remained – as both gay and a porn consumer – doubly exposed.³⁹ Julian Carter of Wimborne, meanwhile, a reader of *Mister International* as well as non-pornographic magazines like *Gay News*, argued that the former as much as the latter had 'done a great deal towards breaking down the strong sense of isolation' he knew as a young man, and which 'no person should have to feel today'.⁴⁰ Contemporaneously with an emergent public politics of gay liberation, letters like these implored the committee to recognise the private use of pornography as a similarly important – and a similarly political – outlet for sexual pleasure, expression, and self-recognition. Furthermore, in following the echoes between responses traced in this and the previous grouping of respondents, we can see how pornographic consumption by the 1970s (and perhaps more broadly the idea of masculinity as a foregrounding at all costs of satisfying sexual desire) was cutting across otherwise still powerful divides between 'gay' and 'straight' masculinities.

A third and final group of male letter-writers put this connection between pornography and politics at the centre of their critiques of the legal status quo. For them, the availability of pornography to adults was a masculinised demonstration of freedom in action, the implications of which reached far more widely than sex. Commonly railing against Mary Whitehouse and other 'self-appointed do-gooders' (A. B. Warburton, Tranmere), dozens of male correspondents stressed their anger at the presumption of those who would tell them what they could or could not read or see, especially, as Mr P. Murlon of Grantham railed, 'in my own home'.⁴¹ These claims were usually supported by reference to either a putative tradition of English 'liberty' – 'the democratic freedom of choice that has up till now been part of the British way of life', as Mr Patterson of Berwick-upon-Tweed put it – or the censorship regimes of Cold War enemies. Celebrating the wholesale legalisation of pornography in Denmark (1969), a country that for a number of writers symbolised a beacon of reason and sanity, male letter-writers asserted their right to spend their money how they wished. In these responses, the dual pursuit of sexual pleasure and realisation was connoted as one that took place in and through the market – a market that any free and liberal society must make more open – by individual men in their capacity as individual consumers.⁴² As Mr Edwards of Crosby noted, 'the only reason for the massive output of pornography in this country is because there is a market for it', for him reason enough to leave it alone.⁴³

For readers like Peter Gardner, meanwhile, such popularity, which stretched across all social classes, was an indication that pornography had in fact become respectable, rendering 'the dirty old man', a recognised archetype of failed masculinity marked by both his age and his perversity, 'a thing of the past'. Pornography, as he argued, was now bought by 'people in every walk of life', not least professionals like himself. The aspirational lifestyle celebrated in the adverts for cars, cigarettes, and alcohol populating most top-shelf magazines was designed to appeal to just such a reader as this: what the Williams letters show is the re-inscription in the 1970s of pornography as a commodity much like any other, and the male pornographic consumer not only as a legible figure but a desirable one.[44] In such sentiments, writers like Gardner positioned pornography as ripe for inclusion in a sexual consumerism more widely in evidence from the 1970s – the masculine subject of sexual liberalism here re-emerging as the prime mover in a growing market for 'the things of sex'. These encompassed everything from the eroticisation of advertising to, in the growth of brands like Durex, the commodification of condoms.[45] In a country that usually put great store in the free market, Gardner and other correspondents suggested, people were already voting for pornography with their wallets. The law just needed to catch up.

In their rethinking and reframing of pornography's effects, the male consumers who wrote to the Williams Committee took part in the consolidation of an idea of sexual freedom that moved beyond the Wolfenden period's negative logic of the (male) citizen's basic right to privacy, towards the positive and public definition of new sexual norms, pleasures, rights, and responsibilities. As I argue elsewhere, between the late 1960s and mid-1980s this new sexual liberalism, which never dislodged the idea that the 'free' sexual subject was putatively straight and male, became the organising ideology of British sexual culture and one of the most lasting legacies of the Sexual Revolution, driven along by an assortment of politicians and other state actors, experts, and publics, non-governmental organisations, and commercial interests, operating in a kind of unintended coordination. This new sexual liberalism, moreover, was an important rampart in the reconsolidation of men and masculinity's dominant positions within the gender order, even at a moment of profound challenge from the combined forces of feminism, the LGBT liberation movements, and a renewed conservative moralism. This was the case even as the champions of sexual liberalism stressed the importance of sexual freedom and autonomy for all, including women, whose hitherto sexually subordinate position was recognised and bewailed, even as they generally counselled the need for women to 'lean in' to equality, for example by becoming more sexually demanding or assertive, rather than for men to 'lean out'.

More than a pure vision of sexual freedom, 1970s sexual liberalism was a gendered and heteronormative regime of learning, looking, showing, buying, and planning that quickly became the 'new normal' and kept radical alternatives in the margins. This new normal did not find its expression in those totemic acts of sexual 'freedom' commonly associated with the revolution – orgies of free love, performances of radical drag.

Instead, the liberal sexual subject learnt techniques of self-improvement and self-realisation from the frank and fun loving advice of popular 'sexperts', looked at sexual images between the covers of new mass circulation top-shelf magazines, showed off their bodies to distant strangers, bought themselves sexual commodities, from branded condoms to sex aids, and rationally planned their free sexual and reproductive lives with the assistance of new state family planning services.[46] To learn, to look, to show, to buy, to plan: to adapt Patrick Joyce's terminology, these were, and arguably remain, the new 'rules of sexual freedom'.[47]

In the letters of the Williams Committee, some of these dimensions of sexual liberalism were made intensely visible, as were the ways in which sexual liberalism failed to dismantle, and indeed helped to secure, patriarchal thinking in British sexual culture. The men who wrote to the Williams Committee positioned themselves to defend a new mass market in pornography that had emerged in the mid-1960s; a market in which most of them were consumers, firming up sexual liberalism as in part a philosophy of buying and looking, at least for men. And in just the same moment that men were being encouraged to rove and spend in a newly sexualised open market, women were instead being guided, as the more responsible 'planners' of sexual liberalism but also (by perception) the less autonomous and assertive, to the more cloistered and directed spaces of the family planning clinic. This national expansion of the 'skin trade', as top-shelf titles like *Penthouse* and *Mayfair* came to be rivalled only by women's weeklies and hobbyist monthlies in popularity, normalised a presumptively male, heteronormative, and 'softcore' pornographic gaze, even as 'harder' or 'perverse' images, including of the bodies of other men, were frequently still deemed by the police and courts as beyond the pale. Yet beyond taking a straightforward pleasure in the kinds of looking enabled by pornography, the committee's letters show that some men went further in claiming pornography's importance in their own development or realisation as happy, healthy, functional, high-performing, or fully realised sexual selves. Like Alex Comfort's manual *The Joy of Sex*, pornography taught gendered lessons in pleasure and performance. The men of the Williams Committee happily learnt them.

At the same time, we must remember that, despite this coalescence in the 1970s of a new male sexual subject, this was a complex historical conjuncture, composed of various possibilities for a different sexual future. In the same moment, as John Tosh and Lucy Delap show in the Conclusion, feminists, and men in the anti-sexist men's movement, were articulating an alternative to this regime of sexual liberalism: from buying commodities to socialist articulations of sharing and making, from learning from sexual experts to practices of group discussion and consciousness-raising, from looking at women as sexual objects to thinking of them as sexual subjects.

In the years around the committee's formation, the feminist film scholar Laura Mulvey and the Marxist art critic John Berger both formalised their ideas of the 'male gaze' and the possibilities of a counter-cinema and a radical visuality; Angela Carter fantasised about a pornography 'in the service of women'; and pro-feminist men's groups expressed the need to evacuate the sexist 'shit and rubbish that clogs our heads'.[48]

So how then can we explain the resilience into the present of this masculinist sexual liberalism of the Williams Committee's male respondents, as well as the longer tradition of patriarchal dominance, in the face of such feminist futures? One thing I would like to return to here is the work of 'crisis' in this story. As I have argued, in the 1970s male consumers of pornography were assailed by two narratives of crisis, gestured towards in different contexts in Colin Hay's research on an adjacent narrativisation of crisis in the Winter of Discontent of 1978–1979, more or less contemporaneous with the committee's work.[49] First, a grassroots conservative narrative of pornography as representing a crisis *of* masculinity. Pornography here was breaking down masculine codes of sexual respectability and mastery in favour of sexual licence. Secondly, a feminist narrative of masculinity *as* crisis. Pornography here, by enacting but also representing violence against women and the objectification of women, was defined as symbolising a masculinity that was destructive of women and their bodies.

These dual crises of masculinity, as I think we begin to see in the letters, were refuted and mocked by many letter-writers in favour of another crisis, at least implicitly, even an urgent politics of backlash: for these correspondents of the committee, the *real* crisis of masculinity was the threat posed to manly independence, and manly sexual well-being, by either neo-Victorian moralism or feminist over-reach. The work of this framing instead was thus to meet criticisms of patriarchy and the masculinity of sexual liberalism with a counter-narrative of male victimhood and the need to shore up men's power. As we in our own historical moment will recognise, such claims now inform the twisted, ironic vocabulary of men's rights activism, with it's talk of men's equality, men's rights, meninism, and men's lives matter. To continue to unravel the origins or the genealogies of this contemporary discourse of masculinity seems necessary.

The articulations of pornography's virtues – the ways dirty magazines did not tarnish, perhaps even encouraged, a clean conscience – as captured in the letters received from men by the Williams Committee of the late 1970s, ventured more widely than I have been able to explain here. Yet they have striking utility for thinking through gender and sexual subjectivities in the era of mass pornographic production and consumption and, more broadly, the era of sexual liberalism. Indeed, by using sources like this, in which mostly male consumers – a group, like the mostly female models they gazed upon, seriously under-analysed in existing research on pornography's past and present – gave voice to the meanings and functions such material held for them, we can better understand how the cultural saturation of pornography in the post-war period was lived and understood. By doing so, I argue, we can gain a better hold on the entangled histories of sexuality and masculinity, discourse and subjectivity, and looking and feeling, in twentieth-century Britain.

Notes

1 National Archives (hereafter TNA), HO 265/77/27, James E. Birkett to the Committee on Obscenity and Film Censorship [Williams Committee] (hereafter COFC), 22 September 1977.
2 *Ibid*. On the ob/onscenity distinction, see Linda Williams, 'Porn Studies: Proliferating Pornographies On/scene: An Introduction', in Linda Williams (ed.), *Porn Studies* (Durham, NC: Duke University Press, 2004), 3.
3 TNA, HO 265/77/27, Birkett to COFC.
4 Home Office, *Report of the Committee on Obscenity and Film Censorship* [Williams Report], Cmnd 7772 (London: HMSO, 1979), 1.
5 *Ibid.*, iv.
6 Home Office, *Report*, 103.
7 For an overview of the Act, see *ibid.*, 9–12.
8 An exception was sometimes made for gay (or gay-friendly) publications. See Harry Cocks, 'Conspiracy to Corrupt Public Morals and the "Unlawful" Status of Homosexuality in Britain after 1967', *Social History*, 41:3 (2016), 267–284.
9 John Sutherland, *Offensive Literature: Decensorship in Britain, 1960–1982* (London: Junction Books, 1982); Home Office and Scottish Home Department, *Report of the Committee on Homosexual Offences and Prostitution*, Cmnd 247 (London: HMSO, 1957), conclusion.
10 Christopher Hilliard, *A Matter of Obscenity: The Politics of Censorship in Modern England* (Princeton: Princeton University Press, 2021), 206–207.
11 Carolyn Bronstein and Whitney Strub (eds), *Porno Chic and the Sex Wars: American Sexual Representation in the 1970s* (Amherst: University of Massachusetts Press, 2016).
12 Home Office, *Report*, 251, drawing upon Audit Bureau of Circulation figures for January–June 1977.
13 Among others, notable here are the Royal Commission on Marriage and Divorce, 1951–1956; the Home Office and Scottish Home Department's Committee on Homosexual Offences and Prostitution, 1954–1957 (leading to the 'Wolfenden Report'); and the Longford Committee Investigating Pornography, 1971–1972.
14 Hilliard, *A Matter of Obscenity*, 212–213.
15 Williams (ed.), *Porn Studies*; Feona Attwood and Clarissa Smith, 'Porn Studies: An Introduction', *Porn Studies*, 1:1–2 (2014), 1–6; Tim Dean, Steven Ruszczycky,

and David Squires (eds), *Porn Archives* (Durham, NC: Duke University Press, 2014); Rachael Liberman, '"It's a Really Great Tool": Feminist Pornography and the Promotion of Sexual Subjectivity', *Porn Studies*, 2:2–3 (2015), 174–191; Jiz Lee and Rebecca Sullivan, 'Porn and Labour: The Labour of Porn Studies', *Porn Studies*, 3:2 (2016), 104–106.

16 Lisa Z. Sigel, *Governing Pleasures: Pornography and Social Change in England, 1815–1914* (New Brunswick: Rutgers University Press, 2002); Jamie Stoops, 'Class and Gender Dynamics of the Pornography Trade in Late Nineteenth-Century Britain', *Historical Journal*, 58:1 (2015), 137–156.

17 H. G. Cocks, 'Saucy Stories: Pornography, Sexology and the Marketing of Sexual Knowledge in Britain, c. 1918–70', *Social History*, 29:4 (2004), 465–484; Sarah Bull, 'More than a Case of Mistaken Identity: Adult Entertainment and the Making of Early Sexology', *History of the Human Sciences*, 34:1 (2021), 10–39.

18 Marcus Collins, 'The Pornography of Permissiveness: Men's Sexuality and Women's Emancipation in Mid-20th-Century Britain', *History Workshop Journal*, 47 (1999), 99–120. See also Laura Cofield, Ben Mechen, and Matthew Worley, 'History from the Top Shelf: The Cultural Politics of Sex in Post-war Britain', *Contemporary British History*, 36:2 (2022), 165–173; and Laura Cofield, '"The Way We Were Razed": Pubic Hair and Permissiveness in 1970s Britain', *Contemporary British History*, 36:2 (2022), 207–226.

19 Ben Mechen, '"Instamatic Living Rooms of Sin": Pornography, Participation and the Erotics of Ordinariness in 1970s Britain', *Contemporary British History*, 36:2 (2022), 174–206.

20 Harry Cocks, '"The Social Picture of Our Own Times": Reading Obscene Magazines in Mid-Twentieth-Century Britain', *Twentieth Century British History*, 27:2 (2016), 171–194; Lucy Delap, 'Rethinking Rapes: Men's Sex Lives and Feminist Critiques', *Contemporary British History*, 36:2 (2022), 253–276.

21 Christine Grandy, 'Cultural History's Absent Audience', *Cultural & Social History*, 16:5 (2019), 1–21.

22 Collins, 'The Pornography of Permissiveness', 105–106.

23 Robin Morgan, 'Check It Out: Porn, No. But Free Speech, Yes', *New York Times*, 24 March 1978, 27; Leeds Revolutionary Feminist Group, 'How Do Men See You?', leaflet, September 1978, collected in Dusty Rhodes and Sandra McNeill (eds), *Women against Violence against Women* (London: Onlywomen Press, 1985), 19.

24 Brian McNair, 'Rethinking the Effects Paradigm in Porn Studies', *Porn Studies*, 1:1–2 (2014), 161–171.

25 Paul Deslandes, 'The Cultural Politics of Gay Pornography in 1970s Britain', in Brian Lewis (ed.), *British Queer History: New Approaches and Perspectives* (Manchester: Manchester University Press, 2013), 267–296.

26 Hannah Charnock, 'Teenage Girls, Female Friendship and the Making of the Sexual Revolution in England, 1950–1980', *Historical Journal*, 63:4 (2020), 1032–1053; Ruby Ray Daily, '"Dear Mr K": Mobility, Sex, and Selfhood in Alfred Kinsey's British World Correspondence, 1948–58', *Twentieth Century*

British History, 32:1 (2021), 24–45; Daisy Payling and Tracey Loughran, '"Nude Bodies in British Women's Magazines at the Turn of the 1970s: Agency, Spectatorship, and the Sexual Revolution', *Social History of Medicine*, 35:4 (2022), 1356–1385; Caroline Rusterholz, 'Teenagers, Sex and the Brook Advisory Centres, 1964–85', in Siân Pooley and Jonathan Taylor (eds), *Children's Experiences of Welfare in Modern Britain* (London: University of London Press, 2021), 247–271.

27 For these, see Ben Mechen, 'Everyday Sex in 1970s Britain' (PhD diss., University College London, 2016); and Ben Mechen, *Responsible Pleasures: Liberalism and the Sexual Revolution, 1967–85* (Berkeley: University of California Press, forthcoming).
28 TNA, HO 265/78/50, Peter Gardner to COFC, 24 September 1977.
29 TNA, HO 265/78/83, Richard Kirk Brown to COFC, 6 October 1977. For *Growing Up*, see David Limond, '"I Never Imagined That the Time Would Come": Martin Cole, the *Growing Up* Controversy and the Limits of School Sex Education in 1970s England', *History of Education*, 37:3 (2008), 409–429.
30 TNA, HO 265/78/54, R. E. Knight to COFC, 24 September 1977. Thomas W. Laqueur, *Solitary Sex: A Cultural History of Masturbation* (New York: Zone Books, 2003).
31 TNA, HO 265/77/32, Robert Hollings to COFC, 23 September 1977.
32 TNA, HO 265/78/50, Peter Gardner to COFC, 24 September 1977.
33 This was both a mainstay of sexual commentary in new mainstream publications like *Cosmopolitan* magazine (1972–), and widely circulated feminist tracts like Anna Koedt's 'The Myth of the Vaginal Orgasm' (1970).
34 TNA, HO 265/75/28, B. Turnpenny to COFC, n.d.; HO 265/75/56, M. Herron to COFC, 27 September 1977.
35 TNA, HO/265/78/83, Brown to COFC; HO 265/78/8, S. Eyre to COFC, n.d.
36 TNA, HO 265/78/83, Brown to COFC. Desmond Morris, *The Naked Ape* (London: J. Cape, 1967).
37 TNA, HO 265/78/37, S. and P. Whiting to COFC, 23 September 1977.
38 Deslandes, 'Cultural Politics'.
39 TNA, HO 265/77/41, M.G. Colgate to COFC, 25 September 1977.
40 TNA, HO 265/77/62, Julian Carter to COFC, 15 October 1977.
41 TNA, HO 265/78/90, A. B Warburton to COFC, 8 May 1978; HO 265/75/9, P. Murlon to COFC, n.d.
42 TNA, HO 265/75/55, R. Patterson to COFC, 27 September 1977; HO 265/75/67, I. C. Hamilton to COFC, 29 September 1977; HO 265/75/35, B. Caine [?] to COFC, 26 September 1977; HO 265/75/9, P. Murlon [?] to COFC, n.d.
43 TNA, HO 265/77/36, H. Edwards to COFC, 24 September 1977.
44 TNA, HO 265/78/50, Peter Gardner to COFC, 24 September 1977.
45 Ben Mechen, '"Closer Together": Durex Condoms and Contraceptive Consumerism in 1970s Britain', in Jennifer Evans and Ciara Meehan (eds), *Perceptions of Pregnancy from the Seventeenth to the Twentieth Century* (Basingstoke: Palgrave Macmillan, 2017), 213–236.
46 Mechen, '"Instamatic Living Rooms of Sin"'.

47 Patrick Joyce, *The Rule of Freedom: Liberalism and the Modern City* (London: Verso, 2003).
48 Laura Mulvey, 'Visual Pleasure and Narrative Cinema', *Screen*, 16:3 (1975), 6–18; John Berger, *Ways of Seeing* (1972); Angela Carter, *The Sadeian Woman: An Exercise in Cultural History* (London: Virago, 1979); Dan Muir, 'Looking at Women', *Men Against Sexism* (October 1973), 8.
49 Colin Hay, 'Narrating Crisis: The Discursive Construction of the "Winter of Discontent"', *Sociology*, 30:2 (1996), 253–277.

11

'It's more what me and my partner feel comfortable with': Gay masculinities, safer sex, and Project SIGMA, 1987–1996

Katie Jones

> What I have presented is the mere 'mechanics' of the sexual activities ... My reservation is that my Diary *appears* to represent a 'Bang wham I've had a man' ... What the mode of recording does NOT allow to show is that there *was* great human warmth (not just a physical-physiological need/pressure) ... What I do and let be done to me is governed/motivated by my very personal needs to give and to receive a human/emotional interaction [sic].[1]

Written on the back of a sexual diary form completed for the social survey Project SIGMA (Socio-sexual Investigations of Gay Men and AIDS), these personal reflections revealed the power of emotion in 'governing' men's sexual decision-making.[2] While the sexual diary was designed as a quantitative rather than reflective exercise, this respondent challenged the brief through his worries 'about the "non-quantifiability" of what to me is the dynamics of my personal sex-life [sic]'.[3] From this perspective, the diary format disallowed the recording of 'human warmth' and bodily affection. In volunteering to be interviewed, the respondent now asked to speak openly about the *emotional* content of his sexual experiences.[4] Denied space to talk about emotion, love, and intimacy by Project SIGMA researchers, at least one man criticised the methods of the survey itself.

This emphasis on the importance of emotion in gay men's sexual decision-making, I argue, reflects a wider transformation in the lives of 'ordinary' men in the 1980s and 1990s. Focusing on the voices of individual men, this chapter explores the relationship between sex, emotions, and social surveys. In speaking back to Project SIGMA men resisted the dehumanising agenda of epidemiological research, its underlying homophobic assumptions, and pejorative notions of gay masculinities. While explicit critiques of the sexual diary method were rare, they nonetheless revealed how the survey (and its implications for public health education during HIV/AIDS) upheld myths that the Project SIGMA team wanted to challenge. Within the gay community, HIV education often focused on 'eroticising' the condom, framing it as a sex aid as well as a prophylactic through adverts featuring men wearing condoms in erotic poses. While these campaigns were successful, they upheld stereotypes of a hypersexual gay community and effaced the association between condomless sex and emotional intimacy.[5]

Although the SIGMA team promised to challenge the assumptions about gay men and to treat respondents as experts in their own lives, their research methodology inadvertently upheld these assumptions. This did not go unnoticed by respondents, who resisted the perceptions embedded both in the interview questionnaires and the sexual diary form by emphasising the importance of emotion in their sexual lives. Respondents, then, were integral to creating knowledge of sexual cultures and subjectivities through their cooperation with and resistance to the survey in which they participated.[6]

The Project SIGMA archive also allows us to explore how gay men negotiated the path towards safer sex between 1986 and 1997. Focusing on the rich qualitative data SIGMA obtained from its respondents rather than the quantitative data, I use the survey responses to explore the role of emotions in decision-making around safer sex among a cohort that overrepresented the urban, middle-class, white gay man.[7] Drawing on this material, I demonstrate the centrality of emotion in gay men's sexual lives and decision-making, especially in the context of a regular relationship where unprotected anal sex carried specific emotional expressions. HIV *was* a significant factor in men's decisions about safety, but that process was predicated on the emotive meanings invested in unprotected anal sex with a romantic partner. By the time SIGMA began in 1986, community mobilisation and behavioural change had made condom use 'the first line of defence against HIV infection'.[8] In the next stage of the epidemic, safer sex was both more 'strategic' and more closely attuned to an individual's relationship status and needs. By the 1990s, established couples had developed conscious risk-minimisation strategies whereby condoms were used primarily *only* with casual partners. This response to HIV occurred in the absence of government campaigns that acknowledged the emotional meanings of gay sex or even a clear understanding of how emotions shaped men's decision-making amongst researchers within the gay community.

If this argument breaks new ground in queer and emotional histories, it also contributes to a burgeoning literature on the production of social scientific knowledge and the relationship between researchers and their subjects.[9] This chapter foregrounds the importance of interpersonal dynamics, and feelings of trust, intimacy, and love in shaping men's decisions about safer sex during the HIV/AIDS epidemic. Foregrounding emotions enriches our understanding of LGBTQ lives in the past, without desexualising these histories and drawing attention away from the importance of sex within gay communities.[10] In this sense, the chapter follows those historians who have begun to focus on love and non-straight relationships.[11] With some notable exceptions, historians of romantic love concern themselves primarily with heterosexuality, so that gay men and women have been marginalised in histories of affective life.[12] Centring emotion in gay men's sexual lives thus uncouples love from heterosexuality, revealing the rich emotional texture of queer lives often overshadowed by stereotypes of the sexually promiscuity gay man. That emotional attachment was central to men's decision-making challenges both our assumptions about sexuality and masculinity and that dominant strand within histories of contraception that emphasises the rise of 'rational' contraceptive use through 'modern' contraceptive technologies like the pill. Taking seriously the non-use of prophylactics complicates the idea that 'rational' contraception became the norm in contemporary Britain.[13] As Tony Coxon, the project's principal investigator, argued, sociologists and public health officials had to face the 'embarrassing truth' of gay men's practice.[14] 'Unsafe' sex, Coxon concluded, did not necessarily indicate irrationality.[15] Instead SIGMA presented unsafe sex as 'a different sort of rationality', in which the logic of 'sexual conversation' outweighed the 'logic of safety'.[16] This 'conversation' – the 'negotiation of meaning between two or more individuals' – allows us to understand the emotional *meanings* associated with sexual acts and the relationship between safe sex and those *feelings* individuals sought to express.[17]

Alongside the qualitative survey data, what follows also uses published and unpublished documents written by Project SIGMA researchers to reflect critically on the politics and practice of their survey methods. This data is compared with findings from other contemporary studies, including the large cohort study from St Mary's Hospital medical school and smaller cohort studies, *A Survey of Gay Men's Sexual Behaviour in Glasgow*, on working-class gay men in a small South Yorkshire town, and a needs assessment of gay and bisexual men conducted by South Essex Health in 1994.[18] The chapter also draws on oral testimony from men who were interviewed for the HIV/AIDS Testimonies Project and my own interview with Frank, who joined Project SIGMA as a researcher after the third wave of interviews.

The first section situates Project SIGMA in its historical and political context to explore the assumptions underlying its methods and questionnaire. The second explores how gay and bisexual men negotiated safer sex by examining responses to those questions. Focusing on men in open relationships and the increasingly common strategy where condoms were used with casual rather than regular partners, the chapter shows how emphasising the emotional dimensions of sex could be a form of resistance to assumptions about gay men's sexuality and masculinity. Despite SIGMA's efforts to treat men as the experts on their own lives, the assumptions shaping the organisation of research limited the project's ability to achieve this. Overlooked or marginalised in the project, emotional and relational dynamics remained hugely important in gay and bisexual men's decision-making around safer sex in the 1980s and 1990s. Understanding this can enrich histories of masculinity, LGBTQ life, and sexual health and decision-making.

Researching safer sex

Project SIGMA was shaped by a deep understanding of its work's place within wider histories of homosexuality and communities. It was, they argued, 'important to situate the responses of gay and bisexual men to AIDS in the 1980s in a very specific historical moment'.[19] SIGMA's genealogy reflected the prehistory of men's sexual behaviour and its regulation, particularly the 1957 Wolfenden Report and the creation of the 'discreet, responsible and heavily privatized' homosexual sanctioned in law by the 1967 Sexual Offences Act.[20] While Project SIGMA ensured anonymity, as the first large-scale survey of its kind it asked men to disclose 'private acts' that had been shrouded in legislative secrecy since 1967.

The context in which SIGMA worked was also specifically British. Itemising the problems associated with extrapolating from published American studies and British clinical studies, researchers argued that 'neither source is capable of carrying the weight of inference currently demanded of it ... First, both rely heavily on information provided by those who are willing to identify themselves publicly as gay or homosexual but these are only a subset of their group which engages in homosexual behaviour.'[21] SIGMA's 'snowball' sample from a non-clinical background reflected a shift towards increasing openness. This shift coincided with AIDS but was also exacerbated by the crisis of the epidemic: understanding men's private – and public – sexual practices was essential to meet the public health needs of 'ordinary' men who had sex with men.[22]

Despite the context of HIV/AIDS, SIGMA was not *initially* focused on health and epidemiology. Unlike contemporary surveys like NATSAL (1990), the project was rooted in a different intellectual tradition in the *social* sciences. Writing to the Department of Health and Social Security (DHSS), Coxon identified 'the duty of the social scientist, as distinct from the clinician or the mere biologist, to provide, in the first place, an account of the *relationships* between sexual acts rather than a simple count of their incidence of prevalence'.[23] In this sense, SIGMA was indebted to empirical rather than epidemiological traditions of British research into homosexuality, particularly the ground-breaking work of scholars like Michael Schofield.[24] Before *The Sexual Behaviour of Young People*, Schofield had published *A Minority: A Report of the Life of the Male Homosexual in Great Britain* (1960) under the pseudonym Gordon Westwood, one of three books prepared for the Social Biology Council.[25] As part of this project, Schofield interviewed 127 homosexual men over two years to understand their sexual activities and social background. Like SIGMA, Schofield advocated that his respondents 'speak for themselves', using verbatim quotations to give his book texture and authenticity.[26] That SIGMA received funding from the DHSS, then, underscored the growing acceptability of what it called a 'fragile and fragmented British tradition of research into male homosexuality which reaches back almost exactly a century'.[27]

Looking back in 2009, Coxon noted that 'the group that became SIGMA originally began in the late 1970s, in what was intended to be a replication of the Kinsey Report for the UK'.[28] While SIGMA's initial aims were 'overtaken by AIDS', its politics became increasingly pertinent with the spread of the virus and prejudice. Addressing the epidemic required an understanding of transmission to prevent catastrophic consequences. From SIGMA's perspective, analysing the '*relationships* between sexual acts' and humanising gay sexual practice became more vital. Nevertheless, both the DHSS and project researchers relied on the strategic language of respectability to justify their research and render it acceptable in the context of growing social and political hostility.[29] SIGMA's 'respectability' reflected its strategic claims to 'scientific' method and the pressure to place its work within epidemiological traditions to secure the necessary funding and legitimacy to begin its planned investigation.[30]

In 1986, SIGMA finally secured funding from the Medical Research Council (MRC) and the Department of Health for a longitudinal survey of the sexual attitudes and behaviour of a non-clinical sample of British gay and bisexual men. Two thousand men were involved in the study, making it the largest empirical study of its kind conducted in Britain. Data was collected via face-to-face interviews over five 'waves' and through sexual diary forms, a technique developed specifically for the project. Postal questionnaires and HIV-testing were also used to collect data on the HIV status of men among the cohort. Due to the HIV context, a large part of the survey was dedicated to monitoring attitudes towards safer sex, largely centred on men's adoption of condoms over the period in which researchers began work.

Reflecting on the survey's 'representativeness', SIGMA acknowledged that its respondents were more educated, belonged to 'a higher social class',[31] and 'over-represent[ed] the middle-aged, middle-class educated white gay man in urban centres of the UK'.[32] The study's social and geographical grounding is key to our understanding how men negotiated risk and relationships. Among researchers, such men were assumed to have greater knowledge networks, and were in closer proximity, which shaped the organisation of their sexual lives.[33] During the pre-test stage of the survey, SIGMA became further interested in issues around 'age-conditionality' and the generational nature of safer sex practices.[34]

Collecting data

The project did not explore the idiosyncratic nature of men's sexual practices until its final stages. Activists critiqued this approach, flagging the problem of targeting men in relationships. Edward King argued that:

> This perspective on the meanings of sex to gay men ... is absent from purely quantitative survey research, which only measures the extent to which gay men have changed their sexual behaviour because of the AIDS epidemic. However it is of fundamental importance to understanding the relatively high incidence of unprotected anal sex among men in relationships [sic].[35]

SIGMA engaged seriously with this criticism. In their first published book, investigators 'refuse[d] to accept that the use of quantitative methods automatically commits us to a dehumanising, cold-blooded view of human behaviour, which exalts quantification over the lived experience of individuals'. Clearly, Project SIGMA was invested in critical research into individual lived experience, but research pressures often limited the study's qualitative aspects.[36]

Data for the main study was collected through successive interviews, sexual diaries, and blood sampling. The evolving interview questionnaires reflected a shift in focus as the survey developed, sometimes in response to men's testimony.[37] Interviews were conducted in five 'waves' at ten-month intervals. Each questionnaire included different 'core' and 'non-core' components.[38] Respondents were asked about some core components at each interview, including questions around 'un/safe and risk behaviour' which were explored in further detail during the second (1988), fourth (1991), and fifth wave (1993). In the second wave, men were asked what they liked and disliked about condoms and whether they used them with each sexual partner. Although these questions suggested that investigators understood that condom use varied depending on whether the respondent was having sex with a regular or casual partner, no further *qualitative* information was elicited to explain the reasons for condom use or non-use.

SIGMA knew that 'what the researchers decide is relevant to their enterprise [and] will in all likelihood change over the course of a long-term project'.[39] By the fourth wave in 1991, researchers added pre-written reasons to explain non-use of condoms into the question schedule. Some of these tick-box responses suggested an understanding of the role of relationship in sexual decision-making, particularly around anal sex – 'only use with casual partners'. However, the proforma responses suggested men were not committed to safer sex and echoed the assumptions of 'relapse' theory: 'got carried away', 'condoms are no guarantee anyway', or 'too drunk' and 'too stoned'.[40] Such answers appeared to assume that men would resort to 'irrational' behaviour once their judgement was impaired by desire, alcohol, or drugs.[41] Yet, another response stated 'only fuck with regular partners (probe why)'. The parentheses indicate that the SIGMA team wanted to know more about the reasons *why* condoms were not being used in regular relationships.

One question in wave four asked respondents to grade their responses to a list of twenty-nine statements about anal sex using a five-point scale. Some statements alluded to the sense of intimacy forged through fucking – 'fucking with someone is the closest thing you can do' – or alluded to the notion of love and trust as preconditions for fucking through statements such as 'I have to love someone before I'll fuck with them'. This supports the evidence that relationship type was the most important predicator of the type of sex in which men engaged.[42] Statements including 'I find I often fuck just to please my partner' and 'I've used fucking as a bargaining tool' underscored how investigators were aware of the communicative power of fucking and the power of love or partner pressure.[43] In this fourth wave, respondents were also 'encouraged to talk freely about their perceptions and experiences' as researchers came to recognise the importance of respondents relaying experiences in their own words.[44]

This iteration of the questionnaire also included questions that implied researchers' interest in the broader links between masculinity and emotion in 1980s Britain. Respondents were asked whether they agreed that 'kissing compromises my masculinity more than fucking does'.[45] The assumption that masculinity was defined by active penetration highlights a hypersexualised gay masculinity, setting up a false dichotomy between the acts of fucking and kissing. No qualitative data exists, so we cannot know if respondents engaged with this critically, but the published report revealed that no respondents agreed that they felt they could be intimate without undermining their masculinity.[46]

By wave five, the investigators were increasingly aware that HIV was not necessarily the most important factor shaping men's decision-making.[47] At this stage, the questionnaire contained a section on 'non-condom use', based on a reflexive reading of responses to previous interviews. 'Many men fuck without condoms for a wide variety of reasons', the questionnaire stated, 'we want to know about these reasons in more detail'.[48] The questionnaire then asked about non-use of condoms with a regular partner, and 'if stopped using condoms all together, when and why (probe fully)'.⁴⁹ This implies an understanding that dispensing with condoms could be a decisive, conscious act, when a relationship was established.

Compared to the dynamic and shifting interview questionnaires, the second strand of SIGMA's methodology, the sexual diary form, remained largely unaltered throughout the survey. Only minor changes were made to the form at the end of 1992, to emphasise *'always* record the use of condoms'.⁵⁰ Recruited as part of the interview samples and via appeals in the gay press, diarists were required to keep daily natural-language diaries of sexual activity for four weeks using forms provided in the Sexual Diary Pack.⁵¹ The form comprised two sections, including a partner list where respondents were asked to describe whether their partner was regular, occasional, or 'one-off', along with their age, how long they had been having sex, where they met, and their HIV status. Respondents completed a tabulated box every day or sexual 'session', defined as 'one or more acts by yourself or with a partner(s) at any one time'.⁵² Respondents were asked to record the time, place, and partner(s) involved before describing the details of the 'sexual session'.⁵³ Respondents' testimony, however, shows them articulating a different idea of the diary's function, shaped by wider cultures of life-writing. Instead of an engagement diary to record events, many men apparently wanted a more reflective personal diary. That the sexual session was framed as an 'engagement', as some respondents pointed out, obscured any possibility that emotions might have been useful in understanding men's sexual behaviour.

The way that SIGMA recorded data also changed in response to its growing understanding of the importance of recording respondents' experiences in their own words. When the project began, investigators devised a unique Sexual Behaviour Code (SBC) for acts described in the diary. This established a list of acts, then substituted the relevant abbreviation, with less common acts substituted for a two-letter code and the most common 'street' term for the practice.⁵⁴ Coding had to be precise so 'computers could read it' and data could be stored digitally and analysed at scale.⁵⁵ Yet this emphasis on behaviour meant important aspects of the 'sexual session' were overlooked, particularly things that did not fit into the schematic code or could not be 'chunked' into modality. The session used as an example by SIGMA was: 'we deep kissed and moved into a "69". Whilst doing it I began to finger him. Then he wanked me (both using poppers) and I came. Following that I wanked him till he came.' In the formal syntax of the SBC this became {MDK MS&AFg PW,XN/p AW,NX}.⁵⁶ While SIGMA initially encouraged diarists to use the SBC, some respondents refused to fill out their diaries in code, preferring 'natural language'. This refusal suggests dissatisfaction with code as incapable of accounting and representing the 'non-quantifiability' of sexual experiences. By the early 1990s, then, researchers increasingly encouraged diarists to 'describe the session in your own words'.[57]

Negotiating safer sex

A large portion of Project SIGMA focused on condom use and safer sex. In this context, men's sexual decision-making followed a particular chronology: by the project's end a particular risk-reduction strategy was evident, where condoms were used primarily with casual partners, but not with regular partners due to the symbolic nature of unprotected anal sex. In the first phase of the HIV epidemic, men's practice of safer sex was primarily tactical, focusing on abstinence, before a more strategic approach developed as men began to fit safer sex into existing sexual, affective, and relational structures.[58] As researcher Frank stated: 'things thought of as "wanton" sexual behaviour ... [reflected] considerations of safer sex strategies that fit in with their lives'.[59]

Before SIGMA began publishing its findings, most research identified two reasons for the rise in 'unsafe sex' in the early 1990s: 'relapse' and 'negotiated safety'. Relapse theory hinged on the assumption that men returned to unsafe sex after a period of improvement, effacing the possibility of more nuanced understandings of selective condom use.[60] Edward King identified the 'subtle homophobia' of this model, its 'pathological connotations', and effects in exacerbating the association between homosexuality and HIV.[61] SIGMA took a leading role in challenging these assumptions:

> At the heart of the relapse account lies a crucial assumption ... that no-one will rationally choose to have 'unsafe sex' and that the reasons for doing so must be sought in the irrational, the pathological or the fatalistic aspects of the self. We believe that the search for reasons in the irrational is misguided and ignores the *experience* of gay men who have lived with the need for safer sex for more than a decade.[62]

Building on this position, researchers identified a process of 'negotiated safety', influenced by Susan Kippax's Australian study, which found men stopped condom use after testing confirmed their mutual HIV-negative status.[63] The model over-emphasised the role of risk, communication, and conscious decision-making. SIGMA argued that it did not go far enough in explaining why men chose to have unprotected sex with a regular partner. As its research showed, however, not all decision-making was explicit. Negotiation could be tacit, shaped by the complicated, emotional bargaining underlying interactions between men. Rules regarding sex outside the relationship were often assumed or implicit or broken and remade over the course of time.

Despite the extent of behavioural change in the 1980s and 1990s, then, approaches to safer sex rarely mapped directly onto the 'official' understanding which urged condom use for *all* instances of anal intercourse and made condom use and safer sex almost synonymous. That men reappropriated and reworked this, then, suggests a growing tension between official and vernacular knowledge by the late 1980s. Gay men understood and practised 'safer sex' in ways that fitted into their lives and relationships. HIV remained a central consideration to most men's sexual decision-making. SIGMA's respondents consciously considered the 'safety' of anal intercourse, particularly. In the fifth wave men were asked about any 'self-reflective changes in behaviour' since the advent of HIV and their 'current approach' to safer sex.[64] For some, strategies followed explicit discussion with a regular partner. This was particularly important where the respondent was HIV positive, to avoid further transmission. One man stated, 'I take it very seriously due to my status (positive).'[65] Of other interviewees, those who remained sexually active developed strategies ranging from consistent condom use (particularly when a partner's status was negative or unknown) to abstaining from intercourse altogether. However, most stressed that receiving a HIV-positive test forced them to revaluate their practices.

Within the SIGMA cohort, some men used HIV-testing as part of courtship to inform their safer sex strategies. One respondent stated, 'I never used condoms with P1 [partner one]. If I have casual partners I never fuck and always practise safer sex so not to infect me or me to pass it onto him.' That 'we both had a negative result last test' meant dispensing with condoms posed minimal risk.[66] A similar strategy is evident in the sexual diaries. One respondent and his partner had been monogamous for two years, received a negative test result, and so only used condoms as a sex aid 'to heighten orgasm' rather than as a prophylactic.[67] Strategies akin to 'negotiated safety' *were* being practised by some respondents.

Yet many more men resorted to similar strategies before taking a HIV test, negotiating the guidelines through their individual perception of risk. One respondent to the fifth wave questionnaire believed he had 'relatively safe sex', choosing not to have either 'active or passive' anal sex with casual partners, 'both *to do with HIV*'.[68] 'Relatively safe' implies he favoured risk-*minimisation* over exclusion, by choosing to have unprotected anal sex with his regular partner. Other researchers reported that at the start of the epidemic, many men reduced their number of partners altogether. By the time the project was collecting data, however, it was apparently common for men to have multiple partners. A key goal of SIGMA was to find out the most common relationship arrangement among men, which they knew would be important to understanding the spread of the virus. The most common relationship type among the cohort were open relationships – 33 per cent at wave four of the project – in which men had one or more regular partner(s) and one or more 'casual' partners.[69] Sexual non-monogamy remained a feature of the 'gay lifestyle' after the initial phase of the pandemic.

In this context, maintaining the safety of partners in an open relationship was both important and involved a deliberate assessment of risk. SIGMA found that '43% of open relationships had some kind of agreement as to what kind of sex partner should have outside that relationship, usually based on safer sex guidelines'.[70] Respondents with a least one regular sexual partner were asked if they 'currently have any rules/guidelines/ understandings about sex outside your relationship?'. The interviewer was then instructed to prompt respondents to reveal what these rules or guidelines were and whether they were explicit or implicit.[71] This question – and the testimony used here – points to another way men chose to organise their sexual lives. Although men's responses were guided by the prompts, they revealed the diverse ways men organised their sexual lives.

One respondent made it clear that his strategy followed negotiation with his partner: 'just to be careful. Just safe sex. Mutual agreement after discussion [sic].'[72] Another stated 'safe sex with others, not with each other. We've talked about it ... no fucking with others without a condom' asserting that this decision was arrived at through *explicit* negotiation.[73] Although respondents could be vague in using the term 'be careful', they assured interviewers that this rule was reached via 'mutual agreement after discussion'.[74] Other responses were clear that safer sex was the 'rule' outside the regular relationship.[75] However, in most cases of non-use within a regular relationship there was still a knowledge that neither partner was 'risky' and unprotected intercourse remained possible. Even though it was clear decisions were being made on an emotional basis, HIV was still considered, even if this was based on 'imperfect knowledge' of one another's HIV status.

Rules and guidelines could also be a product of the breaking, testing, and remaking of boundaries. As one respondent outlined: 'sexually: no fucking at all. Emotionally: not allowed to have regular partner we see more than once. This may change rules and guidelines constantly stretched and broken down by me [sic].'[76] Making rules was an ongoing process, reflecting men's changing needs and circumstances. Other agreements were more tacit. One respondent stated, 'to follow safer sex rules. i.e. then use condom. More common sense rather then explicit. Arrived at this rule through awareness of implications of not using condoms [sic].'[77] That condom use was considered 'common sense', and did not warrant discussion, evoked King's idea of safer sex as a gay 'community' norm rather than conscious decision-making.[78] Such practices were predicated on the assumption that their partner was HIV negative, within any threat located outside their relationship.

Yet guidelines regarding sex outside a relationship were not always about HIV. Instead, they were predicated on maintaining the 'specialness' of a relationship and the emotional significance of anal sex. 'Fucking', the slang term for anal sex, had both political and personal meaning when, as SIGMA argued, 'people started challenging the traditional roles and positions of men and women ... for many gay men, receptive fucking became a liberating experience.'[79] Anal sex was thus central in the gay repertoire, despite a 'collective understanding' amongst SIGMA respondents that it was not a 'defining factor of sex'.[80]

Frank's idea that anal sex was a 'relational thing' underscores the interpersonal significance of anal sex among gay men. In 1992, SIGMA argued that 'the type of relationship a man is currently in is the strongest predictor of the type and frequency of sexual acts he is likely to engage in'. [81] It was on this basis that researchers concluded that 'rules about anal intercourse did not always develop due to safer sex. The symbolic importance of this act in a regular relationship, as an act of love and/or trust, can result in partners not wishing to do this act with others.'[82] As survey responses revealed, some men in open relationships *did* restrict anal intercourse with outside partners.[83] Yet, this reflected the significance of anal intercourse. One respondent observed that 'my sexual practice isn't a result of AIDS. It's more what me and my partner feel comfortable with'. Interpersonal factors remained enduringly important to sexual decision-making.[84]

One respondent thus described fucking as 'a really intimate kind of thing'.[85] This was a common response to the fourth-wave questionnaire, when participants were asked about anal sex and its value or importance within a relationship. Interpersonal aspects were mentioned more than physical aspects, with researchers finding that the 'most common among these was the closeness generated or confirmed by the act'.[86] Qualitative testimony hinged upon positive comments about anal intercourse 'as a sign of love, trust and commitment'.[87] As a result, SIGMA concluded, 'very few men who enjoyed fucking, and got a lot out of it, have stopped doing it all together because of HIV'.[88]

Yet *unprotected* anal sex took on new meaning during the epidemic, particularly given the extensive knowledge about transmission and safer sex amongst the SIGMA cohort. As Frank noted, 'not using a condom is a sign of emotional intimacy ... not using condoms with someone you're in love with is quite a big thing'.[89] In the context of a regular relationship, then, unprotected anal sex conveyed feelings of intimacy, trust, and commitment. Where this relationship was open and anal sex was permitted with casual partners, condomless sex differentiated between sex within and without a relationship.

At various intervals during the study, men were asked about their attitudes to condoms, including the reasons why they disliked them. Reading between the lines allows us to further understand the significance of unprotected anal sex with a regular partner. Asked to explain his dislike of condoms, one respondent stated: 'they aren't very romantic'.[90] Condoms were also bound up with questions of trust, so that their use 'implies lack of trust in partner'.[91] When asked specifically about the non-use with a regular partner, one respondent revealed that 'sense of trust developed. Monogamous if I've got a boyfriend. Only used a condom once the first time. After that he said he didn't like it when we got to know one another better and he reassured me I was his only regular partner then. May be foolish [*sic*].'[92] While this respondent recognised the potential for poor judgement, he revealed how feelings of trust could be privileged over a guarantee of safety. Dispensing with condoms thus also represented reaching a relationship milestone and a sense of commitment – what one man called 'a natural progression really'.[93] In a period when same-sex couples were excluded from the relationship rituals and milestones of heterosexuality, unprotected sex could be a marker of the growing 'seriousness' of relationships between men.[94]

Further responses to SIGMA also commented on condom use causing a loss of intimacy. Many men stated they disliked condoms because they created a 'psychological barrier' as well as a physical one.[95] One man stated that condoms 'come between you and partner'.[96] Others mentioned the loss or removal of intimacy, including this response to the fifth-wave questionnaire:

> I think we tend to feel more passionate on those occasions when we don't use a condom. Either one of us may be feeling low and in need of love, and it's the intimacy of not having the barrier between us.[97]

This also highlights the situational aspect of condom use. In privileging emotion in this decision, the man underscored the importance of encouraging discussion of 'personal feelings' or 'moods' in the diary.

Exemplifying the conflicting influences on men's decision-making, one respondent observed, 'I would like to fuck without a condom, it does increase the intensity of experience and emotional closeness.'[98] Similarly, Lee Botham, interviewed in 2007 for the HIV/AIDS Testimonies project, admitted he always used condoms, but since being diagnosed with HIV he had struggled with the notion that he could no longer 'get close' psychologically to a partner in the way that unprotected sex facilitated.[99] Although these respondents had opposite HIV statuses, their responses reflect the struggle to reconcile safety and pleasure at a specific historical moment. They reveal a 'different sort of rationality', which acknowledges both safety and the emotional significance of sexual acts.

Read as a whole, these responses show how safer sex was embedded into existing understandings of sexual interaction. The result were 'realistic' strategies in which men in open relationships chose to have unprotected anal sex with regular partners due to the emotional significance of the act but used condoms with casual partners.[100] These qualitative responses both echoed the 'romantic rationality' identified in smaller studies of gay men's sexual behaviour and reflected the direct critiques of the inadequacies of the sexual diary method with which this chapter began.[101]

Conclusion

In 1993, Edward King argued that 'safer sex guidelines ... have to reconcile advice intended to enable gay men to avoid giving or getting HIV with the continuing emotional, physical and symbolic value of anal sex in those men's lives'. King reflected growing recognition of the emotional realities of men's sexual behaviour in the 1980s and 1990s.[102] Despite this shift, men in same-sex relationships remained at the margins of safer sex advice until the mid-1990s. That year the Health Education Authority produced a targeted campaign with the tagline 'Choose Safer Sex', in which one advertisement tackled negotiation of safer sex in relationships.[103] On the back of the card, placed in *Capital Gay*, was written: 'decisions about safer sex can feel very different when you are in a relationship. So take time to discuss things with your partner. You may feel pressurised to give up condom use, so be aware of this.'[104] The postcard showed a couple smiling into the camera, in stark contrast with erotic earlier campaigns, as public health campaigners began to respond to the emotional and sexual needs of men in relationships.

Other public health initiatives also paid closer attention to emotion in this period, emphasising the social and cultural nature of actions 'whereby individuals and groups recognise and examine feelings and attitudes about sex to enhance personal growth and development, in order ... to facilitate empowerment to negotiate safer sex'.[105] This approach reflected both how sex and emotion was discussed more openly in the late twentieth century and the growing emphasis on personal accounts in raising individuals' awareness of the constraints militating against safer sex in encounters across the hetero-homosexual binary.[106]

As a case study into the relationship between sexuality, masculinity, and social research during the crisis of HIV/AIDS, Project SIGMA allows us to chart the transition from a focus on epidemiology and condom use to privileging the ways that gay men understood their sex lives. When asked about SIGMAS's legacy, Frank stated that it demonstrated that men had diverse ways of managing their pleasure and risk.[107] Qualitative data dispels monolithic concepts of the 'gay community' and the straightforward equation between safer sex and gay identity.[108] This is key to understanding the multiplicity of the queer past and meeting the diverse needs of gay men in the present. Yet it was not only gay men who questioned the relationship between male sexuality, masculinity, and emotions in this period. Straight men also reflected on their own sexual practices and the codes and feelings that informed them.

Notes

1 Wellcome Library, Project SIGMA Archives, GC/260/B.1; GC/260/B.2. Respondent ID: BR:9001.
2 SIGMA researchers invited respondents to write to them to express their views, though most respondents kept to the format provided. Anthony Coxon, *Between the Sheets: Sexual Diaries and Gay Men's Sex in the Era of AIDS* (London: Cassell, 1996), 176–177.
3 ID: BR:9001.
4 GTX:001. GC/260/B.1.
5 Edward King, *Safety in Numbers: Safer Sex and Gay Men* (London: Cassell, 1993), 114–119.
6 See also *ibid.*, xiii.
7 Mike Savage, *Identities and Social Change in Britain since 1940: The Politics of Method* (Oxford: Oxford University Press, 2010), 18. The SIGMA quantitative database, used to facilitate statistical analysis, has proved largely inaccessible to historians unaccustomed to working with large datasets.
8 Coxon, *Between the Sheets*, 145.
9 See Savage, *Identities and Social Change*; Jon Lawrence, 'Social-Science Encounters and the Negotiation of Difference in Early 1960s England', *History Workshop Journal*, 77:1 (2014), 215–239; and Charlotte Greenhalgh, 'The Travelling Social Survey: Social Research and Its Subjects in Britain, Australia and New Zealand, 1930s–1970s', *History Australia*, 13:1 (2016), 124–138.
10 See Benno Grammerl, 'Ultra Sensitive? How the History of Emotions Can Benefit the History of Homosexualities', talk delivered at IHR History of Sexuality Seminar, March 2019.
11 Matt Cook, *Queer Domesticities: Homosexuality and Home Life in Twentieth Century London* (Basingstoke: Palgrave Macmillan, 2014).
12 Claire Langhamer, *The English in Love: The Intimate Story of an Emotional Revolution* (Oxford: Oxford University Press, 2013); Marcus Collins, *Modern Love: An Intimate History of Men and Women in Twentieth Century Britain* (London: Atlantic Books, 2003).
13 Hannah Charnock, 'Teenage Girls, Hopes for the Future and Contraceptive Practice, 1950–1980', paper delivered at the Modern British Studies Conference, University of Birmingham, 2019.
14 Coxon, *Between the Sheets*, 173.
15 Peter M. Davies *et al.*, *Sex, Gay Men and AIDS* (London: Falmer Press, 1993), 53; see also *ibid.*, 50.

16 *Ibid.*, 53.
17 *Ibid.*, 52.
18 Some results are published in M. Boulton *et al.*, 'Gay Men's Accounts of Unsafe Sex', *AIDS Care*, 7:5 (1995), 619–630; Graham Hart and Paul Flowers, *A Survey of Gay Men's Sexual Behaviour in Glasgow* (Medical Research Council, Social and Public Health Services Unit, November 1999); and Paul Flowers *et al.*, 'Health and Romance: Understanding Unprotected Sex in Relationships between Gay Men', *British Journal of Health Psychology*, 2 (1997), 73–86. See also George Wilson, *South Essex Health Needs Assessment for Gay and Bisexual Men Who Have Sex with Men: First Year* (South Essex Health, 1994).
19 Davies *et al.*, *Sex, Gay Men and AIDS*, 5.
20 Committee on Homosexual Offences and Prostitution, *Report of the Committee on Homosexual Offences and Prostitution* (London: HMSO, 1957); Frank Mort, *Capital Affairs: London and the Making of the Permissive Society* (New Haven: Yale University Press, 2010), 355. In the first Project SIGMA working paper, Coxon stated that the 1967 Sexual Offences Act made research difficult as only sex between two consenting adults aged over twenty-one in private was legal. University of Birmingham, Modern Records Collection, A. M. Coxon, 'The "Gay Lifestyle" and the Impact of AIDS', Project SIGMA Working Paper No. 1, November 1985, University College, Cardiff. See also Brian Lewis, *Wolfenden's Witnesses: Homosexuality in Post-war Britain* (Basingstoke: Palgrave Macmillan, 2016).
21 The National Archives (hereafter TNA), Department of Health Papers, JA367/50, longitudinal study of the sexual behaviour of homosexual males under the impact of AIDS: A. P. M. Coxon, 'Research: Effect of Age and Type of Relationship on Sexual Behaviour among Homosexual Males and Their Impact on AIDS', Social Research Unit, University College, Cardiff.
22 Respondents were not recruited through genito-urinary medicine (GUM) clinics. Project SIGMA researchers were also interested in respondents' experiences of public sex, including 'cottaging' and 'cruising', highlighting a subculture that had been obscured by the 1967 Sexual Offences Act.
23 TNA, JA367/50.
24 Coxon, *Between the Sheets*, 6.
25 Gordon Westwood, *A Minority: A Report of the Life of the Male Homosexual in Great Britain* (London: Longmans, 1960). See also Gordon Westwood, *Society and the Homosexual* (London: Gollancz, 1952); and Gordon Westwood, *Sociological Aspects of Homosexuality: A Comparative Study of Three Types of Homosexuals* (London: Longmans, 1965).
26 John Wolfenden, 'Foreword', in Westwood, *A Minority*.
27 Davies *et al.*, *Sex, Gay Men and AIDS*, 5.
28 C. Overy, L. A. Reynolds, and E. M. Tansey, 'Transcript', in C. Overy, L. A. Reynolds, and E. M. Tansey (eds), *History of the National Survey of Sexual Attitudes and Lifestyles*, Wellcome Witnesses to Twentieth Century Medicine, vol. 41 (London: Queen Mary University of London, 2011), 12. See also

Alfred Kinsey, Wardell Pomeroy, and Clyde Martin, *Sexual Behavior in the Human Male* (Indianapolis: Indiana University Press, 1948); and A. M. Coxon, 'Homosexual Sexual Behaviour', Working Paper No. 4, n.d., Social Research Unit.

29 TNA, JA367/50, 'A Longitudinal Study of the Sexual Behaviour of Non-heterosexual Males and the Seroprevalence of HIV', Medical Research Council, October 1986.

30 *Ibid.* Sex research secured legitimacy through association with the medical profession. Coxon's research methods were also described as 'scientifically sound' in DHSS correspondence. TNA, JA367/50. Letter to Dr Rothman from Dr M. J. Graveney, 'Professor Coxon's Studies in Homosexual Behaviour', 5 March 1987. Margaret Thatcher had quite publicly threatened to get rid of sociology from the Economic and Social Research Council on the grounds that it was 'not scientific'. For the epidemiological tradition, see Kaye Wellings, *Sexual Behaviour in Britain: The National Survery of Sexual Attitudes and Lifestyles* (London: Penguin, 1994).

31 Davies *et al.*, *Sex, Gay Men and AIDS*, 85.

32 *Ibid.*, 175.

33 The St Mary's Hospital study also focused on London. Little systematic research was conducted into working-class, Black, and minority ethnic gay and bisexual men, despite the South Yorkshire study examining working-class men's behaviour. SIGMA was a longitudinal study so the cohort aged over time and this prevented a clear picture of younger men's practices. See Davies *et al.*, *Sex, Gay Men and AIDS*, 72. For the 'St Mary's Project', see Boulton *et al.*, 'Gay Men's Accounts'. For the South Yorkshire study, see Flowers *et al.*, 'Health and Romance'.

34 University of Birmingham, Modern Records Collection, Working Paper No. 4: 'Homosexual Sexual Behaviour' by APM Coxon Social Research Unit; 'A Preliminary Study of Some Aspects of Male Homosexual Behaviour in the United Kingdom' by T. J. McManus and Marian Envoy, Project SIGMA, Working No. Paper 6 (In Press, *Journal of Sexual Behaviour*, 1987), 7.

35 King, *Safety in Numbers*, 158–159.

36 Davies *et al.*, *Sex, Gay Men and AIDS*, 75.

37 *Ibid.*, 78.

38 A. M. Coxon, M. Davies, and T. J. McManus, 'Project SIGMA: Gay Men's Panel Study, 1987–1994', UK Data Service, 2002, https://doi.org/10.5255/UKDA-SN-4476-1.

39 Davies *et al.*, *Sex, Gay Men and AIDS*, 76.

40 Coxon *et al.*, 'Gay Men's Panel Study'.

41 For SIGMA's later challenge to this assumption, see P. Weatherburn *et al.*, 'No Connection between Alcohol Use and Unsafe Sex among Gay and Bisexual Men', *AIDS*, 7:1 (1993), 115–119.

42 Coxon *et al.*, 'Gay Men's Panel Study'.

43 Flowers *et al.*, 'Health and Romance', 81–82.

44 Davies *et al.*, *Sex, Gay Men and AIDS*, 130.

45 Coxon *et al.*, 'Gay Men's Panel Study'.
46 *Ibid.*, 140.
47 *Ibid.*
48 *Ibid.*
49 *Ibid.*
50 *Ibid.*
51 Detailed instructions were provided with the diary form. Wellcome, GC/260/A.1, 'Information about Sexual Diaries'.
52 Coxon, *Between the Sheets*, 176; Wellcome, GC/260/A.1, 'Information about Sexual Diaries'.
53 Coxon, *Between the Sheets*, 177.
54 List of behaviours taken from 'Appendix 1: List of Homosexual Acts' in *ibid.*, 175.
55 Wellcome, GC/206.A1, 'Instructions for Encoding Sexual Diaries', 19 April 1999. See also Savage, *Identities and Social Change*, 246.
56 Wellcome, GC/206.A1, 'Instructions for Encoding Sexual Diaries', 19 April 1999. See also 'Appendix 4: Formal Syntax of Sexual Diary Code' in Coxon, *Between the Sheets*, 183.
57 For the 1996 revised diary form containing these instructions, see Coxon, *Between the Sheets*, 182.
58 Davies *et al.*, *Sex, Gay Men and AIDS*, 55–57, 175.
59 Interview with Frank (b. 1965).
60 See King, *Safety in Numbers*, 142.
61 *Ibid.*, 136, 143.
62 Peter Weatherburn *et al.*, *The Sexual Lifestyles of Gay and Bisexual Men in England and Wales* (London: HMSO, 1992), 28 (emphasis added).
63 Susan Kippax *et al.*, 'Sustaining Safe Sex: A Longitudinal Study of Homosexual Men', *AIDS*, 7 (1993), 257–263. Further results from studies in Australia were compiled in Susan Kippax *et al.*, *Sustaining Safer Sex: Gay Communities Respond to AIDS* (London: Taylor & Francis, 1993).
64 Coxon *et al.*, 'Gay Men's Panel Study'.
65 ID: CF:0073.
66 ID: CF:0088.
67 ID: BI:0262.
68 ID: OT:001 (emphasis added). 'Active' and 'passive' indicated the meaning of giving and receiving partner in anal intercourse.
69 Davies *et al.*, *Sex, Gay Men and AIDS*, 150.
70 *Ibid.*, 170–171.
71 Coxon *et al.*, 'Gay Men's Panel Study'.
72 ID: LC:0049.
73 Hickson *et al.*, 'Maintenance of Open Gay Relationships: Some Strategies for Protection against HIV', *AIDS Care*, 4:4 (1992), 416–418; ID: LO:0009.
74 ID: LC:0026; ID: LC:0049.
75 ID: LO:0009.
76 ID: LO:0135.

77 ID: LO:0133.
78 ID: LO:0133. SIGMA concluded that, for some respondents, HIV was an important issue to be considered in non-exclusive partnerships. Hickson *et al.*, 'Maintenance of Open Gay Relationships', 413.
79 Davies *et al.*, *Sex, Gay Men and AIDS*, 128.
80 *Ibid.*, 139.
81 Interview with Frank; Davies *et al.*, *Sex, Gay Men and AIDS*, 147. See also King, *Safety in Numbers*, 46.
82 Davies *et al.*, *Sex, Gay Men and AIDS*, 171.
83 ID: LO:0135.
84 ID: LO:0054.
85 ID: YO:0084.
86 Davies *et al.*, *Sex, Gay Men and AIDS*, 134.
87 Weatherburn *et al.*, *Sexual Lifestyles*, 29.
88 Davies *et al.*, *Sex, Gay Men and AIDS*, 138.
89 Interview with Frank.
90 ID: CF:0294; ID: LO:0156. Another respondent (ID: L0:0372) disliked condoms as they were 'not romantic'.
91 ID: LO:33. This was highlighted in the analysis of the pre-test study. 'Project Background and Description of Core Component with Publications during the Panel Period (1987–1993)', 26.
92 ID: L0:0189.
93 ID: BR:002.
94 Flowers *et al.*, 'Health and Romance', 81.
95 ID: LO:357.
96 ID: LO:75.
97 ID: CF:0322.
98 ID: LT:0041.
99 Lee Botham, interviewed by Wendy Rickard, British Library, HIV/AIDS Testimonies, C743/14.
100 Davies *et al.*, *Sex, Gay Men and AIDS*, 175.
101 See Flowers *et al.*, 'Health and Romance'.
102 King, *Safety in Numbers*, 88, 93.
103 Wellcome, AIDS ephemera: safe sex education box 2, 'Choose Safer Sex', Health Education Authority, 1994.
104 The campaign advised men to call a dedicated helpline provided by the Terrence Higgins Trust (THT), the LLGS (London Lesbian and Gay Switchboard), or the NAH (National AIDS Helpline) if they felt unsure.
105 Boulton *et al.*, 'Gay Men's Accounts', 628.
106 *Ibid.*
107 Interview with Frank.
108 King, *Safety in Numbers*.

Reflection: Writing the history of male sexuality in the wake of Operation Yewtree and #MeToo

Hannah Charnock

The years since 2013 when I began my doctoral research on the history of heterosexuality in post-war Britain have been turbulent ones for gender politics. In that time, Tarana Burke's #MeToo campaign and a series of elections, high-profile legal cases, and disclosures have drawn attention to ongoing cultures of sexual abuse, harassment, and misconduct in Western society.[1] In Britain, Operation Yewtree, the Metropolitan Police Service's investigation into sex abuse (mainly of children) which began in October 2012, garnered significant media attention, as did legislative campaigns surrounding 'upskirting' and compulsory sex and relationship education and social media activism such as the Everyday Sexism.[2] Drawing upon my own experiences of researching adolescent sexuality in post-war Britain, this reflection situates historical practice within the specific context of gender politics in the late 2010s and asks, what do contemporary discussions about the gender politics of heterosexuality mean for the history of masculinity in modern Britain?

Researching histories of sexuality in the 2010s and after

The #MeToo movement has been instrumental in demonstrating the ubiquity of sexual violence against women in contemporary society and the recent past. Echoing Liz Kelly's articulation of the 'continuum of sexual violence', the wide-ranging nature of disclosures associated with #MeToo have highlighted how unwanted sexual behaviour and acts of sexual harm exceed what is accounted for within legal infrastructures; the range of interactions that women find traumatic, humiliating, and dehumanising do not necessarily conform to legal definitions of lack of consent or harassment.[3] Crucially, for the history of masculinity, in revealing the pervasive normality of sexual harassment, the movement has contributed to a recalibration of understanding in which sexual violence is increasingly correlated 'with the "everyman" rather than the "bad man"'.[4] While it is important that we study the history of rape and sexual assault in its own right, this recalibration encourages us to recognise that patriarchal gender dynamics operated in mundane ways, informing individuals' experiences of work, family, marriage, leisure, and education.

Indeed, many #MeToo disclosures sit neatly alongside the accounts of historic sexual cultures I have encountered in my historical research. Studying the lives of teenage girls in post-war Britain, stories of child sexual abuse, stranger rape, date rape, intimate partner violence, street harassment, misconduct in the workplace, sexual assault, and coercion were far more frequent than I had anticipated and although these accounts became less surprising, they did not become any less harrowing or anger-inducing.[5] Faced with the ubiquity of this material and the contemporary climate, it felt imperative to foreground how the threat and experience of sexual violence and harassment informed women's sexuality and their relationships with men. As such, my thesis dealt explicitly with questions of power within heterosexual relationships, examining the ways in which patriarchal gender politics informed how teenage girls were brought up to think about sex as well as how this played out in girls' own relationships with boys and men.

This type of historical research is important in demonstrating the extent of sexual oppression and illuminating the myriad ways in which patriarchy did/does harm to women. Yet, a potential critique of this work lies in its limited explanatory power: while its focus on female experience is well suited to highlighting the form and effects of male-centric cultures of heterosexuality, in so far as it is unconcerned with these cultures' apparent beneficiaries, it is limited in its ability to explain how exactly these cultures perpetuated themselves. A history of male heterosexuality thus seems essential if we are to fully comprehend the power dynamics of male–female relations.

In this way, then, it seems necessary to interrogate masculinity and the role of sex within it in more depth to 'round out' our perspective. Even a cursory glance at the personal testimonies of men of the post-war generation suggests that there was no singular model of masculine heterosexuality; different boys understood and experienced their sexuality very differently.[6] However, this exercise is more complicated than simply 'recovering' male experiences. Although a desire to understand the sexual cultures of the past seems an important reason *why* we should write these histories, the matter of *how* we go about doing this work is more fraught. The rest of this chapter therefore reflects upon the methodological and ethical issues raised by this type of research. It interrogates the challenges of using oral history to write about pasts that are 'loaded' in the present and it questions, in particular, how we reconcile the desire to tell stories of male experience of heterosexuality with the imperative not to sideline or dismiss women's accounts of oppression and assault. Organised around two questions of approach, the following discussions build towards addressing the larger question: how do we write feminist histories of masculinity when we are not addressing institutions or culture, but studying the lives of individual men, many of whom are still alive?

Whose stories do we tell?

A key question to consider is whose stories should we be telling. While attempting to move histories of sexuality beyond structures of regulation and representation offers immense opportunities for understanding sexual cultures, it also heightens the stakes of our work, especially when writing about the recent past. As Kate Fisher has noted, 'little material on the details and meanings of everyday practices, choices, preferences, and beliefs exists in archival sources', particularly those related to sexuality.[7] As such, historical research into these topics has been particularly reliant on oral histories to 'uncover' these otherwise obscured elements of sexual experience.[8] But what are the implications of using personal testimonies to write histories of masculinity? What responsibility do we have to the men whose stories we draw upon? Is it possible to reconcile a desire to interrogate the gender dynamics of the past with the need to 'do no harm' to research subjects?

The prioritisation of individual experience has been a central theme of 'history from below' and has been championed by scholars working on marginalised groups. Oral history practitioners have been particularly vocal about the power of putting previously unheard voices 'on the record'.[9] 'Raising the voices' of women, ethnic minorities, queer communities, victims of political regimes, and other underrepresented groups has underpinned oral history's identity as a form of radical scholarship and notions of advocacy have been core to the discipline's identity since the 1970s.[10] In this way, there is much overlap between contemporary discourse and historical methodology. The desire at the core of campaigns surrounding Operation Yewtree and #MeToo to bring to light the experience of victims of sexual abuse and to destigmatise disclosures of assault sits quite neatly within feminist research traditions which have seen women's narration of their lives as a powerful act of resistance.

How does interviewing men about their experiences of heterosexuality fit within this frame? Feminists have long identified heterosexuality as an instrument of patriarchy, a system that prioritises men's needs and desires over those of women. For the Leeds Revolutionary Feminists, 'The heterosexual couple [was] the basic unit of the political structure of male supremacy' and 'every act of penetration, even that which is euphemistically described as making love', served the function of controlling and punishing women.[11] Although this has never been an uncontroversial position and many feminists themselves resisted the notion that all male–female relationships were irreconcilably oppressive, individuals of variously radical persuasions have critiqued late twentieth-century sexual cultures as perpetuating, even intensifying, the oppression of women.[12] While differing in their conclusions and proposed remedies, sex-positive feminists, anti-pornography feminists, social conservatives, and historians have all suggested that the so-called Sexual Revolution of the 1960s and 1970s may have worsened women's sexual status. The demise of restrictions on sexual licence in this period, it is claimed, did not 'liberate' women but turned them into sex objects, simply reconfiguring gendered expectations of sexuality.[13]

This culture is evident in the material artefacts that remain from the late twentieth century; the British Library holds entire runs of the mainstream pornographic magazines that emerged following the end of print censorship as well as copies of magazines such as *Jackie*, *Honey*, and *Petticoat* that, week after week, addressed girls' run-ins with boys who were 'only after one thing'.[14] Agony aunts' sympathetic but stoic responses mirrored the attitudes of contemporaneous 'facts of life' literature that argued that 'the strength of the sex urge, in most average boys, is such that ... a great number of them will almost certainly "try it on"',[15] and that boys were 'impelled by [the force of glandular processes] beyond their control' to promise love in exchange for sex.[16] These didactic sources offer insight into how gender relations were represented and articulated in the post-war period and appear to conform to feminist critiques of patriarchal norms but from the texts alone it is difficult to know how they were received; exploring how individual boys and men understood and acted within this culture requires a different source base.

A question remains, however, over the status of this male perspective. If we understand men as having benefitted from sexual cultures that privileged their feelings and desires over women, are men owed a platform from which to narrate their own experience? Asking men to narrate their experience sits uncomfortably within a 'testimonial culture' in which 'testimony is bound up with truth and justice'.[17] As Alison Phipps has suggested, there is a danger in treating all experiences as equal as it 'reinforces the advantage of those who already have access to platforms, while masking their structural power'.[18] A feminist research methodology might therefore plausibly reject any attempt to give space to men's stories; as beneficiaries of these patriarchal cultures, are men's stories the ones we should be prioritising?

One way to justify a focus on male experience might be to approach this history in a similar manner to other studies that have demonstrated the value of exploring the lives of those on the 'wrong' side of history.

In other subfields, the study of perpetrators of violence, terrorism, and other atrocities is deemed not only legitimate, but essential.[19] There are, of course, methodological challenges involved, especially when relying upon individuals to provide oral histories as the basis of this study; Carrie Hamilton has written eloquently on how research dynamics change when our narrators are not 'ideological hero[es]'.[20] However, as Katherine M. Blee has suggested, this work is vital if we are to understand 'the historical attraction of ordinary people to [extreme] politics'.[21] But although there are aspects of the study of masculine heterosexualities that fit this mould, this approach is problematised by the nature of sexual culture. As Hamilton has noted, studies with this approach often presume clear distinctions between the 'victims' and the 'perpetrators' of violence; when studying acts of violence or membership of political parties, participation in these acts and membership of these groups was (even if coerced) usually conscious.[22] Part of the nefariousness of twentieth-century sexual cultures, however, was that they were naturalised and normalised to the point that they often went unquestioned. How much agency do we ascribe to those who knew nothing but this culture? Boys of the post-war generation grew up at a time when respected educators informed them that 'sex is a woman's whole life ... But for the man it can be, and usually is, an incident' and in which men's pursuit of sex was considered a fundamental aspect of their physiology.[23] Men's actions had consequences, often causing immense pain and anguish to the girls they pursued, but their agency within these cultural norms was potentially ambiguous. How, then, do we write about these ambiguities in such a way that does a disservice to none of the individuals concerned?

How do we conduct this research?

Questions of ethics and historians' obligations to their subjects are not confined to oral historians. Many scholars are concerned with treating their historical subjects with care and have wrestled with the implications of using personal sources and individual lives in their work.[24] As historians have turned their attention to private life as an area of research, they have asked whether it is appropriate and ethical to examine letters, diaries, and other historic material that was never intended for public consumption. Similarly, the notion that historical research is an affective enterprise, in which the feelings that sources and narratives evoke in the researcher shape the histories that are written, is now widely acknowledged.[25] As Katie Barclay and Matt Houlbrook have demonstrated, historians can have complicated relationships with their subjects even though the latter are long dead.[26]

While these issues of ethics and emotion are relevant for all historians, however, they are particularly acute for oral historians whose encounters with their subjects are not abstract and separated by time but are conducted face to face in the present. For oral historians, ethical dilemmas not only exist on the page but are writ large in real-life social interactions. How we handle ethical questions as they arise in interviews undoubtedly affects the historical evidence we produce but can also have lasting effects for our interviewees. How we manage our emotions during our engagements with our subjects affects not just how we *might* construct historical narratives but defines the extent to which we *can* write our histories. In contrast to 'falling in love with the dead', oral historians must grapple with the challenge of being charmed (or indeed, disgusted) by the living.

A core tenet of feminist praxis that has become a foundation of good practice in oral history methodology is that interviewees should be allowed to 'speak for themselves', with little interviewer intrusion into the narrative. In their influential piece 'Learning to Listen', feminist scholars Kathryn Anderson and Dana C. Jack stressed that 'the processes of analysis should be ... subordinated to the processes of listening', emphasising that 'the interview provides the opportunity [for a female interviewee] to tell her own story in her own terms'.[27] Another chapter in the same collection warned against the emergence of oral history processes that 'seem progressively to efface the original narrator and diminish her control over her own words'.[28] This approach is thus well justified when interviewing members of underrepresented groups, but how desirable is it when interviewing individuals with hegemonic power? If the goal is to interrogate men's place within the dynamics of heterosexuality, how far do we need to directly question narratives as they are being presented?

For example, in my interview with David, I laughed off his comment that girls were 'a pain most of the time'.[29] From our brief interaction I liked David and my reaction to brush it off with a quip ('I'm sure the feeling was mutual!') speaks to the complicated interaction of social convention and research imperatives at play in interviews. As a researcher I probably should have asked him to clarify his comment and explain what he meant. But in the moment, the risk of social awkwardness prevented me from doing so; I did not want to offend him and the interview was still in its early stages so I just moved past it. Similarly, male interviewees often made reference to 'locker-room talk' in their testimonies. They revealed that it was not uncommon for boys to share stories of sexual exploits (real, exaggerated, and/or fictitious), make sexual jokes, and comment on girls' appearance and attractiveness in all-male settings. Yet, when discussing this culture of teenage boys' sex talk the interviewees always positioned themselves as having been passive and disapproving bystanders; Mark explained, for example, that 'there were some lads who talked about what they did with girls but I always thought that was totally wrong and I never, never did at all'.[30] Taken at their word, then, such testimonies seemingly imply a recruitment bias in my cohort of interviewees: maybe only men who feel they have nothing to fear volunteer to participate in oral history projects of this nature. Alternatively, this framing suggests that my interviewees were self-conscious of the ways in which any confession of participation may have been interpreted by a younger, female researcher. Again, however, I cannot know for sure because in the moment, it did not feel right to push them any further on these claims. As these experiences suggest, while there is a strong intellectual rationale for asking difficult questions, as a junior researcher sat across from a stranger who has given up their time to assist in your research, bearing this out in practice is more difficult.

Moreover, beyond the immediate issue of social awkwardness, making critical interventions during interviews can have consequences beyond the interview itself, potentially disrupting interviewees' sense of self and identity. Interviewing women of the post-war generation in 2014/2015 it was not uncommon for conversation to turn to the Rolf Harris trial (either in the interview or in the pre-/post-amble surrounding it). When asked what they thought/felt about the case, women's responses could be conflicted. Interviewees did not necessarily want to dismiss the claims made by Tonya Lee and other women regarding historic sexual assault, but the interviewees found the legal action difficult to reconcile with what they felt was simply 'accepted' conduct; in the words of one interviewee, 'I think we just kind of accepted things for what they were, y'know, 'cos that was just the way it was'.[31] Interviewees had their own experiences of being touched or 'hassled' in the workplace but seemed uncomfortable with the idea of being labelled as victims of sexual harassment.[32] Penny Summerfield and Lynn Abrams have described this tension as a form of 'discomposure' – critiques of historic gender relations widely articulated in the 2010s pushed against women's own personal narratives, creating new structures of interpretation that were not easily reconciled with the stories women were used to telling about themselves.[33]

In the same way, then, that the interview process may disrupt women's composed narratives of gender and workplace relations in the mid-twentieth century, there is potential for interviews to disrupt how men understand their role in past interactions and relationships. Interrogating, in person, the stories that male interviewees might tell about sexual encounters or relations with women has the potential to be deeply disturbing, casting them as the perpetrators (however unintentional) of violence. Simple-sounding questions such as 'How do you know she liked that?' or 'Did you ask for her consent?' are highly charged. As historians, is our job to confront our research subjects with new, potentially very damaging interpretations of their pasts? A tension exists between our desire to write histories that illuminate power relations and patriarchal structures in the past and our obligation to the individuals whose stories we rely on to compose those histories. If we allow narratives of coercion and privilege to go unchallenged, are we complicit in perpetuating (or even endorsing) a sexual politics to which we object? At the same time, however, how far are we prepared to rewrite individuals' histories, potentially irrevocably altering their sense of self, to pursue a political/intellectual agenda?

Crucially, these questions remain beyond the research encounter itself as we begin to interrogate our 'data'. There are potential problems surrounding the matter of informed consent, for example. If the chosen strategy in the interview was to allow men to recount their life stories uninterrupted, how far should researchers deviate from the given narrative in their write-up of this material? As academic historians tasked with analysing the past, at what point do our critical evaluations become unethical? In analysing men's encounters with women we may be inclined to designate certain behaviours as coercive in ways not identified by the men (and/or women) involved. Even if individuals are anonymised and their identities rendered unknowable to outsiders, there is every possibility that interviewees would recognise themselves. How would they feel to pick up a book and find themselves as the subject of discussions demonstrating predatory behaviour? If we did not intervene in these discussions and ask individuals to clarify, justify, or explain their positions, could they offer informed consent? Viewing the past through analytical frameworks is core to the work of historians but, in writing the history of the recent past, when many of our 'subjects' are still alive, and doing this work in the heightened climate of the #MeToo movement, the consequences of this work are highly charged. Echoing Monica Eileen Patterson's analysis of the Truth and Reconciliation Commission in South Africa, research into heterosexual masculinities is thus defined by 'ethical murk' in which the process of historicising past violence renders individuals vulnerable to new pain and trauma.[34]

Conclusion

Having 'unearthed' historic sexual abuse, Operation Yewtree and #MeToo turned a spotlight on the sexual cultures of the late twentieth century. These movements have served as important prompts to investigate the institutional structures and cultural norms that incubated, obscured, and, at times, challenged sexual abuse in the second half of the twentieth century.[35] For those moved by these campaigns, it is imperative that this work is prioritised.

As the previous discussion has shown, however, there is a potential 'cost' to this research; studying individuals' lives and those of their brothers, fathers, grandfathers, and friends in an attempt to understand a culture is not consequence free.

As the pioneers of women's history in the 1970s insisted, contemporary gender politics matter for historians. They not only form the context within which our work is consumed but they inform the research agendas we pursue and have tangible effects on our historical practice. As this reflection has suggested, the study of male heterosexuality pushes at the boundaries of existing paradigms of research ethics and integrity. It complicates understandings of researcher subjectivity and positionality and asks uncomfortable questions of our relative obligations to 'society' and our individual research subjects. As such, the preceding discussions have raised more questions than they have answered. Nevertheless, for myself at least, pulling at this thread has been a useful reminder that our work is not inevitable; all historical narratives are the result of choices made by researchers, and ethics are not absolute but always contextually contingent. That historicising male heterosexuality is fraught at this moment in time makes this process of choice-making more apparent and highlights the importance of treating 'good practice' as an evolving phenomenon that can take multiple forms and which must be constantly renegotiated.

Notes

1 Tarana Burke began Me Too in 2006; the hashtag #MeToo went viral in 2017 having been used by the actress Alyssa Milano.
2 Victoria Browne, 'The Persistence of Patriarchy: Operation Yewtree and the Return to 1970s Feminism', *Radical Philosophy*, 188 (2014), 9–19; Laura Bates, *Everyday Sexism: The Project That Inspired a Worldwide Movement* (London: Simon & Schuster, 2014).
3 Liz Kelly, *Surviving Sexual Violence* (Cambridge: Polity Press, 1988), chs 4–5.
4 Alison Phipps, 'The Fight against Sexual Violence', *Soundings: A Journal of Politics and Culture*, 71 (2019), 62–74.
5 The extent to which this shocked me is undoubtedly a product of my privileged position as a middle-class, white woman.
6 Hannah Charnock, 'Heterosexuality and Adolescent Masculinity in England, 1950–1980', paper delivered at the Twentieth Century Masculinities Conference, University of Birmingham, June 2018.
7 Kate Fisher, *Birth Control, Sex, and Marriage in Britain 1917–1960* (Oxford: Oxford University Press, 2006), 12–13.
8 *Ibid.*; Nan Alamilla Boyd, 'Who is the Subject? Queer Theory Meets Oral History', *Journal of the History of Sexuality*, 17:2 (2008), 177–189.

9 Paul Thompson, *The Voice of the Past: Oral History*, 3rd edn (Oxford: Oxford University Press, 2000), 8–9.
10 Sherna Berger Gluck, 'Has Feminist Oral History Lost Its Radical/Subversive Edge?', *Oral History*, 39:2 (2011), 63–72.
11 Leeds Revolutionary Feminists, *Love Your Enemy? The Debate between Heterosexual Feminism and Political Lesbianism* (London: Onlywomen Press, 1981), 6.
12 Elizabeth Wilson, *Only Half-Way to Paradise: Women in Post-war Britain, 1945–1968* (London: Tavistock, 1980); Lesley A. Hall, *Sex, Gender and Social Change in Britain since 1880*, 2nd edn (Basingstoke: Palgrave Macmillan, 2013).
13 Marcus Collins, *Modern Love: An Intimate History of Men and Women in Twentieth Century Britain* (London: Atlantic Books, 2003), chs 5–6.
14 *Jackie*, 31 December 1965; *Jackie*, 24 May 1975; *Honey*, July 1964; *Honey*, November 1968; *Petticoat*, 16 March 1968; *Petticoat*, 15 February 1969.
15 Len Barnett, *Sex and Teenagers in Love* (Nuffield: Denholm House Press, 1967), 23.
16 Rose Hacker, *The Opposite Sex* (London: Pan Books, 1967), 99.
17 Sara Ahmed and Jackie Stacey, 'Testimonial Cultures: An Introduction', *Cultural Values*, 5:1 (2001), 2.
18 Alison Phipps, 'Whose Personal Is More Political? Experience in Contemporary Feminist Politics', *Feminist Theory*, 17:3 (2016), 313.
19 Miroslav Vaněk, 'Those Who Prevailed and Those Who Were Replaced: Interviewing on Both Sides of a Conflict', in Donald A. Ritchie (ed.), *The Oxford Handbook of Oral History* (Oxford: Oxford University Press, 2011), 37–50; Wendy Lower, *Hitler's Furies: German Women in the Nazi Killing Fields* (London: Chatto & Windus, 2013); Steven K. Baum, *The Psychology of Genocide: Perpetrators, Bystanders, and Rescuers* (Cambridge: Cambridge University Press, 2008), ch. 3.
20 Carrie Hamilton, 'On Being a "Good" Interviewer: Empathy, Ethics and the Politics of Oral History', *Oral History*, 36:2 (2008), 35–43.
21 Kathleen M. Blee, 'Evidence, Empathy and Ethics: Lessons from Oral Histories of the Klan', in Robert Perks and Alistair Thomson (eds), *The Oral History Reader*, 3rd edn (London: Routledge, 2016), note 3.
22 Hamilton, 'On Being a "Good' Interviewer', 36.
23 Kenneth C. Barnes, *He and She* (Harmondsworth: Penguin, 1973), 54.
24 Julia Laite, 'The Emmet's Inch: Small History in a Digital Age', *Journal of Social History*, 53:4 (2020), 963–989; John H. Arnold, 'The Historian as Inquisitor: The Ethics of Interrogating Subaltern Voices', *Rethinking History*, 2:3 (1998), 379–386; Jill Lepore, 'Historians Who Love Too Much: Reflections on Microhistory and Biography', *Journal of American History*, 88:1 (2001), 129–144.
25 Tracey Loughran and Dawn Mannay (eds), *Emotion and the Researcher: Sites, Subjectivities, and Relationships* (Bingley: Emerald Publishing, 2018); Emily Robinson, 'Touching the Void: Affective History and the Impossible', *Rethinking History*, 14:4 (2010), 503–520.

26 Katie Barclay, 'Falling in Love with the Dead', *Rethinking History*, 22:4 (2018), 459–473; Matt Houlbrook, *The Prince of Tricksters: The Incredible True Story of Netley Lucas, Gentleman Crook* (Chicago: University of Chicago Press, 2016), 20–21.
27 Kathryn Anderson and Dana C. Jack, 'Learning to Listen: Interview Techniques and Analyses', in Sherna Berger Gluck and Daphne Patai (eds), *Women's Words: The Feminist Practice of Oral History* (New York: Routledge, 1991), 11.
28 Kristina Minister, 'A Feminist Frame for the Oral History Interview', in Gluck and Patai (eds), *Women's Words*, 36.
29 All interviewee names are pseudonyms. Oral history interview with David, April 2015.
30 Interview with Mark, April 2015. See also interviews with David, April 2015, and Ed, June 2015.
31 Interview with Sandra, February 2014.
32 Interviews with Jacqueline, July 2015, and Hazel, August 2015.
33 Penny Summerfield, 'Dis/composing the Subject: Intersubjectivities in Oral History', in Tess Cosslett, Celia Lury, and Penny Summerfield (eds), *Feminism and Autobiography: Texts, Theories, Methods* (London: Routledge, 2000), 91–106; Lynn Abrams, *Oral History Theory* (London: Routledge, 2010), ch. 4.
34 Monica Eileen Patterson, 'The Ethical Murk of Using Testimony in Oral History Research in South Africa', in Anna Sheftel and Stacey Zembrzycki (eds), *Oral History Off the Record: Toward an Ethnography of Practice* (Basingstoke: Palgrave Macmillan, 2013), 213.
35 See e.g. Adrian Bingham *et al.*'s work on child sex abuse: 'These Outrages Are Going On More than People Know', History & Policy, 26 February 2015, www.historyandpolicy.org/opinion-articles/articles/these-outrages-are-going-on-more-than-people-know (accessed 23 April 2019).

Conclusion: Histories, historians, and the politics of masculinity

Lucy Delap and John Tosh, in conversation

This conversation between Lucy Delap, John Tosh, and the three editors of this book took place via Zoom on 19 December 2020. We have edited the transcript for length and, where necessary, to clarify meaning and correct mistakes.

John Tosh: Looking back on the moment when *Manful Assertions* was being prepared, what strikes me now is the note of very confident polemic. We were very conscious of innovating, and when you're innovating you want to roll out your agenda as emphatically as possible.

Essentially, we were situated into two fields. First, we were very indebted to socialist feminism, which was the prime ideological influence on the book. Our reading was dominated by R. W. Connell and Lynne Segal. There was also some use of cultural theory, particularly in the work of Graham Dawson on Lawrence of Arabia in the British imaginary and Kelly Boyd on boys' story papers.[1] Fundamentally, however, this was a project which we thought of as in alliance with and in support of socialist feminism. This is not to say, of course, that feminists were necessarily terribly enthusiastic about it: this was a moment when the notion that histories of masculinity could be fundamentally supportive rather than undermining of feminism was relatively novel. We were very conscious of that. Our aim might be summarised as being to put flesh on the idea of the social and cultural construction of masculinity.

The second field which we were conscious of being part of one can label men's consciousness raising. When I first started mentioning the possibility of doing some kind of men's history in my men's group in 1984 there was a distinct lack of interest, despite the fact that my fellow members were mostly schoolteachers. But when I raised the idea with people in the men's anti-sexist movement more generally there was more interest, particularly in the idea of recognising historical 'heroes' as an inspiration for a men's anti-sexist project. We were concerned with following through that agenda in terms of owning men's oppression of women and considering how to relieve the burden on men of subscribing to a patriarchal social order which diminished – and which still does diminish – men.

Two more points about the volume's situation in more specific academic agendas. First: in so far as there was a pre-existing historiography in this area, it was largely identified with one book: *Manliness and Morality*, edited by James Walvin and Anthony Mangan. What characterised this book, despite its title, was an almost exclusive focus on writing the history of men as men, regardless of their relationships with anybody else.[2] One of the things that we were conscious of doing, then, was to explore the idea of the social environment when speaking primarily about men, while also understanding men in relation to women and others as well. Second: although there was a strong link with men's anti-sexism, the influence of practical activism on the contributors was relatively slight. Two of us had been in men's groups for some time: Peter Lewis, who wrote the final chapter on all-male educational institutions, and myself.[3] There wasn't a strong sense of mounting a politically attuned and ideologically astute venture. Instead, we were trying to address what we thought of as a niche audience, rather than a social movement.

The other academic context concerns one of the objectives which Michael Roper and I emphasised in the introduction: to desegregate masculinity from male dominance. What we meant is that we wanted to avoid going to the opposite extreme from *Manliness and Morality* and placing all our analytical interest in the notion of patriarchal masculinities. We needed to leave space for those aspects of masculinity which are not defined by that relationship with a subordinate sexual identity. For example, as I've come to understand more readily since then: the place of military commitment in notions of masculinity has very little to do with differentiation from women and much more to do with an exclusive obligation that society places on men to the point where they might have to consider themselves as being expendable. The other point we were conscious of regarding 'patriarchy', however, is one of its merits: it provides a kind of analytical umbrella for many of our concerns as historians.

Lucy Delap: It is great to hear that the anti-sexist men's movement is a context for your interest in histories of masculinity, and one that pervades beyond this collection. Other historians have been involved not necessarily in only writing about gender, but in bringing a commitment to thinking about gender as a pervasive yet specific kind of experience. James Hinton and Mike Roper, for example, were involved in men's groups and therapeutic groups, respectively. You mentioned that you weren't directly activists: I would say this is one of those moments where people often think about all sorts of things that they can do to get to a point of activism. Sometimes the journey turns out to be the activism itself. So, you publish the edited collection, and you think that that is going to make you activist. But it's bringing together the collection that means there's an enormous amount of learning for those involved. The process of writing *Manful Assertions* was activist in its orientation, even if it didn't involve marches and barricades.

The other historical context that we might bring in here – and I'm surprised you didn't mention it, John – is [Leonore Davidoff and Catherine Hall's] *Family Fortunes* as a unique founding text.[4] This is the gender history moment: *Family Fortunes* came out around the same time as Joan Scott's essay on gender as a category of historical analysis.[5] *Family Fortunes* is quite distinctively able to think about masculinity in a pluralised sense, in thinking about gender relationally, and (before the word is available) in working intersectionally through a sustained attention to how class and gender are co-produced. In one of her later essays Lee Davidoff said that there is more than one way of being a woman. There are, in fact, many gender positions, so a woman and lady are completely different. That is not a language that is born of what we might now think about in terms of non-binary or transgender, but nonetheless it helpfully pluralises gender. *Family Fortunes* is still a significant book that opened up those ideas of relationality and competing genders.

I went back to *Family Fortunes* and looked at patriarchy in their index: it is there, but interestingly they don't use it in the actual text. When an index entry takes you to page whatever, there is no mention of patriarchy. Instead, there are interesting discussions about how male authority was exerted in ways that weren't always workable: families are always at risk of breaking up and patriarchs are always at risk of not having their orders followed. In that sense, the category is about the instability of gender as much as it is about an agenda you might name patriarchal. There's an arm's-length relationship to patriarchy in *Family Fortunes*, then, which I think is useful and characterises a lot of subsequent work thinking about masculine power.

John Tosh: We were very aware of *Family Fortunes*, which was being published when our group began. But the direction we were taking is one that has passed out of currency now: we were thinking about the history of men as a kind of totality and worrying away about what the spine of such a history might be. That meant we were not as attentive as we could have been to the notion of a multiplicity of gender positions. The idea is in the book but was not pursued theoretically and doesn't feature in the introduction. If we're looking for a major distinction between the world of *Manful Assertions* and contemporary contexts for exploring histories of masculinity that would be key.

Matt Houlbrook: You talked about exploring what that project might look like as a group: approaching *Manful Assertions* as a practical project, then, was the book the outcome of a series of workshops?

John Tosh: It was a series of what I call kitchen seminars in my house in Haringey. We started at the end of the 1980s and by 1990 we were actively drafting the book or thinking about what might go in it. It was a sequence of fortnightly meetings where, to begin with, we were really acting as a reading group and looking at the theoretical writings I've mentioned already. Then we gradually moved more towards people trying out their own work with very short papers. That's when we began to think in terms of a volume, which was nowhere near our thoughts when we began. The group was a combination of research students who were preparing their PhDs and, as they did so – I'm thinking of someone like Pamela Walker – realising that there was a gender dimension which needed to be addressed in, for example, thinking about the Salvation Army. Then there were other people like myself, Peter Lewis, and Mike Roper, who had a more – I was going to say more strategic objective, but certainly one that was more concerned with getting something off the ground in terms of a new project with potential for expansion.

Ben Mechen: I'm interested in the liminality of that space: the idea of the kitchen seminar seems to sit somewhere between the academy and activism in the way that it mixes formality and informality. It seems like an interesting thing to think with in terms of the project's origins.

John Tosh: It felt quite creative, and as I took the first steps to get this off the ground I was very conscious of doing something different. I thought the combination of an academic set of people and this very different kind of context would work. There were other people who were part of this group for some or all the time, including Catherine Hall, who came to a couple of meetings. We were drawing on a wider range of expertise than simply those who ended up contributing to the volume.

Matt Houlbrook: It feels like something very much of its moment, born out of the consciousness-raising groups of women's liberation, that kind of – not ad hoc but semi-academic structure. Comparing that to the steps that have shaped *this* project, it's striking how history has become hyper-professionalised: our research is bound up with funding applications, conferences, outputs, and justifying our existence. That the blurring of boundaries you mention was still possible in the late 1980s, though, seems to be intellectually and politically productive with *Manful Assertions*.

But I wanted to think critically about some of the categories that are central to *Manful Assertions*. We've talked about patriarchy and the social and cultural construction of gender, but I'm also interested in how you came to identify 'masculinity' itself as a category that might have a history. Could you say more about the keywords you were thinking with – where they came from and why they seemed intellectual or politically useful at that moment?

John Tosh: Masculinity seemed to us to be the only term which opened the way to deconstructing what it's like to be a man in terms of gender. Our initial stimulus for this move was a meeting of the theoretical branch of the British Sociological Association in Birmingham in 1987, which several historians attended. Our terminology was strongly influenced by sociological takes on masculinity. We had to work out what distinguishes manliness from masculinity or manhood. Those discussions were important because we wanted to be crystal clear about our analytical categories and how they linked together. Patriarchy was there throughout our discussions, with a doubled significance. On the one hand, it was a way of thinking more productively about men's role in the oppression of women and in terms of the structures they were inhabiting. On the other hand, it signalled the significance of being involved in a patriarchal relationship or patriarchal expectations on definitions of masculinity and male subjectivities.

Lucy Delap: As John was speaking, I was thinking about the continuities and different avenues that open through *Manful Assertions*. Since the book was published scholars have been thinking about empire or religion as sites for practising and contesting masculinity. It is easy to say, 'why wasn't this or that included?' What *is* now striking, however, is the absence of sexuality. Whether that's minority sexualities or 'heterosexuality', neither seem to be there in a very powerful way. Perhaps this is one of the areas where the literature has been transformed over the past thirty years.

John Tosh: That's a very good question. It certainly wasn't outside our discussions. I think it just happened that it didn't situate itself in the centre of the concerns people brought to the group. The group wasn't constituted in terms of a wish to cover certain areas but was simply composed of people who had some interest in the field of masculinity. Addressing this issue directly is also one of the ways in which the current volume is so excellent. It is interesting, though, that some of the topics covered in *Manful Assertions* could have addressed sexuality more directly: Norma Clarke's essay on Carlyle and Graham Dawson's discussion of T. E. Lawrence, for example.

Ben Mechen: One way that sexuality does enter *Manful Assertions*, though, is in your opening positioning of the book. The introduction talks about women's history, socialist feminism, and the men's movement – but you also acknowledge the influence of gay history, as you put it. Could you explain more about which texts you were speaking to?

John Tosh: We were speaking to Jeffrey Weeks and Alan Bray, who provided a model of what we should be aiming for precisely because the notion of a gay identity was being conceptualised through its relationship to patriarchy and an expansive definition of the social context in which it should be understood, as opposed to earlier treatments of sexuality, which saw it as a kind of pathology or marginal. There were several interventions that Weeks, for example, made which had wider resonance for how sexuality should be addressed beyond the immediate scope of gay history.[6]

Matt Houlbrook: Like Lucy, I was struck by the absence of sexuality within the substantive body of the book. But what I didn't remember from my first reading was how central that acknowledgement of Weeks and Bray and others was in your introduction. As someone trained in a PhD programme at the University of Essex, that made me think back to Mary McIntosh and 'The Homosexual Role', Weeks's early work, Ken Plummer's work, and what you were talking about around the social, cultural, and historical construction of masculinity. And that was where I saw the overlap in the idea of the construction of identities and categories.[7]

I want to come back to this idea of masculinity as a term that did the critical work of problematising men's identities and roles. Rereading *Manful Assertions* now the power and pervasiveness of ideas derived from psychoanalysis and psychoanalytic histories is striking. Does this mean that masculinity signifies both the problematisation of men's identities and an attribute of personality that men possessed? Or were you conceiving of masculinity as a subjective or emotional formation? I'm trying to think through the relationship between *Manful Assertions* and more recent histories of the emotions and subjectivity by scholars like Claire Langhamer.

John Tosh: These are ways of thinking historically which have been much more clearly and theoretically stated in the last twenty years. They were not absent from *Manful Assertions*, but there wasn't a clear-cut language in which they could be expressed. One of the points we made in the introduction, building on Mike's interests, was the crucial importance of maintaining ideas of subjectivity in an analysis which might seem unduly structurally determined by men's social position.

Lucy Delap: One reason that gender history has been such a thriving field is that you were formulating this project around that moment of the linguistic turn and the growing predominance of cultural history. Gender history kept open a mode of doing history where cultural representations and subjective experiences – the living of the changes, if you like – remained very much in dialogue. Perhaps that again comes back to the anti-sexist men's movement, which was always about what men do (and specifically what did they do to women) as well as the inner experience of being a man or living patriarchy. I like how cultural history was always set alongside other ways of addressing these questions, which has been one of the continued strengths of gender history.

John Tosh: I would agree with that. I've been fighting my own particular campaign about the boundaries between social and cultural history for a long time. One of the things that seems really rewarding is when there wasn't this compulsion on the part of writers to define themselves in relation to one or the other. It's actually – I don't want to use the term 'blurring' because that sounds intellectually lazy – in the meeting ground between the cultural and the social and psychological or subjective that the most productive analysis emerges. This means that our understanding of these passages needs to be kept clean and tidy.

Matt Houlbrook: There's a striking moment in the mid-1980s when suddenly the use of the term 'masculinity' or 'crisis of masculinity' takes off. What might this tell us? At the very least, that *Manful Assertions* was part of the scholarly output that sustained the emergence of 'masculinity' as a commonplace term in public life and popular culture?

John Tosh: There's a chronological answer: in the mid- to late 1980s a lot is happening in which men concern themselves for good or for ill with what's happening on the other side of the gender divide. This is when Robert Bly is making his initial impact, when fathers' rights organisations emerge, and when we see the maturation of the gay rights movement and its relationship to history and sociology. Writing the history of masculinity was a very small part of that fusion of points of view that raised masculinity as an issue.[8]

Lucy Delap: I would add the miners' strike [of 1984–1985], which was a very powerful site for thinking about different kinds of masculinity and experiences of deindustrialisation and unemployment, and which generated a lot of discussion about whether men change as the economy changes.

Katie Jones: This idea is echoed in my analysis of the Family Planning Association's [FPA] 'Men Too' campaign in the mid-1980s. It is striking that this discussion of masculinity or masculinity in crisis really takes off around 1984–1985, which is when the FPA start their campaign to encourage young men to take responsibility for contraception, and act more responsibly in their sexual encounters and relationships.

Matt Houlbrook: So, we can see how a category moves between fields of knowledge, as 'masculinity' becomes increasingly central to thinking about men's lives and identities through the work of the men's consciousness movement and the men's movement, but also through the work of NGOs, social surveys, family planning organisations, and the popular media.

Can we think about our current historical conjuncture in the same terms we've approached the moment of *Manful Assertions*? We have all worked in histories of masculinity over the past decade and participated in the discussions feeding into this volume. Now we've had a chance to take stock of the project, what strikes you about the practice and politics of what we're doing right now?

Lucy Delap: I'm tempted to think historically here and trace the journey between 1991, when *Manful Assertions* comes out, and now. Here I'm thinking about the ebbing prominence of the anti-sexist men's movement, but also how a lot of hopes for change were pinned on the incoming Labour Party, the idea of Neil Kinnock or Tony Blair as 'new men', for example. There's a very interesting interview with Tony Blair in *New Statesman* where they asked him and other politicians: 'What's the first thing you think about when you get up in the morning?' and Blair says: 'Oh, I wonder if my daughter's nappy needs changing.' That's clearly staking a claim to be a new man.

But the experience of New Labour in power was very different. The reality that followed that moment of optimism when all those women were elected was that power was exercised by an increasingly isolated clique of macho men and a laddish New Labour culture which went alongside these aggressive deregulation and pro-market policies that left women experiencing impoverishment. There is a real loss of hope there, which was echoed by the experience of popular culture, particularly through the rise of different categories of laddish masculinity and the lack of any clear realisation of masculinity as a sense that boys growing up have a wider variety of role models and normative ways of presenting themselves. Increasingly, however, we see that even though there are geeks and nerds and hipsters and all these different ways of being a man, nothing much has changed. Proliferating masculinities don't bring in their train what was hoped, which is a more respectful and less scripted way of living gender.

Thinking about where we are today, then: there's been a lessening of optimism that lifestyle changes or central government can deliver anything in terms of changing the gender order. Instead, I see more of a sense of needing to recapture older activist repertoires of marches, campaigning, hashtag activism, or traditional campaigns around period poverty, #MeToo, or Everyday Sexism, or the rise of the Women's Equality Party as an attempt to challenge a status quo in which formal party politics has not taken us where we want to be. We are at a moment where there is a resurgent movement for gender justice. At the same time there are enormous hindering debates going on about non-binary gender. Despite that, there seems to be a renewed impetus towards campaigning that might allow us to reconnect our histories with the activist sensibilities that gave rise to *Manful Assertions* and histories of masculinity. My students are much more politically committed than they were ten years ago, for example, and are way ahead of me in their politics. They see themselves as changemakers, and they're doing history because they want to give a history to change. In that sense, I'm optimistic about what might happen, though I recognise that there have been a lot of cul-de-sacs in this question of problematising masculinity and enabling multiple ways of being a man.

Matt Houlbrook: We might come back to that question of reconnection and think about what we might do as historians and activists to reconnect our histories with the activist impulse and powerful sense of civic responsibility we see in a younger generation of students.

John Tosh: I am struck that the men's anti-sexist movement has disappeared. It was a very small set up, but at least it took the idea that there was not only a common interest but a common obligation that men had in terms of how they behave and treated the other sex. That connects with another concern about how activism is focused on particular social groups, some of which has to do with identity politics. One of the dangers is that we end up with a range of histories, which deal with one take on the social order, but lose sight of – not what unites people, but how those experiences or relationships to the social world are often held in common. That's what *Manful Assertions* had in mind, but it raises questions about the case study approach which has become central to histories of masculinity.

Matt Houlbrook: You're right that the proliferation of histories and politics has perhaps come at the expense of dismantling those overall structures of male dominance or patriarchy. What have been the implications of this political shift for the development of the field, though? We might think about how the field has changed since *Manful Assertions* or how future generations of scholars might do things differently.

John Tosh: Recent work underscores how there is no reason why there should be any limit to the diversity of histories that we write. Think about the relationship between masculinity and race or ethnic identity – addressed through contributions to this volume by Jonathan Saha on Burma and Hilary Buxton on West Indian service people experiencing disability in Britain. While previous scholarship might have sought to think about racing masculinity, it often focused on articulations of masculinities in a colonial setting. That is a vital project, but what is equally important are those encounters within metropolitan Britain. Buxton's work explores what happens to soldiers from the Caribbean when they end up in hospital in Liverpool. This case study sits right at the cutting edge of encounters between racially diverse groups in Britain itself, going beyond Graham Dawson's work on Lawrence of Arabia, interactions between different ethnic communities in Arabia, and their cultural and political mediation in Britain.

Lucy Delap: There are now wonderful histories of race and racial encounters by scholars like Kenetta Hammond Perry, Rob Waters, and Kieran Connell, all of whom are attentive to gender.[9] This comes back to one of our initial questions, about the extent to which gender history or histories of masculinity stand alone as a field. I would say that a lot of the productive work that gender is doing is not as a cordoned-off field, but through being routinely written into histories like Connell's account of Dread and Rasta culture in 1980s Handsworth and the relationship between these kinds of macho masculinities and women's ability to feel at home in those subcultures. The work of whiteness is also worth drawing out. It has been useful to think about whiteness as a racial category that works to stabilise masculinity. As Jonathan Saha has shown, whiteness does an enormous amount of work in colonial governance to establish different hierarchies and make certain things seem like colonial common sense.

To come back to our point about the politics of this field: one interesting way in which Black Lives Matter has played out in Britain is in making prominent this category of white ally-ship. While these debates have encouraged people to embrace the idea of ally-ship, they have also drawn attention to the idea's limits, and how it can be tokenistic and exhausting for people of colour to be with so-called white allies but find that ally-ship doesn't really change anything. That echoes debates about the men's anti-sexist movement, which was both welcomed in socialist feminist circles and recognised as an exhausting distraction for women who were being asked to pay attention to men. The political opportunities offered by those moments of ally-ship mean that there is a lot of resonance between today and 1990.

Matt Houlbrook: This takes us back to your earlier point about reconnection, Lucy. Something that's been implicit in our conversation is how much of the progressive hope of the late 1980s has been lost through the political and economic shifts of the past three decades. I wonder, though, if really what we're saying is that historians have stopped that work – that we have not done enough to reconnect our histories with the political contexts or activist groups for whom they might be important. What might historians of masculinity do to recapture the progressive energy that characterised *Manful Assertions*?

Lucy Delap: The impact agenda was never intended to be about radical history, clearly, but it has sometimes been used against the grain to authorise and found ways of reaching beyond the academy that *do* have radical potential. It will be interesting to look at the different ways in which impact is framed in the current REF [Research Excellence Framework]. As opposed to previous incarnations, which had a lot of quite conventional 'we'll talk to ministers' approaches, I suspect this REF will include a much wider range of impact case studies.

Another thought about activist history is to acknowledge that while we might need to get out of the academy, the academy is itself political terrain. Higher education has been so enrolled into these systems of marketisation and austerity, whether that's manifested through the precarity of early career scholars, students paying high tuition fees, international students being treated as cash cows, that politics infuses higher education through issues around gender justice, race justice, thinking about homophobia and transphobia, and so on. We can do activist politics in our institutions, disciplines, and profession as well as acknowledging how we need to connect beyond that.

Matt Houlbrook: I have been struck by how the Royal Historical Society has taken a lead in driving forward progressive political change through their reports on gender, race, and ethnicity, and – most recently – LGBTQI histories and historians. As well as the reflective way in which they have approached these issues, it has been impressive to see how their attention has been on both the discipline and the profession – histories and historians. It has been our professional organisation that (alongside other initiatives) has taken challenging or reworking structures of inequality within our institutions as its remit.

Katie Jones: I have been thinking about how I can use my project to create change. For example, part of my work with Tracey Loughran's Body, Self, and Family project on the history of women's health and well-being involves designing an educational activity for use in schools that allows young boys to engage with sources on sexual health and responsibility from the 1980s and inviting them to think critically about the impact of gender norms on their emotional health and well-being.

Ben Mechen: As Lucy said, teaching is also a form of political engagement, and history offers a political education to students. Teaching and doing gender history or histories of masculinity within a university, I am still struck by the utility that students find in approaching these fields for the first time in making sense of their own lives and the world around them. It is also striking how many of the contributions to this volume are rooted in reclaiming feminist history as an endeavour. Feminist politics and a feminist reflexivity about our discipline and institutions are the starting point for many of our contributors, most obviously those reflections by Hannah Charnock and Charlotte Riley. That means the book feels like a product of the post-#MeToo/Everyday Sexism moment and the resurgence of feminism in the social media age.

Lucy Delap: That is exactly where I feel like I've learned as much from my students as they have from me. Thinking about Everyday Sexism and agendas around neurodiversity shaped how I'm thinking about trans issues and how prominent young voices have been in pushing for non-binary gender to be taken seriously. In thinking about race, Black Lives Matter, and decolonising the curriculum, similarly, the impetus is coming from people at undergraduate or even school level. That is why it's so important that we don't think that we need to get out of institutions to effect change.

John Tosh: It is interesting to compare *Manful Assertions* and this volume. Both are structured around case studies. In terms of content or political direction, however, those case studies are very different. The bigger question is about what these different cases are offering us, how they work together, how they might form part of a broader inquiry. What can we do to create a setting for those discussions which will lead to a more systematic and holistic understanding of histories of masculinity in modern and contemporary Britain?

Matt Houlbrook: Lucy challenged us to think about reconnection, but another way of phrasing that idea, John, would be to think about reintegration: looking at the development and diversification of histories of masculinity over the past three decades, what is the whole that can be more than the sum of these parts? In part we're talking about the limits of the edited collection of essays as an academic form, but are we also implying fragmentation is a particular problem for this field?

Lucy Delap: Studying masculinity is most successfully done in the doing. The field is most compelling at those intersections where different stories come together. Possibly the most compelling and challenging work, though, is recent literature that does not take the binary of gender for granted but asks instead if (and how) masculinity becomes a workable category at a particular historical moment. If pushed on where are we going, I would focus on absorbing the contributions made by Adrian Kane-Galbraith. That essay pushes us to ask how people do transgender and how our provisional stabilisation of gender animates certain historical moments. I find it energising to think through the implications of taking gender seriously as a performance which comes in different kinds of sexual difference. Although we have had that framing since Judith Butler's work, we haven't worked through its implications for understanding the past.[10]

Matt Houlbrook: Adrian's piece is the key that unlocks this volume, and reading it made me think differently about the project and the threads running through it. Now I would emphasise the importance of engaging in the work of radical critique you have identified, Lucy. The premise is simple yet far-reaching: men, like masculinity, are made, and those processes of making are embedded in wider social, cultural, economic, political, and psychic formations. Paying attention to those processes might also provide a way to move from histories of masculinity back out to some of the bigger debates in the modern and contemporary British field.

John Tosh: Thinking about histories of men and mental health would be extraordinarily productive, then, not least because it brings together issues around the intersection between subjectivity and social, cultural, and economic conditions. One way to understand the slump of the 1930s, for example, is through the spike of male suicides – men who were clearly giving up on life when there was no means of supporting it. There are classic works that touch on this issue – Olive Anderson, for example – but there is a huge amount more to be done.[11]

Katie Jones: I have been thinking about this recently through a new project on men's health in modern Britain, which will historicise concerns over men's mental, sexual, and emotional health. All these aspects become big concerns for NGOs in the 1980s as more holistic ideas about men's well-being emerge.

Lucy Delap: We might add to that work on the relationship between masculinities and disabilities. I'm working on learning disabilities and the labour market, for example. But histories of disability also underscore the importance understanding the negotiations between men and the state, which is where Kane-Galbraith and Jessica Meyer have found such rich sources. Thinking about men's experiences of different kinds of institutions – the immigration system or the growth of Britain's prison population since the 1980s – suggests there is more work to do exploring the relationship between the modern state and gender order.

Ben Mechen: This collection comes out of a particular moment around Trump, Brexit, the men's rights movement, #MeToo, and pressing debates around male violence and women's safety. Perhaps it reflects a place of pessimism around the effects of masculinity on contemporary politics, society, and culture. With the COVID-19 pandemic, the end of Trump's term as president, and the finalisation of Brexit it will be interesting to see if this moment is passing. The collision of home and working lives, for example, might be reshaping conversations around the family and the burdens of different kinds of labour within and without the home. If this is a point of transition between one political moment and another, will we begin to see new conversations around masculinity and its politics emerging?

Lucy Delap: The fact that this project has been prolonged has made it more interesting. From our first meeting through to this conversation, the pace and scale of social, cultural, economic, and political change has been extraordinary. We might no longer recognise the world we are in. Our experiences of Trump and the wider emergence of right-wing populism might not so easily be put aside. What we might take away from that experience, however, is the loss of any residual wishful sensibilities that somehow things are just going to get better – that we can look to the past and see the resurgence of men's rights in the 1980s while consoling ourselves that somehow things will inevitably get better. My students don't invest in that progressive narrative anymore. I think ten years ago they would say, 'yeah, yeah, things are getting better.' Now, though, economic and environmental crises have suggested to them that progress is no longer inevitable – that change needs work. That's a useful prompt for continued work on histories of masculinity.

Notes

1 Graham Dawson, 'The Blond Bedouin: Lawrence of Arabia, Imperial Adventure, and the Imagining of English-British Masculinity', in Michael Roper and John Tosh (eds), *Manful Assertions: Masculinities in Britain since 1800* (London: Routledge, 1991), 113–144; Kelly Boyd, 'Knowing Your Place: The Tensions of Manliness in Boys' Story Papers, 1918–39', in Roper and Tosh (eds), *Manful Assertions*, 145–166.

2 J. A. Mangan and James Walvin (eds), *Manliness and Morality: Middle-Class Masculinity in Britain and American, 1800–1940* (Manchester: Manchester University Press, 1991).

3 Peter M. Lewis, 'Mummy, Matron, and the Maids: Feminine Presence and Absence in Male Institutions, 1934–63', in Roper and Tosh (eds), *Manful Assertions*, 168–189.

4 Leonore Davidoff and Catherine Hall, *Family Fortunes: Men and Women of the English Middle Class* (London: Routledge, 1987).

5 Joan Scott, 'Gender: A Useful Category of Historical Analysis', *American Historical Review*, 91:5 (1986), 1053–1075.

6 Jeffrey Weeks, *Coming Out: Homosexual Politics in Britain from the Nineteenth Century to the Present* (London: Quartet Books, 1977); Alan Bray, *Homosexuality in Renaissance England* (London: Gay Men's Press, 1982).

7 Mary McIntosh, 'The Homosexual Role', *Social Problems*, 16:2 (1968), 182–192; Kenneth Plummer (ed.), *The Making of the Modern Homosexual* (London: Hutchinson, 1981).

8 Robert Bly, *Iron John: A Book about Men* (Shaftesbury: Element, 1990).

9 Kennetta Hammond Perry, *London Is the Place for Me: Black Britons, Citizenship, and the Politics of Race* (New York: Oxford University Press, 2016); Rob Waters, *Thinking Black: Britain, 1964–1985* (Berkeley: University of California Press, 2019); Kieran Connell, *Black Handsworth: Race in 1980s Britain* (Berkeley: University of California Press, 2019).

10 Judith Butler, *Gender Trouble: Feminism and the Subversion of Identity* (New York: Routledge, 1990); Judith Butler, *Bodies That Matter: On the Discursive Limits of 'Sex'* (New York: Routledge, 1993).
11 Olive Anderson, *Suicide in Victorian and Edward England* (Oxford: Clarendon Press, 1987).

Index

Abbott, D. H. 52–53, 57, 60
African Telegraph 98–101, 103–104
agency 61, 68, 122, 203, 229, 232, 235, 255, 292
  male 18–19, 126, 198–199, 240, 292
ambiguity 21, 229, 233, 292
anti-sexist men's movement 5–6, 27, 178, 263, 299–300, 304, 306–308
anxiety 4, 13, 18–20, 23, 50, 78, 95, 97, 113, 158, 163–165, 167, 169, 183, 214, 231
apprenticeships 145, 182
authenticity 17, 71–72, 129, 168, 183, 221, 273
authorising institutions 161, 163–164
Avery family 233, 239–240
Ayers, Pat 19, 24, 189–207

behaviour
  male 6, 28, 50–51, 70, 80, 114–115, 137, 163–164, 183, 195, 202–203, 214, 295
  sexual 270, 272–278, 282, 288
Belmont Road Auxiliary Hospital, Liverpool 91, 96–103
Bengali Hindu middle classes 67, 69
biography 22, 51, 69, 141, 211–212
biosociality 101–103
Birchwood family 241
Birkett, James 253, 256, 258
birth certificates 21, 49–50, 52, 56, 60
Black, Alistair 210–211, 221

Black
  embodiment 22, 91, 93
  masculinity 89, 93, 95, 104
  servicemen 22, 88–105
Black Lives Matter 308, 310
Blackness 88–105
Bobbin Works, Garston 192, 196–197
Bourke, Joanna 89, 100
bravery 12, 90, 95, 99, 101, 165, 168, 214
  see also courage
breadwinner role 11–12, 19, 21–22, 50, 54–55, 57, 60, 62, 89, 137, 165–167, 169, 193, 195, 200, 213, 240
Brexit 16, 151, 311
British West Indies Regiment 22, 88, 90–101, 104
Brown, Richard Kirk 259, 260
Bryant & May 24, 191
Burgoyne, Frank 213, 219
Butler, Judith 310
Buxton, Hilary 7, 10–11, 21–22, 25, 88–110, 307
BWIR *see* British West Indies Regiment

camaraderie 90, 99, 145, 150–151
Carden-Coyne, Ana 94, 97, 122
Carlyle, Thomas 214, 220–221, 303
change
  cultural 15, 17, 148, 162, 171, 228, 254, 311
  in masculinities 2, 4, 9–11, 14, 16–17, 20, 128, 136, 140, 142, 159, 162, 165, 179–180, 182–183, 306
  political 15, 127–128, 255, 309, 311

sex 21, 49–54, 57, 59
social 3, 15, 58, 127, 143, 148, 158, 161, 221, 228, 243, 311
Chan-Toon 21–22, 70–71, 76–81
see also Mabel Cosgrave
Charnock, Hannah 8, 27–28, 288–298, 309
Church
  as authorising institution 161, 163–164
  importance for socialisation 200
citation practices 27, 116
citizenship 21–22, 49–50, 52, 57–58, 61–62, 81, 90, 234–235
class
  consciousness 167, 236–239
  differences 2, 12, 23, 74, 102, 136, 236–237, 250
  gender and 5, 14, 141, 189, 301
  hierarchies 7–8, 67, 229, 241
  histories of 139–140, 171
  identities 24, 136, 139, 148, 189, 201, 235–238
  solidarities 12, 24, 197, 228
  status 75, 81, 213, 241–242
classes
  middle 24, 67, 69, 123, 127, 160–162, 167–168, 178, 208, 213–215, 218, 220, 229, 237, 239–242, 270, 273
  upper 71, 137, 214, 218, 229, 242
  working 13, 24, 113, 136–151, 159, 161–162, 166–167, 170, 181, 192, 198–199, 201, 208, 211, 213, 217, 219–221, 229, 235–242, 271
Cohen, Deborah 123, 230
Collins, F. M. 53, 56, 57, 60
Colonial Masculinity 67, 69
Comfort, Alex 258, 260, 263
Committee on Obscenity and Film Censorship 253–259, 262–264
communication communities 23, 161–163, 166, 168, 171
community
  colonised 68–69
  communication 23, 161–163, 166, 168, 171
  emotional 12, 141–142, 147–151
  gay 269–270, 279, 282, 290
  local 19, 100, 137, 141, 189–193, 195–197, 199–202
  occupational 137, 140–141, 147–148, 150, 182, 196, 201
  sense of 102, 140–141
condoms
  commodification of 262–263, 269
  use 26, 270–271, 273–282
  see also safer sex
Connell, R. W. 9, 137, 159, 178, 184, 299
conscientious objectors 162, 170
consciousness raising 27, 263, 299–300, 302, 305
consumerism 16, 166, 228, 262
contraception 271, 305
Cosgrave, Mabel 21, 70–76, 79–81
  see also Chan-Toon
courage 162, 165, 183, 214
  see also bravery
Coverley family 231–232, 240–241
Cowell, Peter 209, 217
Coxon, Tony 271–273
crisis of masculinity 3, 9, 14–15, 17, 23, 29, 77, 148, 150–151, 158–160, 162–164, 166–171, 180–181, 184, 221, 256–257, 264, 305
cultural
  activities 143, 146, 200
  change 15, 17, 148, 162, 171, 228, 254, 311
  contestation 159–160, 163–164
  history 3, 11, 20, 122, 124–125, 127, 139, 165, 179, 299, 304–305
  models 19, 159–160, 162, 164, 167
  scripts 19, 228–229
culture
  consumer 13, 15, 17, 19
  of masculinity 8, 14, 27
  norms 159, 161, 163, 169, 171, 215, 230, 262, 291–292, 295
  patriarchal 27, 80, 291
  popular 17, 191, 254–255, 305–306

Index

culture (*cont.*)
  sexual 26, 262–263, 270, 289–292, 295
  work 137–140, 143, 149–150, 182
Curd family 231, 235–237

Davidoff, Leonore 28, 167, 178, 249–250, 301
Dawson, Graham 299, 303, 308
deindustrialisation 14, 23, 137, 140, 147, 151, 235, 305
Delap, Lucy 4, 7, 16, 29, 161, 180, 230, 250, 263, 300–301, 303–306, 308–312
Demeritte, John 88–89, 91, 96, 98, 100–103
Department of Health and Social Security 60, 272–273
Deslandes, Paul 257, 260
DHSS *see* Department of Health and Social Security
disability 62
  Black experience of 22, 88–92, 94–104, 307
  First World War and 22, 25, 88–92, 94–104, 122–124, 126, 128–131, 166
  histories of 122, 126–127, 171, 311
  images of 91, 93–95, 100–101, 103–104
  masculinity and 89, 91, 96, 100, 122, 124, 131, 311
  pensions 21–22, 54, 103, 121–132
  white experience of 88–89, 94, 99
DIY *see* do-it-yourself
docklands 24, 189–191, 194–199, 202
do-it-yourself 232–233
domesticity 20, 73, 129, 137, 150, 181
  male 20, 183, 192, 231–232
Domney, John 4, 18–20

education 19, 24–25, 81, 127, 139, 142–143, 146, 167, 213, 219–220, 228, 230, 235–236, 239, 289, 309
  female 76–77
  health 269, 282

  male 3, 159, 165, 167, 300
  sex 253, 259, 288, 309
embodiment 25
  Black 22, 91, 93
  male 11, 21, 51, 54, 70, 80–81
  processes of 14, 22, 68
emigration 128–131
emotional
  bonds 12, 20, 23, 26, 148, 270–271, 281
  communities 12, 141–142, 147–151
  labour 114, 116, 215
emotions
  history of 17, 70, 270, 304
  in gay relationships 270–271, 277, 279–282
employment 12, 24, 52–53, 61, 75, 151, 190, 230
  male 181–182, 190–191, 193–200, 232
  masculinity and 132, 194–197
  female 116, 167, 190–191, 193, 196, 200, 232, 233
  see also unemployment; work
everyday life 10, 17–18, 136, 138, 148, 150, 229
Everyday Sexism Project 6, 164, 288, 306, 309–310

family
  conceptualisation of 2, 11, 69–70, 242
  extended 215–217, 239
  finances 189, 193, 200, 202, 240
  life 12, 22, 55, 137, 203, 228–243
  masculinity and 20, 24, 192, 231
  nuclear 54–55, 229–230, 232, 234
  planning 263, 305
  structures 79, 131, 158, 170, 230–231, 234, 240
Family Fortunes 249, 301
fashion 14, 148–150
fatherhood 127, 131–132, 192–193, 200, 229
fathers 20, 25, 127, 131–132, 150, 165, 170, 192, 219, 221, 228–243, 296, 305

femininity 14, 62, 73–75, 181, 210, 214, 219, 221
feminism 6, 26–27, 54, 77, 115, 164, 169, 178–179, 181, 231, 299, 303, 308–309
  first-wave 74–75
  pornography and 256–258, 262–264, 291
  second-wave 14, 113, 184
  third-wave 3
feminist histories 6–7, 28–29, 116, 127, 249, 290–291, 293, 309
First World War
  Black servicemen 88–104
  disability from 88–104, 121–132, 166
  histories of 89–90, 122
  masculinity and 90–91, 130, 158, 162, 167–168, 192
  pension records 121–122, 124–126, 128–132
  white servicemen 90–92, 96–97, 100–102, 104
  see also conscientious objectors
Fisher, Kate 232, 290
Foskett, Edward 217–218
Foucault, Michel 179–180
fucking see anal sex

Gagen, Wendy 89, 123
Gardner, Peter 259, 261–262
Garston 190–203
gay
  community 151, 269–270, 279, 282, 290
  history 4, 6–7, 179, 272, 303–304, 309
  identity 282, 304
  liberation 7, 14, 158, 178, 261–262
  marriage 170
  masculinities 261, 269, 271, 275
  pornography 260–261
  rights movement 305
  sexual cultures 26, 269–283
  see also homosexuality
gender
  class and 5, 14, 141, 189, 301
  dysphoria 58–59

hierarchies 8, 92
history 4, 6, 17, 25, 28–29, 127, 140, 159, 163, 178, 183–184, 249–250, 301, 304–305, 308–309
identities 2, 5, 24, 58–59, 101–102, 123, 132, 138, 141, 148, 167, 189, 192, 249
inequalities 4, 6, 22–23, 26, 115
non-binary 301, 306, 310
norms 13, 94, 123, 165, 257, 309
order 5, 9, 14, 16, 23, 27, 158–160, 171, 231–232, 262, 306, 311
performances 19, 21, 49, 51, 53, 67, 69, 80–81, 130, 138, 159, 162–165, 167–169, 171, 231
politics 4, 9, 14, 26, 28, 73, 167, 256, 288–289, 296
power and 9, 12, 27–28
reassignment 25, 58–59
relations 7–8, 27, 70, 77, 123, 181, 203, 231, 235, 291, 294
roles 233–234, 242
sex and 51, 58–59
General Register Office 49, 52, 58
gentlemanliness 19, 70, 159, 160, 162, 165–168, 242
Gladstone, William 218, 220
Goldthorpe, John 232, 235, 239
Goss, Charles 208, 215
Griffin, Ben 9, 15, 19, 22–23, 137–138, 158–171, 202
GRO see General Register Office

Hadfields, Sheffield 139, 140
Haggerston, William, librarian 208, 217
Hall, Catherine 69, 167, 178, 249, 301–302
Hall, Richard 16, 20, 24–25, 228–243
health
  education 269, 282
  men's 137, 219, 311
  mental 3, 6, 19, 159, 234–235, 242, 311
  sexual 127, 272, 309, 311
Henry family 241–242

318 *Index*

heroism 15, 22, 24, 89–91, 93, 95, 97, 100–101, 103–104, 146, 160, 162, 165, 208–209, 214–221
heteronormativity 27, 131, 137, 234, 262–263
heterosexuality 221, 230–231, 257, 271, 281, 288–290, 292–293, 295–296, 303
hierarchies
 class 7–8, 67, 229, 241
 gender 8, 92
 of masculinities 104, 127, 140, 159–162, 168–169
 occupational 213, 215
 racial 7–8, 92, 102
 of sexualities 7–8, 159
 social 240–241
history/ies
 of class 139–140, 171
 cultural 3, 11, 20, 122, 124–125, 127, 139, 165, 179, 299, 304–305
 of disability 122, 126–127, 171, 311
 of emotions 17, 70, 270, 304
 feminist 6–7, 28–29, 116, 127, 249, 290–291, 293, 309
 gay 4, 6–7, 179, 272, 303–304, 309
 gender 4, 6, 17, 25, 28–29, 127, 140, 159, 163, 178, 183–184, 249–250, 301, 304–305, 308–309
 of masculinities 3–8, 11, 14–15, 18, 26–27, 61, 67–69, 90, 104–105, 122, 124, 136, 158–159, 171, 178–185, 249–250, 288, 290, 299–301, 303, 305
 oral 11, 20, 28, 138–139, 141, 228–229, 234–235, 239, 271, 289–290, 292–294
 present, for the 10, 27, 180–181
 present, of the 29, 179–180, 184–185
 queer 7, 9–10, 17, 127, 270, 283
 of sexualities 7, 9, 70, 265, 290
 social 3, 6–7, 20, 23, 89, 122–123, 125–127, 138–139, 165, 305
 women's 4, 6–7, 9, 28–29, 122, 126, 179, 249, 296, 303

HIV/AIDS 26, 169, 269–282
homemaking 230–232, 240
 see also domesticity
HOMME (history of men, masculinity, etc.) 29, 178–179, 250
homosexuality 51, 181, 231, 260, 272–273, 277, 282
 law reform 12, 51, 170, 231
 see also gay
homosociality 102, 181–182

identity/ies 7, 9, 12, 16, 21, 23, 124, 130, 139, 141–142, 145, 148–149, 161, 218, 220, 236, 241, 294, 304
 class 24, 136, 139, 148, 189, 201, 235–238
 collective 101–102, 104, 140, 143, 189–190, 200
 documents 52–53
 gay 282, 304
 gender 2, 5, 24, 58–59, 101–102, 123, 132, 138, 141, 148, 167, 189, 192, 249
 legal 49–51, 61
 lived 51, 56, 62
 masculine 3, 13, 16–17, 24–25, 49, 90, 129, 136–137, 140, 146, 150–151, 181–183, 189, 195, 198, 200, 203, 304–305
 professional 27–28
 racial 71, 96, 101, 307
 sexual 52, 58, 300
 trans 14, 54, 61
incels 3, 169
inequality 2–3, 22–23, 98, 102, 171, 240, 309
 gender 4, 6, 22–23, 26, 115
intersex people 51–52, 58–59

Johansen, Michelle 24, 208–221
Johnston, Ronnie 195–196
Jones, Jack, trade unionist 194, 198–199, 201–202
Jones, Katie 16, 25–26, 269–283, 305, 309, 311
Jones, Vincent 49–53, 56
Joy of Sex, The 258, 263

Kane-Galbraith, Adrian 7, 10–11, 13–14, 16, 21, 25, 49–66, 310–311
King, Edward 274, 277, 279, 282
King, Laura 20, 163, 180, 192, 231
Kitten, James 1–4, 12–13, 17, 18, 22
Koven, Seth 94, 123

labour 161, 165–166, 170, 198, 210, 219–220
  division of 24, 232, 311
  markets 6, 8, 11, 15, 23–24, 30, 68, 128, 158, 170, 181–182, 190–191, 193–196, 199, 202–203, 311
  servicemen's 88–89, 91–93, 95, 103
Langhamer, Claire 230–231, 235, 304
Leeds Revolutionary Feminists 257, 290–291
legal profession 13, 80–81, 161, 163–164
leisure 8, 12, 23–24, 137, 140–145, 147, 150, 162, 170, 182, 193, 200–202, 219–220, 228, 239, 289
Lewis, Peter 179, 300, 302
liberation
  gay 7, 14, 158, 178, 261–262
  women's 4, 7, 27, 178, 183, 302
librarians 208–211
libraries 212–214
life cycle 3, 20, 22, 122, 126–128, 130–132, 160, 166
lived experience 19, 70, 72, 123–125, 127, 129, 131–132, 138, 228, 230, 274
Liverpool 22, 24, 89, 91, 96, 98, 100, 137, 189–203
Livingstone family 238–239
London, Midland and Scottish Railway 198, 201–202

magazines
  top-shelf 165, 254–255, 258–264, 291
  women's 164, 258–259, 263, 291
  works 138–139, 143, 146–149, 216
Manful Assertions 4–11, 27–29, 178–180, 184–185, 250, 299, 301–308, 310

manhood 2, 6, 13–14, 17, 62, 69, 100–101, 104, 127, 137, 158, 166, 183, 189, 191–192, 202, 214, 220, 303
manliness 2, 5, 9, 13, 16–19, 23–24, 27–28, 67, 74, 90, 93, 166, 181, 183, 198, 203, 209, 215–216, 219–221, 303
see also masculinity/ies
'manosphere' 4, 6
mansplaining 111–117
marginalisation 7, 68, 122–123, 131, 136–137, 139, 159, 271–272, 290
marriage 56, 70, 74, 78–79, 122, 131–132, 193, 200, 216, 231, 289
  bar 191, 196
  between those of same birth-assigned sex 56–58
  companionate 216, 232
  gay 170
masculine
  identities 3, 13, 16–17, 24–25, 49, 90, 129, 136–137, 140, 146, 150–151, 181–183, 189, 195, 198, 200, 203, 304–305
  subjectivities 4, 14, 16, 20, 123, 228, 231, 234, 243, 303
masculinity/ies
  Black 89, 93, 95, 104
  British 10, 61, 67, 69–70, 74, 80–82, 105, 122, 126, 129, 131, 184
  as category 2–3, 11, 69–70, 130, 151, 183, 303–306, 310
  change in 2, 4, 9–11, 14, 16–17, 20, 128, 136, 140, 142, 159, 162, 165, 179–180, 182–183, 306
  colonial 67–82
  crisis of 3, 9, 14–15, 17, 23, 29, 77, 148, 150–151, 158–160, 162–164, 166–171, 180–181, 184, 221, 256–257, 264, 305
  cultures of 8, 14, 27
  disabled 89, 91, 96, 100, 122, 124, 131, 311
  employment and 132, 194–197
  family and 20, 24, 192, 231

masculinity/ies (*cont.*)
  gay 261, 269, 271, 275
  hegemonic 9, 15, 17, 29, 89–90, 130–131, 137–138, 147, 159, 162, 182, 184
  hierarchies of 104, 127, 140, 159–162, 168–169
  histories of 3–8, 11, 14–15, 18, 26–27, 61, 67–69, 90, 104–105, 122, 124, 136, 158–159, 171, 178–185, 249–250, 288, 290, 299–301, 303, 305
  imperial 21, 67–68, 81–82, 90, 129
  military 68, 89–91, 130, 147, 162, 168, 182–183
  models of 9, 19, 23, 89–90, 137, 159–162, 164, 168–169, 192, 240, 289
  normative 2, 21, 26, 124, 126, 128, 132, 160, 165, 221, 258
  norms of 55, 70, 89, 94, 161, 164, 215
  performance of 19, 49, 51, 67, 80, 130, 138, 151, 159–160, 165–169, 171, 202, 229
  queer 26, 137, 290
  race and 74–76, 90–91, 93, 95–96, 100–105
  toxic 137, 151, 164, 181
  white 67–68, 77, 80, 82, 89–91, 104
  see also manhood; manliness
McIvor, Arthur 195–196
Mechen, Ben 25–26, 29, 253–265, 302, 303, 309, 311
medical profession 121, 161, 163–164, 234
Men's History Group *see* HOMME
men's rights activism 3, 6–7, 14–15, 17, 26, 164, 264, 311–312
mental health 3, 6, 19, 159, 234–235, 242, 311
Men, Women and Care project 122, 124–125
#MeToo 6, 137, 164, 288–290, 295, 306, 309, 311
Meyer, Jessica 9, 18–19, 22, 94, 121–132, 311

middle classes 24, 67, 69, 123, 127, 160–162, 167–168, 178, 208, 213–215, 218, 220, 229, 237, 239–242, 270, 273
miners 4, 12–13, 149, 213, 305
Ministry of Pensions and National Insurance 22, 49–51, 54–57, 59–61, 121
mobility 70, 90, 101, 121
  occupational 236
  social 19, 113, 162, 166, 208, 213, 214, 229, 238–242
models
  cultural 159–160, 162, 164, 167
  of masculinity 9, 19, 23, 89–90, 137, 159–162, 164, 168–169, 192, 240, 289
  role 139, 160, 195, 214, 217, 219, 221, 306
Moncrieff, Alexia 125, 128–129
morality 2, 52, 102, 163, 170
MPNI *see* Ministry of Pensions and National Insurance
Mullins, John, librarian 209, 217

National Assistance Boards 53–54, 57
National Insurance card 21, 49–52, 54, 57, 60–61
normality 16, 148, 230, 235, 242, 288
norms
  cultural 159, 161, 163, 169, 171, 215, 230, 262, 291–292, 295
  gender 13, 94, 123, 165, 257, 309
  masculine 55, 70, 89, 94, 161, 164, 215
nostalgia 141, 151, 229

Obscene Publications Act 253, 256, 258
Operation Yewtree 288, 290, 295
oral history 11, 20, 28, 138–139, 141, 228–229, 234–235, 239, 271, 289–290, 292–294
ordinariness 4, 12–13, 16, 20, 23–25, 136–138, 150, 229, 234–235, 237–243, 255, 257–258, 269, 272, 292
Owen family 56–58

patriarchy 4–6, 8, 10, 17, 24–28, 30, 80, 89, 94, 116, 130, 189, 203, 216, 249, 263–264, 289–291, 295, 300–305, 307
Pelmanism 18–20
pensions 54, 59, 128, 131
  disability 21–22, 54, 103, 121–132
  military 21
  records 22, 121–122, 124–126, 128–132
  widow's 56, 58
periodisation 20, 122, 126–128, 130, 171
permissiveness 163, 231, 255, 258
'Persons of Doubtful Sex' 14, 53, 56, 58
political change 15, 127–128, 255, 309, 311
Poole, Richard 142, 145–146, 150
pornography 253–265
poverty 71, 167, 170, 190, 202, 221
power
  gender and 9, 12, 27–28
  inequalities of 2–3
  male 4–6, 10, 17, 23, 26, 29, 89, 93, 115, 137, 189, 284, 301
  relations 5, 8, 12, 23, 102, 123, 127, 138, 158–159, 168, 170–171, 179, 232, 289, 295
press 2, 89, 161, 163–164, 231, 254, 257
privacy 8, 254, 262
professionalism 27, 115, 211, 215, 302
Project SIGMA 26, 269–283

queer
  histories 7, 9–10, 17, 127, 270, 283
  masculinities 26, 137, 290
  men 14, 62, 137, 271

Rabinow, Paul 101–102
racial
  difference 2, 70, 75, 79–81, 93
  identities 71, 96, 101, 307
  prejudice 71, 73, 75, 77, 79–80, 190
racism 2, 76, 79, 93, 100, 102, 171, 190, 199
Randell, John 59, 61
rape 72, 164, 257, 289

Regan, C. M. 60–61
relations
  family 12, 16, 25, 130–131, 192, 228–243
  gender 7–8, 27, 70, 77, 123, 181, 203, 231, 235, 291, 294
  power 5, 8, 12, 23, 123, 127, 138, 158–159, 170–171, 289, 295
  same-sex 13, 231, 270–271, 273–282
  sexual 26, 56, 259, 305
  social 3, 5, 8, 10, 14, 21, 69, 101, 104, 170, 201–202, 236
religion 5, 8, 170, 199, 303
  Catholic 193, 197, 199, 200–201
  differences in 74, 78, 90, 94, 199, 200–201
  Protestant 193, 197, 199, 200
Riley, Charlotte Lydia 27–28, 111–117
Robb, Linsey 147, 160, 162
role models 139, 160, 195, 214, 217, 219, 221, 306
Roper, Michael 4–5, 11, 16, 27–28, 131, 161–162, 165, 178, 249–250, 300, 302, 304
Royal Antidiluvian Order of Buffaloes 201–202

Saha, Jonathan 10–11, 21–22, 67–82, 307–308
Salmon, Lady Austin 4, 13–14, 18
St Pierre, Joshua 127, 131
Savage, Mike 235, 240, 242
Scates, Bruce 123–124
Schofield, Michael 272–273
Scott, Joan 8, 18, 181, 301
seafaring 193, 196, 199
Second World War 15, 147, 160, 162
Segal, Lynne 178, 299
self-fashioning 3, 14, 18, 20, 129, 193–194
self-forgetting 209, 215–216, 218–219
self-fulfilment 25, 231, 235, 238, 239
selfhood 10–11, 16, 23, 25, 29, 53, 104, 150, 228–229, 231, 241

self-improvement 18–19, 214, 216, 220, 235–236, 260, 263
sex
  anal 26, 270, 274–275, 277–282
  assignment 25, 50–51, 53–54, 56
  binary 21, 50, 52–53, 59, 61, 183, 310
  change 21, 49–54, 57, 59
  education 253, 259, 288, 309
  gender and 51, 58–59
  safer 26, 270–275, 277–282
  unsafe 271, 277
sexual
  abuse 230, 288–296
  behaviour 270, 272–278, 282, 288
  cultures 26, 269–283, 289, 291–292, 295
  decision-making 269–270, 277–278, 280
  diaries 26, 269–270, 273–274, 276, 278, 282
  difference 2, 12, 158, 183, 310
  experiences 28, 137, 253, 257–258, 269, 271, 277, 290
  harassment 28, 115, 288, 294
  health 127, 272, 309, 311
  identities 5, 52, 58, 300
  impropriety 21, 56
  knowledge 57, 256, 258–259
  liberalism 254, 260, 262–264, 291
  orientation 14, 115, 257
  pleasure 26, 258–261
  politics 28, 158, 256, 295
  relations 26, 56, 259, 305
  subjectivities 10, 25, 258, 264, 270
  violence 6, 26, 28, 230, 288–289, 294
sexuality/ies 10, 14, 25, 58, 136, 258–260, 282, 290, 303–304
  female 75, 123, 127, 289, 291
  hierarchies of 7–8, 159
  histories of 7, 9, 70, 265, 290
  male 74, 263, 269–283, 288–296
Sheffield 23, 138–141, 144, 150
Shepard, Alexandra 127, 184
Sinha, Mrinalini 67–69
Smith, Bracewell 1–4, 17

Smith, Helen 15, 22–23, 136–151, 161, 182
Smith, Richard 90, 92–93
social
  change 3, 15, 58, 127, 143, 148, 158, 161, 221, 228, 243, 311
  media 4, 163–164, 288, 309
  relations 3, 5, 8, 10, 14, 21, 69, 101, 104, 170, 201–202, 236
  status 161, 168, 214, 240–241
socialisation 102, 140, 161, 163, 195
sociology 4, 9, 16, 113, 151, 158, 163, 179, 271, 303, 305
solidarity
  class 12, 24, 197, 228
  interracial 98–99
  masculine 96, 102–104, 181, 195, 198–199
  workplace 12, 23, 182
Solnit, Rebecca 112–113, 116–117
Songs of Steel 138–139, 141, 150
Sorrell, Alan 230–231, 237–238
status 1, 12, 81, 89, 92, 95, 126, 208
  class 75, 81, 213, 241–242
  HIV 273, 276–279, 281
  masculine 5, 22, 25, 130–132, 137–138, 147, 158–160, 162, 165, 167–168, 171, 182, 189
  occupational 140, 144, 147, 150–151, 161, 198, 211, 218, 221, 236, 240–241
  outsider 114–115
  social 161, 168, 214, 240–241
  soldier 2, 89, 92, 95, 97, 100–102, 104, 182
Steelos see Steel, Peech & Tozer
Steel, Peech & Tozer, Rotherham 139–145, 147–150
steelworks 138–151
strength 12, 23, 162, 168
subcultures 149–150, 308
subjectivities 3, 11, 14–15, 25, 70, 82, 101, 184, 235–236, 238, 242, 255, 265, 296, 304, 311
  masculine 4, 14, 16, 20, 123, 228, 231, 234, 243, 303
  sexual 10, 25, 258, 264, 270

suicide 6, 19, 311
Sullivan, David 254, 256
surveys, social 11, 269–274, 276, 305
Sutcliffe-Braithwaite, Florence 237, 241
Szreter, Simon 61, 161, 232

Taylor family 233–234, 238
temporality 122, 126–128, 130
Tillett family 237–238
Todd, Selina 126, 228
Topham, Will 4, 12–13, 18
Tosh, John 4–5, 7, 9, 16–17, 27–29, 62, 122–123, 127, 129–130, 158, 178–185, 189, 263, 299–312
trade unions 12, 23, 24, 166, 168–170, 182, 194, 197–198, 239
training 92, 144–146, 148, 208, 211, 216–217
transition 50–55, 58–61
trans
　histories 7
　identities 14, 54, 61
　men 10–11, 14, 16, 21, 49–62
　people 10, 50, 58, 60–61, 301, 310
　women 51, 54–55, 58, 59
transsexualism 51, 58
Trump, Donald J. 137, 311–312

unemployment 6, 12, 14, 19, 23, 54–55, 137, 151, 166–167, 170, 181, 183, 197, 305
upper classes 71, 137, 214, 218, 229, 242

Vaughan, J. 52–53
violence
　domestic 72, 74, 170, 200, 230, 289
　male 4, 6, 10, 17, 137, 181, 256, 264, 311
　racial 89, 96, 98, 103
　sexual 6, 26, 28, 230, 288–289, 294

War Office 91–92, 94–95, 99, 104
Weeks, Jeffrey 180, 304
welfare state 11, 21, 49–62, 95, 127, 142, 230
　see also pensions

West Indian Contingent Committee 92, 99
West Indian servicemen 88, 90–104
Westwood, Gordon *see* Michael Schofield
Whitehouse, Mary 256, 261
whiteness 22, 70, 72, 81–82, 89–90, 116, 308
widows 56–58, 196, 215–216
Williams Committee *see* Committee on Obscenity and Film Censorship
Willmott, Peter 161, 236
Wolfenden Report 163, 254, 262, 272
women's
　education 76–77
　employment 116, 167, 190–191, 193, 196, 200, 232, 233
　history 4, 6–7, 9, 28–29, 122, 126, 179, 249, 296, 303
　liberation 4, 7, 27, 178, 183, 302
work
　blue-collar 144, 228, 242
　culture 137–140, 143, 149–150, 182
　dangerous 91, 144–145, 146, 165, 194–196, 198
　domestic 20, 24, 191–193, 196, 232
　impact on masculine identity 12, 23, 136–137, 139–140, 143, 145, 149, 182, 195–197, 236
　skilled 55, 140, 144, 151, 182, 190, 213, 220, 236
　status 140, 144, 147, 150–151, 161, 198, 211, 218, 221, 236, 240–241
　unskilled 137, 190, 196, 213
　white-collar 55, 137, 140, 211, 214, 218, 221, 228, 249
　see also employment
working class 13, 24, 113, 136–151, 159, 161–162, 166–167, 170, 181, 192, 198–199, 201, 208, 211, 213, 217, 219–221, 229, 235–242, 271
works magazines 138–139, 143, 146–149

Young, Michael 161, 236

EU authorised representative for GPSR:
Easy Access System Europe, Mustamäe tee 50,
10621 Tallinn, Estonia
gpsr.requests@easproject.com